ATHENS, OHIO

The Village Years

ATHENS, OHIO

The Village Years

ROBERT L. DANIEL

OHIO UNIVERSITY PRESS • ATHENS

Ohio University Press, Athens, Ohio 45701
© 1997 by Robert L. Daniel
Printed in the United States of America

Ohio University Press books are printed on acid-free paper ∞ ™

01 00 99 98 97   5 4 3 2 1

Publication of this book was made possible with support from the Athens Bicentennial
Steering Committee, the O'Bleness Foundation, and Cornwell Jewelers.

Library of Congress Cataloging-in-Publication Data
Daniel, Robert L., 1923–
    Athens, Ohio : the village years / Robert L. Daniel.
       p.   cm.
    Includes bibliographical references (p.) and index.
    ISBN 0-8214-1195-0 (cloth : alk. paper). — ISBN 0-8214-1196-9
(paper : alk. paper)
    1. Athens (Ohio)—History. 2. Athens (Ohio)—Biography.
I. Title.
F499.186D36 1997
977.1'97—dc21   97–17328
                                         CIP

Credits:

Pages ii–iii: Panoramic view looking both north and south on Court Street and east on Washington Street, courtesy of Margene Bush and the *Athens Messenger. Page 2:* S. P. Hildreth's map of The Plains area reproduced from E. G. Squier and E. H. Davis, *Ancient Monuments of the Mississippi Valley,* 1973. *Page 12:* Engraving of Rufus Putnam, courtesy of Archives and Special Collections, Ohio University Libraries. *Page 38:* Photograph of Jacob Lindley, courtesy of Archives and Special Collections, Ohio University Libraries. *Page 70:* Drawing of original First Presbyterian Church by P. Mitchell, courtesy of First Presbyterian Church, Athens. *Page 116:* Postcard of "Old Brick," Athens Public School, courtesy of Margene Bush. *Page 138:* Sgt. Major Milton M. Holland, courtesy of Michel and Connie Perdreau. *Page 168:* Portrait of Charles Grosvenor, courtesy of Archives and Special Collections, Ohio University Libraries. *Page 188:* Photograph of the Bank of Athens, courtesy of James Anastas. *Page 228:* Postcard of State Hospital, courtesy of Margene Bush. *Page 290:* Photograph of racing at the Athens County Fair in 1890, courtesy of the *Athens Messenger. Page 322:* Photograph of McBee Binder Co., 1916, courtesy of The Dairy Barn and Archives and Special Collections, Ohio University Libraries. *Page 368:* Photograph of an unknown student, courtesy of The Dairy Barn and Archives and Special Collections, Ohio University Libraries.

To the People of Athens

Contents

CONTENTS

CONTENTS

Illustrations

Following Page 110

Peter Finsterwald, respected, longtime village marshal

Alston Ellis, president of Ohio University, 1901–20

Lydia Carpenter Armstrong, matron of Athens County Children's Home, c. 1905

"Mother" Eliza Daniel Stewart, internationally famous temperance speaker

Isaac and Lydia Taylor, proprietors of the Eagle House

Maria Foster Brown, c. 1850s

Admiral Louis Rudolph de Steiguer

Following Page 174

Herrold's Mill and Dam

Herrold Place and West Bridge, 1875

Woolen factory and flour mill of D. B. Stewart and East Bridge, c. 1875

Daniel Bertine Stewart, entrepreneur

Otto Barth's Mill and Dam, c. 1907

South Bridge, steel span of 1908

South Bridge, covered bridge of 1876 with steel span over railroad

East-bound Baltimore and Ohio Engine No. 172 with old South Bridge in background, 1878

Bishop David Hastings Moore

Methodist Church of 1812, South Congress Street

Methodist Church of 1908, College Street

Methodist Church of 1837, College and Washington streets

St. Paul's Catholic Church, North Congress Street, as pictured by the *Athens Journal*, 1892

St. Paul's Catholic Church, North College Street, 1895

Fife Brothers' Tabernacle, Carpenter and Court streets, 1913

Booker T. Washington literary club, Mt. Zion Baptist Church, 1909

Reverend Joseph Wilson, pastor, Mt. Zion Baptist Church

Presbyterian Church as remodeled in 1865

Presbyterian Church of 1903

East Side School, 1911, Wallace Drive at Ohio Avenue

Athens High School, 1906

Athens County Children's Home, c. 1900

Athens State Hospital, c. 1900

Nurses of Athens State Hospital

Preface

Two hundred years ago, Rufus Putnam, leader of the Ohio Company, sent eleven men to found what is now the City of Athens. By 1797, having guided the settlement at Marietta, Putnam's next order of business was to get a settlement underway on lands set aside for a college. This new settlement, later designated Athens, was in the Ohio Company lands in the valley of the Hockhocking River. More specifically, it was some forty-five miles west of Marietta and a similar distance from the mouth of the Hockhocking River. As one of the oldest communities in Ohio, Athens has a heritage that merits recording and appreciating. Now, as we look ahead to the third century of our community, we pause a moment to assess our community's past.

Using surviving reminiscences, newspapers, institutional records, and the manuscript census, I've sought to illustrate how the Athens community grew, how it changed over the years, and what it was like to have lived in Athens in the past. I've tried to identify the problems the community faced and how it went about resolving them. Thus, this account looks at the community's efforts to provide local government, the changing ways its people kept house and earned a living, the ways they worshiped, their efforts to educate their children, what they did to amuse themselves, how they dealt with sickness, accidents, and aberrant behavior. It traces the transformation of an isolated hamlet that was rooted in a self-sufficient agrarian economy into a cosmopolitan small city with a diverse, interdependent economic base. It deals with the village years.

Along the way, many people have contributed to the furtherance of this project. Above all, I'm indebted to the letter writers, diarists, organizational secretaries, journalists, and hometown historians whose writings provide an insight into our community's past. But there are also my contemporaries, without whose aid this would have been a far more difficult or even impossible task. There are those specialists at the Ohio University Library—Judy Daso, Joyce Hamby, and Elizabeth Story, who have pointed the way to government documents. Access to manuscript materials has been eased by repeated assistance from George Bain, Sheppard Black, and Karen Jones. Similarly, Ted Foster has aided in expediting access to newspaper and census materials.

This project would not have been completed at this time without the aid of the personnel of the Athens County Historical Society and Museum, whose holdings complement and supplement those of Ohio University. Beverly Schumacher has aided greatly at critical moments in overcoming the obstacles of that demon of our age—the computer. Above all, my thanks to Joanne Prisley, Director of the ACHS&M, who made the facility available, who has given wise counsel, and who has critiqued the manuscript. My thanks to Michel Perdreau who generously shared with me his exceptional knowledge of Athens' black community and to Robin Lacy who led me on an exploration of the route of the Marietta and Cincinnati railroad from Athens to Harmar. Carolyn Murphree wielded a critical red pencil in her reading of the manuscript, while Professor Ivan Tribe of the University of Rio Grande has, with good humor and a meticulous reading of the manuscript, saved me from otherwise embarrassing errors. For those errors and glitches that survive, I plead the old maxim: "To err is human." I leave to the reader to decide the measure of forgiveness he can muster and wish him a state of divinity.

I would be remiss if I did not also express my gratitude to Doctors Henry Croci, Philip Kinnard, William Burak, and Nik Shaw, whose medical skill has enabled me to complete this work.

To the Athens Bicentennial Steering Committee and its chair, Verda Jones, go thanks for their help in the publication of this work, in seeking to make it more accessible to the public by underwriting part of its publication costs. The O'Bleness Foundation and Cornwell Jewelers have graciously provided additional support.

At this point, I look forward to exploring Athens: The Urban Years.

Robert L. Daniel

January 30, 1997

ATHENS, OHIO

The Village Years

1

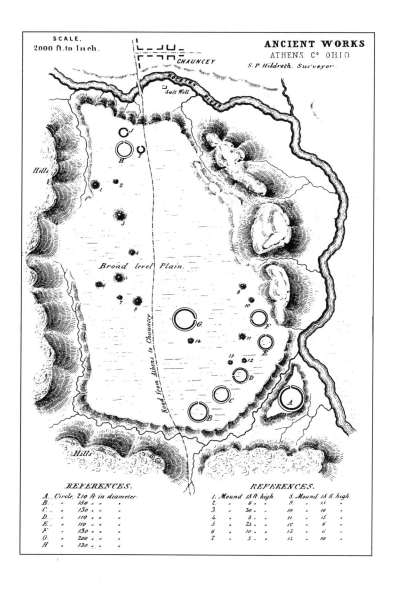

SCALE,
2000 ft. to Inch.

CHAUNCEY

ANCIENT WORKS
ATHENS Cº OHIO
S.P. Hildreth. Surveyor.

Salt Well

Hills

Broad level Plain.

Road from Athens to Chauncey

Hills

REFERENCES.

A.	Circle,	210	ft. in diameter.
B.	"	150	" " "
C.	"	150	" " "
D.	"	110	" " "
E.	"	110	" " "
F.	"	130	" " "
G.	"	200	" " "
H.	"	130	" " "

REFERENCES.

1. Mound 18 ft. high.		8. Mound 18 ft. high.	
2. " 6 " "		9. " 15 " "	
3. " 30 " "		10. " 10 " "	
4. " 8 " "		11. " 15 " "	
5. " 24 " "		12. " 6 " "	
6. " 10 " "		13. " 6 " "	
7. " 5 " "		14. " 10 " "	

The First Athenians

Long before Rufus Putnam set in motion the founding of Athens village, a succession of Indian Americans utilized the area. No one, of course, knows the names of the first humans who camped or settled in what is now Athens. From the artifacts left behind, however, it is certain that parties of Paleo-Indians hunted and camped in the Hocking Valley and the Athens area.

PALEO-INDIANS

The Paleo-Indians, whose ancestors had crossed the Bering land bridge from Siberia to Alaska some 10,000 to 25,000 years ago, were hunter-gatherers who followed such animals as the mammoth and mastodon. Relatively few in number, the Paleo-Indians hunted and camped in the area of the Hocking Valley, which was largely untouched by the Wisconsin glacier, the most important local site being at Doanville near the mouth of Monday Creek. Artifacts have also been found at five other sites: the Gabriel site near Beaumont; at Harmony; two miles down the Hocking from the Stimson Avenue bridge; the finest spearpoint from Canaan Township on the south side of the Hocking; and the Lindsay site along the headwaters of Margaret Creek.

Relatively little is known of these first visitors. As hunter-gatherers, they did not establish permanent living sites, but over the years the remains of the mastodons they hunted have come to light. The first notice of a mastodon was in August 1828, when the Hocking River ate away its bank a mile and a half upstream from the village, exposing an upper and lower jawbone with eight teeth. The second to be found, the "Courtney mastodon," stirred much interest when it was unearthed along the

Hocking a mile north of the village in 1832. The remains of other mastodons have provided further evidence of these elephantine animals in this area.

Although Paleo-Indians camped in the Athens area, the region did not offer the best of all possible environments. The rugged terrain was difficult for both the hunters and their giant prey to negotiate. The local flint used to fashion tools was inferior to that found near Newark and Coshocton. The one "exportable" resource locally available was hematite, a brownish-red iron ore, which when heated produced a much-valued red pigment.

ARCHAIC INDIANS

About 8000 B.C. the effects of the retreat of the Wisconsin glacier on Ohio's climate brought a change in Indian culture. The cool, moist climate that had supported the plants and animals of the Paleolithic era gave way to the humid, continental climate that prevails today. It encouraged the growth of deciduous trees whose leaf mold in turn promoted the growth of a wide range of plants that had hitherto struggled to survive. Bear, elk, and deer displaced the mastodons. The population of smaller animals such as hare, raccoon, and opossum exploded. The net effect was to force the Indians to develop a new lifestyle.

The Archaic Indians, as the hunters and gatherers who adapted to the new environment are called, persisted from roughly 8000 B.C. to about 1500 B.C. These people pursued elk, bear, and especially the white-tailed deer. They became increasingly skilled in gathering nuts, berries, roots, herbs, and seeds. As with their predecessors, they lived a migratory existence, although the evidence of the Koster site in Illinois and Meadowcroft in southwest Pennsylvania documents that some of them founded semi-permanent settlements. They made baskets and leather items, kept domesticated dogs, carried on trade with distant Indian communities, and developed special rituals for burying the dead. There is even evidence that those at the Koster site built permanent homes.

In and about Athens, the Archaic Indians utilized temporary campsites. Where stone suitable for shaping tools was found, they might create a "work camp." They might also establish a temporary camp where the hunters stayed long enough to butcher their deer kill, then move on. There are campsites at Haydenville, Doanville, Chauncey, and Athens. The Athens County Children Services site, at East State and the Route 33 bypass, yielded ground stone celts as well as a fragment of an axe. The imperatives of highway construction completely destroyed the site before a systematic archaeological dig could be completed.

ADENA VILLAGERS

The major element in the pre-white heritage of Athens is the presence of Adena Villagers, some within the village limits, others at The Plains. By any standard the Adena and the chronologically overlapping Hopewell culture represent the golden age of prehistoric Indian culture east of the Mississippi River. The Adenas' principal center was at Chillicothe, with The Plains being the second largest center in Ohio. The time frame—dates are approximate—ran from 1000 B.C. to as late as 200 A.D.

The Adena economy remained one based on hunting and gathering. What differentiated it from the Archaic was the tentative beginnings of horticulture, the deliberate cultivation of seed crops such as marsh elder and goosefoot. By the start of Adena culture seeds had become a more important component of the Indian diet than nuts. Whether they had learned to plant maize (corn) remains doubtful, though they probably planted squash. Their food sources—a mix of the fish, fowl, and game they hunted; the herbs, berries, nuts, and seeds they gathered; and the seeds they cultivated—gave them a food supply sufficiently stable to enable them to become sedentary. They lived in small communities of two to five family units—all the people who could be sustained by the plant and animal food accessible within a radius of two or three hours' walk.

The Adena also developed pottery, a means of safeguarding foodstuffs from rodents and moisture far superior to baskets. They learned to mix grit with the clay for added strength, to bake the pots to enhance their durability, and to apply a glaze that allowed them to hold water.

Adena houses were round with a conical roof covered with sheets of bark or thatch. They might be on the order of twenty feet in diameter, producing some 314 square feet of space—small, but better protection than rock shelters in rain and cold weather. But most domestic activities were conducted outside. The Adena cooked on an open hearth, bathed and laundered at a nearby stream, and prepared hides, processed foodstuffs, and made tools out-of-doors.

The Adena are known primarily through the burial mounds for their dead, their graves typically including the tools and ornaments of the departed. Most if not all of The Plains earthworks were constructed between 300 B.C. and 200 A.D.—that is, during the latter years of the Adena Culture.

The presence of Adena mounds in the Athens area, especially at The Plains, was recognized almost from the beginning of white settlement. Samuel P. Hildreth, a Marietta doctor, surveyed The Plains, and his map of the earthworks appeared in E. G. Squier and E. H. Davis's classic *Ancient Monuments of the Mississippi Valley*, published by the newly established Smithsonian Institution in 1848. The identification of these earthworks was subjective, inexact. When E. B. Andrews surveyed The Plains area in the 1870s, he identified thirty mounds and eight "sacred circles." Many of the mounds were only four to six feet high, and not all have survived. Further, as property changed hands, the names attached to the mounds also changed. Thus, the Beard or Baird Mound is now the Coon Mound; the George Connett Mound, the largest mound at The Plains, is also called the Hartman Mound. Never excavated, the Hartman Mound was 40 feet high and 140 feet in diameter. In April 1989 its ownership passed from private hands to the Athens County Historical Society and Museum.

When the Adena mounds at The Plains have been opened, they have often yielded one or more burials and a miscellany of grave goods, including rolled copper beads, a unique tubular pipe of copper, rolled copper bracelets, and discoidal beads of marine shell. The most unusual find, from the School House–Post Office site at Chauncey, was an ornamented dress covered with copper beads, which the excavators proceeded to cut into pieces and distribute to bystanders as souvenirs. One fragment made its way to Harvard University's Peabody Museum.

If The Plains is a suburb of Athens today, what is now Athens was a suburb of the Adena settlement. And in Athens three mounds—the Daines Mounds—rise above the small ridge that separates Coates Run from a tributary of Dairy Run—that is, the area west of Richland Avenue and south of Dairy Lane. These three mounds date from late in the Adena era. Another mound, some 160 feet in diameter and 5 feet high, sits on a high spur of land at the head of a small tributary of Rock Riffle Run. It contained eight burials and two cremations. The fill of the mound also contained the skeletal remains of preadolescents, suggesting, as James L. Murphy declares in his *An Archeological History of the Hocking Valley*, that "not all children and infants were given elaborate burials."

One last site deserves mention, a mound along what is now Harmony Road just downstream from the old Mill Street Bridge. In 1828 the Athens *Mirror* reported matter-of-factly that students had opened a mound that was solitary and conical. Two human skeletons had been unearthed, both found in a seated position facing east with feet stretched out. An ornament found with one body, a stone with two holes, was probably worn around the neck.

If the Adena found The Plains and the Athens area a congenial place to live, the Hopewell and subsequent Indian cultures did not. The Hopewell, contemporaries and successors of the Adena, surpassed them in the extent of their agricultural and craft skills. As agriculturists, they preferred the richer glaciated areas such as Chillicothe, Lancaster, and Newark. But although they chose not to live in the Hocking Valley, they hunted in the area. Their small prismatic "flake knives" have been found there. And for temporary campsites, they made use of locations their Paleo and Archaic forebears had found attractive—the Gabriel site, the McCune site (West Union Street across from the cemetery), and the Children Services site. The pottery fragments found at the McCune site suggest that the Hopewell may have lived there briefly.

LATE PREHISTORIC CULTURE

In the thousand-year interval between the end of the Hopewell era and the arrival of the first white intruders, various Indians occupied sites in and about Athens, but never on a long-term basis.

Indian cultures continued to evolve. They developed the bow and arrow and expanded their mastery of horticulture. Their populations grew. The major permanent site in the Hocking Valley of the Late Woodland Indians was the Wright Village site near Logan, twenty-five miles northwest of Athens. The Gabriel site and the McCune site were occupied intermittently. The latter site seems to have been especially attractive to successive Indian peoples, for it yielded a Paleo fluted spearpoint, identifiable Archaic points, Early Woodland points, and Late Prehistoric artifacts. In addition there were endscrapers, knives, pendants, beads, awls, and nearly six hundred pottery shards. Carbon dating of charcoal remains indicates that both the Gabriel and McCune sites were occupied about the same time, 1300 to 1400 A.D., then abandoned.

WHITE INTRUDERS

By the time Spanish, French, and English colonists arrived on the Atlantic coast in the 1500s and 1600s, the Indian cultures had organized themselves into tribal structures. Still locked into the Stone Age, these Indians were limited to working with stone, bone, clay, and wood; the whites had metals—brass, copper, tin, lead, and iron—with which to fashion saws, hatchets, axes, hammers, and knives—tools far more efficient than their Indian counterparts. The Indians were skilled in fashioning leather into moccasins, leggings, breech clouts, robes, and skirts, clothing eminently suited to life in their wooded habitat. The whites, though, had learned to work wool—to spin and weave it for a variety of uses such as blankets and clothing, or to knit it into scarves, gloves, sweaters, and stockings—clothing more flexible, though less durable, than the Indians' leather goods. Indian weapons—the bow and arrow and tomahawk—were lethal, to be sure, but had reached the upper limit of their development. The English musket, initially less efficient than the bow and arrow, was at the threshold of its development, and by the 1790s, the Pennsylvania rifle was far more deadly than the Indians' best weapons. Furthermore, with the sailing ship and the horse or oxen harnessed to the wagon, the whites could move people and goods with a speed and in quantities Indian societies could not match.

At the political level, Indian societies were fragmented by tribal and village attachments that precluded common responses to challenges. The whites, on the other hand, had developed political and economic institutions capable of mobilizing the manpower and economic resources of large regions. Perhaps of greatest significance, Indian societies lacked a natural immunity to a host of diseases that the white man imported. Smallpox, highly contagious, swept through Indian communities that came in contact with whites, and was passed through Indian trade channels from village to village. Venereal diseases left Indian women sterile, while childhood diseases of the white man—measles, mumps, and chickenpox along with whooping cough and scarlet fever—were deadly for Indians. Indian communities lost far more people to disease than to warfare.

Despite their cultural differences, whites and Indians had a fatal mutual attraction. Indians, on first seeing the metal weapons, tools, pots, fabrics, and trinkets of the white man, were driven to acquire these goods. The whites, for their part, found profit in the export of the Indians' furs and hides to Old World markets. Indian communities that had been self-sufficient became hooked almost immediately into a dependence on European goods. Nor was this loss of self-sufficiency limited to Indians on the Atlantic coast.

The efforts of the Dutch, French, and English to develop the fur trade with the Indians is fascinating but not a part of this account. What is relevant is that in the 1600s, Indian economies shifted to commercial hunting and trapping, in which the white traders had the upper hand in setting the terms of trade. In the 1700s, and especially at midcentury, the English and French governments came to realize the economic and political value of controlling the fur trade, and they went to war to gain that control. The French and Indian War, 1754–1763, resulted in the exclusion of the French from North America. Between 1760 and 1775, colonial fur-trading companies—especially those in Pennsylvania and Virginia—jockeyed for dominance.

It was George Croghan and Christopher Gist, the chief of the colonial fur traders, who in 1751 were the first white men of record to enter the Hocking Valley, crossing the northern portion of the valley. The fur traders were the first whites to gather general knowledge of the terrain, and the Lewis Evans map, the first map of the Ohio Country, dating to 1755, notes the Hockhocking River and the outcroppings of coal along its banks. The first whites to take note of the river used the Indian name Hockhocking, a usage that continued until after the War of 1812, when it was shortened to Hocking.

LORD DUNMORE'S WAR

The Virginian colonists were stubbornly determined to claim exclusive use of the area east of the Ohio River from Pittsburgh to the Great Kanawha, while the Shawnee, understandably, were unwilling to relinquish their hunting lands. Lord Dunmore's War resulted from this clash of wills. The initiative lay with John Murray Dunmore, "a rather heavy, pompous" man, who, while royal governor of Virginia, also had a pecuniary interest in the Indian trade and in western land speculation. Dunmore planned a three-pronged attack. One element, led by Colonel Angus McDonald, moved against the Wapatomica towns on the Muskingum River in June 1774. By the time McDonald reached the Indian towns, the Indians had fled, but he destroyed their villages. The principal operations called for the use of some 3,000 militiamen. A group under Colonel Andrew Lewis was to march from the Greenbrier area along the Great Kanawha to Point Pleasant on the Ohio, while Lord Dunmore, who had taken his army to Fort Pitt, would float his force of 900 down the Ohio. In point of fact, Lewis and Dunmore were bitter rivals.

Aware that an invasion of the Ohio Country was imminent, Chief Cornstalk, the Shawnee leader, nonetheless counseled his people to keep the peace. But the Shawnee were bent on resisting the whites, and rather than yield his leadership role, Cornstalk reluctantly agreed to head the forces. With 800 Shawnee and 200 Delaware warriors, Cornstalk opted to attack Lewis at Point Pleasant (now West Virginia) before he could be joined by Dunmore, who was still descending the Ohio River. Cornstalk crossed to the Virginia side of the river at night preparatory to launching a surprise attack at daybreak, only to be discovered while still three-quarters of a mile from Lewis's camp. In a day-long, seesaw fight, Lewis lost half of his commissioned officers and sustained a total of 75 dead and 140 wounded. Although Cornstalk's forces lost only 22 dead and 18 wounded, he broke off the fighting at day's end, recrossing to the right bank of the river. While Cornstalk's Mingo, Delaware, and Wyandot allies went home, Cornstalk and the Shawnee withdrew to the Pickaway Plains.

When Dunmore reached the mouth of the Hocking River, he learned of the encounter between Lewis and Cornstalk. He paused long enough to build Fort Gower at the mouth of the Hockhocking, then proceeded to lead his men up the Hockhocking Valley, camping overnight at a series of sites along the Hockhocking (Beebe, just downstream from its junction with Federal Creek; the old state hospital grounds in Athens; the west end of Nelsonville; and the Great Falls at Logan) before turning west toward the Pickaway Plains. As Dunmore approached the Shawnee villages, Cornstalk offered to make peace. Dunmore negotiated a settlement reflecting his concern with land speculation, in which the Shawnee abandoned their claims to the Virginia side of the Ohio and conceded to the whites the right to travel unmolested on the Ohio River. Satisfied that the Virginians could now proceed to settle the area of the Monongahela, Great Kanawha, and Ohio valleys, Dunmore returned home. Ohio was left to the Indians, but Dunmore's party was the first group of white men of record to pass through what became Athens.

In a sense the peace settlement gave the Shawnee and Delaware a reprieve. For the next generation the acquisitiveness and aggressiveness of the colonials was to be concentrated in the areas to the east and south of the Ohio River. In reality, however, the peace made by Lord Dunmore and Chief Cornstalk did not bring security to the Ohio Indians. They might continue to hunt in the Hockhocking Valley, but they could not safely locate villages anywhere on the river below present-day Logan.

THE FORT GOWER RESOLVES, 1774

While stopping briefly at Fort Gower en route home, the American colonials with Lord Dunmore's army learned of the debate in the First Continental Congress over an appropriate response to the "Intolerable Acts." At this point, some of the colonial officers and men drafted a set of resolves that pledged "the most faithful allegiance" to George III, but then went on to affirm that "the love of liberty and attachment to the real interests and just rights of America outweigh every other consideration," and pledged "every power within us for the defence of American liberty and for the support of her just rights and privileges." In February 1775, the Fort Gower Resolves were published verbatim in the *Virginia Gazette* and reprinted elsewhere. Spurred by the Point Pleasant Chamber of Commerce, some local residents have argued that the Battle of Point Pleasant marked the opening of the American Revolution—hardly true. The contest between Colonel Lewis and Chief Cornstalk had nothing to do with colonial differences with the English over the Intolerable Acts. Dunmore's War had nothing to do with the Fort Gower Resolves.

THE WAR FOR INDEPENDENCE

The War for Independence, of course, began in the East and most of the fighting took place there. Yet, as with the French and Indian War, the War for Independence had great consequences for the future of what would become Athens. First, because the Ohio Indians supported the English military against the American frontiersmen, when the war was over the new American government took the position that the Ohio Indians had forfeited their rights to land and could continue to remain in Ohio only on whatever terms the American government chose to grant. Second, in the course of the war, George Rogers Clark persuaded the Virginia government to outfit an expedition to strike at Vincennes, Kaskaskia, and Cahokia, the French settlements in the Wabash Valley and in the Illinois Country that the British had taken over. At the war's end, the area between the Ohio and Mississippi rivers was in the nominal possession of the Americans, and in the peace that followed, the British relinquished their claim to the area south of the Great Lakes and east of the Mississippi River. The Ohio Country was to be American henceforth.

Enmity between the various Ohio Indians—especially the Miami and Shawnee—and the whites flooding into Kentucky continued unabated. Periodic attacks by Colonel Benjamin Logan and George Rogers Clark in the Scioto and Miami valleys forced the Indians to retreat from southern and southeast Ohio, even for the purposes of hunting. More ominous, as the Constitution was being framed in Philadelphia in 1787, veterans of the Revolutionary Army were completing plans to establish a settlement in the Ohio Country.

2

From Middletown to Athens

THE FOUNDING OF ATHENS was bound up in the organization of the Marietta settlement by a group of New England veterans of the American Revolution. Faced with an expanding population and a limited terrain with still more limited tracts of fertile soil, foresighted New Englanders at the end of the Revolution were looking for new areas to settle.

RUFUS PUTNAM'S VISION

The leading figures in the events leading to the founding of Athens were Rufus Putnam and Benjamin Tupper. Born in 1738 and orphaned at age seven, Putnam was self-taught, making his mark as a surveyor. As a member of the colonial militia, Putnam participated in the French and Indian War, and in 1773, he joined a group of veterans of that war who sought to redeem the land warrants they had received for their services by founding a colony in West Florida. He sailed there, in fact, only to find that the governor had no authority to grant them land.

At the outset of the Revolution, serving as lieutenant colonel in Brewer's Regiment, one of the first regiments organized, Putnam distinguished himself as "ardent, active, and efficient," as Charles Walker wrote in his *History of Athens County, Ohio*. In August 1776, he was commissioned a colonel in the Continental Army, a post he soon resigned in favor of the command of a Massachusetts regiment. In January 1783, Congress appointed him brigadier general. Putnam, who at forty-five found his postwar prospects none too bright, chaired the officers' committee and drafted the Newburgh Petition, requesting that the Continental Congress make definite provisions for a land grant in the Ohio Country by way of redeeming the land bounties promised to the soldiers and officers for their service. In a separate letter to General Washington in June 1783, he described such a grant "as of great consequence to the American Empire." His vision focused on a plan for opening the Ohio Country to white settlers. He suggested the creation of townships six miles square, reserving within these townships lands that could be used to support the ministry and schools. He also urged that one-eighth of the new lands be reserved for veterans, the shares being distributed according to rank. He concluded by averring that many veterans, lacking a satisfactory means of making a living in New England, were prepared to become adventurers in the Ohio Country. Putnam's petition was not timely: the Treaty of Paris had not yet been concluded, and the land in question still belonged to Virginia.

Benjamin Tupper, the same age as Putnam, had likewise seen service in the French and Indian War. As a militia officer at the start of the Revolution, he had arrested the loyalist members of the Massachusetts Bay Supreme Court. From 1776 to the end of the war, he had seen extensive service in New England, on Long Island, and at Saratoga and Monmouth. Before retiring from the service in 1783 with the brevet rank of brigadier general, he had joined Putnam and the 288 Continental officers in signing the Newburgh Petition.

THE LAND ORDINANCE OF 1785

Preoccupied with major foreign and domestic issues, Congress did not respond to the petition. In fact it waited until 1785 before enacting a law providing for surveying the Ohio Country. The Land Ordinance of 1785 contained several provisions of importance to the subsequent development of Athens. First, the surveyors were to take note of all the "mines, salt-springs, salt-licks, and mill-sites" that came to their attention. Second, the odd-numbered townships were to be sold entire; the even-numbered townships, in square-mile blocks. Finally, the Ordinance reserved Section 16 in each township "for the maintenance of public schools." In that it provided for a survey of the Seven Ranges, that is, an area west of the Ohio River from the Pennsylvania border southward almost to the Muskingum River, and opened the land to sale, the Land Ordinance of 1785 was a necessary element in opening Ohio to settlement; but the conditions of sale—both in terms of the minimum land unit of 640 acres and the price of $1.00 per acre—were onerous. While these provisions precluded the creation of baronies such as those attempted by

Richard Henderson in Kentucky and Tennessee or by Simon Kenton in Kentucky and western Ohio, no bona fide farmer could make efficient use of a plot of land as large as a square mile, let alone a township. Nor was it reasonable to tie up so much money in land that could not readily be put to productive use. Furthermore, the ordinance was defective in that it made no provision for civil government, without which settlement could not safely proceed.

After Rufus Putnam declined the job, Benjamin Tupper was appointed to the corps of surveyors and personally conducted the survey of ranges three and four of the Seven Ranges. Tupper's on-site experience convinced him that "the garden spot" of the Ohio region was the Muskingum Valley, an area to the west and south of the Seven Ranges and guarded by Fort Harmar. These lands, he reported, were "of a much better quality than any other known to the New England people." On returning home, Tupper went directly to see Rufus Putnam to share his appraisal of the Ohio Country.

Determined to realize their vision of a veterans' colony in the Ohio Country, Putnam and Tupper placed an "Information" in Boston and Worcester papers in late January 1786. They described the Ohio Country in positive terms, assuring the public that "the climate, seasons, produce, etc., are, in fact, equal to the most flattering accounts which have ever been published of them." They went on to outline a plan for colonizing the Ohio Country and called on those veterans interested in pursuing such a plan to meet in their respective county seats at 10 A.M. on Wednesday, February 15, 1786, to choose delegates who were to assemble at the Bunch of Grapes Tavern in Boston on March 1 to agree on a plan. Putnam and Tupper read the spirit of the times correctly. Eleven delegates assembled on schedule.

The assemblage at the Bunch of Grapes Tavern, in addition to Putnam and Tupper, included Gen. Samuel H. Parsons, Winthrop Sargent, Jr., and Manasseh Cutler. General Parsons had been a negotiator of the Treaty of Fort McIntosh with the Ohio Indians only the year before. Sargent, a Harvard graduate and the son of one of the most prominent shipowners of Massachusetts, served as secretary of the meeting. Cutler, a veritable Renaissance man—doctor, lawyer, scientist, teacher, clergyman—proved to be an effective lobbyist for the company.

With Putnam chairing the meeting, a committee of five was selected to draft articles of association. The committee, which included Putnam, Sargent, and Cutler, completed its work in two days. It proposed to generate a fund of up to $1 million in certificates of the Continental Congress with which to buy land under the Ordinance of 1785, each share to cost $1,000 and no one person to own more than five shares. The object was to allow veterans of the Revolution to redeem the land warrants given them in partial payment for their military service by letting them form a new settlement in the Ohio Country. Thus, the Ohio Company of Associates came into being.

THE NORTHWEST ORDINANCE

A year passed before a sufficient number of shares were subscribed to enable the Company to proceed. Then, at a meeting on March 8, 1787, General Parsons, Rufus Putnam, and Manasseh Cutler were directed to make application to the Congress for "a private purchase of land." General Parsons was dispatched to New York to initiate the negotiations with Congress but was unsuccessful and returned home. Manasseh Cutler then tried his hand. Winthrop Sargent joined him in New York.

Cutler proved to be the right man in the right place at the right time. He reached New York on July 1st, just as Congress resumed its session. He had two tasks—to negotiate the purchase of land on behalf of the Ohio Company, and to lobby for the establishment of a civil government for the Ohio Country.

Congress, which had confronted the problems of governance of the Western territories since the early 1780s, was at last prepared to act. By the Treaty of Paris (1783), Great Britain had relinquished its territorial claims to the Ohio Country, and in 1784, Virginia abandoned its claims to Ohio, reserving title only to the area between the Scioto and the Little Miami rivers. At the moment, the need for Congress to deal with the "State of Franklin" (Tennessee) was equally urgent. As a member of Congress in 1784, Thomas Jefferson had proposed dividing the Western territories into as many as ten districts, each to be administered by Congress until they attained a minimum of twenty thousand persons, when they would be admitted into the Congress of the United States "on an equal footing with the said original states." After Jefferson went abroad as minister to France, Congress put off action on this measure. Subsequently, Nathan Dane modified the proposal, and his report to Congress in April 1787 was debated the following month. Action on it was pending when Congress reassembled in July.

While the basic bill was the product of many persons, including its chairman, Nathan Dane, Manasseh Cutler, a lobbyist rather than a delegate, was allowed to critique the bill, and Congress incorporated many of his suggestions into the final measure, adopted on July 13. In its final form, the bill provided for three steps: 1) a preliminary government by appointed officials; 2) an intermediate stage in which the residents of the territory might express their will through an elected legislative assembly; and 3) full statehood. Other notable provisions, probably the result of Cutler's input, included an enumeration of the individual rights of citizens, a precursor of the Bill of Rights, and finally, the work of Dane, a provision excluding slavery from the area. As a consequence, as historian Theodore Pease saw it, for the first time Americans "could now leave the older states assured that they were not surrendering their political privileges." Clearly, much of the liberal character of the Northwest Ordinance was owing to the remarkably effective lobbying of Manasseh Cutler. With a framework of civil government for the Ohio Country assured, Cutler was free to devote all his energies to the negotiations for land.

THE OHIO COMPANY LAND PURCHASE

Adoption of the Northwest Ordinance spurred the Treasury Board, headed by William Duer, to enter into negotiations to sell land to the Ohio Company of Associates. The history of the sale of this land remains clouded in controversy. Ironically, Putnam's original proposal to Congress had called for no land grant in excess of a township—36 square miles or 23,040 acres. Now the associates sought title to over a million acres, and, worse yet, they had raised only $250,000. Negotiations did not proceed as quickly as Cutler had expected. By July 20, he was preparing to leave for home in despair. As Cutler tells it, at that point he threw down the gauntlet. He had $250,000, money that the Congress desperately needed; for its part, Congress had land for which it otherwise had no buyer, land the Ohio Company wanted. In the test of wills, Congress blinked. Cutler had his way.

In fact the land purchase was facilitated by the cupidity of William Duer who, as secretary of the Board of Treasury, had charge of land sales but who also represented a "number of principal characters in the city," a group that included members of Congress. In the assessment of historian Theodore Pease, Duer and friends were "an unsavory crew," "peculiarly shifty and tricky specimens" who sought to reap where they had not sown, seeing "an opportunity to hide behind the coattails of Revolutionary veterans" to promote their own selfish ends. Duer approached Cutler, offering to support the plans of the Ohio Company. Over an oyster supper in Brooklyn, Duer and Cutler concocted a scheme that historian Ray Allan Billington has condemned as being "as simple as it was dishonest." Some have argued that Duer had neither "transgressed the law" nor "exceeded the limits set by the standard of commercial morality of the times."

At this point Cutler and Duer amended the proposal of the Ohio Company. Now the Company asked Congress for 1.5 million acres to be paid for in two $500,000 installments, the first when the sale was made, the second when the land survey was completed. In addition, the Company sought an *option to buy* an additional 3.5 million acres. In reality this second transaction was on behalf of Colonel Duer's associates who were organized as the Scioto Company. The latter proposed a schedule of six installments. For incorporating the Scioto Company's proposal into its own, the Ohio Company received a loan from the Scioto Company of the funds it needed to make the down payment; Cutler and Winthrop Sargent became silent partners in the Scioto Company. Cutler was willing to wheel and deal.

The Scioto Company had thirty-two shares. Duer and friends received thirteen of these shares; Cutler and Sargent split thirteen shares between them; the remaining six shares were to be sold in Europe to raise the cash needed to make the installments until such time as the Scioto speculators could unload their option to buy the lands on some other group of speculators at a handsome profit.

Duer and Cutler concluded their secret deal on July 21. On July 24, Cutler again threatened to return home if Congress did not promptly agree to the sale of land to the Ohio Company. Three days later, having allowed time "to create an impression of deliberation," the Board of Treasury accepted the terms. What stands out is the self-serving dealings of Duer and those members of Congress who used their public positions to further their private interests, while the Reverend Manasseh Cutler, acting as agent for the Ohio Company of Associates, secretly secured a substantial share in the Scioto speculation for himself and Winthrop Sargent.

To be sure, the operations of the Ohio Company and the Scioto Company were as different as day and night. The founders of the Ohio Company, veterans who had been compensated for their military service in a combination of depreciated notes and land warrants, expected to move with their families to the new country. This was a bona fide colonization proposal. In contrast, the Scioto Company was pure fly-by-night speculation. Its founders had no interest in moving to Ohio; their only interest was in making a quick profit by selling options to buy Western lands. Ultimately, for this and other shenanigans, William Duer ended his life disgraced and in prison. Cutler agreed to let the Ohio Company provide a cover for the speculations of the Scioto schemers, while he and Sargent looked forward to pocketing their share of the profits from the Scioto Company's operations. Because the Scioto Company proved to be a business failure, neither Cutler nor Sargent realized any profits from this scheme. Indeed, Cutler and Sargent conveyed to Duer the right to half the land included in their second contract in exchange for enough money to make the first payment for the Ohio Company. Even so, Cutler and Sargent retained options to buy in excess of 650,000 acres.

One element of the purchase was of transcendent importance to the development of Athens. Buried in the terms of sale was a requirement that the Ohio Company set aside two townships to be used to support a university. (To the extent that Ohio University, later dubbed "Harvard-on-the-Hocking," had its origins in the lobbying of Manasseh Cutler, it was the work of a Yale graduate.) This provision further stipulated that the two college townships should be "as near the centre [sic] of the whole tract, as may be." In addition, one section of land (640 acres) in each township was reserved for the purposes of religion and a second section for the support of public schools.

PLANNING FOR MIGRATION

The Northwest Ordinance served the Ohio Company well. With Rufus Putnam in overall command, the company proceeded with plans for opening a settlement at the mouth of the Muskingum. Far from being an expression of unfettered free enterprise, the settlement was a corporate undertaking. The company employed four surveyors and twenty-two support personnel. In addition, it hired six boat builders, four house carpenters, one blacksmith, and nine common laborers to facilitate the migration. Each member of this advance party, all men, was to arm himself with "good small arms, bayonet, six flints, a powder horn and pouch, priming wire and brush, half a pound of powder, one pound of balls, and one pound of buckshot" (Walker, 8). The company furnished one hoe and one axe and agreed to transport thirty pounds of baggage per person. The men would be housed and fed at company expense and in addition were to be paid $41 per month, very good wages for the day and recognition of the arduous and potentially hazardous nature of the undertaking. Putnam aggressively and efficiently pushed forward the plans. Eight months after the enactment of the Northwest Ordinance, Putnam and party were on their way to the Ohio Country.

The West was thriving in spring 1788. There were, of course, the old French settlements at Detroit, Vincennes, Kaskaskia, and Cahokia that went back to the beginning of the century. The Kentucky settlements were booming: what in 1775 had been scattered, vulnerable outposts now, little more than a dozen years later, had become small "cities with populations running into the thousands, each with streets and churches, shops and stables and schools," as Allan W. Eckert phrases it. Also in the works were the real estate promotions of John Cleves Symmes planned for the area between the two Miami rivers. And finally, there was already in place Fort Harmar, constructed in 1785 on the west bank of the Muskingum River.

Not surprisingly, traffic on the Ohio River was active. Joseph Buell, one of the first arrivals at Marietta, noted in his journal for May 6, 1788, that thirteen boats bound for Kentucky and loaded with families, goods, and cattle had passed during the day. The next day twenty-one boats passed with 509 souls, "many wagons, goods, etc."

Putnam arrived April 7 with fifty men to begin a settlement (briefly called Adelphia but changed to Marietta in honor of Marie Antoinette, on July 2, 1788) on the east side of the Muskingum, across from Fort Harmar. His party began with "a great spirit." Three weeks later General Parsons, Winthrop Sargent, and a number of other settlers arrived. In midsummer, in keeping with the terms of the Northwest Ordinance, Arthur St. Clair, an experienced administrator and old soldier, was appointed territorial governor; Winthrop Sargent, secretary of the Ohio Company and silent partner in the Scioto Company speculations, was named territorial secretary. Among the judges appointed for the new territory were Samuel H. Parsons, Rufus Putnam, Benjamin Tupper, and Return Jonathan Meigs, Jr.

THE INDIAN WARS

The arrival of settlers at Marietta and the volume of river traffic were a direct challenge to the Shawnee, Miami, and Delaware Indians—an indication that the whites, not satisfied with having taken their hunting lands east and south of the Ohio River, now would be vying for lands within the Ohio Country. The Shawnee and Miami struck back, attacking the Kentucky settlements as far from the Ohio River as Harrodsburg, Danville, and Stanford. Scores of boats coming down the Ohio were waylaid, the occupants more often killed than taken prisoner. New settlements in the Symmes Purchase—Symmes City, Losantiville, and Columbia—experienced frequent attacks. The depredations of the Indians prompted President Washington to apprise Congress of the fact that in the preceding seven-year period, more than 1,500 settlers had been killed and scalped on the Ohio River alone. And so, Congress authorized the first of what would be three campaigns against the Indians of Ohio: Josiah Harmar's in September 1790, Arthur St. Clair's in November 1791, and Anthony Wayne's in August 1794.

The first consequence of the Indian wars was a virtual stop for the time being to further migration to the Ohio Country. A survey of the Hockhocking area was put on hold. Although the three campaigns were all fought in the Wabash or Maumee river valleys, far from the Hockhocking, the Indians' decisive victory against Harmar emboldened the Shawnee, who staged a raid on Big Bottom, an outlying settlement north of Marietta. By "stealth and sudden surprise" (as related in *History of the Hocking Valley, Ohio*) they descended on the unsuspecting community at dawn on January 2, 1791. The resulting massacre and scalping left twelve persons dead and caused utter panic at Waterford, Marietta, and Belpre. The evening of the attack at Big Bottom, the residents of Belpre were alerted to an impending raid. Roused from their sleep, some thirty persons crowded into the largest and strongest cabin. Water secured, windows and doors barred, they waited through the night. At dawn the Indians arrived, but seeing that the settlers had anticipated their attack, they departed. The Big Bottom Massacre and the threatened attack on Belpre made a lasting impression on persons who later came to Athens.

Although the Miami chieftain Little Turtle and his Shawnee ally, Blue Jacket, routed first Harmar and then St. Clair, the Indian coalition sustained a devastating defeat at the hands of Anthony Wayne. The Treaty of Greenville, which Wayne negotiated with the vanquished Indian tribes, had enormous consequences for the occupation of the Hockhocking Valley. By this treaty the entire Hockhocking Valley was off-limits to the Indians. There was peace. White settlement of eastern and southern Ohio could safely resume.

UP THE HOCKHOCKING

As the Treaty of Greenville removed the Indian threat to the occupation of southeast Ohio, migration to the Ohio Company lands resumed. Inevitably, the major focus was on Marietta and the Muskingum Valley. But times had changed since the start of the Indian Wars. Kentucky, already admitted to statehood in 1792, was by 1795 the major attraction for settlers going down the Ohio. Within Ohio, the Muskingum Valley had to compete with the Scioto and Miami valleys and with the Western Reserve. At the same time Putnam, Tupper, Sargent, and the other stockholders in the Ohio Company, aside from finding new homes for themselves, had to promote the sale of the company's lands. They had particular responsibility for the two townships that were to be used to support a college, townships that could provide a focus for further town developments. As early as June 30, 1790, the Company had taken note of its obligation to "fix on the two townships" it was obliged to set apart for the university, and at its November 1790 meeting, had appointed a committee of five to tend to this task. This selection of land, however, had to be put off because of the Indian wars.

In January 1795, Putnam sent a party of surveyors, with fifteen guards, from Marietta to the Hockhocking. They encountered no Indians, and in the course of the spring and summer they completed their survey. They recommended that the townships we know as Athens and Alexander were most central in the Ohio Company's purchase and that "the lands are of an excellent quality." On a map of the land holdings of the Ohio Company, Athens appears on the western edge of those holdings. The college lands were, however, midway between Marietta and the southernmost point of the Company's land. They were also midway between Marietta and Chillicothe.

Later in 1795, at a time Indians typically engaged in their fall hunt, a second party consisting of the Fleethart brothers and a man remembered only as Gillespie came to the Hockhocking. They ascended the Hockhocking to its confluence with Federal Creek. Finding many signs of Indians, they built a large fire, hung up a blanket and other articles to advertise their presence, then slipped into the darkness and quietly fled. The experience of the Fleetharts further delayed sending settlers to the Hockhocking Valley. Returning a year later, one of the Fleetharts maintained the camp, while the other brother went up Federal Creek and Gillespie, accompanied by his dog, ascended the Hockhocking to its junction with Sunday Creek. They concluded that it was safe to occupy the area.

FIRST FAMILIES

From Putnam's point of view, although the Treaty of Greenville had ended the Indian menace, a new threat had emerged—a handful of squatters, unnamed, living on the college lands. In the account of Samuel P. Hildreth in 1797, Putnam, always the prime force in pushing the settlement of the company's lands, recruited a party of roughly a dozen "substantial men" from the Marietta and Belpre settlements, men already accustomed to life in the Ohio Country, "men possessing firmness of character, courage, and sound discretion" to occupy the college lands (as yet unnamed), to expel the trespassers, and to commence a permanent settlement. These included the Bingham brothers, Silas and Alvan; Isaac Barker; John Chandler, a brother-in-law of Alvan Bingham; the Dorr brothers, Barak, Edmund, and William; William Harper; Robert Linzee; Jonathan Watkins; and John Wilkins. That the process of settlement was both risky and arduous is reflected in the fact that no women or children were in this initial group. A second party followed in the spring of 1798: Solomon Tuttle, Christopher Stevens, John and Moses Hewitt, Cornelius Moore, Joseph Snowden, John Simonton, Robert Ross, the Brooks, and the Hanings. In addition, there was Margaret Snowden, the wife of Joseph, and the first white woman to settle in this part of Athens County. These firstcomers did not all congregate in what became the village of Athens, nor was it the intention of the Ohio Company that they do so. During 1797, George Ewing brought his family to what is now Ames Township, while the following year Ephraim Cutler and Captain Benjamin Brown built cabins there. Solomon Tuttle would remove to what is now Glouster.

An account of the founding of Athens, written late in the nineteenth century and apparently apocryphal, suggests that Putnam, who previously had reconnoitered the area, had intended the college site and its village to be located on the broad plateau at what is presently The Plains. Certainly this area, once occupied by the Adena, offered easy access to the Hockhocking River while constituting a "beautiful level plain." The legend further avers that the pioneer party coming up the Hockhocking mistook the high bluffs bounded by the river, the site of the present-day College Green, for Putnam's site. They were further impressed that this was a defensible position in the event of future Indian troubles. If the first party of settlers gave any thought to replicating Marietta's Campus Martius in Athens, however, they certainly made no effort to plan a compact settlement. In fact, these first settlers dispersed over a wide area. The story that the settlers located at the wrong site seems specious, for the site allegedly preferred by Putnam is on the left side of the Hockhocking, going upstream; the site selected is on the right. There is no report of Putnam remonstrating against the choice of location.

The diverse interests and backgrounds of the first settlers of the area account for their dispersal. William Harper, who would serve variously as county treasurer and township trustee, established a ferry some hundred yards upstream from the juncture of the Hockhocking and Margaret Creek. Harper's ferry became a nucleus of a settlement that he called Elizabethtown. The elder Isaac Barker, onetime sea captain, also located along the Hockhocking near Elizabethtown. A year later, Isaac Barker, Jr., poled his way up the Hockhocking; he settled near the ferry, tended it, and eventually married Harper's daughter, Christiana. Around 1815, Isaac Junior moved to Athens, eventually becoming a tavern keeper and judge.

Captain John Chandler is acknowledged as having constructed the first house in Athens, located at the north end of College Street between what is now Mill Street and East State Street. William Dorr acquired a lot on President Street and built a double log house at College and Mill Streets. The other two Dorrs, Barak and Edmund, located north of Athens. John Wilkins, "a man of considerable learning," laid claim to the property on West Union Street that became the site for the handsome limestone building that long housed the Athens post office.

In the forefront of those who settled what is now uptown Athens were the Bingham brothers. Veterans of the American Revolution, they represented law and order. Alvan, the older of the two, had been appointed justice of the peace; Silas was deputy sheriff. They were to persuade the squatters in the area to make arrangements to buy the land or leave, and otherwise to keep the peace. The brothers worked hand in glove. Alvan was a serious, no-nonsense person; Silas, a man with an exuberant sense of humor. On one occasion, when an accused felon refused to plead before Judge Alvan, Sheriff Silas suggested that the accused had but two alternatives. One was to be taken to Marietta, where he could expect to be dealt with very harshly; the other was to get on his knees and crawl back into the court before Judge Alvan and throw himself on the judge's mercy. The man crawled, and Silas saved himself an arduous trip to Marietta. While the brothers developed a variety of interests, their base was in what became the village.

Robert Linzee, a native of western Pennsylvania, settled in Alexander Township, became the first elected sheriff of Athens County, and served several terms in the state legislature as its representative.

Moses Hewitt, one of the most colorful of the first settlers, had left New England in 1789 in the company of his uncle, John Hewitt, and had settled near the mouth of the Little Kanawha. A man of extraordinary strength, he reputedly could lift a blacksmith's anvil by its horn. Although he was only marginally literate, Hewitt is described by his biographer, Susan L. Mitchell, as possessing "a clear, discriminating and vigorous mind." Hewitt settled along Margaret Creek and is remembered as the first white settler of Waterloo. He spent his last years in Athens village, living at the southeast corner of Congress and Washington.

As a group, these were men who were old enough to have acquired experience and to have demonstrated their skills, yet young enough to provide vigorous leadership for the new community. Picked as "men possessing firmness of character, courage, and sound discretion," they did the work cut out for them.

THE ROAD TO ATHENS

Migrating to Athens from New England, New York, or western Pennsylvania was physically exhausting. Rufus Putnam set the pattern. Typically the settlers proceeded by horse or oxen and wagon to western Pennsylvania, aiming for the banks of either the Youghiogheny or the Monongahela. East of the Allegheny Mountains the migrants traveled through farm country. Beyond the crest of the Alleghenies they encountered wild turkeys and deer at the water's edge and perhaps "a dusky Indian." On reaching the Monongahela, Putnam's party constructed a flatboat some 45 feet long by 12 feet wide. Roofed over, it provided shelter for all. If the river was high enough, the migrants could float downstream to Marietta in five days. Typically, the trip from New England to Marietta took three months. Customarily, those bound for Athens followed the route Putnam pioneered.

Although the general outlines remained similar, each migrant had a special story to tell. For Isaac Barker, Jr., who left Massachusetts in 1788, the trip was made in the company of the Joseph Dana family. Barker began with a wagon, two oxen, and a horse. By the time the party reached Pennsylvania Dutch Country, the oxen were footsore. Barker traded them with a "Dutch" tavern keeper. Immediately after resuming the trip, he reached a bad point in the road. The oxen stopped and refused to proceed. The Dutchman was summoned, and, Charles Walker has recorded, "by dint of considerable swearing at the oxen in good Dutch," the team moved on. Barker located at Belpre for nearly a decade before poling a flatboat up the Hockhocking.

For the Eliphaz Perkins family the trip was especially memorable. A medical doctor, Perkins had set out alone for Marietta in spring 1789, but was persuaded to stay in Clarksburg, Virginia. Then, with the onset of the Indian wars, he had returned to his family in Connecticut. By the time Perkins resolved to migrate permanently to Ohio in June 1799, he and his wife had seven children and Mrs. Perkins was again pregnant. To relieve herself of the "tiresome motion of the wagon," she rode a gentle horse part of the time. After passing through Reading, Pennsylvania, she gave birth to twin daughters. The family remained three weeks before resuming the trek, but by this time other members of the family were ill, an illness attributed to "hot weather, bad water, and an abundance of fruit." As Perkins's daughter Julia recalled the experience, they found the Pennsylvania Dutch "not very friendly to strangers," but as the children were too sick to travel, they took refuge in an abandoned blacksmith's shop with a fireplace and earthen floor, "better than nothing." They remained ten days, then pushed on, traveling six or seven miles a day to McKeesport on the lower Monongahela. As the children were sick again, the Perkinses were detained several weeks. By the time the children recovered, the river level was too low for travel with a full load. To reduce the weight, the two oldest boys took the team overland, while the rest of the family proceeded by flatboat, taking three days to reach Pittsburgh. By this time it was November. Three miles below Pittsburgh their boat struck a rock and was in danger of breaking up. Forced to proceed by land, the mother rode a horse holding one child in her lap with a second one hanging on behind her. An older daughter did the same, riding with one child in front and one behind her, while the father walked, holding one of the babies in his arms. Sometimes following "little paths" and sometimes no trace at all, the family took a week to reach Wheeling. Here they were able to board a flatboat again. A week later, they arrived in Marietta—five months and two weeks after their trek began. A suitable house was not readily available, and it was the end of December before one was found. Exhausted from her ordeal, Mrs. Perkins was "seized with a nervous fever." A few days later she died.

In spring 1800, Dr. Perkins was invited to move to Athens. He came alone and secured a home—a log cabin—one room, one window, one door. A spring of "excellent water" was nearby as was a shed for horse and cow. Perkins sent for the five older children. Accompanied by a guide, they walked to Athens. "Here," his daughter concluded, "we enjoyed peace and happiness."

From Marietta, Athens-bound settlers had two routes. In the summer of 1797, the first year it was safe to settle on the Hockhocking, Ephraim Cutler, the son of Manasseh Cutler, and George Ewing, father of Thomas, cut a pack-horse trail from Waterford on the Muskingum to Federal Creek. Women and children generally traveled by horseback from Marietta, ascending the Muskingum Valley to Waterford, where they turned west along Wolf Creek, then hiked or rode cross-country along the Cutler-Ewing trail to Federal Creek and Amesville, and thence another ten miles to Athens. The men, in the meantime, loaded the family's goods into a pirogue, a hollowed-out log canoe, or onto a flatboat, floated down the Ohio past Belpre to the mouth of the Hockhocking River, and then poled or towed their canoe or flatboat up the Hockhocking to Athens.

For decades travel remained difficult. The overland route between Athens and Marietta via Wolf Creek was only gradually widened to accommodate a wagon; even then, after a rain, the roadbed was impassable sea of mud. The river route always was dependent on the water level. One of the first problems the Athens community faced was improving the lines of communication and transport with the outside world.

SETTLING IN

The first imperative was housing. Among the most essential tools of every pioneer was an axe and an auger, while someone in the party brought a crosscut saw to share with neighbors. Thomas Ewing recalled in a reminiscence the pioneer's belief that "with an axe and an auger a man could make everything he wanted except a gun and bullet molds." The dense woods provided the materials. The first homes were log cabins, such as pioneers had been building since the Finns and Swedes introduced them along the Delaware River in the middle 1600s. The individual settler could fell the trees; he could even square the logs and cut them to the desired length. When the requisite number of logs had been cut to the desired length, the able-bodied men in the area assembled for a cabin raising. As nails were a rarity, puncheon floors, a section of a tree that had been split lengthwise, were anchored with wooden pegs. A mixture of mud and sticks or mortar was pressed into the open spaces between the logs to shut out rain and cold, a task that had to be repeated each fall. Doors were hung on clumsy wooden hinges; they were held closed with wooden latches. A leather latchstring was used to lift the latch from the outside but could be pulled back inside to "lock" the door for the night. The roof was initially of bark; later shingles were laid on in rows and weighted down with straight logs. The finished cabin was likely to be no more than 12 to 14 feet wide and 15 to 18 feet long—the length of a log that two men could comfortably lift into place.

For cooking, there was an open fireplace. This might initially be built of logs coated on the inside with a thick layer of mud—inherently dangerous, for as the mud cracked, the wood was likely to ignite, setting the cabin afire. Preferably, field stones were gathered and, set in mortar, fashioned into a massive fireplace.

Windows were few, and in the absence of glass, the openings might be covered by greased paper or greased parchment. During inclement weather and at night, the window area could be closed by shutters. The interiors of houses, then, were ordinarily dark. Candles were too expensive to use frivolously; so, too, were whale-oil lamps. The pioneer's life was regulated by the rising and setting of the sun.

As time permitted, additional space was gained by adding a lean-to behind the original building and using it for storage, an extra bedroom, or a kitchen. Alternatively, one might literally raise the roof, building a second floor, thus doubling the floor space and separating the living and dining area from the sleeping quarters. Or one might extend the house sideways, essentially building a second log house adjacent to the original structure. In time, a log house might be incorporated into a frame house, the combined structures being enclosed in clapboard to give the house a unified, updated appearance.

Furnishings were simple. The migrants could bring no more than one or two pieces of treasured furniture. For the most part, they started from scratch. A large bed built into one corner of the cabin with a trundle bed for the children would suffice, although older children might sleep in the loft above the living quarters. The bedding might well be a bear skin; for a long time, straw ticks—long sacks filled with straw or even dry leaves—were articles of luxury. A cupboard might be built into another corner. In addition, there would be a rough, heavy table, fashioned somewhat like a modern picnic table, while hewn slabs served for seats. Clothes would be hung on pegs along the walls. The one-room living-dining-bedroom-kitchen afforded little privacy.

THE PIONEER ECONOMY

Athens was isolated. That basic fact shaped its economic life for decades. The reminiscences of the pioneers emphasize repeatedly the narrow trail through dense forests and over rough hills that they had traversed en route to Athens. For years, the only alternative to the pack-horse path cut by Ephraim Cutler and George Ewing was the Hockhocking. To navigate the Hockhocking, one had first to construct a raft, canoe, or flatboat, steered by a sweep, and, then, perhaps, wait for floodwaters to recede or for rains to raise the water level to the requisite depth. To ascend the river with a cargo, one had to pole the boat upstream—slow, exhausting work.

Isaac Barker, Jr., recalled that to get grain milled, he had to go to Devol's mill, located five miles upstream from Marietta, a trip made by pirogue that took four days, requiring that he camp overnight each way. Whether by land or water, the dangerous trip took several days, and exposed the individual to attack by wild animals and snakes. The difficulties deterred all but the most essential travel and trade.

Hunting

In the face of this isolation, the pioneer, while providing a cabin to house himself and his family, had to take time out to secure food. For at least a generation, Athenians secured much of their protein from hunting white-tailed deer and turkey.

Isaac Barker, not especially distinguished as a hunter, nonetheless was able to kill "great numbers of deer and turkeys." Deer were killed with "great ease," but "panthers, black bears, and wolves were sufficiently plentiful" to provide variety. Indeed, Captain Pratt, on one occasion, brought down a panther that measured "nine feet from tip to tip." Again Thomas Ewing reports "our meat—bear meat or raccoon, with venison or turkey, cooked together and seasoned to taste (a most savory dish) —was cut up in morsels and placed in the centre of the table, and the younger members of the family, armed with sharpened sticks, helped themselves about as well as with four-tined forks." For the first generation of settlers, beef, pork, and mutton were rarities. In fact, Ewing recalled vividly the first beef he ever tasted: "I thought it coarse and stringy compared to venison."

Planting

The pioneer also had to prepare for the future. The first season the pioneer planted in the nearest natural clearing. But for the future, the settler had to expand his arable land. By girdling trees (that is, stripping the bark around the trunk) and clearing underbrush, he could clear three to five acres of land, enabling him in the following spring to plant in the open area between the trees. Such clearings were small, irregular, and scattered. At best they provided corn for corn bread, mush, and hominy.

Each year, additional land would be cleared, a process that continued for years. Clearing was done in winter months, the underbrush cut and piled. Logs already on the ground were either burned or cut into pieces to facilitate their removal. Timber suited for use as fence rail was cut into appropriate lengths and split. Larger trees, having been girdled, were eventually chopped down. Some of the cut logs would be utilized for construction of houses, barns, and other outbuildings; other timber was cut and split for fuel. But the supply so far exceeded local demand that timber had little commercial value, and consequently much was simply burned in the field to get it out of the way. Ashes from the burned timber were collected, leached, and processed into lye that might be traded at stores and eventually processed into potash for Eastern markets.

These first settlers farmed much as the Indians had farmed. Whereas Indian women had used a dibble stick to punch a hole in the ground in order to plant corn, squash, and beans, the white Athenians used a hoe or axe to lift the soil. To be sure, the whites had a plow, but the plows of this era had wooden moldboards;

only the plowshare and point were made of iron. Such plows were clumsy and could not be widely used until the roots of the virgin forest had decayed. This might take a half-dozen years or longer. To level the soil after it was plowed, the pioneer employed a makeshift harrow—dragging the crotch of a tree across the plowed field. It also sufficed to cover grain that had been sown by hand and was rugged enough to be used in fields still studded with stumps and roots.

Corn was the grain of necessity, if not choice. A bushel of seed wheat produced fifteen to twenty bushels; a bushel of seed corn, four hundred bushels. Furthermore, it was far easier to prepare the soil for corn than for wheat. When the corn was a few inches high, the farmer returned to the field and chopped the weeds with his hoe. At harvest time, the corn might be picked and husked in the fields; or it could be cut, shocked, and husked at a later date.

The growing of wheat had to be deferred until the land had been cleared, fenced, and plowed. Even then, the grain was sown by hand, a traditional method that produced low yields. After being cut with a sickle, the wheat had to be shocked to dry, then hauled to the barn, where it was spread on the ground and threshed either with a flail or by using horses to tread out the grain. Finally, the grain had to be winnowed, that is, the grain had to be separated from the chaff. Given the broadcast method of planting and the use of the handsickle to harvest, crop production was severely limited.

To facilitate planting and harvesting, Athens pioneer farmers used animals. For clearing land and general farmwork, oxen were preferred. They were less expensive than horses and more easily kept. The yokes for oxen were less costly than leather harnesses for horses, and the oxen could work more steadily. Ultimately, they could be put to pasture, fattened, and eaten. Only after the land was cleared of stumps, roots, and rocks did the use of horses become more feasible.

In short, most Athenian pioneers farmed as well as hunted to assure food for their families. Of necessity, Athens-area farms were small, primitive; the produce, largely for use of the family. Surpluses, if any, could be sold to a newly-arrived neighbor or to a local miller or storekeeper for cash or, more likely, bartered for goods the farmer could not produce himself. Such subsistence farming was the norm to 1825 and beyond. Villagers, too, might engage in limited agriculture as house lots were huge, permitting a large kitchen garden, while five-acre out lots were within easy walking distance.

Livestock

As agriculture was limited in scale, so too was the raising of livestock. In the first instance, until the predatory animals—especially wolves and bears—were exterminated, pioneers could not safely let cattle, swine, or sheep graze loose, nor, given other urgent demands on their energies, could they provide fenced pastures for their herd. The choice, then, was to forgo raising livestock altogether or else to let the animals scavenge the woods and take their chances with the predators, admitting them to the enclosed fields only after harvest. In these circumstances, it was a case of survival of the fittest. The common hog, called a "rail splitter," was small, its meat low in quantity and quality. An additional bar to raising cattle was the prevalence of the bloody murrain, a fatal ailment that afflicted American cattle in those years. Dairying, too, was impractical, for there was no commercial market for butter or cheese, much less for fluid milk. At most, a family kept a cow to supply itself with milk and butter. Even so, a year-round supply was not certain. Village dwellers, no less than farmers, kept cattle, pigs, and sheep, all too often letting them run loose or grazing them on the commons.

Household Industries

Of necessity, then, Athenians pieced together a living by pursuing a variety of economic activities. Not to be overlooked were the household industries of the women. In the first instance, they shouldered conventional domestic responsibilities—caring for the children, preparing meals, keeping house—freeing the adult males of the household to devote their full energies to the care of the large animals, to clearing land, to planting and harvesting, and to hunting and fishing. But there was far more hard physical work for the women than these conventional responsibilities imply. Cooking was done from scratch. Preparing meals over several open fires, a woman might well begin her day by stirring the embers into a suitable fire, splitting kindling, hauling the wood inside the cabin. She, or the children, had to fetch water from the well or nearby stream. Soup, for later in the day, had to be started. If her family was to have bread, the dough must be mixed, kneaded, allowed time to rise, kneaded a second time, allowed to rise, and finally baked—a process possibly spread over two days. Meat that was being roasted had to be turned on a spit.

Food preparation also entailed going into the woods to gather herbs for seasoning and medicine; boiling maple sap gathered in late winter by her husband and the children; gathering honey from a "honey" tree throughout spring and summer; collecting nuts, fruits, and berries in season to supplement the diet; planting and tending a vegetable garden; drying, smoking, salting, pickling or otherwise preserving vegetables, fruit, and meat for consumption later in the year; making sausage; churning butter and making cheese.

Nor was keeping house simple. To wash clothes, water had to be drawn and then heated, the clothes stirred, wrung out, rinsed, wrung out, and spread on bushes or the grass, and, when dry, shaken out, folded, and put away, an all-day chore. But there were other essential economic activities for the woman: collecting ashes, leaching out the lye, and adding grease to make soap; collecting tallow and hand-dipping wicks to make candles or pouring hot tallow into molds to make a dozen candles at a time; gathering bayberries in season to make candles for special occasions; collecting feathers to stuff pillows and comforters; selecting straw for mattresses; piecing quilts. As soon as sheep could be raised, women sheared the sheep, carded the wool, spun it, dyed it, and then knitted it or wove it into cloth, and finally cut the cloth and sewed it into garments for their families' use. A woman might also process flax, which used alone produced linen or, when woven in combination with woolen yarn, produced linsey-woolsey—the equivalent of today's denim. Many of the woman's economic activities were highly seasonal and generally were discontinuous, but they formed an indispensable part of her family's support. The division of labor between men and women inexorably kept males and females in family units. The frontier environment did not allow men or women to live alone.

Life in the first years of a frontier community was in some respects a "Robinson Crusoe" existence. What a family did not produce for itself, it had to do without. The pioneer Athenian combined subsistence agriculture with gathering and hunting, much as the Indians had done. For the Indian, such an economy had represented the highest achievement thus far; for the Athenian, it was a temporary expedient. Having come from communities where a variety of specialized goods and services had been available, these new Athenians had to mark time before turning to commercial agriculture and replicating those goods and services. For a generation, the best they could do was to piece together a living by pursuing several activities.

The Fur Trading Economy

The first major "export" commodities for white Athenians, as for the Indians, were furs and hides. Elk, deer, wolves, and panthers abounded. Despite the heavily wooded terrain of the Athens area, there had been enough open spaces for bison to graze the Hockhocking Valley; by the late 1790s, however, they were scarce. A member of the party sent out by Putnam in 1795 to explore the Hockhocking spotted a bison on the present site of the Athens County Fairgrounds, wounded it, and pursued it to the vicinity of the present county courthouse where, finding it "tearing [at the ground] in great rage and pain," he killed it. The last bison in the Raccoon Creek area was captured in the spring of 1799 and exhibited publicly until it gored its owner. Bison, elk, and bear, which required the largest areas to forage, were the most vulnerable to human encroachment. Bison and elk were gone by 1800. The last great bear-hunting season occurred the winter of 1811–12.

The fur trade was a part-time activity for most pioneer farmers, for until they radically reduced the population of deer and predatory animals, they could not press forward with either agriculture or grazing. For a short time, then, 1797 to 1812, bear skins would be taken. The always pesky raccoon was "especially troublesome" when it snacked on the ripening corn. Active boys would set out with their dogs in quest of raccoons. This was likely to be more sport than business, for raccoon pelts had limited commercial value.

The principal staple was the white-tailed deer, as it had been for the Indian. Until the War of 1812, parties of Wyandot, in particular, despite the Treaty of Greenville, hunted in the Hockhocking Valley in the winter months when the pelts were at their prime. "Large" parties visited Raccoon, Monday, and Sunday creeks and the headwaters of Federal Creek. Among white Athenians, some deer hides were retained for family use, since deer skin remained the ideal material for wear in the woods. Venison, as mentioned earlier, formed a major component of the meat supply. For those seriously involved, hunting was a group activity; a party of men, employed the "surround" to corner a number of deer in order to maximize the kill. Initially, the individuals would have to tan the hides, which then might be bartered with local merchants, who, consolidating the catch of a large number of hunters, would bale the hides and market them outside the area.

One pioneer stands out as a specialist in the fur business—Moses Hewitt. Thirty years old when he came to Athens County, Hewitt lived first on Margaret Creek. He had been a professional hunter and trader prior to coming to Athens and continued these activities once in the Athens area. The extent of his business remains undocumented, but it was of sufficient magnitude that he took his furs to Pittsburgh to market them. Like others, Hewitt used the fur trade to get a start. He was, in fact, an aggressive, enterprising businessman who, by the time of his death in 1814, developed extensive real estate holdings, built up a farm with horses, cattle, sheep, and hogs, planted a 200-tree orchard, and held two mail contracts. He was one of the original landowners in the village. His business affairs were of sufficient magnitude that he engaged Henry Bartlett, a fellow townsman, to take care of his business correspondence.

For most white Athenians, unlike either the First Athenians or the white intruders of the 1740s and 50s, the fur trade was never more than a short-term enterprise. The pioneers of 1797 looked forward to acquiring land and becoming farmers or merchants. The fur trade was a means of producing a cash income while the land was being cleared. As their basic interest was in agriculture and animal husbandry, the pioneers had no interest in conservation to assure long-term prosperity to fur trapping, hunting, or trading. Rather, the dominant interest was in exterminating the predators as quickly as practicable as an essential precondition of introducing livestock. By the same token, they had to clear the timber as a precondition of pursuing agriculture. The coming of the white settlers meant major changes in the area's ecosystem.

Milling

From the arrival of the first settlers, obtaining flour or corn meal was one of the most trying problems of frontier life. The first residents of Athens, like the Indians before them, might use a mortar and pestle to pound their corn into meal. A mortar was "dug out of a large stump, with a spring pole fastened to an iron wedge for a pestle." Alternatively, settlers had to transport their own grain either to a floating mill, powered by the current of the Ohio River, located between Parkersburg and Marietta or to one of the mills on Wolf Creek. In recognition that travel was physically difficult, time-consuming, and dangerous, the Ohio Company had offered free use of a tract of land 150 by 200 feet to the person who built the first mill near the mouth of the Muskingum.

As Marjorie Stone, the co-author of *Getting to Know Athens County*, reminds us, going to a mill on Wolf Creek, the Muskingum, or Ohio River was a real hardship for the pioneer. With so many physically taxing tasks to be done, the man of the house could not be spared to spend three or four days taking grain to a distant mill to be ground. It was a better use of personnel to send the teenage son. But, as Stone points out, if the sack of grain or meal became unbalanced on the horse's back, the lad was in a jam. If he was unable to hoist the sack back into place on the animal's back, he might have a long wait before another person happened by who could assist him.

Joseph Bobo recalled that as late as 1815, when as a thirteen-year-old he was sent from Lodi to a mill at Coolville, there was but one house along the fifteen-mile distance. Young Thomas Ewing, while a boy living near Ames, made numerous trips to the Wolf Creek mills at Beverly or to Barrow's mill on Federal Creek— trips that required stopping overnight along the way. Ewing made the best of an arduous task, for he found he might spend the night with Doctor Timothy Jones, a graduate of Brown University, whom local lore claimed had been banished to the frontier by his family for his intemperance. Jones, however, had books which he invited young Ewing to read to him. In recalling this period of his life, Ewing wrote: "going to the mill and intemperance contributed to my education."

By 1800, hand-powered mills became available. Resembling a large coffee mill, a handmill might be fastened to the side of a house or to a tree close by. In Ames, George Ewing apparently acquired a small handmill that he permitted neighbors to use, as did George Cassell, who lived southwest of Athens village. Indeed, Cassell not only let his neighbors use his handmill for a price, but he seems to have fabricated such mills from local stone and marketed them. In a community where labor was in short supply, handmills were at best a temporary expedient when one ran short of ground meal.

An alternative was a horse-powered mill, the first of which was that of Christopher Herrold of Ames in 1800–1801. Silas Bingham also operated a small horse-powered mill in the vicinity of present-day Mill Street and the Hocking River. A horse-powered mill, like a handmill, could be operated wherever its services were required. But the capacities of such mills were decidedly limited. For the area to mature economically, a water-powered mill was essential.

PLATTING A TOWNSITE

The first settlers of the college lands dispersed—some in Alexander Township, others along Margaret Creek, and still others in the immediate vicinity of the "high bluffs" of what is now the College Green and uptown Athens. This latter area was denominated "Middletown," probably because of its location roughly halfway between Marietta and Chillicothe. By 1799, the nucleus of settlers at Middletown merited recognition as a community that necessitated formal organization. One factor, external to be sure, was the growing sense of Ohio as a political entity apart from the Northwest Territory. Congress removed the Territorial capital first to Cincinnati, then in 1800 to Chillicothe. In light of this latter development, Middletown gained importance. For itself, the Middletown community was spread out.

At this point, the question of opening the college lands to settlement came to the fore as the Territorial legislature directed Rufus Putnam, Benjamin Ives Gilman, and Jonathan Stone to lay off in the most suitable place within Athens and Alexander townships "a town plat which shall contain a square for the college, also lots suitable for house lots and gardens." Putnam executed the survey promptly, and at its next meeting the legislature, on December 6, 1800, "confirmed and established" a town called Athens. Middletown, thus, passed away.

Putnam's plat gave the village a focus, consisting of an area essentially five blocks by five. From south to north there would be Mulberry (Park Place), President, Union, Washington, and State streets; from east to west: Vine (University Terrace), College, Court and Olive, Congress, and High. Altogether, the plat designated seventy-seven in-lots. The College Green was bounded by Vine, Mulberry, Olive, and President streets. The Green, however, was bisected by College Street which ran from Mulberry to State. In addition, the plat designated two commons, one on the south side of Union Street, occupying the northern third of what is now the College Green; the other, north of State Street, that is, in the area presently occupied by the Armory and North Hill. In addition, Putnam's plat provided a substantial number of five-acre out-lots that might be farmed. Essentially, Putnam's plat encompassed the high bluffs that had attracted the pioneers of 1797.

As of 1800, there were no more than five or six cabins on the town plat. Captain John Chandler, who located on in-lot number 1 at the north end of College Street, had as his near-neighbors John Havner and Solomon Tuttle. A Mr. Earhart located on "the brow of the hill," Christopher Stevens's cabin was on Mulberry Street, and a Mr. Brakefield lived in the vicinity of present-day Shively Hall and Morton Hall. Alvan Bingham, who lived "a half mile to the northeast" on the northwest side of East State Street near its intersection with Elmwood Place, and Othneil Tuttle, whose cabin was at the southwest corner of the West State Street Cemetery site, were outside the village. Few of these persons remained long.

In 1803, as Ohio became a state, the Rev. Thaddeus M. Harris, a clergyman from Massachusetts, passed through the community. "Athens," he reported, "is regularly laid out, on elevated ground of easy assent, round which the river [Hocking] forms a graceful bend. The situation is healthy, and the prospect delightful beyond description. The town is abundantly supplied with never-failing springs of excellent water, and the adjacent county is thought superior to any in the state for pleasantness and fertility." As a *place* Athens had achieved official recognition. To realize its potential, two additional steps were required: formal legislation to charter the college and legislation to authorize village government.

3

Pioneer Athens: 1800–1825

WHILE THE TERRITORIAL LEGISLATURE recognized Athens by according it a name and directing Rufus Putnam to plat the town site, Athens was still without a government of its own, the land still largely in its natural state, the college still on the agenda for the future. That future would lock the Athens area into a legal embrace with the university in which the growth of one depended on the growth of the other. The first need, however, was a functioning government.

FASHIONING A GOVERNMENT

Progressing from territorial status to statehood was not easy. The territorial bureaucracy—Governor St. Clair, Secretary Sargent, and the three judges—had economic ties with the Ohio Company and were Federalist in their political sympathies. Those settlers who in the late 1790s took up lands in the Virginia Military District west of Chillicothe or in the Symmes Purchase in the Miami Valley, predominantly Jeffersonian Democrats, sought immediate statehood as a means to gain political power. But St. Clair, a confirmed Federalist, had a vested interest in delaying statehood.

Having ties with the Ohio Company, Athenians sided with St. Clair. The most persuasive argument against immediate statehood, however, was economic. While statehood promised a larger degree of political autonomy, it would increase the costs of government, requiring higher taxes that land-poor Athenians were not eager to absorb. (While residents of the college lands were exempt from state property taxes, other county residents were not.) When a state constitutional convention was elected in 1802, Alvan Bingham opposed statehood, arguing that "in our opinion, it would be highly impolitic and very injurious to the inhabitants of this territory, to enter into a state government *at this time.*" Bingham, like the Washington County delegates, hoped to defer statehood until the population of Ohio had grown to the point that the western boundary of Ohio would be set at the Scioto River. This would make the Muskingum Valley central to the new state and preserve the Federalist influence. The convention, however, meeting in Chillicothe, was of a different mind. When the convention delegates voted on a resolution that "it is expedient, at this time to form a constitution and a State government," Ephraim Cutler was the only delegate voting against the measure. The convention then proceeded to draft a constitution. Accepting the reality of the situation, Cutler actively participated in drafting the Ohio constitution and was largely responsible for the provisions for the county court system and for language barring slavery from Ohio. In the end Cutler was pleased with the Ohio Constitution. The following year, on March 3, 1803, Congress accepted Ohio as a state. The new state had its imperatives. One was to fashion the requisite levels of government—first the county, then the village.

County Government

As soon as Ohio became a state, the legislature addressed two questions of special importance to Athens: separating the Hocking Valley area from Washington County and chartering the university. Early in 1805 Athens County came into existence.

As established by the legislature, Athens County encompassed 1,053 square miles, double its present size, bounded by Washington, Fairfield, Ross, and Gallia counties and the Ohio River. The county seat was fixed as the town of Athens. The county was inaugurated March 1, 1805, and the election of the first commissioners occurred five weeks later. In the course of the next two decades, the county's boundaries were repeatedly modified, whole townships being transferred to new counties—Jackson, Hocking, Vinton, and Meigs. In 1825, Athens County, much reduced in size, still included Homer and Marion townships, now part of Morgan County, as well as Ward Township, now part of Hocking County.

OFFICE HOLDERS

Most of the county's officials were paid on a fee basis, so public office was at best a part-time activity. Some names recur: Abel Miller, for example, served as an associate judge of the Common Pleas Court from 1806 to 1812, a task that occupied four or five days each quarter, leaving him ample time to serve also as public surveyor for several county roads, to lay out the foundations for a county jail, and to pursue his private interests. Another major figure in the governance structure was Henry Bartlett, whose name first appears in connection with preparing for the county commissioners a list of non-resident landowners, and who thereafter repeatedly performed a variety of services for the county's officialdom. On December 1, 1806, Bartlett became the first salaried employee of the County, being offered thirty dollars for one year's service as clerk of the Board of Commissioners, scarcely a full-time position.

Robert Linzee and Alvan Bingham likewise wore several hats. Linzee's major role as sheriff did not preclude his serving as a viewer of roads. As sheriff, he was paid on a fee basis. For summoning a grand jury in July and November of 1806, he was paid four dollars. In 1814, Linzee was elected county commissioner, a post he held for two years, and from 1819 to 1825 he was a common pleas judge. Bingham became a county commissioner in December 1806, for a three-year term. Years later, in 1824, Bingham, who had been the area's first judge, was elected to the Court of Common Pleas, remaining there until 1838. Sylvanus Ames appears first as an associate judge of the Common Pleas Court in July 1805. Two years later, he vacated the bench to become sheriff. Returning to the bench in 1813, he remained there until his death in 1824.

If Abel Miller, Robert Linzee, Henry Bartlett, Alvan Bingham, and Silvanus Ames formed a courthouse gang, it is worth remembering that, except for Bartlett, none had a fixed salary, and none of their positions was full-time; county officials had to derive the bulk of their living from their private endeavors. If personal concerns sometimes precluded giving attention to public affairs, these officials developed a degree of expertise in the conduct of public business. They never monopolized public office. In fact, by 1825, twenty different Athenians had served as county commissioners; ten different men had served as justices. In the office of prosecuting attorney, no person served longer than three years, and a total of eight persons, among them the youthful Thomas Ewing, occupied that office between 1806 and 1825. Even with Robert Linzee holding his place as sheriff six years, by 1825 six different men had filled the office.

PUBLIC STRUCTURES

Inevitably, to function effectively the county government required housing. The highest priority went to building a jailhouse and sheriff's residence. At their first meeting in April 1805, the commissioners called for the construction of a log jail and jailer's house, the jail to be 13 feet wide, 24 feet long. Progress was slow, for not until June of the next year did the commissioners authorize payment to Abel Miller for "laying out jail bounds"; this first jail stood on the southern portion of the lot occupied by the present courthouse.

Initially, the county commissioners met in private homes, the session of the commissioners in June 1806 meeting at the South College Street home of Silas Bingham. Having authorized the construction of a jail, the commissioners sought a courthouse of their own at Court and Washington. Work began in summer 1807, the land first having to be cleared of timber. During the late summer and fall, a two-story structure of hewn logs was erected with "a sturdy chimney." Subsequently a pale fence and a "necessary"—an outhouse—were built nearby.

From the beginning the courthouse served as a multipurpose building, providing permanent quarters for the commissioners' business and for the Court of Common Pleas as well as for a school. A resolution of December 11, 1811, enjoined the person in charge of the school to furnish ready-cut wood for use of the court and required him to keep the building in good repair and well swept. In December 1813, when the schoolmaster failed to meet the expectations of the commissioners, they evicted the school from the courthouse.

The log courthouse was a temporary expedient. The commissioners, needing a place of their own, had lacked the resources in 1807 to erect a building suited to the county's long-term needs. The commissioners' exasperation with the operation of a school in the building in part reflected the fact that the building was no longer adequate. Thus, in spring 1814, the commissioners began the process of securing a large, permanent structure. As construction was about to commence, Eliphaz Perkins, then Athens postmaster, bought the original log building, disassembled it, and reassembled it at the northeast corner of Court and Union.

Forty-feet square, the new building was a two-story structure and had a hip roof topped by a cupola. The courtroom occupied the first floor; county offices, the second. The pale fence which had surrounded the log courthouse was replaced with a board fence on Court and Washington, access to the building being gained by a stile.

Creating a Village Government

Not until 1811 did Athens village have a government of its own. The legislation of January 28, 1811, created a corporate entity that, subject to the provisions of state law, could enact ordinances for the village and impose taxes to meet its expenses. Ohio law provided for an elected council of five persons, the council electing a presiding officer and recorder (secretary) from its own membership. In addition the village had an elected marshal, a treasurer, a tax collector, an assessor, and a supervisor. This machinery of government called for a total of ten persons. To put this in perspective, in the March 1826 elections forty-three votes were cast. To the extent that there was one village office for every four voters, village government was close to the people. As with the county government, these were only part-time, unsalaried positions.

While the state let counties and villages address many purely local problems, it retained powers that had a significant bearing on the economic development of the area. Prodded by Alexander Hamilton, the Federalists had already established the precedent that the federal government ought to use its powers aggressively to create an economic climate that would facilitate national economic growth; such measures included instituting protective tariffs to promote industrial development; initiating federally financed internal improvements to facilitate the transportation of goods from one region to another; and establishing a Bank of the United States to provide a nationwide banking system.

For its part, the Ohio General Assembly reserved the right to license the building of dams and the operation of mills. A long-established principle of English law held that navigable streams, such as the Hockhocking, could not be obstructed except with the permission of the legislature. In 1805, the state legislature authorized Jehiel Gregory and John Havner "to erect a mill dam" across the Hockhocking. They were required to provide "a good and suffcient lock," such that free navigation of the river would not be obstructed. Located on the right bank of the river at the end of present-day Mill Street, the dam and mill were in operation by 1806. Subsequently, in 1816, Silas Bingham secured legislative authorization to build a mill dam and mill on the Hockhocking at the rapids below the confluence of Margaret Creek. These mills provided farmers in the immediate vicinity of the village with critically needed facilities for grinding their corn. The farmer had a choice of selling his grain to the miller, who assumed the problem of marketing it, or he could have it custom ground, in which case the miller was entitled by tradition to retain one-eighth of the grain as the fee for his services.

While the state regulated the building of mill dams, the counties were responsible for regulating ferries and taverns. Thus, in June 1805, only four months after the state legislature enacted the basic legislation, the Athens Commissioners set license fees for ferries operating on the Great Hockhocking at two dollars and for ferries on all other streams within the county at one dollar. In addition, they spelled out a detailed schedule of rates: Foot passengers, for example, could be charged three cents; a man and a horse, ten cents; a loaded wagon and team, fifty cents; larger animals—horses, mules, asses, or neat cattle—six cents each; smaller animals—sheep and hogs—three cents. License fees for taverns were tailored to the potential clientele, varying from a stiff eight dollars a year in Athens to four dollars for Ames Township. In practice government intrusion in private business was slight, but at the same time there was no blind commitment to laissez-faire doctrine.

OHIO UNIVERSITY

The creation of a university within the Ohio Company's land was mandated by the company's contract with Congress in 1787. That seventeen years passed before the college was chartered suggests a degree of foot dragging. In truth, little could be done until settlers had moved onto the college lands in sufficient numbers to generate the funds needed to commence building and to provide a student clientele. Surprisingly enough, the territorial legislature took the first steps toward organizing a university per se in January 1802, three years before Athens County was created and nine years before Athens village was authorized.

The charter of 1802 created the American Western University. The language of the charter was primarily the work of Manasseh Cutler; the bill itself was introduced by his son, Ephraim Cutler, then a member of the territorial legislature. Manasseh Cutler, who remained in Ipswich, Massachusetts, studied the charters of both American and English institutions. He thought a college charter should enunciate mere principles, and those should be as clear and as few as may be. In the end he patterned his draft charter on those of Harvard and Yale, and especially the latter, his alma mater. It was Cutler's idea to name the institution the "American Western University," a name that seemed to be the "most natural, easy and agreeable."

The American Western University was never more than a paper institution. No effort was made to implement the legislation, for the territory's leaders were fully occupied by partisan in-fighting over statehood, in drafting a state constitution, and in creating a bureaucracy for the new state.

Once statehood was achieved and the administration of Governor Tiffin launched, the governor urged the state legislature to draft a new charter. Adopted February 18, 1804, the new charter largely reenacted the charter adopted by the territorial legislature. The salient changes began with a new name: Ohio University. The governor of the state became an *ex officio* member of the board of trustees and was charged with calling the first meeting of the board. The initial board, while including residents from the Marietta area, also included members from Chillicothe, Cincinnati, and Columbus. However, the legislature made no effort to provide either capital funds or operating monies.

The charter assigned the trustees two major tasks. First, they had the oversight of an educational institution. Accordingly, they were to select the president, secretary, and treasurer as well as the professors, instructors, and tutors; in addition, they were charged with oversight of the physical plant and finances of the college. The president and faculty were "to ordain, regulate, and establish the mode and course of instruction" and to formulate and administer "such code of rules, regulations, and by-laws" as they deemed necessary.

A second responsibility of the trustees, and of critical importance, was to supervise the leasing of the college lands. The university charter made the university trustees the landlord of every resident of Athens village as well as of Athens and Alexander townships. The 1804 charter directed the trustees to lease tracts of no less than 80 nor more than 240 acres for ninety years at a rental of 6 percent per year on the appraised value of the lands. Moreover, the land so leased was subject to revaluation at the end of thirty-five years and again at the end of sixty years from the commencement of the lease. By way of starting, a statute of February 21, 1805, set the minimum valuation at $1.75 per acre. Thus, a farm of 80 acres would be valued at not less than $140.00 and carry a minimum rent of $8.40 per year. While such a rental fee seems innocuous, as historian Thomas Hoover has pointed out, a settler on Ohio University lands would pay out $294 in rent over a thirty-five-year period for 80 acres, while a person settling in the rich upper Scioto Valley would have paid $320 for 160 acres, land which he owned outright. However, at the end of thirty-five years, the farmer on the college lands could look forward to an increase in the annual rental fee which would go on indefinitely. To many Athenian farmers, these terms would seem odious. Finally, the university trustees were assigned the administration of the lands within the village plat. They could alter Putnam's plat. Property and buildings actually used by the university were exempted from all state taxes.

To get the university underway, Governor Tiffin summoned the trustees to meet in Athens in June 1804. Seven of the trustees—Governor Edward Tiffin, Elijah Backus, Rufus Putnam, Dudley Woodbridge, Daniel Story, Samuel Carpenter, and James Kilbourne—gathered at the home of Dr. Eliphaz Perkins. The governor chaired the board, while Woodbridge and Perkins were elected secretary and treasurer, respectively. The first order of business was to force squatters already on the college lands to obtain leases and to pay rent. Steps were taken to have the lands appraised. In effect, the trustees offered to let squatters have first right to secure a lease for land they had staked out, except where the squatter had "for a valuable consideration" sold the property to another.

By way of leasing the lots within the "village" of Athens, Rufus Putnam and Samuel Carpenter were charged with holding a public auction on the first Monday in November, 1804, to offer twenty-seven house lots and an equal number of out-lots for lease. Successful bidders made a cash payment for a ninety-year lease and obligated themselves to an annual rental fee set at six percent of the appraised value of the land. Lessees were exempt from state taxes on the land; on the other hand, the university was authorized to have the land reappraised at future times and to raise the rent to six percent of the new value. The leaseholder could sell the lease to another party but never secured a fee simple title to the land. Athenians talked about "buying" and "selling" the lots or land, but in law they were buying and selling leases.

"Selling" town lots proved no easy task. While sixteen persons, including John Havner, Silas Bingham, Rufus Putnam, and Eliphaz Perkins, bid for lots, many of the sixteen bidders, Putnam included, failed to make the requisite payments and subsequently forfeited their claims. As a result, a second auction was held in November 1806, and both the forfeited and unsold lots were put up for auction. At this second auction forty lots were leased, the prices varying from a high of $72.00 to a low of $6.00. Of the forty lots, twenty-nine went for $20.00 or less. There was a message here: The leasing of land as a means of raising an endowment for the college-to-be would not generate a large fund. By the end of 1806, all but sixteen town lots had passed into private hands, and the college had gained but $800. Nor did the college fare much better in leasing farm lands. State appraisers identified 154 claimants of college lands, the farm lands being appraised at from 43¢ to $4.43 per acre. This posed a problem since the statutes constrained the trustees to accept no less than $1.75 per acre. This obstacle was overcome in January 1807 when the legislature authorized leases at less than $1.75 per acre.

At the 1806 meeting the trustees also took several actions with respect to the village. They accepted the bids on the town lots, subject to payment of the lease price plus interest. The board then set aside the southwest corner of Court and Washington for the county courthouse and the adjacent lot on Court Street for the jail, while it assigned lot 18 (the site of today's City Building) to the town of Athens. Finally, the trustees allocated five acres of land along West State Street for a burying ground. One further bit of business relating to the college lands stipulated that the annual rents on improved lands should begin as of January 1, 1806, and on unimproved lands a year later. The university was about to acquire a continuing, if barely adequate, income with which to commence operations. In fact, Manasseh

Cutler's mechanism for financing the university locked the institution into a strait-jacket. Had the university been able to lease all of its land in the two townships at an average value of $2.00 per acre, it would have been limited to an annual operating income of just over $9,200.

The Athens Academy

The April 1806 trustees meeting turned to the problems related to operating a college. The board chose Jacob Lindley—a trustee, a graduate of Princeton College, and pastor of the Presbyterian Church at Waterford, Ohio—along with Rufus Putnam and William Skinner to contract for a building in which to house an academy. Lindley's plan for the building—a two-story, brick structure 24 feet by 30 feet—was accepted by the board in December. Construction, begun in 1807 by Jehiel Gregory, was completed in 1808 at a cost of $500.

While Gregory proceeded with construction, the board charged Lindley, Eliphaz Perkins, and Rufus Putnam with formulating a plan "for opening the Athens Academy, providing for a preceptor, and conducting that branch of the Ohio University." The committee did its work promptly; the board appointed Lindley to be the preceptor, his duties to begin when the academy opened in October 1808. Indeed, Lindley was all: president pro-tempore of the board, administrative head of the academy, and its sole teacher.

Ohio University began operation as a secondary school for the simple reason that there was no one in the region prepared to undertake collegiate study. The three students who enrolled—Joel Abbott, Brewster Higley, and John Perkins—took courses in arithmetic, grammar, Latin, Greek, geography, mathematics, logic, rhetoric, natural philosophy, and moral philosophy. They paid no tuition but were assessed a fee of two dollars a quarter for "fire wood and other contingent and necessary expenses." They were advised that "Good boarding and washing may be had in respectable families, on reasonable terms." Classes met six days a week. Trustees examined students quarterly, while once a year students faced a public examination.

In hopes of attracting college-level students, the board also set standards for the conferral of a baccalaureate degree. Such students had to demonstrate an "adequate proficiency in Virgil, Horace, Cicero, Xenophon, Homer, the Greek Testament, Geography, Logic, Arithmetic, Algebra, Surveying, Navigation, Conic sections, Natural Philosophy, the general principles of History, Jurisprudence, English Grammar, Rhetoric, Belles Lettres, and Criticism."

Academy enrollments remained small. The three students of 1808 grew to fourteen in 1812, yet in 1815 only nine students appeared for the examinations. Of these, one, Gustavus Everts, was from Athens and one, John Doland, was from out of state. The others hailed from nearby areas of Ohio. Finally, in May 1815, two students, Thomas Ewing of Lancaster and John Hunter of Circleville, were examined by a trustees' committee in "grammar, Rhetoric, the Languages, Natural and Moral Philosophy, Logic, Geography, Astronomy, and the various branches of mathematics." Satisfied with their performance on the examinations, the trustees voted to award each man "the Bachelor of Arts and Science degree in the Seminary." There was no formal commencement exercise. Months later the board decided to confer the degrees at formal exercises. Hunter pronounced the Salutatory in Latin; Ewing, the Valedictory. Finally, on September 24, 1816, they received their baccalaureates. At the time Hunter and Ewing were awarded their degrees, there was no separate college program as such.

The early student population was young, not surprisingly, since the Academy was a secondary school. Some youngsters were evidently less than twelve years old when they began. Archibald G. Brown, long a major figure in Athens, was fourteen when he first enrolled. On the other hand, Thomas Ewing was twenty when he first entered. Under the necessity of earning his own keep, Ewing attended off and on, working at times in the Kanawha salt works and as surveyor for the Athens County Commissioners. He was twenty-five when he completed his studies.

The College

Obviously, the academy, though a start, did not fulfill the dream of Manasseh Cutler to create a college in the Ohio Country. Not until March 1812 did the board appoint Rufus Putnam, Eliphaz Perkins, and Seth Adams to draft plans for a college building, but three and a half years passed before Putnam's design was presented. Having approved it, the board charged Lindley, Perkins, and John L. Lewis with contracting for the necessary building materials. They also petitioned the state legislature 1) to close College Street south of the Commons so that the college building could be centered on the green facing College Street and 2) to loan the college $8,000 for the building. The legislature agreed to vacate the street but declined to loan the money.

Despite this setback, the board proceeded. Putnam's design was revised by Benjamin Corp, a Marietta architect. Contracts were let with a variety of Athenians for the necessary bricks, lumber, and stone and to commence construction. Absent the loan, construction had to be geared to the college's cash flow. The cornerstone was laid in the summer of 1816, but not until March 1818 was the board in a position to let the contracts for the roof, to glaze the windows, and to install locks on the doors. At the last minute, the whole project was imperiled as lightning struck the east end of the building, starting a fire that caused much damage, which would have been far worse had not an accompanying downpour doused the fire. As it was, the College Edifice, having cost $18,000, was ready for occupancy the following month.

Beginning Collegiate Instruction

In October 1819 the first students enrolled in the baccalaureate program. The stated object was "the evolution of the intellectual and moral faculty and the formation of habit." The curriculum was top-heavy with Latin and Greek literature. Although there were courses in Latin and Greek history, there were none in American history, a field that had not yet developed. The curriculum went no further than algebra in mathematics, and its offerings in the sciences were limited to astronomy and natural philosophy. For the first time, the college assigned students to one of four classes—Freshman, Sophomore, Junior, and Senior—and instructed them in organized classes.

In 1822 the curriculum was expanded in an effort to attract students. Whereas "natural philosophy" had offered a general survey of the sciences, now the college introduced separate courses in anatomy, mineralogy, botany, and "chymistry." While this departed from the rigidly classical curriculum outlined three years before, it reflected the direction American collegiate education was taking. In keeping with the practice of the day, President Lindley taught a senior class in moral philosophy. College students received a broad general education.

As in 1808 Lindley had full charge of the institution, for there were no vice presidents, provosts, deans, or administrative assistants to share the responsibility. He had day-to-day charge of the buildings, grounds, and property. He collected the student fees, decided when students were ready for graduation, and presided over the board of trustees. The president got some assistance in that the Board employed a treasurer and a secretary, both of whom were primarily concerned with administering the college lands and oversight of construction contracts.

A beginning was made in creating a faculty. Joseph Dana, an attorney, was the first regular faculty member. Employed in 1821 as professor of ancient languages,

Dana held the post until his death. Next, the Reverend James Irvine was hired to teach mathematics, and when he succeeded Lindley as president, the Reverend Samuel D. Hoge replaced Irvine as a professor of mathematics, making a total of four professors in 1825. In addition, having employed a Mr. Ward and then A. G. Brown as tutors in the academy, the trustees appointed Daniel Read the preceptor in April 1825.

Although this was a "state" school, students were required to attend religious exercises each Sunday. University regulations carried stiff sanctions for indecent behavior, profane cursing or swearing, for rioting, gambling, or "any other known immorality." Nor were these mere pious declarations. Among the explicit duties of faculty, who were expected to be on duty five and one-half days per week, was the responsibility for exercising discipline, the rules being those of Lindley's alma mater, Princeton. The university took its *in loco parentis* responsibilities seriously.

Because of its homogeneity, the student community had a life of its own. Undoubtedly, given that the students were in their teens and early twenties, there was much informal activity—horseplay—for which no record remains. There were no organized sports. Jacob Lindley's curriculum for the academy and college, unlike Benjamin Franklin's program for the College of Philadelphia a half-century earlier, made no provision for physical exercise. What the record discloses is the organization of literary societies, of major importance to the social and intellectual life of students throughout the nineteenth century. Although there are references to a Zelothian Society and a short-lived Polemic Society, the first significant literary society was the Athenian, dating from 1819. Its object was to pursue "the attainment of knowledge, the improvement of the mind, in taste, genesis, and criticism; the cultivation of morality and friendship, and the perfecting of the power of eloquence and reasoning." Sophomores and juniors gave recitations and wrote themes; seniors debated, delivered original orations, and wrote essays. The members criticized each other's presentations. The society met regularly on Saturday afternoons at two o'clock. The first composition presented to the group was on "Hope." The first topic debated: "Is the love of fame as an actuating principle productive of more good or evil?" Reflecting the age of the members, many of the topics concerned love and marriage.

The early membership of the Athenian Literary Society included Archibald G. Brown, founder of the *Athens Mirror and Literary Register*, Wilson Shannon, two-time governor of Ohio, and Daniel Lindley, son of the president, who later won distinction as a missionary in Africa. The university leadership—President Lindley and Professors Dana, Irvine, and Whittlesy—were ex-officio members.

However separated from the town population, students were not oblivious to the principal issues of the day. As townspeople organized a Bible Society, university students formed their own, selling and giving away Bibles—presumably to a student constituency. In 1825, a second literary society surfaced, the Philomathean Society, which met at the courthouse with its meetings open to the public.

Management Problems

As the academic program evolved, the trustees continued to struggle with collecting the rents due the university, conflicting land claims, and claims not established. While the board indulged some lessees with unpaid rents, in other cases it repossessed the properties. Indeed, in April 1825, Secretary of the Board Henry Bartlett warned lessees who had not paid their rents for 1825 to pay up in 30 days or "be dispossessed according to law."

As landlord to the community, the board exercised a veto on the kinds of enterprises undertaken in Athens. The straight-laced Presbyterians of the board who frowned on student immorality sought to protect the town as well. The board declined to lease two acres of land to William Weir for a brewery and rejected Ebenezer Currier's bid to acquire land on which to locate a distillery. So, too, the bids of Jacob Wolfe and John L. Lewis to secure land for a tanyard and a potash works, respectively, were denied, and although the state legislature in 1812 directed the trustees to grant a tract of land to the local Methodist Society, the board delayed compliance for three years. Once Currier, who was on his way to becoming one of the most substantial citizens of Athens, became collector for the college in 1813, the board relented and leased an acre of land to him for five years on which to locate a distillery.

The board also had to cope with personnel problems of its own. Due to problems of weather and travel conditions, trustees could not invariably attend meetings. Even with a board of twelve members, a quorum of seven could not always be counted on. In 1808, the state legislature increased the board to nineteen members. Even so, the university was always seriously handicapped by discontinuities in the attendance of personnel. Thomas Ewing, a trustee from 1822 to 1832, seems never to have attended a single session of the board. Ultimately the board got by on the strength of a membership that was composed of a sufficiently large number of persons from Athens to assure the necessary quorum and continuity. The price was a board that was provincial and at times self-serving.

Exit Lindley, Enter Irvine

A final problem had to do with the university presidency. In September 1820, President Lindley, having organized first the Academy and then the College, asked to be relieved of his duties. The board reluctantly accepted his resignation and appointed a committee to select the "most suitable character" as his successor. The committee did nothing until April 1822, when a report to the trustees indicated that President Lindley had failed to pass on to the treasurer a considerable amount of tuition money paid him by the students. Spurred to action, the search committee had a candidate the next day: James Irvine, professor of mathematics, whom the board elected unanimously and offered $900 a year; the board tendered Lindley the post of professor of rhetoric and moral philosophy and thanked him for his "most laborious and unremitted exertions."

Irvine's tenure as the second president was brief. Born in New York, he had graduated from Union College in 1821. That same year he was appointed professor of mathematics at Ohio University. Experiencing poor health, he was unable to devote much time to his presidential duties. He left the university in April 1824 to accept a pastorate in his native New York state, where he died shortly thereafter.

At this point, the board expressed concern at the state of the university: there was a need for a larger faculty, more extensive physical equipment, and additional income. In 1821 Ephraim Cutler, once again in the state legislature, had secured an appropriation from the State of Ohio, but it was a one-time-only grant of $1,000 for some "philosophical" equipment. In an age when Ohio had yet to create a public school system, the state was not ready to underwrite the operating expenses of a state university. The board uttered a cry of desperation: "our finances are in a deranged state, our treasury is exhausted, we are in debt." In this frame of mind, the board elected as the university's third president Robert G. Wilson of Chillicothe. To 1825, then, while the university had become functional and had overseen the transfer of the college lands to private individuals, it had not succeeded in stimulating the economic development of the Athens area nor had it achieved financial stability.

AN EXPANDING ECONOMY

In 1800, Athens was no more than a hamlet with a vision of what might be. A quarter century later, Athens village was a going concern. With a corporate existence of its own, the village served as the center for both the township and county. Although the county had lost territory as its boundaries were adjusted, its population grew from 2,787 in 1810, the first census in which Athens County was enumerated as an entity, to 6,439 in 1820 and 9,763 in 1830.

Athens Township contributed to this growth. With 1,114 persons in 1820, it had far and away the largest population of any of the townships. The village itself had about 500 residents in 1825 and in addition 50 to 100 university students. With 729 persons in 1830, the village was nearly nine times larger than any other village in the county. Lest one be swept away with images of runaway growth, it is well to realize that in 1800 the village, with five or six households, counted perhaps 30 persons. The 729 persons of 1830 represented a net accretion of 24 persons a year. Athens was the Queen City of the Hocking; it was not the Queen City of the West.

In assessing this growth in 1825, A. G. Brown, the editor of the *Athens Mirror and Literary Register*, the community's first weekly newspaper, expressed a dim view of the original settlers, the squatters, who "in general were of the lowest order." The opening of the academy in 1808 under Jacob Lindley had marked "the beginning of solid and general improvements in the appearance of the town and the moral character of the inhabitants." In this scenario, Brown credited the university, especially after it began systematic collegiate instruction in 1819, with promoting "the growth and prosperity of the town." According to the *Mirror*, in 1825 the village had 75 dwelling houses, roughly half of them large, two-story, brick structures. The pride of the community were the three-story "College Edifice," now Cutler Hall, the Academy Building, and the Courthouse. In addition the town boasted a Methodist meeting house, a Masonic hall, and a school building. There was a sense of pride in that achievement.

The Village Economy

The village economy was rooted in agriculture. Athens Township in 1820 reported 253 persons with an occupation, of whom 3 were merchants and 28 were engaged in manufacturing. The census does not list their specific occupations, nor can one sort out which of these persons were clustered in the village and which of them pursued their business or craft from a base in the rural areas. From the names in the census and the files of the *Athens Mirror and Literary Register* a general outline of the development of the village economy is possible.

The Professionals

At the professional level, the village had four clergy, two physicians, and three lawyers. Four clergy may seem excessive for seventy-five families, but in 1825 denominational rivalries were keenly felt and Methodists, Baptists, and Presbyterians tended to go their separate, if roughly parallel, ways. While a number of Methodist and Baptist clergy served Athens during these years, most were circuit riders, so that while they brought support and consolation to their flocks and fashioned viable organizations led by the laity, they were not in a position to put down roots and provide day-to-day leadership within the community.

By contrast, Athens Presbyterians from the first had resident clergy because of the presence of the university. Jacob Lindley made his mark no less as the founding pastor of the Presbyterian Church than as president of Ohio University, positions he occupied simultaneously. As with most colleges of the antebellum era, Ohio University was led by a succession of clergyman presidents—first Jacob Lindley, then James Irvine and Robert Wilson. Because Presbyterian clergy were college-educated, ordained clergy, such as Irvine and Samuel D. Hoge, were regularly recruited to teach at the university. Their presence assured the Presbyterians and the village alike of well-educated leaders.

The first doctor in the area according to local legend was Dr. Samuel Barnes. The good doctor came to Athens in the late 1790s, died in Athens in 1799, and was buried in what became the Old Cemetery on West State Street. For a time, Eliphaz Perkins and Leonard Jewett were the only doctors in Athens—or for that matter between the Muskingum and the Scioto, between Zanesville and the Ohio River. Like all doctors of his age, Perkins was primarily an herbal doctor. But Jewett came to Athens after having trained at Boston Medical College and with four years experience as an assistant surgeon at New York Hospital. Even so, there was no scientific knowledge of germs as a cause of disease and infection, no knowledge of antiseptics nor of anesthesia. What a doctor might do by way of treating a patient was extremely limited. There was a heavy reliance on the bleeding of patients and on the use of calomel and opium. In many ways a white physician of the early nineteenth century could do little for his patients that an Indian medicine man could not do equally well. Be that as it may, Eliphaz Perkins's rounds, according to his son, Chauncey F. Perkins, were "often accompanied with great exposure, fatigue, and danger." He was highly respected by fellow citizens and was a man of many parts. Acquiring the northeast corner of Court and Union, Perkins doubled as the town postmaster and merchant while also serving as a leading member of the university's board of trustees and its treasurer. Jewett served four years as a state senator, 1806–10, and was a surgeon with General Harrison during the War of 1812. His life was cut short by blood poisoning in 1814.

By 1825, the town's doctors were Chauncey F. Perkins, Eliphaz's son, and Columbus Bierce. The doctors organized a County Medical Society in 1824 and were bent on raising the standards of medical practice. State law charged the county medical societies with examining those who aspired to be licensed to practice "physic and surgery." The requirements were "an acquaintance with Latin and Greek" and three years of prior study under some "reputable physician or surgeon," including study of anatomy, chemistry, materia medica, surgery, obstetrics, and the theory and practice of medicine. At the time, Columbus Bierce was secretary of the County Medical Society.

As the county seat, Athens was the center of the legal community. Legal training was acquired by "reading" law with a practicing attorney. County judges examined candidates for admission to the bar, that is, the right to accept pay for legal services and to plead cases before the courts. Although by 1800, trained lawyers had displaced the untutored attorneys-in-fact who had served throughout the colonial era, one did not need to be an attorney to serve either as a judge of the court of common pleas or as a justice of the peace. Society still trusted laymen of good judgment to exercise the judicial role in local courts.

Because the presiding judge moved from county to county, so did most of the trial lawyers. Thus most of the attorneys who practiced in Athens County during this period resided elsewhere. A surprising number of these were, or became, men of distinction. Thomas Ewing, initially from Ames, was constant in his practice of law in Athens in the first years after he was admitted to the bar. So, too, Samuel F. Vinton, who, in 1817, made Gallipolis his home base, had business interests in Athens and served as its representative in Congress for twenty-two years. Other lawyers who practiced in Athens and attained distinction were General G. Goddard of Zanesville, Henry Stanbery, Hocking H. Hunter, John T. Brazee, and Simeon Nash. Second in ultimate distinction to Thomas Ewing was the youthful Lewis Cass, who argued his first case in Athens. Cass went on to a major command in the War of 1812, became a governor of Michigan Territory, was United States secretary of state, and a candidate for president of the United States in 1848. William Woodbridge of Marietta practiced in Athens briefly before removing to Michigan where he, too, went on to become governor and United States senator.

The first resident lawyer in Athens, Artemus Sawyer, settled in 1808, became prosecuting attorney in 1810, and then faded from the scene, a victim of intemperance. Dwight Jarvis, the second resident attorney in the village, remained until 1830. So far as the practice of the law was concerned, Athens was not a good base before 1832. The only attorney who resided in town for an extended period, Joseph Dana, was primarily a professor of ancient languages at Ohio University and only occasionally represented a client in the local courts. He did serve, however, as prosecuting attorney off and on for a total of eight years.

The Mercantile Community

The preeminent merchant of Athens in the mid-1820s was Joseph B. Miles. Miles made a special point of the broad range of fabrics he offered for sale: "Broad cloths, cassimiers, Flannels, Callicoes, Painted Jackonets, Domestic Plaids and Stripes, Domestic and Cambric Muslins, and Fancy Goods of different descriptions." But his trade was not limited to dry goods, for he claimed "a general supply" of groceries, hardwares, men's and women's leather and Morocco shoes, powder, lead, salt, and whisky. Later in the year, proclaiming a new stock of goods, Miles advertised the availability of cravats, umbrellas and parasols, hats, books, stationery, tea, coffee, and a range of spices, dye stuffs, and paints. Miles also assumed a civic role, serving as county auditor one term.

Ebenezer Currier, a native of New Hampshire, came to Athens in 1806 at age thirty-four, becoming one of the pioneer merchants of Athens. Like other merchants, he imported his goods from the East Coast. In 1811, for example, he engaged Archelaus Stewart to take a light wagon to Baltimore to pick up the merchandise and to return to Athens, a trip taking two months! In common with other Athenians, he pursued a variety of business activities simultaneously. A merchant for over forty years, Currier also served variously as university treasurer, county treasurer (1807–8), county commissioner (1808–10 and 1812–14), and county judge (1814–26).

The mercantile community also included Charles Shipman and Thomas Brice. Shipman, like Miles, was brought by his parents to Marietta at the start of the Indian Wars, but did not come to Athens until 1813. He, too, claimed "a general and elegant assortment of staples and Fancy Goods Suited to the Season." Brice similarly claimed a wide variety of goods—piece goods, including "Sheetings and Shirtings, and bedticking, finished merchandise such as handkerchiefs, shawls, shoes, hats, gloves, and hose." His line of groceries mentions French brandy, Jamaican Spirits, Lisbon and Port Wines. His leather goods included saddles and bridles.

The store of Ezra Stewart, son of Daniel Stewart, the Revolutionary War veteran, offered the community "Seasonable goods," dry goods, hardware, Queen's-ware, glassware, nails, nail rods, hoop and bar iron. Stewart's was also the place to purchase paints, medicines, dyestuffs, ropes, cordage, school books and stationery. Whereas Stewart was located on Court Street, John Perkins's emporium faced Union Street and offered the usual array of groceries, hardware, china, shoes, schoolbooks, saddlery, medicines, and paints as well as Du Pont's best rifle powder. Perkins also housed the post office.

Clearly, these were general stores, focusing on staples. While their advertisements refer to groceries, there are no references to fruits or vegetables. Piece goods, including sheetings and shirtings, are referred to, but clearly the purchasers expected to hem their own sheets and make their own shirts and dresses. At most one might walk out with ready-made boots and shoes, a shawl, or handkerchief, but no ready-to-wear coat, jacket, skirt, dress, or trousers. While reliance on homespuns was passing, this was still very much a do-it-yourself age.

Several aspects of the mercantile community are remarkable. First, the goods came from the East—Philadelphia, Baltimore, and Pittsburgh. Charles Shipman was typical of the merchants in that he went to Philadelphia at least once a year to purchase goods for his store, some years, twice. Reportedly, he made the trip nineteen times, always by horseback. Second, while the merchants had no aversion to cash, the Athens economy was not yet sufficiently mature to operate exclusively or even primarily on a cash basis. Barter was the norm. Prices were never advertised. Merchants traded their merchandise for "wheat, oats, whisky, paper-rags, bee's wax, tallow, buckhorns, and beef hides." Fur skins, butter, and cheese were also items for barter, as were feathers, wool, ginseng, deer skins, and country linen and flax. As a result, the merchant of the 1820s was as much involved in finding a market for the agricultural and domestic manufactures of the Athens area as he was in marketing the manufactured goods he imported from the East. Annually, Stewart's hired men drove cattle overland to East Coast markets. Other merchants floated the pork and other products down the Hocking to the Ohio and Mississippi to find a market. Third, most of the business was done on credit. Periodically, anguished merchants published general notices urging delinquent customers to settle their accounts.

Craftsmen and Manufacturers

That the 1820 census lists so few merchants (three) and so many manufacturers (twenty-eight) for Athens Township reflects the fact that many Athenian businessmen were both producers and merchants and that their identity was linked with the specialized product they made and sold. On closer examination the "manufacturers" were craftsmen producing a variety of goods by hand labor, seldom with more than one or two employees.

Data for the 1820s does not permit organizing the manufacturers into a hierarchy. Extrapolating from later years, it seems reasonable to suggest that the mill operators ranked at or near the top of the business community. The operation of a grain, saw, or woolen mill required a major outlay of capital for the mill dam or mill race, wheel and equipment for grinding, sawing, or carding and spinning as the case might be. To be profitable there had to be a plenitude of farmers, lumbermen, or sheepherders in the vicinity to keep the mill busy. As noted earlier, two mills stood in close proximity to Athens: that of John Havner and Jehiel Gregory at the foot of present-day Mill Street and that of Silas Bingham, located at a fall on the Hocking (the variant of the name Hockhocking that became standard in the early nineteenth century) where White's Mill stands today. Bingham, who always had a variety of business interests, often rented the mill out to others.

Two other players in the milling business were Silas Pruden, who in 1816 bought the Gregory mill, and, more important in the long run, his son Samuel Baldwin Pruden. A dynamic figure, Baldwin, as he was commonly known, recognized that money was to be made in processing wool. By the mid-1820s, it was feasible to graze sheep on the steep hillsides and floodplains of the Hocking Valley—land that could not profitably be put to the plow. In partnership with Isaiah Cranston, young Pruden set up a wool-processing operation in connection with Bingham's mill, offering wool carding, fulling, dyeing, and cloth dressing. W. W. Bierce also entered the business. Located at an unspecified site, his fulling mills were ready, Bierce averred in the *Mirror* in 1825, and a journeyman was on duty. While all local farmers and consumers alike were dependent on the services of the mill operator, the business was risky, contingent on a river level that was neither too high nor too low to drive the mill wheel. Furthermore, it was a seasonal business, tied to shearing season for processing wool and to harvest times for processing wheat and corn. Periodic floods could, and did, destroy the mills.

Given that the town was adding four or five households a year, there was a modest continuing demand for the services of carpenters, joiners, bricklayers, plasterers, painters, and cabinetmakers. The Athens hillsides furnished an ample supply of clay suitable for brick. In this era the clay was brought to the building site and the brick made on site. The three sons of Nathan Dean—William, Gulliver, and John—were among those who were active in making brick, and it was William Dean who made the bricks for the College Edifice. For a time, William D. Bartlett and Isaac N. Norton together engaged in making chairs and cabinets. In late 1825, the two men parted ways, Norton continuing in "the old shop" on Washington Street, while Bartlett set up a new shop on College Street.

Reflecting the agricultural character of the community, the village craftsmen included three blacksmiths, two saddlers, and three tanneries. The smiths and saddlers, of course, served farmers and townspeople alike in shoeing horses and in repairing plows and other farm tools. The tanyards provided a market for the hides harvested by local hunters and herders. To this list of craftsmen should be added the cooper, who made containers for storing and shipping farm commodities.

The isolation of the community pushed it toward self-sufficiency in clothing itself. Two hatters, three tailors, and seven shoemakers served the community. Of the tailors, Benjamin Baker, Jr. took pains to let the community know that he had set up shop at Brown's Tavern. Hull Foster, a son of Zadoc and Sally Foster, and a self-taught shoemaker, began as an itinerant, traveling at times into rural Kentucky, but returned to Athens, where he established himself as a shoemaker for the next four decades. While the census lists only men's occupations, it requires no stretch of the imagination to assume that a number of women, working in their own homes, functioned as milliners, dressmakers, and coat makers.

Not the least of the town's businesses were its several taverns. From 1809 to his death in 1814, Zadoc Foster kept a tavern, and for a time thereafter his widow, Sally Foster, continued the operation, becoming the first businesswoman in Athens. She sold the tavern to Isaac Barker, Jr., who in the early 1820s replaced the double-log tavern building with a brick structure. General John Brown was undoubtedly the leading hotelier, the census of 1820 reporting twenty persons in his household. His household would include several women servants or chambermaids, one or more cooks, a laundress, and a hostler to serve his guests. In addition, a few townswomen supplemented their family incomes by boarding one or more students or some of the single businessmen and craftsmen. When local merchants and craftsmen housed their unmarried employees, their wives found themselves running a de facto boardinghouse. It is also more than likely that a number of young women in their teens, some as young as twelve, and early twenties were engaged as live-in domestic servants.

Overall, craftsmen greatly outnumbered merchants and service providers. Athenians had to rely on one another to provide food, shelter, and clothing to a far greater degree than in any subsequent time. For the most part, what they did not produce, they did without.

RECONSTITUTING A SOCIETY

The first families of Athens were keenly aware of their isolation. One sees silent testimony in the Old Cemetery where grave markers bear witness to the homes they left behind in Old England, New England, and Pennsylvania. While the pioneers went about creating a government, clearing farms, and starting shops and businesses, they also directed their energies toward resurrecting the cultural and intellectual life they had known before coming to the new country.

To the degree they could, they maintained contact with the society they had left behind. Athens merchants traveling downstream to New Orleans and east to commercial centers such as Baltimore, Philadelphia, and Pittsburgh had an annual or semiannual glimpse of the broader world. So, too, the slow, steady influx of settlers provided an ongoing flow of information. Yet it remained true until the coming of the telegraph and railroad in the late 1850s that Athenians had no day-to-day contact with the outside world.

The creation of private schools afforded an indispensable means of exposing the community's youth to the shared culture of the nation. To be sure, at the elementary level, the focus of these schools had to be on the Three R's. Without those skills an individual might be able to acquire the traditional skills of farming or homemaking by observing a parent, but would find it increasingly difficult to keep the records required in the business world of the village or to make a career as a professional. In the absence of a public elementary school, Athens relied on private schoolmasters and mistresses. As noted earlier, secondary education for males became available at the university's Academy in 1808; college classes, in 1819, greatly extended the diffusion of the cultural heritage. Migrating to Athens did not condemn the pioneers or their children to regressing in matters cultural and intellectual.

Securing access to the outside world by mail service was as important as creating a transportation network. Initially the pioneers on the Hockhocking relied on private individuals to carry letters. Mail entrusted to the U.S. Post Office came to Pittsburgh from the East and went by land to Wheeling; from there it traveled by river on a small boat about twenty-four feet long with a crew of five well-armed men to Marietta and on downstream to Cincinnati. Mail was dispatched to Athens once every two or three weeks. At last in 1802, with Chillicothe having come to the fore politically, an overland mail route was established from Marietta through Athens and Chillicothe to Cincinnati.

It was 1804 before Athens had a post office of its own, and that was located briefly at the mill of Jehiel Gregory. Shortly afterward the postmastership was shifted to Dr. Eliphaz Perkins, who served until 1817, when his son, John, succeeded him. The elder Perkins kept the post office on State Street temporarily, then moved it to the corner of Court and Union. Throughout the nineteenth century the addressee had to pick up the mail at the post office. Creation of a post office serving Athens made it possible for ordinary citizens to send mail with the assurance their letters would reach the intended recipient. The mail service intermittently brought two or three residents copies of the *United States Gazette* or the *National Intelligencer* with news of national and international events. Mail service always had to be slow. As late as 1825, mail reached Athens only twice a week from Marietta; news of the deaths of John Adams and Thomas Jefferson, which had both occurred on July 4, 1826, did not reach the village until after the 15th, and the published notice of their deaths appeared in the weekly *Athens Mirror* of July 22, 1826.

A giant step forward in ending the cultural and intellectual isolation of Athens was the founding of the *Athens Mirror and Literary Register.* The youthful founding publisher, Archibald G. Brown, had come out of the Ames community, the son of Captain Benjamin Brown. An 1822 graduate of Ohio University, Brown began publication of the *Mirror* in April 1825, a paper that with numerous changes in titles, publishers, and editors continues as the Athens *Messenger.*

The *Mirror* reflected the intelligence and broad interests of its publisher. In a sense the beginning of the *Mirror* marked the end of the pioneer era as Brown introduced his readers to a host of events and ideas. In an early issue, readers learned of George Guess, known today as Sequoya, who designed a phonic syllabary that enabled the Cherokee to communicate in writing and to publish books in their own language. Through the *Mirror* Athenians followed the triumphal tour of the Marquis de Lafayette. A "scissors-and-paste" paper, the *Mirror* secured most of its copy by snipping it from Eastern papers and magazines. It regularly printed short stories and long-winded political speeches. Caught up in the excitement of the Greeks' efforts to free themselves from the Ottoman Turks, editor Brown published the appeals beseeching relief supplies for the beleaguered Greeks. Brown kept Athenians abreast of events in the outside world.

Given his wooden press and limited space, Brown had to be selective in what he printed. He was acutely aware that the well-being of the Athens community rested on the quality of agriculture practiced in the region. Accordingly, Brown ran an item taken from the *Boston Gazette* that called attention to the changing attitude of Americans toward farming. The author deplored the view, of relatively recent origin but gaining acceptance, that held agriculture to be "a low and servile occupation fit only for drudges and menials." Likewise, the author deprecated the desertion of rural areas for "the noise and ribaldry of towns and the disqualifying pleasures of a town life." The reader was reminded that the "Specious promises and flattering prospects" of commerce afforded "temptations, . . . sudden gains and rapid prospects."

Pursuing the same theme, Ohio University President Robert G. Wilson told the commencement audience of 1825 that agriculture, commerce, and manufacturing were not mutually hostile. The employees of industry provided a market for the surpluses of farmers, and commerce furnished the means of moving goods from producer to consumer. Agriculture, Wilson reminded his audience, was "the most natural, and obvious means, by which a people can provide a regular and adequate supply for their bodily wants."

While Brown chose not to follow in his father's footsteps as a farmer, he recognized that the well-being of the area required a prosperous agricultural base. To this end, he published a notice of a meeting in Marietta to organize an agricultural society designed to promote better agricultural practices. This was the beginning of an ongoing campaign to lift area agriculture from the realm of traditional practice to intentional innovations. Better agricultural practices meant more prosperous farmers; more prosperous farmers meant more lucrative markets for Athens merchants and craftsmen.

THE CONSOLATION OF RELIGION

For many Athenians, the church was the most important social group beyond the family. Whether or not they had been churchgoers before leaving for the Hockhocking, the settlers had come from a society that had been shaped by Protestant Christian values. The church, the preaching, affirmed traditional values; the services also afforded opportunities for all—husbands, wives, children, and single adults— to enjoy varying degrees of social contact before and after services. Apprehensive that frontiersmen might lose touch with their Christian heritage, Easterners took pains to send missionary clergy to the frontier.

The first clergy known to visit Athens was the Reverend Mr. James Quinn, an itinerant Methodist clergyman. Coming to Athens by way of the Cutler-Ewing trace, on the first Sunday in January 1800 Quinn preached a sermon on a text from St. Paul's message to the people of ancient Athens. In the first years, preaching was decidedly intermittent. Not until 1804 was the Reverend Mr. Quinn assigned to the Hockhocking Circuit, responsible for ministering to the settlements along the Muskingum and Scioto as well.

The late eighteenth and early nineteenth centuries were marked by the rise of evangelical Christianity, and on the frontier this produced the camp meeting, which brought large crowds to a central point for preaching, prayer, and repentance. In 1806, the youthful Reverend Mr. Peter Cartwright, who gained fame as a major force in frontier Methodism, preached and organized Methodist societies in both Alexander and Athens townships. Four years later, Mr. Quinn and the aging Bishop Francis Asbury held a camp meeting near the village. In the course of four days, Bishop Asbury delivered two "powerful" sermons. The appeal of Methodism was such that, in 1812, the state legislature directed the university trustees to lease "a piece of the public commons" to the Methodist Society on which to build a meeting house. The trustees, all Presbyterians, dawdled and the Methodists went ahead on their own. Having met in private homes heretofore, the Methodists in 1812 proceeded to build a brick church on Congress Street near the site of the present Beta Theta Pi fraternity house. In 1815, the Reverend Mr. Thomas Morris, a brother of Athens businessman Calvary Morris and later a bishop, was appointed to the congregation in Athens, 1816–18. In 1825 the Methodists added a brick parsonage.

The Presbyterians organized in fall 1809. Reflecting the role of the university, the first pastor was the Reverend Jacob Lindley, whose office as college president did not preclude pastoring the small flock of Presbyterians: Joshua Wyatt and wife, Elizabeth, Josiah Coe, Arthur Coates, Dr. Eliphaz Perkins, Alvan Bingham, and Sally Foster, and his own wife. The organization was informal. For the time being, they worshiped in a little brick schoolhouse that stood where the Athens City Building currently stands. As the group grew, it moved its meetings to the courthouse. The Presbyterians flourished, there being 47 members in early 1815. A revival that year added another 43 members. By 1820 the congregation numbered 177, a sizable portion of Athens' adult population.

Organized religion enabled Athenians to share once more in rituals that had been part of their lives in the East, to resurrect a continuity in their lives that their migration to the new country had disrupted. Though separated from the society they had known, religion assisted immeasurably in the re-creation of a similar culture and society in the west.

ORGANIZED SOCIETIES

Women had a low profile in Athens. Homemaking, child care, and home industries kept them busy from sunup to bedtime. Yet, from time to time, their presence was noticed. The first notice of a women's society in Athens was the call for a meeting of the Athens Female Cent Society to meet at the home of the university president, Dr. Robert Wilson, early in July 1825. Of its membership, nothing is known other than that E. R. Hoge was secretary. Such organizations, designed to raise money to enable pious young men to attend seminary, had started in New England a decade earlier. Another evidence of women's out-of-home activities was a report in the *Mirror* in September 1826 that the women of the Presbyterian Church were supporting one student at Ohio University. Other religious societies, the Athens Sunday School Union, the Athens County Bible Society, and the Domestic Missionary Society, were male-led, evidence that piety was not restricted to women. The existence of these societies provides evidence that by 1825, despite its isolated location, Athens was moving along the same paths as the large cities of the East Coast. It was reconstituting the society it had left behind.

ATHENS AND THE WORLD

Aaron Burr Visits Athens

As isolated as Athens was, the village was nonetheless touched by the new nation's first scandal—the Burr conspiracy. In 1804, Burr had challenged his political nemesis, Alexander Hamilton, to a duel and had killed him. In the wake of this duel, Burr came west and visited Athens. The precise nature of Burr's plans is not known, though he had arranged to buy a half-million acres of land in northern Louisiana. By way of fulfilling his plans, Burr linked up with Harman Blennerhassett, an Irish-born opportunist, who had built a mansion on an island in the Ohio River just below Parkersburg, Virginia. Dudley Woodbridge—a trustee of Ohio University and sometime property "owner" in Athens—was a business associate of Blennerhassett.

At least three Athenians crossed paths with Burr. Burr visited Blennerhassett in May 1805, en route to New Orleans. On that occasion Zadoc Foster, who then operated a gristmill on the Little Hocking, supplied the Burr party with cornmeal for their trip downriver. On his way back to Marietta in October, Burr stopped over in Athens, staying with Moses Hewitt. A year later, 1806, Burr was back, lodging this time for several days at Silas Bingham's tavern. He was remembered as "a very elegant appearing gentleman." At this level Burr was simply one of the famous and infamous to pass this way. Bingham was no more than a host. The connections with Moses Hewitt were of a different character, as revealed by a conversation with Burr Hewitt subsequently reported: "He [Burr] came out on the stoop and sat down and asked me if I had heard the reports of dividing the Union by the Allegeny [*sic*] Mountains." Hewitt also met with Harman "Blannerhasset," who tried to recruit him. There is no suggestion in surviving records that Hewitt was in any other way interested in Burr's plans or that he shared Burr's views. Burr expressly denied that he had "any design to separate the western from the eastern states." But in the fall of 1806, Blennerhassett contributed some articles to the Marietta paper in which he did raise the possibility of such separation. It was after the publication of these articles that first President Jefferson, then Governor Tiffin became convinced that Burr and Blennerhassett must be thwarted.

One can characterize Burr as an infamous American whom fate brought briefly to Athens. His conspiracy, if that is what it was, sought to exploit the acute difficulties that frontier farmers and merchants alike faced in selling their surpluses in a market in which they could not buy, while compelled to purchase their manufactured goods in a market in which they could not sell. Such problems continued long after Burr departed from the scene.

Ohio and the British

The difficulties of marketing their surpluses at New Orleans prompted residents of the Ohio Valley to vent their frustrations on the British, because Britain had blockaded the Caribbean and Atlantic ports of the French and Spanish colonies and was interfering with American ships. The attack of the English man-of-war *Leopard* on the American ship *Chesapeake* in 1807 ended the neutrality of Ohio newspaper editors. Fear of Indian attacks still lingered among Ohioans, but for Athens the dangers were more imagined than real. Certainly, British agents in Canada had been guilty of inciting Indians to conduct outrages against American settlers. After Harrison's destruction of the Indian village at Tippecanoe Creek in 1811, Tecumseh, despite having been betrayed by the British in the past, nevertheless felt he had more to gain from the British than from the Americans. Even so, Athens was in no danger from the Indians.

In 1811, the election of Henry Clay—Harry of the West—as speaker of the United States House of Representatives brought much rejoicing that "the supposed 'wilds of America' will no longer be looked upon with indifference." War with England seemed thereafter to be a matter of time, and Ohioans generally seemed to welcome it, primarily as a means of eliminating British influence in the west. Yet in June 1812, when President Madison asked Congress to approve a declaration of war against Great Britain, Ohio's representatives in Congress divided on the question. Its single congressman, Jeremiah Morrow, voted for war; one of its senators, Alexander Campbell, who was probably pro-war, was away from Washington at the time and did not cast a vote, while the other senator, Thomas Worthington, voted against declaring war. Worthington's opposition was less ideological than pragmatic. As events demonstrated, he correctly perceived that the nation was ill prepared for conflict.

Athens in the War of 1812

Participation by Athens in the War of 1812 was supportive in spirit but otherwise short-lived. In common with others who lived in the Ohio Valley, Athenians supported the war. They blamed the British naval blockade for the unsatisfactory market conditions at New Orleans; they blamed the British in Canada for keeping the Indians in northern Ohio and Indiana stirred up.

When Congress declared war in mid–June 1812, the United States already had an army in the field. On approaching the Detroit area, General William Hull, the cautious, superannuated American commander, asked Ohio Governor Return J. Meigs, Jr., to send supplies or "the army will perish." The governor had the requisite supplies, guarded by a militia company, on the way two days later. Shortly afterward, Hull called for militia troops. Again Governor Meigs responded with dispatch, calling for three corps of three hundred men each. It was to this call that Captain Jehiel Gregory, who, with his brother Nehemiah, ran the mill east of the village, raised a company of fifty-three men and officers. Indeed, brother Nehemiah was second in command. Little survives of the record beyond the roster and dates of service. Jehiel's company was mustered into service August 9, 1812. On the 15th, it was at Chillicothe. Upon reaching Urbana, it learned of Hull's surrender of Detroit. Enlisted for six months' service, the company returned to Chillicothe to await discharge on February 19, 1813.

During this interval, Nehemiah Gregory was detached from the company to return to Athens and recruit a company of his own. At this point General William Henry Harrison, who had supplanted Hull as the American commander, was considering a winter campaign to retake Detroit. This was not to be, for an American detachment, operating contrary to orders, sustained a crushing defeat at the River Raisin, losing two hundred dead and wounded and seven hundred captured. With all hope of a winter campaign gone, Nehemiah's company of sixty-three men and officers was discharged two days after brother Jehiel's unit.

In early summer 1813, an American force at Fort Meigs on the rapids of the Maumee was under siege. In response to a request from General Harrison, Duncan McArthur, acting as major general of the Ohio militia, ordered out his whole division. Among the ten thousand militiamen who were shortly on the march for Upper Sandusky was Captain Jehiel Gregory's newly recruited company, this time with Jacob Dunbaugh as lieutenant and Thomas Ewing as ensign. That Gregory's company numbered but thirty-seven men reflected a degree of demoralization following the ill-fated campaigns the Athenians had been involved in some months before. As it turned out, the English siege of Fort Meigs was lifted before the militia reached the rendezvous point—Upper Sandusky. Aware that Harrison planned to invade Canada, the militiamen were eager to join him. But for the moment, Harrison's hands were tied; he could not move against the English in Canada until Oliver H. Perry cleared Lake Erie of English ships. Meanwhile the Ohio militia units sat idle at Upper Sandusky.

Uneasy, Harrison dispatched a letter to Governor Meigs expressing his "alarm at the astonishing consumption of flour at Upper Sandusky." He asked the governor why he was retaining "so many militia which from the nature of their organization and period of service could be of no service and cannot be permitted to accompany him to Canada." Distrustful of Ohio militiamen generally, Harrison had planned a campaign that would rely on seven thousand regular U.S. Army troops supplemented by two thousand militiamen from Kentucky. At most, he was willing to have two thousand Ohio militiamen in reserve as replacements. Otherwise he directed Governor Meigs to march the rest of the Ohio militiamen back to Chillicothe for discharge. Distressed, Governor Meigs reluctantly sent the men home, but not before congratulating them for having "done their duty" by being "usefully employed in escorting public stores, munitions of war and provisions" for more than seventy miles through the wilderness. Gregory's second tour with the militia ended September 3, 1813. For the Athenians the war was over.

On September 10, Harrison received a message from Perry: "We have met the enemy and they are ours." Harrison moved promptly. On the 26th of September, Perry disembarked Harrison's army three miles south of Malden, Ontario. Soon his men were in hot pursuit of the English. On the fifth of October, Harrison overtook General Proctor's force on the Thames River. In the brief battle that followed, the British were quickly overwhelmed; Proctor's Indian allies were crushed, and the great Shawnee warrior Tecumseh was killed. The war in the Great Lakes Country was over.

The impact of the war on Athens was minimal. There were no widows, no orphans, no disabled veterans, no dead. The periods of militia service, as little as thirty-eight days, as long as six months and ten days, worked relatively little hardship on the men or their families.

On the economic front the war had a positive, short-term impact. The presence of Harrison's forces in Ohio generated a high demand for farm produce. In Cincinnati flour fetched five to six dollars a barrel; the demand for pork and beef likewise was strong, obviating for the moment the need to ship goods to New Orleans or to drive livestock to the East. Once the war ended, Athenians would again have difficulties marketing their surpluses and securing easy access to manufactured goods.

The political front produced a reaction. At the national level, the war was badly managed and militant Federalists led the opposition to the war. The Washington Benevolent Societies of Zanesville and Putnam—in which Ephraim Cutler and Rufus Putnam were known members—were at the center of Ohio's opposition to the war. This was a minority position, and while it did not win popular favor for Cutler, it was not fatal. Thomas Worthington, despite having voted against the declaration of war, won the Ohio governorship by a 5–2 margin in fall 1814. Cutler went on to one of the most productive periods of his legislative service.

The end of the war, however, did confront Athenians with new problems. The end of the Indian "menace" opened the far richer farm lands in northwestern Ohio, Indiana, and Illinois to settlement, diverting the main flow of westward migrants to those areas. The disruption of foreign trade prior to and during the war had provided motive and time for the textile and metalworking industries of New England to get a solid start.

Post-War Years

In the absence of a local newspaper or private papers, one can only speculate as to the Athens posture vis-à-vis the world beyond the Hocking Valley, as it would be called hereafter, between 1815 and 1825. The major issues, pretty much defined by Henry Clay, focused on the chartering of a Second Bank of the United States, a protective tariff, internal improvements, and slavery.

Athens did not have an organized bank during these years, nor, indeed, did it get one until the late 1840s. The largely subsistence economy of the community with its heavy reliance on barter minimized the need for a bank. As local business emphasized craftsmen producing for a local market, such Athenians were likely to support Clay's proposals for a protective tariff, though, in fact, the high costs of shipping goods across the mountains effectively barred imported goods—either English-made or of American east-coast origin—from reaching Ohio in volume. The all-consuming concern of farmers and merchants alike was access to eastern markets to sell their products and access to goods that could not be produced locally. The solution to the Athens transportation problem would be the key to promoting the community's growth.

4

The Country Village: 1825–1850

ATHENIANS MUST HAVE FELT disappointed in 1850. The growth anticipated in 1825 had never materialized. To be sure the county's population more than doubled between 1825 and 1850 as newcomers occupied much of the best of the remaining farmland. Even Athens Township—which, because it had led in development before 1825, had a smaller potential for continued growth than other areas of the county—grew by some 60 percent in population. But, alas, the village counted but 882 persons in 1850, an unimpressive increase of only 161 persons in two decades.

The plodding growth of the village reflected the character of its economic base as a county seat—market town for its rural hinterland. It reflected the difficulties associated with the area's subsistence agriculture, its limited industry, the financial problems of Ohio University, and the continuing physical isolation of the community. Most residents of Athens County still were farmers, while villagers provided a center for marketing their surpluses and dispensing diverse goods and services. The industrial revolution that was fueling economic expansion in New England and even at Pittsburgh and Cincinnati bypassed Athens.

THE AGRICULTURAL BASE

Agricultural potential continued to be shaped by the region's unglaciated terrain; the bottoms afforded limited level floodplains safe for farming. The steep hillsides generated rapid runoff that produced sudden, sometimes devastating floods. The crests of the hills held little humus. Of the roughly 310,000 acres encompassed by the county in 1850, little more than one-fourth was improved land and another one-third remained unimproved. The rest was nonagricultural. After a half century of settlement, Athens-area farms remained small.

The agricultural base was fragile. Athens Township in 1850 reported 132 farms, a number that would have allowed at least a quarter section of land to each farmer and the prospect of a reasonable living. The reality was that no more than four or five of the township's farmers operated on a commercial scale. Men such as Nathan Kinney, Horace D. White, John D. White, and Andrew Kessinger did well, combining grain production with raising livestock. Kessinger's herd of forty head of cattle was the largest in the township. The great majority of the township's farmers devoted no more than seven to fifteen acres to corn and even less land to wheat. Farms cultivating three or four acres of corn and even less of wheat were common. Such farmers—and they constituted some 30 percent of the township's farmers—faced an austere life. To supplement their incomes, many area farmers raised a range of products that may or may not have found their way into the stream of commerce. Some cultivated small tracts of tobacco. Others, like Eben Foster, planted small orchards of apples and peaches; a few continued to tend a patch of flax, which the women processed at home to spin and weave into country linen and linsey-woolsey. There were modest productions of Irish potatoes, maple sugar, and beeswax and honey. Most farmers still engaged in subsistence agriculture, producing a variety of goods, most of it for home consumption. Having little surplus to sell or barter with village merchants, area farmers lacked the wherewithal to avail themselves of the merchants' goods or services. To many it seemed that in the absence of accessible, inexpensive transportation for bulk goods, Athens-area farmers and merchants alike got smaller rewards for their efforts than did those with easy access to canals or railroads.

THE VILLAGE ECONOMY

In an expansive moment in the summer of 1827, A. G. Brown, editor of the *Mirror,* assessed Athens village. The village, he reported, had 678 white inhabitants and 3 blacks. Of the 109 dwelling houses, 55 were two-storied, brick buildings. He went on to provide a breakdown of the occupations pursued by the villagers, who included 9 professionals—4 physicians, 2 lawyers, and 3 clergy. There were 8 mercantile stores, but as some of the stores were partnerships, there were perhaps as many as 16 merchants. Most of the adult males, by Brown's analysis, were craftsmen. There were 9 carpenters and house joiners along with 5 plasterers and bricklayers. To these must be added 3 cabinetmakers and 2 chairmakers. Five persons specialized in clothing—2 hatters and 3 tailors. There were 8 metalworkers—5 blacksmiths, 2 silversmiths, and 1 tinner. The 2 coopers and 3 tanners served the agricultural community, the cooper by fabricating the barrels needed for shipping cornmeal, wheat, bacon and hams, lard and butter; the tanner, by processing animal hides. The one druggist—an apothecary—formulated the village's ointments, salves, and elixirs and dispensed herbs. The four taverns provided accommodations for persons passing through and for single persons who worked in town. Finally, there was the printer himself, A. G. Brown.

His list is hardly exhaustive. Almost certainly a handful of young women worked as domestic servants, some in private homes, others in the taverns. In addition, a number of housewives unquestionably supplemented family income by furnishing board and room to one or more of the seventy Ohio University students or else by boarding the single workers, perhaps their husband's employees. Just as certainly several women earned incomes as seamstresses or as milliners. But Brown did not include any women or common laborers in his list of occupations. Nor did he list any public officials, presumably because public office remained a part-time post and did not rank as a form of employment. The picture Brown outlined was of a largely self-sufficient village economy—a community producing goods and services for community consumption.

The Professionals

Comparison of the occupations reported in the 1850 census with Brown's list of 1827 provides a rough measure of the village's economic growth in the intervening quarter century. At the professional level, there was a substantial broadening of the occupations. Now the town had 11 lawyers, 3 clergy, and 8 physicians, and in addition there were new professionals—6 teachers and college faculty, and 8 public officials. The town also boasted a dentist, 2 druggists, and a phrenologist, along with 2 publishers. (Phrenology, extremely fashionable in the mid- to late nineteenth century, was the analysis of personality traits as revealed by the shape of the skull.)

Whereas the lawyers of the pioneer era had tended to live elsewhere and traveled to Athens in the company of the president-judge, after 1825 Athens was served primarily by resident, locally trained lawyers. The lawyer with the longest service was Joseph Dana, a man who combined a limited practice of law with serving Ohio University as a professor of languages. The professor-attorney served several terms as county attorney and clerk of court as well as training young men in the law. His most distinguished student was John Welch, who met with Dana for a tutorial once or twice a fortnight. So, too, Joseph M. Dana got his training from his father. This one-on-one training also provided the means by which William Reed Golden and Lot L. Smith began their legal education. But reflecting new methods, Golden attended lectures at the National Law School, Ballston Spa, New York, graduating in 1851.

While this first generation of resident lawyers escaped the need to travel the judicial circuit, they were likely to pursue a variety of interests. Thus, John Welch, who had migrated to Rome Township with his father in 1826, bought the Beebe Mill from his father and pursued the milling business before taking up the law. A. G. Brown first worked as a preceptor in the Academy, founded and published the Athens *Mirror*, and dabbled in politics before becoming a lawyer. Early in their legal careers, many of these men, including both Danas, Welch, and Brown, took an active role in the management of village and county business. Of the lawyers, John Welch and A. G. Brown had clearly arrived in terms of worldly goods by 1850. Many of the others—Henry T. Brown, Samuel Knowles, William Reed Golden, and Lot L. Smith—were in their twenties, with a long future ahead of them.

Of the eight physicians practicing in 1850, Pardon Cook, Jacob Swett, and Eben G. Carpenter were the elders. In an age when medicine still lacked a scientific basis, doctors did not accrue the income that would characterize the practice of medicine in the late twentieth century. On the periphery of the medical profession were the community's dentist, druggists, and phrenologist. John Wilkins, an Ohio-born twenty-four-year-old, practiced dentistry. Oliver Pickering and H. K. Blackstone, both young men, were the druggists. Along with patent medicines, they offered a variety of merchandise ranging from lard and tanner's oil to wines and liquors, dyestuffs, paints and groceries. They also sold patent medicines. The phrenologist was Sumner Bartlett. None of these four owned any real property.

The number of village clergy remained unchanged during the period, only three persons identifying themselves as clergymen either in 1820 or in 1850. The number, however, seriously understates their influence in the community. In fact the clergy had maintained a most active role in the community from the days of Jacob Lindley onward. Presidents Robert Wilson, William Holmes McGuffey, and Alfred Ryors had all been ordained Presbyterians. So, too, three faculty members of 1850, Addison Ballard, Aaron Williams, and William J. Hoge, were ordained Presbyterian clergy. James Campbell, while minister at First Presbyterian, also ran a girls' school. Of these men only Campbell and Ryors claimed any real property.

The Mercantile Community

The Athens mercantile community had grown to twenty persons by 1850. Nominally, these were persons involved in selling goods imported from elsewhere. Their advertisements indicated that while they welcomed cash, they still stood ready in 1850 to accept country produce, which they then had to find ways of marketing. Their repeated published warnings to customers to pay up underscores the fact that many transactions were based on credit. The range of mercantile enterprises, reflected in the advertisements in the *Messenger,* includes dry goods, hardware, clothing, and groceries. These were still general stores, different from those of 1825 chiefly in the wider variety of merchandise.

Of the twenty merchants, fourteen owned property and probably were employers. The other six, without property, were likely employees. Two merchants—John Ballard and Rudolph de Steiguer—were in business with their sons. De Steiguer, a Swiss, was the only foreign-born merchant; the rest came, in roughly equal numbers, from New York, Massachusetts, and other parts of New England. To this time, the Ohio-born had not succeeded in becoming merchants. As a group, the merchants had fared well. Ezra Stewart and Rudolph de Steiguer each claimed property valued in excess of $20,000. Mahlon Atkinson reported property worth $13,000, while John Ballard, Rufus W. Carley, and Samuel Pickering claimed $7,500 in property. These merchants numbered among the economic pillars of the village, men who were comfortably well off but not rich.

Decade by decade, the merchants expanded the variety of goods available to the community. The merchants of 1825 had offered a narrow range of staples—tinware, dishes, cloth—goods that could not easily be fabricated in Athens. The passing of the make-do lifestyle of the frontier era was marked by tailor John Brown's notice in 1825 that he offered "the NEWEST FASHIONS" from Philadelphia. Other tailors who passed through Athens emphasized that they had just come from New York or Philadelphia and were fully acquainted with the latest styles. In 1830, Edward Hatch marked a change when he offered "toys for children." He also advertised that hot coffee and oysters were available "at all times." In 1840, H. W. Develling offered "a choice lot" of groceries, including a variety of fish—cod, salmon, shad, mackerel, and pickled herring. He also offered soft-shell almonds, English walnuts, and ground nuts, lemons and raisins, tooth powder and shoe blacking, and Turkish opium. Reflecting the passing of the open fireplace as a means of heating and cooking, stoves and grates—Franklin stoves—were available. While candles were for sale, so, too, was sperm oil (obtained from sperm whales), indicating the use of oil lamps. By 1850, several businessmen sold property insurance. R. P. Crippen stocked a variety of ready-made clothing—coats, pants, shirts, drawers. By the end of that year the village had a bookseller and stationer. The austere pioneer village of 1825 had become a modest, comfortable country village by 1850.

Establishment, in 1848, of an Athens branch of the Ohio State Bank gave important evidence of growing economic maturity. Appearance of the bank in Athens marked the waning of the barter economy and emergence of a money economy, the supplanting of a self-sufficient economy by an interdependent economy. Capitalized at $100,000, the bank had forty-nine local investors. Its board of directors was a *Who's Who* of the local establishment: John Ballard, Ezra Stewart, and Samuel Pickering, all leading merchants, A. B. Walker, the salt magnate, and Joseph M. Dana and Leonidas Jewett, attorneys. John Welch, a prosperous lawyer, was president. The bank set up quarters at the southeast corner of Court and Washington Streets.

The Industrialists

A few Athenians tried their hand at manufacturing. These manufacturers—millers, lumbermen, brickmakers, salt boilers, and ironmakers—relied on exploiting natural resources: water power, timber, salt, clay, and iron. None of their enterprises was large. Only one employed a steam engine. Either individually owned or partnerships, the enterprises had an ephemeral quality, frequent changes in ownership being common. Milling was the "big" enterprise, relying on the water power of the Hocking River. In 1825, the Bingham and Pruden mills were already in operation. Given the periodic rampages of the Hocking, the mills and mill dams were frequently damaged or needed to be replaced altogether. In 1833, Silas Bingham engaged his stepson, Joseph Herrold, to work at his mill. Herrold also picked up additional employment by building bridges, and in 1839, he bought out Bingham and thereafter operated the mill himself. It should be noted that the various mill owners—Bingham, Herrold, Pruden, and Miles—owned the dam and the mill wheel—the power supply—as well as owning and operating the mill itself, but often leased their mills to others. Milling was a seasonal enterprise.

The Pruden mill, in 1825, solicited custom work, promising same-day carding of wool at 6¼¢ a pound—half cash, the rest in the produce of the country. Although it was Silas Pruden who bought out Gregory, by 1825 it was Silas's son, Samuel Baldwin Pruden, who operated the mill. A year later, W. W. Bierce and Nathan Stewart installed machines for cloth dressing in connection with Pruden's mill. For the convenience of customers, they arranged to receive cloth for processing at either of two stores in central Athens. While Baldwin Pruden was a mill operator, he was also a merchant who bought corn, wheat, and flax seed; he sold whiskey, "good pickled pork," and wheat. In 1827, Pruden announced he preferred flax seed to any other country produce and offered to pay "CASH!!" for it. As Samuel B. Pruden began developing an oil, grist, and sawmill along with a salt-boiling works at Harmony, he sold his operation at Mill Street to J. B. and R. W. Miles in 1832. Court Street merchants, the Miles brothers built a flour mill on the site and then a covered bridge across the Hocking to afford easier access to the village. Shortly after acquiring the property, J. B. Miles left Athens for Tazewell County, Illinois, leaving the business to R. W. Miles. By 1850, the mill was being operated by Andrew Kessinger.

LUMBERING

The Athens area had abundant timber, much of which had to be cleared if agriculture was to expand. While some of the cut timber was converted into building material (the Miles mill, for example, could produce three to four thousand feet of lumber in twenty-four hours), the local market could absorb only a fraction of the cut timber. Much timber, then, was either burned to get rid of it or formed into rafts and floated down the Hocking. One observer reported eleven rafts passing Athens in a single day. The venture of Daniel Herrold, Jonas Rice, and Captain Crippen is known only obliquely—from an obituary notice reporting their drowning in the late spring of 1829 after their raft came apart on the Ohio somewhere near Evansville, Indiana.

BRICKMAKING

A little-heralded industry of the era was brickmaking. Builders made their bricks on site, underscoring that this was an ad hoc enterprise. The leading brickmaker was Nathan Dean, who had learned the craft in New England. As Marjorie Stone points out in *Getting to Know Athens County*, the university trustees were prompted to make regulations concerning the use of the Commons for brick making. Dean and his sons had contracted to supply the thousands of bricks used in the construction of the College Edifice (Cutler Hall). In 1835 his son, John N. Dean, made the bricks for the East and West Wings, now Wilson and McGuffey halls, respectively. As early as 1823, Eben Foster operated a small brick business. His bricks, according to his daughter, were eight-sided "like a honey comb design" and were used for pavement. The brickmakers did not advertise, and their highly utilitarian product did not attract much attention. The *Messenger* did note in passing, however, that in 1850 alone some 700,000 bricks had been manufactured in the town, largely for the local market. The enterprise was not large, only two persons, Thomas Stevens and his son Daniel, being brickmakers at that time.

SALT

In 1850, the *Messenger* reported that some 200,000 bushels of salt were produced yearly in Athens. Indeed, the production of salt, indispensable to preserve meat, was the major industry of the Athens area. One of the first actions of the leadership of the Ohio Company in the 1780s had been to locate salt springs and salt licks. The earliest source of salt for Athens was the salt springs upstream from Marietta, first used by area Indians, and the salt licks in Jackson County.

An effort, in 1820, by Ebenezer Nye to secure salt water by sinking a well near the mouth of Bailey Run in Dover Township ended in failure. A decade later, John Pugsley of Dover struck brine at 800 feet and proposed to produce salt "in quantity for this season." Obviously the start-up costs were minimal. About the same time, Resolved Fuller, who owned land along Sunday Creek from Chauncey to Millfield, struck brine on his own property, launching what for the next fifty years would be "the most lucrative industry in the county." Salt brine, in fact, underlay the Hocking and Sunday Creek valleys at depths between 570 and 1,000 feet.

Within a decade, the Resolved Fuller enterprise became a thriving business. Almost from the start, coal was the fuel for boiling the brine, creating a local market for coal. In 1833, Fuller sold his land and saltworks to Calvary Morris and Norman Root, who in turn sold out to Thomas Ewing and his partners—Samuel F. Vinton and two Philadelphia capitalists, Nicholas Biddle and Elihu Chauncey. Anticipating growth of the business, Ewing and company founded a town, named for Chauncey, and built a large hotel to accommodate the anticipated business clientele. The coming of the Hocking Canal in 1842 greatly expanded the market for salt.

Two young Athens entrepreneurs became involved in the salt business. James J. Fuller, a son of Resolved Fuller, and his brother-in-law, A. B. Walker, had become partners in 1832. Their initial venture—buying cattle in Kentucky in the spring, summering the animals on "the barrens" west of the Scioto River, then driving them to market in late summer—had ended in a five-hundred-dollar loss. Nonplussed, they spent the winter of 1832–33 buying pork and produce, especially flour, loaded a boat, and took off down the Mississippi, selling what they could as they went. This was the beginning of a business of shipping pork and flour that lasted "through many years." James Fuller, whose house still stands on the northwest corner of Washington and College, did his packing in the side yard. Their need for salt and the fact that Fuller already had a family connection to the business led Fuller and Walker to expand their partnership interests into salt manufacture. First they developed a salt furnace across the Hocking from Chauncey; then in the 1840s they expanded with a second operation a short distance upstream near present-day Beaumont, founding a community called Salina. Here they developed a multipurpose industrial complex—salt furnaces, a coal mine for fuel, a gristmill, and a loading dock. Houses were built for workers as well as a store and church. By 1850, J. J. Fuller and A. B. Walker were among the top businessmen of Athens. Fuller reported real property worth $20,000; Walker, $18,000.

In the mid-1840s, Samuel B. Pruden, well-established in the milling business, bought out the Fuller-Walker interest at Chauncey; then developed his own salt wells at Harmony; much of this salt found its way downstream to Ohio River towns, but at least some of it was poled upstream to Athens, then transshipped on the Hocking Canal to markets farther north. In his *Reminiscences*, A. B. Walker avers that he was associated with S. B. Pruden in the development of the saltworks on "the Connet place," boring wells, constructing two new furnaces, and sinking a coal shaft. Salt production was the big industry of the county by 1850.

IRON WORKS

In February 1850, the *Messenger* carried a notice of the Athens Foundry, a new enterprise of two New York–born iron molders, Eliazer Smith and Phillip Wheeler (listed as Phillip Whaler in the 1850 census). Initially the enterprise was small, employing three men, two of whom boarded at Wheeler's home. They produced a variety of iron goods—plows, kettles, stewpots and skillets, stoves, grates, and fire irons, testing the market to see where the demand was.

The essence of industrialization was the substitution of machines for people on the assumption that machine production would give investors a higher return on their investment than would hand production. And often, machines could. The reality of Athens, however, was that transportation costs severely limited the market for the products and this, in turn, kept the firms small. The largest of the firms—the Daniel B. Stewart woolen mill—was capitalized at $25,000; the next largest enterprise, his grain mill, along with Joseph Herrold's woolen mill and W. S. Love's foundry and plow factory represented investments of from $8,000 to $10,000 each.

Craftsmen

Far more Athenians continued to be engaged as craftsmen than as merchants, underscoring the extent to which Athens still had to produce much of its own goods and services. Yet, it is apparent that the variety of goods produced locally had grown appreciably since 1825. Eight craftsmen specialized in food products; Athens now had bakers, butchers, confectioners, and a brewer. Seventeen persons produced clothing—a weaver, fourteen tailors, and two hatters. The building trades, which employed twenty-seven persons, included a brickmason, stonemason, painter, and plasterer as well as cabinetmakers and carpenters. The metal trades now included a machinist in addition to the specialists in copper, tin, silver, and the ubiquitous blacksmiths. One was a gunsmith. Other craftsmen fabricated wagons, carriages, and coaches. The leather trades, as earlier, included boot and shoemakers along with harness- and saddle-makers. This proliferation of crafts reflected a growing affluence, which allowed the consumer to purchase goods made by specialists rather than relying on made-at-home products. The craftsmen, like the professionals, merchants, and manufacturers, were self-employed, setting their own work schedules and at most directing the labors of one or two employees.

Laborers

The Athens economy of 1850 occupied relatively few wage laborers—indeed only twenty-three identified themselves as laborers, although the sixteen manufacturers listed in the 1850 manufacturing census reported thirty-two males and two children as employees. D. B. Stewart—the largest employer—had five men working in the woolen mill and six men and two youths in the grain mill. Alex Cochran employed four men in his boot and shoe operation. No other firm engaged more than three employees. Primarily young men—a third of the laborers were less than twenty-one years of age and another third ranged in age from twenty-one to twenty-nine—these were men who had yet to master a skill that would give them a leg up in the world. Six of the group, however, were heads of households, households that were at some financial risk, since none of the six reported owning real estate. Furthermore, their addresses as given in the census rolls suggest that, even in that bucolic era, Athens had one and possibly two working-class neighborhoods. Overall in 1850 labor-management relations retained a high level of personal contact. Even so, these laborers depended for their wages—their food, shelter, and clothing—on the ability of their employers to find profitable markets for the goods so as to provide steady employment. But the working-class population remained a small fraction of the village labor force in 1850.

Even the most cursory comparison of Athens village with Chillicothe and Marietta, villages with comparable dates of origin, further underscores the limited growth experienced by Athens village in its first half century. Of the three communities in 1850, Chillicothe boasted over 6,000 residents, Marietta claimed 3,100, while Athens counted 882. Both Chillicothe and Marietta served agricultural regions that were far more productive than the Hocking Valley. And unlike Athens, both were served by navigable streams that facilitated the export of the produce of farmers and villagers.

TRANSPORTATION

Athens was not alone in needing the means for moving the products of its farms to East Coast markets. And as New York neared completion of its Erie Canal, Ohio decided to tie into it by building its own canal that would link Lake Erie at Cleveland with the Ohio River at Portsmouth. On the nation's forty-ninth birthday, July 4, 1825, Ohio broke ground for the Ohio Canal. Thomas Ewing, the principal speaker of the day, pointed with pride to "the vast extent and matchless fertility" of Ohio's soil, to its advance in industry and "progress in the arts." Yet he noted that Ohioans still could not reach Atlantic Coast markets by water because of Niagara Falls; and while New Orleans was accessible, it was more remote from foreign markets than the Atlantic ports, its climate caused goods to spoil, and it was often flooded with goods, depressing prices. The most important single requirement for Ohio's growth, Ewing concluded, was "adequate transportation."

Maria Foster Brown cast the transportation problem of Athens merchants in more graphic terms. The daughter of Eben Foster, one of Athens village's more successful businessman-farmers, she was the wife of Daniel Brown who, in the 1840s, had served an apprenticeship in the Court Street store of Ezra Stewart before undertaking a general store of his own in Amesville. Mrs. Brown voiced the perspective of merchants dealing in grain, dry goods, and hardware. Like other merchants of the 1840s, her husband accepted farm produce in trade for his goods, produce for which he had to find a market. As the hogs he received in trade could not be driven to market profitably, he fattened and slaughtered them to be marketed as pork and bacon; he stored wool and hides in his barns. In addition, he raised sheep, baled their wool, tanned their hides, and fed their carcasses to his hogs. In fall, he cut timber with which he built a flatboat. Come a spring freshet, he hastened to load his scow with grain, bacon, wool, tobacco, and dried fruits in time to ride the crest down Federal Creek to the Hocking and on down the Ohio. Grain and tobacco he sold at Cincinnati. At plantations along the Mississippi, Brown bartered bacon for molasses, while at New Orleans he traded the molasses for refined sugar. The remaining goods, including the scow, were sold for cash.

Brown packed his cash—Mexican silver—in a small, black, horsehair trunk which he kept in his stateroom on his return upstream by steamboat. But no sooner was he home than he had to be off to Pittsburgh to purchase hardware and to Philadelphia for dry goods, household furniture and general merchandise, and farming implements that had to be carried to Ohio by Conestoga wagons drawn by six horses. Daniel Brown did well. In the course of eleven years, he parlayed his initial investment of $500 into $5,000. Yet the fact remained that merchants like Ezra Stewart and Daniel Brown had to spend several months each year away from Athens to market the accumulated surpluses of their customers and to purchase a new stock of goods to sell.

All-Weather Roads

Badly as Athens farmers and merchants needed an inexpensive means of delivering their goods to Eastern markets, the most urgent need was local all-weather roads. Ohio had already authorized a state road from Marietta to Athens and on to Chillicothe. It had been widened from a trace to a wagon road of sorts. A sense of progress was implicit in the notice of an 1825 petition to open a state road from Gallipolis to Athens and thence northward through Perry County to Newark, Mount Vernon, and Mansfield, what is now essentially Route 13. Often as not, these roads were inadequate. The economic resources of the state permitted little more than laying out a road, typically with no crown nor culverts to drain the roadbed. Smaller streams might be bridged, but larger streams had to be forded or crossed by ferry. With the Hocking forming a loop around the village, access to Athens village from the west, south, and east depended on ferry service until the mid-1830s. Then, in the course of six years, privately owned toll bridges were thrown across the river at three points—the East Bridge in 1834, the West Bridge on the state road to Chillicothe in 1836, and finally the South Bridge to Pomeroy, Alexander, and Albany in 1839. In time, through a combination of volunteer subscriptions and county funds, these were made toll-free, public bridges.

Village, township, and county governments devoted much time and much of their limited resources to laying out roads. They were constructed for the most part by the local residents themselves who by law were required to work on the county roads two days a year. The results were poor. Neither the townships nor the county could provide knowledgeable supervisors; many of the residents failed to report for work. There were inadequate funds for supplies.

At a different level, one notes that seven persons in 1850 made a living by providing transportation services to townsmen. Details are sketchy, but this almost certainly included livery service—providing carriages and wagons when needed as well as servicing stagecoaches running north to Lancaster—an all-day experience —and south to Pomeroy. One of the memorable experiences of the Reverend Mr. John Spaulding, a Presbyterian clergyman who served Athens for several years, was that the stage carrying him and his wife overturned while en route to Athens.

Canal Fever

Building the Ohio Canal, on which so many hopes rested, proved far harder than the optimistic words of Thomas Ewing suggested when the first spadeful of earth was turned. The canal was to be: "The great artery of America, which will carry abundance to all the extremities of the Union." The expansive enthusiasm was contagious. Immediately every Ohio community wanted a canal or river improvements of its own. The state legislature gave in, agreeing to finance canals linking the Maumee with the Wabash River and both with the Great Miami. Not to be outdone, Marietta insisted on river improvements that would open the Muskingum to steamboat travel as far upstream as Zanesville. With Ohio's resources spread thin, canal construction was slowed. And as exciting as the Ohio Canal proved to be, it bypassed Athens and the Hocking Valley, crossing north of the Hocking Valley as it passed overland from the Tuscarawas Valley to the Scioto and then descending alongside the Scioto through Chillicothe to Portsmouth.

No matter. Athenians quickly were attracted to the possibilities of two other ventures—a proposal by Baltimore entrepreneurs to build a canal linking Chesapeake Bay with the Ohio River and a second proposal to build a railroad from Baltimore to the Ohio River. As canals had long been used in Western Europe and steam railroads were virtually untested, attention centered on the possibilities of the Chesapeake and Ohio Canal. From the first, the project excited businessmen in Marietta and Athens. They promptly raised objections to proposals that would route the canal from the crest of the Allegheny Mountains to the Youghiogheny River and thence rely on the Ohio River, arguing pointedly that from Pittsburgh to the Muskingum the Ohio was often too low for navigation. Rather, they lobbied for a canal route leading to the mouth of the Muskingum, giving Ohioans "a market at their door." Failing this, they argued, the Ohio trade so coveted by Baltimore would make its way northward to the Ohio Canal and thence be delivered via the Erie Canal to New York City.

In fact, Athenians had to wait a decade and a half for access to a canal. As it became apparent that the Chesapeake and Ohio Canal would not reach out to the Muskingum and Marietta, Athens had to look to a connection with the Ohio and Erie Canal. A private Lancaster venture dug the Lancaster Lateral, an eleven-mile canal linking Lancaster to the Ohio Canal. As the Ohio Canal neared completion, pressure on the state to finance canal routes serving other areas of the state increased. Finally, in 1836, thanks to the skillful lobbying of Calvary Morris, who had a major interest in the local salt business, the Ohio Legislature approved the Hocking Valley Canal, a project by which the state acquired the Lancaster Lateral and constructed a canal down the Hocking Valley to Athens. The great selling point of the Hocking Canal was the access it would afford to the salt and coal deposits of northern Athens County.

Much delayed, the Hocking Canal reached Athens in 1843. The village rejoiced. Hand-written bills proclaimed the "Canal Celebration" to be held Friday, October 25, 1843. The "Committee of Arrangements" with band and citizens met the first boats and passengers. As the band played, a thirteen-gun salute was fired from Mason Hill, the present-day site of the Athens Middle School. After the boats with passengers departed on their return trip, bound for Chauncey, Nelsonville, and Logan, again to the accompaniment of band music and the firing of cannon, the citizenry assembled at the courthouse for a celebratory address.

Because the market for the salt and coal lay to the north, Nelsonville became the major shipping point for those products. As helpful as the canal proved to the salt producers, it was no panacea. It was of limited use to coal mines not adjacent to the canal, for such coal had to be loaded into wagons at the mine, hauled to the canal, then reloaded onto the barges; furthermore, during the winter months, when the demand for coal was at a peak, the canal was often frozen, traffic at a standstill. Although far better than the river route to New Orleans, the Hocking Canal route required repeated loading and unloading as cargoes made their way north and east to New York City. Athens still needed a direct, inexpensive mode for shipping goods eastward.

Railroad Fever

Suggestions in 1827 of building a railroad between Baltimore and the Ohio River were greeted with a mix of skepticism and hope. Editor Brown's first reaction in the *Mirror* was one of skepticism. He clearly saw the implications. If such a railroad did indeed reach the Ohio River, he predicted the proposed Chesapeake and Ohio Canal would be abandoned. On the other hand, Brown recognized that the

Baltimore and Ohio firm had already sold nearly forty-five thousand shares of its stock and that Marietta citizens had already formed a committee to communicate to the railroad's directors that they regarded a point opposite the mouth of the Muskingum as the optimal place on the Ohio River for the western terminus of the railroad.

Rather promptly, Athens joined other southern Ohio communities in enthusiastically applauding the Baltimore and Ohio project. Chaired by Ebenezer Currier, a leading merchant-farmer and sometime public official, the Athens meeting endorsed the project, praising it as "a means of a more convenient, expeditious and less expensive transportation of the products of the soil to the Eastern market." The meeting further endorsed the extension of the rail line from Marietta to Athens and thence to Chillicothe and on to Cincinnati. Foreshadowing later controversies, "A Subscriber" argued that a rail line from Belpre to Athens would be far easier to build than a line from Athens to Marietta, since the countryside along the Hocking was more level than the rugged hill country between Athens and Marietta. A subsequent community meeting in Chillicothe also urged the Baltimore and Ohio to come to Parkersburg and to connect with an Ohio extension at Belpre.

On July 4, 1828, three years after Thomas Ewing's address, the Chesapeake and Ohio Canal and the Baltimore and Ohio Railroad both broke ground, but there were many miles to traverse before either would reach the crest of the Allegheny Mountains, much less the Ohio River.

Progress toward an Athens rail link with the Atlantic Coast proceeded at a snail's pace. In May 1830, the Baltimore and Ohio began limited operations in the east, the first railroad in the United States open to the public, but not until 1842 did it reach Cumberland, Maryland. As it began building west of the Appalachian Summit, Ohio's interest in a rail line across southern Ohio became serious, and on March 8, 1845, the Belpre and Cincinnati Railroad—the B & C—was chartered, with authorization to place its eastern terminal either at Harmar, across the Muskingum from Marietta, or at Belpre and to run west to Cincinnati. The leading figures in the Belpre and Cincinnati Railroad were William Parker Cutler, son of Ephraim, the erstwhile patriarch of Amesville, and Noah Wilson, a Chillicothe banker. Two Athens businessmen, A. B. Walker and John Ballard, became members of the board of directors, and in time, the railroad named two of their engines for them. While Cutler represented Marietta interests, the center of power for the Belpre and Cincinnati was at Chillicothe. Athens would be a way station whose rail service would depend on decisions and policies made elsewhere.

At the time construction of the B & C began, a controversy arose over whether to approach the Queen City via Hillsboro or via Greenfield, a matter of small concern to Athenians but of such vital concern to the rival communities as to delay construction. Not until the end of 1850 was the B & C ready to solicit bids on the route from Greenfield to Chillicothe.

As of 1850, Athens had only partly solved its market problem. The need to rely on ferries to enter or exit the village from the west, south, and east had ended as the Hocking was bridged. The network of roads had grown, easing local traffic. The Hocking Canal offered an inexpensive, if roundabout, means to move the area's agricultural surpluses to New York City. But direct rail transportation to the East Coast still lay in the future.

Verbal communication with other communities remained limited and slow. Over time, new mail routes expanded the channels by which mail moved to and away from Athens. However, the irregularity and slowness of the postal service, sometimes ten days late, remained the norm. The problem of irregular delivery continued to midcentury, though in November 1850, the post office was not held responsible when some "fiendish scoundrel" stole the newspaper bags from the Lancaster-Athens stage.

By 1850, the technical barriers to nearly instantaneous communication had been broken. Samuel F. B. Morse had demonstrated a commercially viable telegraph in 1844. Relatively inexpensive to construct, relatively simple to maintain, telegraph service connecting Athens to the rest of the country was only a matter of time.

THE UNIVERSITY

In 1825, Ohio University was a going institution looking forward to the future. It had two buildings—the Academy and the College Edifice. A five-man faculty was on board. As landlord to the village as well as of Athens and Alexander townships, the school enjoyed a modest—very modest—income. Leadership of the college fell successively to Robert G. Wilson (1825–1839), William Holmes McGuffey (1839–1843), the university's best-known president, and Alfred Ryors (1846–1852). In President Robert G. Wilson, it had reasonably competent leadership. Nonetheless, during the next quarter century, the college proved no more able to stimulate the growth of the village than the village was to spur the growth of the college.

Enrollment was a problem. The university offered collegiate education in an area with a sparse population in an age when few farmers, tradesmen, or craftsmen were likely to find a college degree necessary to vocational success. Nor was a college degree prerequisite to entering a profession. There were no public secondary schools and few private college preparatory schools in the region. Furthermore, after 1815, the major population growth in Ohio had occurred in the Miami Valley and in northern Ohio—areas in which, starting with Kenyon College in 1824, a number of private colleges emerged to compete for the limited pool of Ohioans seeking a college education. As it was, Ohio University's enrollment fluctuated from year to year, making it difficult to budget or to efficiently employ its faculty. Before 1839, the enrollments seem never to have reached 100. Temporarily, a year and a half into McGuffey's presidency, enrollments reached 120, then plummeted. In August 1845, enrollment dropped to thirteen, three of whom were in the prep school. This was disastrous to an institution that derived 30 to 33 percent of its income from student tuition.

Student discipline was a continuing problem. Presidents Wilson and McGuffey as well as the faculty were overwhelmed by problems of unruly students. The presidents and faculty were stern. The demanding student schedule began before dawn. Morning prayers and breakfast were already out of the way before the first study period began at 6:00 A.M. Recitations ran from 7:00 A.M. to noon and from 1:30 P.M. to evening prayer; from early candle-lighting to 9:00 P.M. was study time. A student was expected to "remain in his room and pursue his studies with diligence." "Strict and undeviating regard" was to be paid to "virtuous conduct and to exemplary diligence, fidelity, and punctuality."

An older man and a stern Calvinist, President Wilson was "paternalistic and harsh" in his approach to student behavior. Unable to distinguish between youthful exuberance that resulted in rambunctious actions and genuinely antisocial behavior, he assumed that the best way to deal with the "bad" boy was to expel him. At the same time, the school afforded no relief from the grind. No organized athletic or social activities provided a change of pace. Exasperated with what they perceived as "a state of disorder" among students, university trustees in 1835 provoked a crisis by requiring each student to sign a pledge to "tell on" disorderly students. Of the school's seventy students at the time, forty refused to sign and departed; thirty acquiesced, twenty in the college, ten in the prep school. With enrollments so precipitously reduced, the trustees balanced the school's accounts by dismissing three of the college's five faculty members.

The university's most serious problem was the ongoing conflict with the community, the product of its role as the village and area landlord. Even before R. G. Wilson began his presidency, there remained unsold land both in the village as well as in Athens and Alexander townships, land from which the university realized no income. This undoubtedly goaded trustees to enhance university revenues by reappraising the leased lands at their current value. Trustee-legislator Ephraim Cutler had supported this effort by securing the enactment of the requisite legislation by the Ohio General Assembly in February 1820. Townsmen were upset.

On becoming president, Wilson sought a way out of the difficulty. He proposed the outright sale of land to the leaseholders, the sale price to be deposited with the state. The money so generated would constitute a perpetual endowment fund from which the university would draw six percent interest. Leaseholders would also be required to pay all rents in arrears to the university before securing title to their lands. Leaseholders voiced no objections, but in fact few availed themselves of this opportunity to acquire a fee simple title to their land and thus free themselves from their economic tie to the university.

In a second move to bolster the school's finances, Wilson and the trustees commissioned the Reverend Mr. Randolph Stone to "diffuse correct information" regarding the university. Stone was also appointed professor of English and history contingent on his raising an endowment of $12,000 from "individual liberality." A year's effort proved unavailing, and in April 1839, the trustees discharged Stone as its agent. Stone never taught a class.

Differences with the community became further strained when the university sought possession of the South Commons, the area along Union Street. President Wilson complained of "the accumulation of filth about our doors from the sheep, hogs, and cattle." As the original plat of the village had disappeared, various stratagems were employed. In April 1835, Wilson sought a deed from the village council relinquishing the green and assenting to its enclosure by the university. Before the council responded, a traveling circus pitched its tent on the green, although it had been denied permission by the university to do so. An irate President Wilson charged the circus with trespass and won a judgment of $5.00 and costs. This action so angered townspeople that the council refused to deed over the Commons to the University. Next, the university petitioned the legislature to vacate the disputed area, but townsmen countered that the Commons was useful to pasture animals, and the local militia company claimed it as their drill grounds. When the legislature delayed action, Wilson asked the Ohio Supreme Court to clear the title to the Commons. Again nothing came of this approach. Finally, in spring 1838, the trustees' building committee was authorized "to enclose . . . the College Green . . . with a neat substantial fence." The committee was circumspect; the fence was erected close to the buildings rather than along Union Street.

Despite his frustrations, when Wilson retired in 1839, the university was in tolerably good order. There was again a full faculty of five. The dismissal of three faculty members in 1836 had generated savings sufficient to allow the trustees to

construct the East and West Wings—present-day Wilson and McGuffey halls—
to house students, thereby making enrollment more attractive to students. For its
day, the university was "a solid institution of higher learning."

William Holmes McGuffey, Wilson's successor, proved unable to build on that
foundation. Although widely known for his *Eclectic Readers,* McGuffey arrived in
Athens under a cloud, for he had been charged with plagiarism, and his publisher
had settled out of court. Further, he had great difficulty in working with
colleagues, a factor that made it especially hard for him to resolve the college's
problems. Student disciplinary problems continued, and the university's financial
problems recurred. To increase income, the trustees now moved to revalue all the
college lands that had been under lease for thirty-five years as well as all houses and
town lots in the village. The Athens County members of the board of trustees opposed this move, but they were outvoted. When a test case came before the Ohio
Supreme Court, the court held for the university. Furious, the leaseholders turned
to the state legislature for relief. In this move, they were supported by Elijah
Hatch, Jr., a trustee, Henry Bartlett, the university secretary, and Thomas Armstrong, the university collector. In March 1843, the legislature granted the townsmen the relief they sought, agreeing that the February 1805 legislation, indeed,
meant what townspeople had long claimed, that the original valuation of the land
was the only value that the university could employ in determining rents on the
college lands. Delighted with the outcome, townsmen scheduled a victory celebration featuring a bonfire, speeches, and the firing of the "great gun"—a six-pounder.
The bonfire blazed; orators poured forth; but "the boom of the cannon was not
heard," for the night before the event, Samuel Sullivan Cox, as brassy a student as
ever attended the university, spiked the cannon. However pleased the villagers were
with the legislature's action, as historian Thomas Hoover observed in *The History of
Ohio University,* the university was "virtually stripped of its birthright of land." Forever after, the university was restricted to an income of approximately $4,500 a year
from the college lands, imposing "years of hardship and frustration, limited facilities, enrollments, and equipment. . . ." Distressed by "the chaos of the university's
finances," in 1843, McGuffey resigned.

At this point relations between the university and the village reached their nadir.
McGuffey's departure was "a crippling blow," and the university virtually collapsed.
Daniel Read and Alfred Ryors, faculty members, departed; only twenty students
remained. Three Athens trustees, in an effort to clear the air of rumors, took space
in Athens and Columbus papers to deny that McGuffey's departure grew out
of "a cherished and bitter hostility" on the part of citizens toward the university.
Certainly McGuffey, who had supported revaluation of the college lands, had

"incurred the odium of a large majority of the people." Whether citizens actually stoned McGuffey on the streets of Athens, as local lore would have it, remains unverified.

The university's growth was also inhibited by its own internal problems. All too often, the trustees exhibited a "boundless optimism" that blinded them to realities. They were extraordinarily casual about attending meetings; at a time the university could scarcely meet its financial obligations, they talked blithely of starting up a medical college and botanical garden. Ebenezer Currier, the treasurer, was, at the least, careless in his bookkeeping. Townspeople complained—evidently with reason—that some trustees had used their public position for private gain in the administration of the college lands. In dealing with the enrollment problem, as Thomas Hoover concluded, the trustees were "slow in recognizing the necessity for a more progressive attitude toward many fields of learning." In financial matters, they were "lax and inefficient," failing to budget properly or to adhere to their budgets. Even when compelled to close the college for three years, they failed to reduce the college debt. Desperate to generate income, the trustees proposed to sell scholarships for $30, permitting the holder to attend the university for nine terms. Fortunately, few of the scholarships sold, since each one, if fully used, deprived the university of $60 in income. Indeed, when McGuffey left in 1843, conditions were so bad that the trustees were unable to find a suitable candidate willing to accept the presidency. After two prospects rejected their offer, the trustees closed the college for three years, though not the preparatory school, before turning to Alfred Ryors, a former faculty member.

Called back from Indiana University to become president in 1846, Ryors promptly reopened the college. In the course of four years, he cut the college's debt in half. A New School Presbyterian, he abandoned the stern manner of Wilson and McGuffey, which had engendered so much conflict with students. When students inevitably misbehaved, probation, not dismissal, was Ryors's first recourse. His embrace of New School Presbyterianism, in addition, paved the way for a transfer of control of the university from the Presbyterians to the Methodists, whose membership was approaching one-third of the state's population. By 1852, when Ryors resigned, the university was again a viable institution. But the fact remained that leases of the college lands had failed to provide the university an adequate income while engendering a legacy of ill will toward the university. To 1850 the university, far from sparking the growth of the community, may have retarded it by the unattractive terms under which land was available.

THE POLITICAL SCENE

Since 1811, when it first incorporated, the village had operated under a five-man council, which elected a president from among its own members. Then, in 1828, in response to new statutory authority, the village government reorganized. A nine-man council with staggered, three-year terms governed. Beginning in 1829, the mayor and town marshal were also elected by the citizenry, while the council chose all other officials, including the town treasurer and recorder.

Necessarily with so small a population, the village government was close to its citizens. Jacksonian democracy presumed that every man was qualified to hold public office, and rotation in office rather than continuity became the norm. Over the twenty-one years for which there is a record, the office of mayor was occupied by seven persons. John Brown 2d, known as General John Brown, held office nine years, Samuel Miller four, and Joseph Dana four. Even so, the office changed hands at least nine times during the interval. The mayors were men with relatively high public visibility. Brown headed the local militia and operated the major tavern in the village. Miller was the town's leading carpenter; Dana, a professor at the university.

The council seats were occupied by forty-nine different persons over the quarter century. Considering that the village had fewer than five hundred qualified voters in 1850 and thirteen village offices to fill, roughly one voter in forty held some local office at any single time, and close to one voter in ten had served on town council at one time or another. This was still government by friends and neighbors.

By and large, the village fathers were preoccupied with making the environment safe for its residents. An ordinance of April 1826 banned swine, the village "garbage collectors," from running at large. Owners who failed to confine their pigs risked having the town marshal impound them, then auction them off to the highest bidder. Sheep, the village's "live-in lawn mowers" might run at large during the daytime, but at night the sheep were to be "yarded." Still another ordinance forbid residents to obstruct streets, alleys, or sidewalks with wood, lumber, or stone.

New urban problems surfaced. In May 1827, the council prohibited galloping a horse or horses in town on pain of a $5.00 fine. In the interest of preventing shows and exhibits "contrary to good morals," the council instituted licensing requirements—the mayor screened the applicants, and the council granted the license—constituting, in fact, prior censorship. As in every generation, Athenians were troubled by the condition of the streets. In December 1829, council set standards for placing curbing on the outside of sidewalks for gutters "sufficient to carry off the water." To what extent curbs and gutters were actually installed remains un-known. Maria Foster Brown remembered the streets as a sea of mud after every rain, requiring that women, whose skirts in the fashion of that time brushed the ground, be carried by horse from one side of the street to the other.

THE COMMUNITY

Despite the village's slow growth, the community shed its frontier character. This was evidenced as it faced problems of health and crime, and as it developed a va-riety of community institutions.

Community Health

To romantics of a later age, this era—when most Americans lived on farms or in small villages such as Athens and enjoyed an abundance of fresh air, pure, clear spring water, and healthy, rosy-cheeked children—seemed ideal. The reality in-volved recurrent epidemics of influenza, typhoid fever, malaria, and yellow fever as well as a high level of infant and maternal mortality. Of the 123 Athenians buried at West State Street Cemetery between 1825 and 1850 and whose age at death is known, 30 had not reached their second birthday; an additional 5 did not reach their third birthday. The median age at death for females was 25.5 years; for males, 29 years. The difference in these median ages at death seems attributable to the risk women assumed in childbirth. Of the persons who died between ages 18 and 36, the prime years of child bearing, 20 village women died as opposed to 13 males.

The high infant mortality and maternal deaths reflected the prevalence of life-threatening diseases and infections that were beyond the ability of nineteenth-cen-tury doctors to treat. Men, too, were cut down by disease. Whether in 1825 or 1850, Athens County had vast areas of unimproved land; the village relied on wells and privies. Horses, dogs, hogs, sheep, and cattle, flies and mosquitoes abounded. If farm folk were exposed to the ague, to malaria promoted by an abundance of poorly drained lands, the villagers who lived in close proximity to one another were especially susceptible to contagion.

In spring 1827 a number of students were suffering from a mild form of typhus fever, according to the *Mirror*, which expressed relief that there had been no casu-alties. The condition returned that fall, and the *Mirror* noted that the village had just been "severely visited" by "slow Typhus or Nervous Fever." This time it found satisfaction that fewer fatalities than usual had accompanied the disease, that this epidemic was less serious than the "Bilious" kind. The tombstone of Enoch Hannaman bears mute testimony to this epidemic. It was erected at West State Street by his eldest brother "from the sentiment of brotherly duty." Hannaman was "twenty one years, five months, two days at the time of his death." The *Mirror* may have erred in its appraisal of the epidemic, for at least ten persons died in 1827, a higher proportion of the population to die than in any other year before midcentury.

In 1832, Ohio was hit by an epidemic of cholera of sufficient magnitude that Governor Duncan McArthur called for "a day of fasting, humiliation and prayer to God" that Ohio be spared "this dreadful malady." Cholera returned periodically to Ohio. Asiatic cholera was especially devastating among those who traversed the California Trail during the gold rush of 1849, and in August 1850, the *Messenger* noted that this summer, as several summers before, cholera had afflicted communities along the Ohio River. The *Messenger* noted that it was of epidemic proportions in Columbus, and that an outbreak in Circleville had caused panic there. For once Athenians could be grateful that Columbus and Marietta were still two to three days' travel distant; Athens escaped this plague on both occasions.

In the winter of 1834–35, the village was hard hit by scarlet fever and at least three students and one faculty member were stricken. While six town children died, including the three children of Daniel Read, principal of the academy, no college student did. When an unidentified epidemic struck in winter 1837, one student "in feeble health," died en route home. For all the personal trauma occasioned by the loss of infants and of women in childbirth, the discomforts of malaria, and the ravages of contagious diseases such as scarlet fever, the community was helpless to protect itself.

Athens was too small to host organized groups that embraced the various health movements of the day—those that rejected tea and coffee, or that endorsed graham flour or spas for the benefits of their mineral baths. The *Spectator*, however, did bring to the community's attention the danger of the corset. In a three- to four-column-long address on "Health as Affected by Dress," a Professor Munsey of Dartmouth College warned the ladies of the community of the serious consequences of tight-lacing. Corsets restricted the development of the lungs, interfered with digestion, deformed the spine, and had an adverse effect on complexion, he warned.

Crime

Of course, a small number of persons upset the public decorum. The *Spectator* hints at the range of such offenses in reporting the escape of three inmates of the local jail: Joseph Atkinson, being held for horse stealing; Marcus Frost, for rape; and Henry Brand, for assault and battery. Atkinson and Brand were Pennsylvania Dutch and it is not clear whether the offenses with which they were charged had been committed locally. Security of prisoners apparently was a problem, for in June 1826, the *Mirror* reported a $20 reward for the capture of Matthew Watkins, who had escaped from jail three weeks earlier. In general, the community was tranquil. Reports of a stolen horse, assault, or counterfeit bills were the exception. The crimes that drew the most attention were crimes of passion, robberies, and thefts that had occurred elsewhere. The efforts of lodges and church bodies to discipline wayward members affirm that some members of the community abused alcohol, that some husbands and some wives were unfaithful, that petty thievery did occur. That such disciplinary efforts were abandoned by the Presbyterians suggests not so much the attainment of perfection as a reflection of the growing secularization of the community, a willingness to leave law and order to civil authorities.

Organized Society

In confronting its problems, the residents of Athens, like those of other communities of the day, made liberal use of voluntary organizations. The community fashioned a variety of ad hoc organizations to deal with special problems or interests.

When it came to organizing fire protection for the community in 1831, citizens chose to form a volunteer company independent of the village. The leadership included both town and gown. Robert G. Wilson, the university president, was director; Charles Shipman, a leading merchant, was the assistant director. Many of the town's merchants and craftsmen were officers of the brigade. However good the intentions, absent a municipal water system or a mechanical pump, the fire brigade was not likely to be of much help in a big fire. Volunteer fire companies would come and go. Until 1850, even on Court Street, buildings were generally far enough apart that most fires could be contained to a single structure.

Temperance

Throughout this period Athenians grappled with the problem of alcohol. Convention required the host of a log-rolling or house-raising to provide an ample supply of liquor. Employees, too, expected a ration of whiskey as part of their daily compensation. This social pressure was sufficiently great that although Eben Foster was a teetotaler, he nonetheless gave his employees the traditional daily ration of whiskey. The alcohol problem was further accentuated by the propensity of local farmers to convert their corn to whiskey. Denison University historian William Utter, writing of early nineteenth-century Ohio, put it succinctly: "The land would produce nothing but corn, but as there was no market for corn, they made it into whiskey; as there was no market for whiskey, they drank it." Evidence that the consumption of alcohol was out of hand is found in the records of local church bodies as they censured members whose drinking had become a source of public embarrassment.

In 1828, students at Ohio University organized a Temperance Society. Condemning the "unmoderate use of Spirituous Liquors," they referred to the "deleterious consequences" of drinking and invoked the image of "Sodom and Gommorow" (sic). They ended by urging members to commit themselves "to refrain from the use of ardent spirits." Townsmen followed the next year in organizing a temperance group of their own.

The pressure to limit drinking had some impact. In June 1832, the tavern operated by Isaac Barker, Jr., stopped the sale of hard liquor and restyled itself the Temperance House. Emphasizing moderation rather than total abstinence, the Temperance House advertised itself as a place where "travellers may find undisturbed rest and plenty." But it assured patrons that "wine, cider, and soda water were available."

As with the nation as a whole, the temperance campaign in Athens began as a male-dominated effort to restrict the consumption of liquor, directed by the Washingtonian Society. As his contribution, Eben Foster stopped providing his laborers the traditional daily ration of whiskey and dumped two barrels of whiskey into the gutter. In time, the thrust of the reform movement shifted from emphasizing moderation in drinking to total abstinence. Thus in February 1850 a blue-ribbon committee of notables called on local merchants to desist altogether from dispensing alcohol. The committee included Alfred Ryors, the University president, Nelson Van Vorhes, editor of the town newspaper, Ezra Stewart and A. B. Walker, leading businessmen, and A. G. Brown and John Welch, members of the local bar. By way of stimulating interest in an upcoming community meeting, the committee reported that most merchants had agreed to halt the sale of liquor— once they had sold the stock on hand.

The community gathered to celebrate their seeming success, "an enthusiastic affair." Agreed on attacking the evil, they pointed to "the new-made graves in the cemetery, the hungry and half-clad orphans, and the unequaled wretchedness" that "the sale and use of ardent spirits has brought to the community." This meeting was followed a month later by a mock trial of "alcohol." The trial occupied two nights, the courtroom almost overflowing with townspeople. The intensity of community pressure was reflected in the advertisements of Pickering and Blackstone— the town's leading distributors of patent medicines and drugs—hedging even as they acquiesced with the community will: henceforth wines and liquors would be available, but "exclusively for medicinal purposes." By spring 1850, the "Friends of Temperance," intoxicated with their success, were no longer willing to settle for voluntary compliance. They aimed at a constitutional amendment that would prohibit the state legislature from enacting laws that licensed the sale of drinks or that made the liquor traffic legal.

The Agricultural Society

By the mid-1820s, an interest in improving the quality of agriculture was apparent. Editor A. G. Brown, son of a farmer, noted that Athens still lacked an agricultural society. "Nothing," he wrote, "would more effectually promote the farming interests of the county." Indeed, Brown might have added, the economic well-being of the village depended on a productive farm community able to buy the diverse goods and services offered by the merchants and craftsmen of the village.

Generating interest in an agricultural society took time. Not until spring 1828 did Brown succeed in scheduling a community meeting. The organizers were, for the most part, villagers with Brown as the secretary of the meeting. Thomas Brice, a village merchant, chaired the gathering while Calvary Morris, another businessman, and Daniel Read, head of the Academy, were among the sponsors. Together, Read, Morris, and Brown directed an "Address to the Citizens of Athens County," making three points: 1) that agriculture had not enjoyed the advances that had marked manufacturing; 2) that the expenses of transportation had "swallowed up the profits of almost every marketable product"; 3) that the society should promote a county fair in which "specimens of the best our county can produce" might be exhibited, affording an opportunity for a comparison of goods and "an interchange of opinions on agricultural subjects."

The society, indeed, was organized. To provide a grass-roots base of support, the structure provided for a vice president from each township in the county. Of the other officers, Robert Linzee, the president, was a farm owner widely known for the political offices he had held, but Thomas Brice and A. G. Brown were townsmen, as were several other members of the board of trustees. In October 1828, the society staged its first county fair. Despite its initial success, the society did not endure. Finally in December 1850, the *Messenger* carried a new call to assemble at the courthouse to organize a County Agricultural Society, hoping once again to raise the level of agricultural productivity.

Library and Lyceum

While Belpre, Ames, and Dover organized subscription libraries early in the century, Athens village waited until 1826 to take its first tentative steps. In late June, the *Mirror* published a call for interested citizens to meet at the courthouse for the purpose of organizing "a Public Circulating Library Association." Little is known about the progress of the group. But a year and a half later, the *Mirror* noted that a tax of 25¢ per share was due and that some of the original subscribers had still not paid for their shares. A. G. Brown, the *Mirror*'s publisher, was the librarian. He reported the collection was not large. One possible factor was that the professional men of the village—the doctors, lawyers, and clergy—had their own personal, specialized libraries, while the university as well as the literary societies maintained libraries of sorts, blunting the demand for a community collection. Although few adults were illiterate, even in 1850 few persons remained in school to the eighth grade. The demand for a library was not likely to be very strong.

In the 1830s, the Philomathean Society at the university and the new lyceum movement expressed interest in the establishment and support of a town library. Both societies, however, placed more stress on sponsoring orations, lectures, and debates than on the promotion of libraries. The Philomathean Society continued, as in earlier years, to meet at the courthouse. Its December 1827 meeting, for example, scheduled for "early candlelight," featured two orations by members, identifying neither the titles nor the speakers; its April 1832 meeting offered orations (still by unnamed speakers) on "Liberality of Sentiment" and "Our Country."

By 1833, Athens boasted its own lyceum. The first speaker, Professor Wall of

Ohio University, lectured on history. The professor's lecture was coupled with a debate on a proposal to abolish the office of the county assessor and to assign the task to the respective townships. Unlike the Philomathean Society, dominated by students, the lyceum featured townspeople, usually adults, as speakers and the topics for discussion, as in the case cited here, were matters of vital concern to taxpayers and lessors of college lands. The lyceum met at the offices of A. G. Brown, who, having sold the *Mirror,* had launched a legal career. Under one sponsorship or another, Athenians would maintain a series of public lectures for entertainment and edification through the rest of the century.

The Masons

The wave of anti-Masonic sentiment that swept the nation in the late 1820s and early 1830s led Paramuthia Lodge to suspend its activities from 1831 to 1842. As it resumed operations, many prominent Athenians, such as Norman Root, Archibald B. Walker, James McAboy, Calvary Morris, and Samuel Pruden, were members, and numerous grave markers in the West State Street Cemetery affirm the importance of Masonic affiliation to the individual. At one level, the Masons attracted because they offered assistance to a member's widow and children in the event of his death. But in an age without movies, radio, television, or organized sports, lodge meetings afforded a night out with the boys, a chance to hobnob with the village respectability, even the possibility of becoming a Worshipful Master.

Churches of Athens

The various churches of the village remained the most important groups in which Athenians participated. Of necessity, Athenians who belonged to a church in 1825 were either Presbyterians or Methodists. Yet during the quarter century following, other denominations appeared.

As of 1825, the Presbyterians still lacked a building of their own, relying instead on the facilities of the county courthouse. Nonetheless, they had prospered, and their congregation, numbering in excess of 177, included a large part of the adult population of Athens. The employment of Presbyterian clergy as faculty members by the university gave the Presbyterians an edge in influencing the character and leadership of the community.

To 1827, the church had operated informally, but in that year the Presbyterians incorporated in anticipation of erecting their first church house. The Articles of Association, drafted by Joseph B. Miles, speaks of "the importance of religious and moral instruction." To the trustees was assigned the duty of hiring "preaching," the sermon being central to worship. "Owing to the scarcity of money," country produce, that is, "wheat, flour, rye, oats, corn, beef, pork, flax, wool or country linen" was accepted in payment of one's subscription. The lay leadership included many of the village's most prestigious citizens: Joseph Miles, Charles Shipman, Eben Foster, John Perkins, and Cephas Carpenter. The Presbyterians also gained a degree of prestige from the fact that the successive university presidents—Robert G. Wilson, William Holmes McGuffey, and Alfred Ryors—were ordained Presbyterian ministers who at times served as pastor. In addition, most of university faculty were Presbyterian clergy.

Having incorporated, the Presbyterians proceeded to call their first regular minister, John Spaulding. "An earnest, energetic man," Spaulding worked not only for the Athens church, but organized the church at Amesville and assisted in forming a congregation in Hocking County. With a minister in place, the congregation built a church house in 1828. A plain brick building, cater-corner from the courthouse, it had a basement but no Sunday School room and no bell tower. The pulpit was located so that the congregation had to face about in the pews in order to look up at the preacher. An organ was secured for the new church, prompting some who disapproved of such a worldly instrument to leave the church and join the Methodists. Some of these, however, returned to the Presbyterian fold after they were dismissed by the Methodists for dancing, a practice of which the Methodists disapproved, while the Presbyterians regarded it as "not necessarily sinful." As early as the 1840s, the Presbyterians had a choir. And Maria Foster Brown recalled that even in the course of the church service a moment of levity might intrude, as when her uncle, Hull Foster, made faces and twitched his shoulders in an effort to make her and her sister choristers break into a giggle.

Just as the clergy-presidents of the university sought to suppress the hijinks of their students, so the Presbyterians devoted long hours to hearing charges regarding wayward members. These cases ran the gamut from members charged with public intoxication to those accused of fornication or adultery. A particularly trying case involved Mary Pruden, wife of Samuel B. Pruden, who, following a month-long "trial," was excommunicated for disseminating the infidel views of the utopian socialist, Robert Dale Owen. Ultimately, in the course of compelling moral rectitude, the lay leadership became burned out, while a few members, alienated by the unbending ways of Lindley and Wilson, left the church. The defection was aggravated by a tussle between the Old School and New School Presbyterians, a nationwide phenomenon. A question over whether or not to permit a Cumberland Presbyterian clergyman to speak from the Athens pulpit triggered a split in the church. For a period of several years in the 1840s the church's governing body did not meet, at a time when the university, undergoing its own traumas, was drifting leaderless. As of 1850, the church was rebuilding, but whereas in 1825 the Presbyterians had been the dominant congregation in the village, by 1850 they had to share leadership with the Methodists.

Well-established in their brick church on South Congress and with a new parsonage, the Methodists in 1825 were very active. The national church had been invigorated by a revival in 1827 that had brought new leaders into the church, one of whom was E. R. Ames of Athens County, who subsequently became a bishop of the church. More important, the local church included Calvary Morris, Daniel B. Stewart, and Eliakim H. Moore, whose prominence in the Athens community gave the local Methodists a degree of respect the church had lacked at the start of the pioneer era. Having outgrown its first building, in 1837 the Methodists constructed a new edifice on College Street, slightly to the north of the present building. By 1850, the Methodists were solidly established.

The religious scene altered with the organization of a Cumberland Presbyterian church in the early 1830s. A product of the Great Revival of the early 1800s, this group of Presbyterians placed particular importance on the spiritual state of their clergy and abandoned the requirement that its ministers be seminary graduates. In 1831, Jacob Lindley, then a minister in Pennsylvania, accompanied a missionary named Morgan to Athens. The stirring sermons of Mr. Morgan won a number of converts in Athens village and subsequently at Hebardville, as it was then called. As a result, the Alexander Cumberland Presbyterian Church was organized in 1832 and, a year later, the Athens Cumberland Presbyterian Church. The organizational meeting at the Athens County Courthouse in July 1833 elected elders and trustees. Leaders in this move included such local notables as Isaac Norton, A. B. Walker, and General John Brown. They held services in a building on West Washington Street, a site now occupied by the General Telephone Company. In 1835, the church reported forty-two members, too few to support a permanent pastor. A series of itinerant clergy held communion, while others contracted to serve for six months to a year at a time. In 1843 the church in Athens disbanded, turning over its cash resources to the church at Alexander.

By 1850 Athens was a far more heterogeneous community than it had been in 1825. Certainly the village churches offered more than just a place for public worship. They afforded social contacts especially important for wives who were homebound during the week. Membership tended to confer an aura of respectability, given the penchant for disciplining the wayward. To those who enjoyed singing, the churches provided an opportunity for self-expression. At the same time, keen denominational rivalries precluded cooperation between the churches.

School Days

Until the 1840s, the operation of schools for the community's children rivaled the churches as a private activity in support of creating a better community. One of the first village schools was kept by Sally Porter Foster, a widow. "Lithe and active," she was remembered for her kindly face, ruffled cap, and three-cornered kerchief worn about her neck and shoulders. Like many dame schools, it met in her home. Boys and girls as young as three or four attended. Although Sally Foster's school was coed, boys and girls did not receive the same instruction. Certainly some of the formal instruction was sex neutral. The children used Webster's *Elementary Spelling Book*, learning useful tidbits of knowledge as they learned to spell. They also read from the *New England Primer* and were taught Roman numerals "so that we could open the Bible and know what chapter it was." However, in formal and informal ways, girls and boys were socialized to be different. Girls were taught to sew and knit. Maria Foster Brown, who attended the school, recalled that at age six she pieced a patchwork quilt, nine pieces to a patch. She learned to turn a hem and to knit her own garters and stockings. "Never," she reminisced, "was a more useful school." At recess, girls played together under the apple tree, while boys romped in the street. At ninety-nine, Maria still recalled that when she had laughed boisterously, her teacher-grandmother had called her aside, then quietly admonished her: "My child, if something amuses you laugh, but not so loud." When school was dismissed, the girls lined up, curtseying to their teacher, then the boys "marched by, cap in hand."

In looking back, Maria Brown evaluated her schooling, "You see, I had a rather severe course in Domestic Science, but the rest of my education didn't amount to much." At age ten, her formal education was "about completed." Even in her school days, her attendance depended on whether she could be spared from work at home. "Some days we could go to school, some days not." David H. Moore, the bishop, also recalled Foster's school, especially the walnut dunce block on which the disorderly sat or stood.

To the end of her life Maria Foster Brown believed she got too little education; the fact is that before she had finished school, she had read *Pilgrim's Progress, Paradise Lost,* and *Paradise Regained*, books few college graduates of the 1990s have read—or their instructors. In her nineties, she still recalled lines of the poet William Cowper. She recalled, too, the successive newspapers—the *Spectator*, the *Hocking Valley Gazette*, and the *Athens Messenger*. She also remembered with special fondness a present she had received at age fourteen—twelve bound copies of *Godey's Lady's Book*. The fact that her reading was so broad suggests that the elementary offerings of Sally Foster's school were tailored to the abilities of the individual pupil and the level of culture of the teacher. Foster's school served some unusual students. Among others, David H. Moore and Charles Cardwell McCabe, both of whom became bishops of the Methodist Church, got their start with Foster. So, too, did Elizabeth Sampson (Hoyt), who became one of the first women in the United States to earn a Ph.D.

Sally Foster's school, which operated from 1822 to 1847, was not the only private school in the village, as attested by notices in the Athens papers. Most of the other schools were ephemeral. Data about them is fragmentary. Charlotte E. Hindman opened a school in September 1829, charging $1.50 per quarter. Children were taught reading, writing, English grammar, and geography. Those who paid $2.00 were taught rhetoric, natural philosophy, history, and arithmetic.

On the path to a tax-supported, public school system, neither Athens nor the college townships followed the route of the rest of the county or state. Because the village's house lots were not subject to state taxes, not until the 1840s did Athens village get authority to create a public school board of its own. Once authorized, the village acted expeditiously, voting to proceed with a free school to open in winter 1844–45.

SECONDARY SCHOOLS

Because of their need to recruit students aggressively, the secondary schools of Athens—all proprietary operations, that is, schools operated as a private business —left a more visible trail than the elementary schools. From the first, the major burden of secondary education was carried by Ohio University's Academy, which by 1825 was seventeen years old. The Academy, serving males only, continued on its course even during the troubled years when the university suspended collegiate instruction. During much of this time, the leadership fell to Daniel Read, an able educator who ultimately became president of the University of Missouri. The Academy, besides providing Athens residents with easy access to secondary education, drew some of the abler, more ambitious youth of the region into the village, preparing them for careers or for entrance to the university itself.

The secondary education of Athens women was left to the proprietary schools. Emma Willard's Troy (New York) Female Seminary, beginning in 1821, set the pat-

tern for women's secondary education, and while Athens village was in no way prepared to emulate Willard's school, it did what it could. The first serious effort was
by the Rev. James McAboy, one of the Presbyterian ministers drawn to Athens by
Ohio University. A member of the Athens School Committee, McAboy organized
his own School for Young Ladies, instruction beginning June 12, 1826. Within a
year, he reported having eighty students enrolled. Tuition was $5.00 per term, the
terms congruent with those of the college. Reflecting local conditions, he accepted payment in goods in lieu of cash. McAboy, however, ran into trouble, becoming the subject of some now-forgotten gossip which led him to leave town.

Others took up the challenge. J. P. Weethee, assisted by a Miss Jewett, began a
school in December 1832. Their school operated at both primary and secondary
levels. At the upper level, its offerings included history, rhetoric, philosophy, chemistry, astronomy, and mathematics, all for $4.00 per term. In the mid-1830s, Mrs.
Maria Gay operated the Athens Female School. A formal prospectus announced a
program designed "to improve the minds, morals, and habits of young ladies . . .
(thus aiding) in *elevating* the female *character*. . . ." The course of instruction, she assured parents, would be *"thorough,"* preparing young women for "those *various* and
responsible duties incumbent upon the female part of our community." While Gay
recognized the desirability of affording women access to secondary education, she
also regarded women as having a separate sphere of activity. Her school had an
ambitious curriculum. "Orthography [spelling], reading, writing, arithmetick,
geography, Grammar and Composition" were "essentially important." Other subjects such as ancient and modern history, rhetoric, natural theology, and evidences
of Christianity were termed "requisite to good education." As one does not continue to hear of this school, it was presumably short-lived.

The Athens Female Academy fared no better. It began its first quarter Monday,
October 23, 1839, claiming to offer "all the branches of a liberal female education."
The school had a board of trustees that included William Wall of the university
faculty along with local businessmen such as A. B. Walker. Initially, instruction was
offered by Ohio University faculty until a separate staff was employed, and the
academy advertised that it had access to the college's philosophical apparatus and to
the "chimical [*sic*] laboratory." In 1840–41, after the university hired away the principal of this school, its board of trustees proved unable to keep the school running.

In 1850, the young women of the village had a choice of three schools. One, run
by Helen O. Crippen and M. Price, operated in the Cumberland Presbyterian
Church rooms. Its curriculum included both elementary and secondary instruction.
For the first time, instruction in domestic economy was listed as well as piano,
drawing, and painting. A second school, the Athens Female Seminary, offering a

preparatory department and three classes, was managed by the Rev. James Camp-bell and his wife, Laura. The third, terming itself a select school, occupied the school room over the Market House (8 North Court) and was operated by Julius C. Stedman. The transient existence of these schools casts doubts upon the qual-ity of instruction. The concern with adapting women's education to their peculiar feminine roles reinforces these doubts.

What of school enrollments? The earliest solid data is for 1850 and that indi-cates that 80 percent of the village boys of elementary school age, youngsters 6 through 13, were enrolled in 1850, as compared to 76 percent of the girls, a modest difference. Males and females aged 14 through 17 attended at the same rate—57 percent—a surprisingly high rate for the day. It may well be the case that some of these youngsters were still enrolled in elementary school. The chief difference in educational access in 1850 lay in the fact that for women, a secondary education marked the upper limit of education; for males, it opened the door to college. If any Athens woman attended college during these years, there is no record of it.

The Black Community

Although Athens was a largely white village to the 1850s, throughout the period it had a small, often shadowy black population. The first black of record in Athens is Violet Burrington, a member of the Eliphaz Perkins household. She came from Connecticut to Marietta with Catherine Greene, and in 1803 to Athens when Miss Greene married Dr. Perkins. After Catherine died, Violet remained in the Perkins household and stayed when he took his third wife, Ann Culver, widow of Bezaliel Culver. In 1829 Violet died at an advanced age. Presumably she was a household servant.

Several blacks of distinction had a short-term connection with Athens as they passed through Ohio University. The first of these was John Newton Templeton. Born in slavery in 1805 and emancipated in 1813, Templeton entered the university in 1824. As a student he lived in the household of President Robert Wilson, main-tained an excellent academic record, participated in the activities of the Athenian Literary Society, and graduated in September 1828. The fourth black college grad-uate in the United States, Templeton went on to a career as a clergyman and teacher. In 1833, Edward James Roye, the son of a prosperous Newark, Ohio, family, en-tered the university, remaining until 1835. A career as teacher in Chillicothe and businessman in Terre Haute, Indiana, followed. Offended by the discrimination he faced as a black, Roye responded to the blandishments of the American Colonization Society and migrated to Liberia, where he pursued a distinguished career as a businessman, and in January 1870, he took office as the fifth president of Liberia. His proved a troubled presidency. Turned out of office in a coup d'etat in October 1871, he was tried and sentenced to death. In an effort to flee Liberia in early 1872, he died, whether by being shot or by drowning remains unknown.

Joseph Carter Corbin entered Ohio University in 1850 at age 17. As an undergraduate he took an active part in the Philomathean society, where he developed his skills as a public speaker. He graduated in 1853. He received an AM degree 1857. A multitalented individual, Corbin distinguished himself as a mathematician, linguist, and musician. During Reconstruction he was elected superintendent of public instruction in Arkansas. For thirty years he presided over Branch Normal College at Pine Bluff, Arkansas, and for his impact on black education was compared to Horace Mann. The university bestowed a second AM degree on Corbin in 1889 He died in 1911.

Overall, the number of blacks in Athens village down to 1850 never exceeded twenty. Nor were they a cohesive group. In the 1820s and 1830s, a third of the blacks lived as individuals in private homes, probably as servants. In 1830, for example, the households of Thomas Brice, John Brown 2d, Thomas Drake, Isaac Taylor, and Robert G. Wilson each sheltered one black. The two who lived with hoteliers Brown and Taylor likely were employed in connection with the hotel. So, too, in 1840, the five blacks living in the household of George W. Barnes, a manufacturer, were likely to have been his employees.

At all times up to 1850, a majority of the blacks in the village lived in a household headed by a black. Yet given the small black population, there were never more than two black households at any one time, and only the household of John Flowers provided continuity from 1830 through 1850. Indeed, there were too few blacks to constitute a community. The most one can observe is that the two black wives of 1850 had married in early adolescence, and that the Moses Morgan family sent both of their school-age children to school, while none of the children of the much larger Flowers family attended.

Slavery

The attitude of white Athenians toward blacks and slavery cannot be documented with precision. Certainly those settlers of New England origin who spent time at Marietta or Belpre before moving to Athens acquired some exposure to slavery since there were slaves on the Virginia side of the river. Frances Dana Gage, who grew up in the Marietta area, has recorded her awakening to the meaning of slavery and her unremitting hostility to it, becoming one of the foremost leaders of the anti-slavery cause in Ohio. One knows, too, that Moses A. Hoge, onetime pastor of the First Presbyterian Church, reportedly manumitted his slaves before leaving his native Virginia for Athens. And Ephraim Cutler persuaded the Ohio Constitutional Convention to ban slavery within Ohio.

As editor of the *Mirror*, A. G. Brown kept fellow citizens well posted on the views and activities of the American Colonization Society, an organization that would buy the freedom of slaves and then send them to Liberia. Athens had a closer connection to the Colonization Society, for Robert G. Wilson was in the forefront of the movement as vice president of the Ohio Colonization Society, a factor underlying his hosting John Newton Templeton while the latter was a student in Athens.

Athenians were likewise apprised of the "peculiar institution" by advertisements offering rewards for the apprehension of runaways. The advertisements personalized the slave's plight in assigning names to the runaways—"Tom" and "Eliza"—and in detailing their physical appearance. The degree to which Athenians were moved by the arguments of the Colonization Society or by the reports of runaways is partly a matter of conjecture. Maria Foster Brown, however, makes clear that at least some Athenians had personal contact with the runaways. Of the Foster and Brown families she remarked: "We were abolitionists. . . . It was bred in our bones to hate slavery." Her recollections were that from her "earliest youth," she had been accustomed to seeing runaway slaves, to seeing slave owners from Kentucky "with chains and whips, looking for their slaves." An event etched indelibly in her memory was seeing in the Brice House, the hotel her stepfather operated on Court Street, a slave owner who had caught his slave, and the slave "weighted with irons" attempting to eat. Challenged on one occasion to explain the differences between Democrats and Whigs, she had replied testily: "Democrats believe in buying and selling people, and Whigs don't." She reported, too, that her husband, on a trip home from New Orleans, had seen a slave sale in St. Louis, "saw men and women exposed for sale on a block in front of the courthouse, saw the auctioneer trying their ability and running his finger around their mouths exactly as if they were horses. We all *hated* slavery." What Maria Brown saw and heard, other Athenians would have seen and heard, too.

Clearly Athens was a station on the Underground Railroad. Even allowing that the number of persons able to gain their freedom in this manner has been much exaggerated, as Larry Gara has pointed out in *The Liberty Line* (1961), the "railroad" did operate. Will Brown, a son of Maria Foster Brown, recalled an incident from his childhood. His "Uncle Jack" Brown, "a big fat man who lived at Albany," along with his father, Daniel, were conductors. Jack Brown was accustomed to driving an open phaeton with his wife Susan sitting beside him, wearing "a poke bonnet that had a green veil hanging over it." On the remembered occasion, Uncle Jack and Aunt Susan had arrived at Daniel Brown's store in Amesville. But Aunt Susan, who ordinarily made "a great fuss" over Will, brushed him aside, refusing even to speak to him. "Aunt Susan," he learned later, was a runaway slave the Brown brothers were conducting to freedom.

The feelings of Athenians about slavery or their attitudes toward blacks resist quantification, but voting patterns give a sense of community sentiments. Athenians' opposition to Lewis Cass, in a sense "a local boy," in the 1848 presidential campaign is consistent with the *Messenger's* stance against opening the Western territories to slavery. Likewise the steady growth in votes Athenians cast for the abolition candidates, James Birney and Martin Van Buren, suggests that a small but growing number of Athenians felt strongly enough about slavery to reject the mainline parties and to vote for the extreme position—immediate, uncompensated emancipation. Few, if any, Athenians in 1850 had any inkling of the impact the slave issue would have on their lives; that fall, they were far more concerned about the prospect of the Belpre and Cincinnati Railroad reaching Athens and being completed to the Ohio River.

Women in Athens

To understand the Athens experience, it is necessary to look at the role its women had in society. The women of Athens were a paradox. Numerically, they formed half the population, yet despite the development of Jacksonian democracy, they never appeared as officeholders or voters and only occasionally in public roles. Yet in 1850, one-third of the 15- to 19-year-old females in the village had some kind of employment, chiefly as domestic servants; a handful of older women were teachers, but none were doctors, lawyers, or clergymen. Women did, however, act as midwives—although in the East the midwife had been displaced by the doctor. When in 1850, the ladies of the Athens Female Benevolent Society sponsored a fund-raiser for which tickets were sold, the ladies remained anonymous. Only occasionally did women's names appear as members of an organized group. Yet they were a presence in the community.

The period 1820–1850 was one in which the roles of both men and women in urban America were changing dramatically. Urban males began to work away from home—typically from dawn to dusk, six days a week. While professionals, merchants, and craftsmen were ordinarily self-employed, an increasing proportion of the male labor force worked for others. By default, urban wives were left at home to manage the household alone. As the urban husband shouldered the load as the provider for his family, the wife was gradually released from some of the burden of contributing to the family income through her domestic production. Urban women could buy yarn for knitting or cloth for sewing; they might buy bread, lard and sausage, butter and soap. Released from domestic production, urban women were enjoined to practice the virtues of purity, piety, submissiveness, and, above all, domesticity. Taken together, the practice of these feminine virtues produced the Cult of True Women. The cult provided the village woman with a sense of direction and a meaningful lifestyle.

Among Athens village women during this period, there was often a lack of congruity between the ideal "true woman" and the reality of women's lives in the village, which precluded many women from living in a husband-wife relationship. In 1850, one household in seven in the village was headed by a woman. Such women collectively had responsibility for forty-eight children. The vulnerability of the woman without a husband is revealed in the plaintive advertisements of Mrs. J. T. Johnson in 1828 as she announces in the *Mirror* that she takes in laundry and of the Widow Gilman who takes in boarders. Maria Foster Brown affords additional insights. When her mother's sister was widowed, her father, Eben Foster, drove a team to Sandusky and brought the family back to Athens, housing them in his own home. They were given several rooms, including the use of a second kitchen to allow them a degree of privacy. He bought his widowed sister-in-law a loom so that she could weave and "earn a little." He also built a home for his mother, Sally Foster, when she became a widow. While few other Athenians could afford Foster's generous mode of taking care of widows, orphans, and dependent parents, the community did have a sense that somehow kinfolk would find a way. After her father died, Maria's mother remarried, apparently badly. In reduced circumstances, Maria waited table at the Brice House, the hotel her stepfather managed. Indeed, a substantial proportion of young women fifteen to eighteen years of age lived in households headed by persons other than their parents, quite likely in the role of domestic servant. Another forty-one adult women, in 1850, lived in households in which they were neither the head nor the wife of the head of house.

Certainly, the records of the day confirm the piety of women. There are references to the Female Cent Society and to the Female Benevolent Society. The church rolls of the Cumberland Presbyterians indicate a higher proportion of women members than of men. Sunday was a day of rest, "a day of quiet leisure." In the Foster household, and likely many others, no cooking was done on the sabbath. At most a fire might be made to boil coffee; food for the day was prepared the day before. It was the day for family togetherness. Maria Foster Brown recalled this as the day her father had time "to hold me on his lap." It was a day for dressing up and for attending church.

Yet, the nature of piety needs to be kept in context. Men were pious, too. Athens men supported the Sunday School Union and the Bible Society. Eben Foster, as head of the household, led his family in prayer and expected the hired men who lived in his household to participate. Indeed, the Presbyterians insisted that men lead their families in prayer and that they engage in private prayers of their own. Piety was a coed value.

There is a dearth of evidence that permits a precise evaluation of "purity." The *Mirror* periodically reminded villagers that if marriages were made in heaven, they were lived in this world. Complaining that his wife Anna had "forsaken and renounced" his "bed and board," George Gilbert rejected her agency, that is, he would no longer pay debts incurred by her. Samuel Colvin had problems; he charged his wife Rachel with committing adultery with Jefferson Pickens. Mary Wells, on the other hand, complained of her husband's "extreme cruelty" as well as of his willful absence. Eliza Thomas charged her husband Elza with "willful absence, adultery, and total neglect of duty." And wives found husbands capable of "committing the most extreme and cruel violence." Session records of the Presbyterians further document that both men and women on occasion engaged in fornication or adultery. Such behavior the church strongly condemned, yet those who openly confessed their transgressions were readmitted to the fellowship. Within the religious community purity, too, was a coed value.

Female submissiveness was so engrained in American society, that it did not elicit comment. Even in the perennial war of the sexes, the humor does not allude to women failing to subordinate themselves to father or husband. At most, the editor of the paper was upbraided on one occasion by an anonymous correspondent demanding more news about women. The letter writer requested the publication of poetry and essays by and about women. Husbands and fathers had the final say where a difference of opinion existed between husband and wife or between father and minor children. But in day-to-day affairs, as the husband went away from the home to work, the wife gained practical charge of her household.

While domesticity was affirmed, there were evidences of changes in its nature. Maria Brown recalled that as a girl during the 1830s she did the dishes before she was seven; she was surely not the only Athens child to do so. Her mother raised flax, processed it, spun it into linen yarn, and wove it. In turn, she taught Maria's older sister, Libbie, to spin, but by the time Maria was of an age to learn, her mother concluded that a modern miss no longer needed this skill, and Maria was not taught to spin. Yet Maria appreciated homespun. Weaving "gave a woman an opportunity to exhibit her taste." "But, oh, it was hard work." While Maria learned to make candles, her mother ordinarily bought them instead from the Deans, for whom candle-making was a cottage industry. Like other girl-children of her age, she learned to sew and embroider, to make wax flowers. She recalled, too, that little girls took knitting with them wherever they went, and they were expected to complete a minimum amount before they were free to play. There is no indication that she asked her daughter to follow suit. She noted, too, that her mother had major responsibilities for drying and preserving fruits and vegetables. But in her own home, milking and making a garden was work for boys and men. As a young woman in the 1840s, she had acquired skills to cook, roast, and bake in an open fireplace; she also registered her disappointment with the first "little iron stove" that she acquired in the mid-1840s. In warm weather, she washed outdoors under the quince bushes, using homemade soap and starching her clothes either with starch made from flour dough or from grated potatoes. She accepted domesticity, but she noted: "It was a hard life for women."

To be sure, the Athens community was made aware of the Cult of Womanhood. Periodically, the *Mirror*, the *Western Spectator*, the *Hocking Valley Gazette*, and the *Messenger* affirmed these values. The *Mirror*, for example, in August 1826, remarked: "There is an ease, delicacy, refinement, confidence, and expansion which the mind never feels, but in the friendship of a sensible, interesting woman." This friendship, it explained, produced "softer manners, gives morals their purity." Again, in September 1829, the *Mirror*, taking the posture of "A Mother to Her Daughter on Marriage," enjoined the daughter to be "no longer the flighty, inconsiderate, haughty, passionate girl, but ever, with reverence and delight, have the merit of your husband in view." The daughter was cautioned to be "moderate in your private expenses, and proportion your great expenditures to the standard of his future, or rather his wishes." Again, the *Mirror*, in an essay on maternity, commented that while "Women's charms are certainly many and powerful, . . . the charm of maternity is most sublime." Comparing the Old Testament woman with the modern woman, the writer preferred the latter as "a valuable mistress of a family, and a useful member of society."

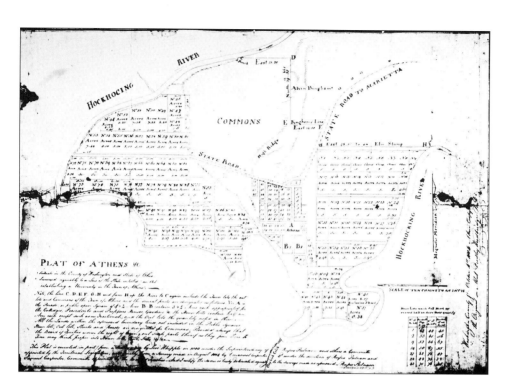

Plan for the new town of Athens, drawn in 1804, included lands for the college buildings and the homes and gardens of the president and professors (see sections B1 and B2). The Hocking River set the southern boundary of the town. *(Courtesy of Archives and Special Collections, Ohio University Libraries.)*

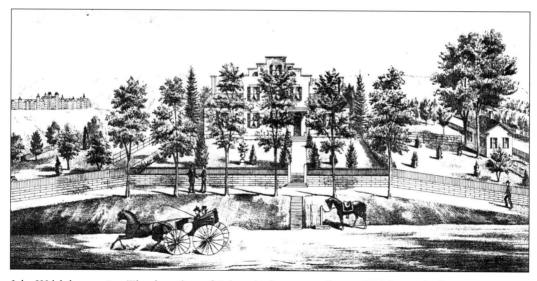

John Welch house, 1875. The showplace of Athens in the 1860s and 1870s. Welch was chief justice of the Ohio Supreme Court for two terms. *(Reprinted from D. J. Lake, ed.,* The Atlas of Athens County, Ohio, *1875.)*

The Daniel Read house, built in 1840s. Court and Union Streets. Read was preceptor of the Academy; later in life he was president of the University of Missouri. *(Courtesy of James Anastas.)*

General Charles Grosvenor, Ohio University graduate, Civil War officer, and congressman. *(Courtesy of Archives and Special Collections, Ohio University Libraries.)*

General Thomas F. Wildes, editor of the *Athens Messenger* and commanding officer of the 186th OVI. *(Reprinted from Mattox, ed.,* The Athens Home Coming Reunion, June 14 and June 15, 1904.)

Major Charles Townsend, Ohio University graduate, Civil War officer, and Ohio secretary of state. *(Reprinted from* The Athens Home Coming.)

Earliest known view of Ohio University. This was used in 1838 on the masthead of the *Hocking Valley Gazette and Athens Journal*. *(Courtesy of Archives and Special Collections, Ohio University Libraries.)*

Ohio University campus, c. 1908. Ellis Hall with its north wing, East Wing, the College Edifice, West Wing, and Ewing Hall. *(Courtesy of The Dairy Barn, Southeast Ohio Cultural Arts Center, and Archives and Special Collections, Ohio University Libraries.)*

Ohio University campus, c. 1909. Carnegie Library, Ewing, West Wing, Chapel, East Wing, Ellis (background), and Boyd Hall. *(Courtesy of The Dairy Barn, Southeast Ohio Cultural Arts Center, and Archives and Special Collections, Ohio University Libraries.)*

The McGuffey Elms at their peak, 1926. Victims of the Dutch elm disease, the last of these trees succumbed in the late 1950s. *(Courtesy of the* Athens Messenger.*)*

Ewing Hall, 1898. Administration building and class building. *(Courtesy of the Athens County Historical Society and Museum.)*

William Holmes McGuffey. President of Ohio University, 1839-43. *(Courtesy of Archives and Special Collections, Ohio University Libraries.)*

Thomas Ewing, class of 1815, Athens County prosecuting attorney, United States senator, secretary of the treasury, secretary of the interior. *(Reprinted from Hoover, The History of Ohio University.)*

The first gymnasium, 1909. *(Courtesy of James Anastas.)*

Business students learning shorthand, 1908. The ladies are in blouses with high collars and long sleeves, hair up. The men are in jackets with ties. *(Courtesy of the* Athens Messenger.*)*

The State Normal School (Ellis Hall), 1904. Growth of this school triggered the growth of the village as well as the university. *(Courtesy of ACHS&M.)*

The Ohio University football team of 1897. This was the age of the sixty-minute player. *(Courtesy of James Anastas.)*

The university baseball field, 1909. *(Courtesy of ACHS&M.)*

Academy coeds of 1873. Despite Margaret Boyd's example, women students remained concentrated in the Academy to the end of the 1870s. *(Courtesy of James Anastas.)*

Parade to support prohibition. Prohibition and woman suffrage were the stirring issues of the war years. *(Courtesy of the* Athens Messenger.*)*

Music Hall, originally the chapel (1883). The building was characterized by the exquisite detailing of its wood, brick, and stone work. *(Courtesy of James Anastas.)*

Coeds in their Sunday best at the State Hospital fountain, c. 1908. *(Courtesy of Joanne Prisley.)*

The Baltimore and Ohio Southwestern Depot, West Union Street. After remodeling and expansion, this became Athens' Union Depot. (*Courtesy of the* Athens Messenger.)

The Hocking Valley Railroad Depot, Shafer and Dean Streets. The HVRR enabled Athenians to go to Columbus and back in a single day. (*Reprinted from* The Athens Home Coming.)

William Parker Cutler, chief engineer of the Marietta and Cincinnati Railroad. This grandson of Manasseh Cutler was also a congressman. (*Reprinted from* History of the Hocking Valley, Ohio, *1883.*)

Hocking Valley and Sunday Creek Traction Line, c. 1910, on a Sunday outing. The traction line brought customers to Court Street merchants but never turned a profit. (*Courtesy of the* Athens Messenger.)

Milbury M. Greene, president and chief engineer, Hocking Valley Railroad. Thanks to Greene's expertise, the Hocking Valley was profitable from the very start. (*Reprinted from* The Athens Home Coming.)

John Brough, typesetter for the *Athens Mirror*, Ohio University student, and Civil War governor of Ohio, 1864-65. (*Reprinted from* The Athens Home Coming.)

Calvary Morris, "Father of the Hocking Canal" and member of Congress. *(Reprinted from* The Athens Home Coming.*)*

Dr. William Parker Johnson, prime mover of the Athens Lunatic Asylum. *(Reprinted from* The Athens Home Coming.*)*

Margaret Boyd, first woman graduate of Ohio University, 1873. *(Courtesy of Archives and Special Collections, Ohio University Libraries.)*

Irma Voigt, the university's first dean of women, on an outing with Ohio University coeds. *(Courtesy of The Dairy Barn, and Archives and Special Collections, Ohio University Libraries.)*

Edward C. Berry, nationally respected hotelier. *(Photographs of the Berrys courtesy of Archives and Special Collections, Ohio University Libraries.)*

Mattie (Mrs. Edward C.) Berry, an active participant in bringing distinction to the cuisine and service of the Berry Hotel.

Eliza Brown Davidson, cooking for General George Custer. Athens school children collected pennies for her memorial plaque. *(Reprinted from Custer,* Tenting on the Plains, *1915.)*

Andrew Jackson Davidson, Athens' first black attorney, drew criticism for being an active Democrat. *(Courtesy of Archives and Special Collections, Ohio University Libraries.)*

Peter Finsterwald, respected, longtime village marshal. *(Reprinted from* The Athens Home Coming.*)*

Alston Ellis, president of Ohio University, 1901-20. Under Ellis's leadership, Ohio University grew more in twenty years than in the preceding century. *(Courtesy of James Anastas.)*

Lydia Carpenter Armstrong, matron of Athens County Children's Home, c. 1905. *(Reprinted from* The Centennial Atlas of Athens County Ohio, *1905.)*

"Mother" Eliza Daniel Stewart, internationally famous temperance speaker. *(Reprinted from Willard and Livermore, eds.,* A Woman of the Century, *1893.)*

Isaac and Lydia Taylor, proprietors of the Eagle House, which was destroyed by fire in 1854. *(Reprinted from* The Centennial Atlas of Athens County Ohio, *1905.)*

Maria Foster Brown, c. 1850s. Her memories provide an understanding of life in Athens in the 1830s, 1840s, and 1850s. *(Reprinted from* Grandmother Brown's Hundred Years, 1827-1927, *1929.)*

Admiral Louis Rudolph de Steiguer accepted the surrender of the German Fleet at Scapa Flow at the end of World War I. *(Courtesy of Archives and Special Collections, Ohio University Libraries.)*

SENSE OF THE WORLD

In freely reprinting news items snipped from other newspapers and magazines, the *Mirror, Western Spectator, Hocking Valley Gazette,* and *Messenger* gave Athenians a sense of the world beyond the Hocking Hills. The exotic always appealed. Thus, Athenians read of Captain Weddell's account of his approach to Antarctica. So, too, they might read Peter P. Pitchlynn's account of the education of Choctaw youth, follow Commodore David Porter's court martial, keep up with the progress of the Greek War for Independence and the removal of Indians from Ohio, or read George Catlin's account of life in a Mandan Indian Village.

Intellectual life was enriched by the stories printed in the weekly editions of the town paper as well as by the programs of the Athenian and Philomathean societies and lectures by Ohio University faculty. The various organizations—missionary societies, Sunday School Union, and Bible Society, the American Colonization Society, and Temperance groups—afforded opportunities for social interaction, but they also put Athenians in step with other communities across the nation. Occasionally villagers were favored with a visit and address by the governor. In the Log Cabin campaign of 1840, Governor Wilson Shannon spoke. In many years the Fourth of July was the major social event—typically observed with oratory and a community dinner served on the College Green followed by interminable toasts, an experience duplicated in thousands of other communities.

Although Athens was too far removed from the Ohio River to enjoy performances by theatrical companies that traveled up and down the Ohio River, it did receive traveling shows. One attraction was an exhibition of such exotic animals as a South American cougar, a spotted tiger, and an Arabian camel. In September 1829, the excitement centered about the exhibition of "the celebrated *solar* microscope" [sic]. By 1840, Athens boasted a brass band. In 1850, Crane's Great Oriental Circus favored the village with a visit. The advance notice promised "240 men and horses, children, and ponies." It would enter Athens with "the Monster Dragon Chariot" drawn by ten camels and a "Fairy Chariot." The reality entailed more drama than the advance publicity promised, for as the circus crossed the Margaret Creek bridge, there was a near-fatal accident to the driver of one of the wagons.

The successive editors of the Athens paper closely followed the proceedings of the Ohio General Assembly and the Federal Congress. Presidential and gubernatorial messages were reported verbatim. The great debates over the Second Bank of the United States and Jackson's veto were reported in detail, as was Calhoun's statement on nullification. Athenians kept abreast of events elsewhere.

Mexican War

Athenians participated in the Mexican War through E Company, Second Regiment, Ohio Volunteer Infantry. The E Company organized in Athens in June 1846, as other units were organizing at county seats such as Chillicothe, Logan, Lancaster, and Mt. Vernon. Robert McLean was chosen captain of E Company, while William Wall became 1st lieutenant, and J. K. Blackstone, 2d lieutenant. The company initially numbered 61 privates plus 17 non-commissioned and commissioned officers. Drill began immediately. Within three weeks, the regiment came together at Camp Washington, near Cincinnati, and, in another three weeks, it was on its way to Mexico. Before leaving for Mexico, Lt. Wall was appointed major, becoming the third-ranking officer in the regiment. Michael Earhart prompty replaced Wall as E Company's 1st lieutenant.

Arriving in Mexico at the end of July 1846, the unit was ordered to Comargo, a hundred miles or so south of the Rio Grande. With Comargo as its base, the regiment guarded General Taylor's supply route between Comargo and Monterrey. Duty in Mexico was wearing, often unhealthy. Some of the men were not suited to military duty under the best of circumstances, and several men were discharged on a surgeon's certificate of disability as soon as the regiment arrived at the Rio Grande. In mid-September, after only six weeks in the field, another six men received medical discharges. There were fatalities, too. George Full drowned in the Rio Grande, while others took ill and died in camp or in hospital.

General Taylor began active military operations against the Mexicans at Buena Vista in February 1847, and on leaving that place for Saltillo on the night of February 22, he ordered the 2d Regiment to assemble at Ceralvo and march forthwith to Monterrey. Responding with dispatch, the 2d Regiment began its march toward Monterrey the morning of the 24th. In this move, the 2d Regiment accompanied the First and Third Ohio Volunteers. Part of the force came in contact with Mexican forces and sustained some casualties, but none in E Company. Apparently the Second Regiment thereafter made permanent camp on the battlefield of Buena Vista where it remained until mid-May 1847. Its year of service nearly completed, the regiment was sent to New Orleans, where it was mustered out.

Although General Taylor still had need for Ohio militia troops in mid-1847, the Athenians evidently had satisfied their curiosity about the glories of war and the exotic nature of Mexico. A second Ohio volunteer infantry was recruited in Ohio, but without a company from Athens. When all was said and done, the E Company had lost one man by drowning, six had died from disease, and twelve had become ill. No one died at the hands of the Mexican Army. Of the men, Rudolph de Steiguer would become a county judge; Edward Hatch, the stepfather of Maria Foster Brown; and J. C. Stedman, an officer in the Civil War.

Buckeye Rovers in California

Gold! When President Zachary Taylor confirmed reports of the discovery of gold at Sutter's Mill in December 1848, the response was immediate. On the West Coast, thousands of men had already dropped whatever they were doing and headed for the western slopes of the Sierra Nevada. But the flood of prospectors from the Mid-West and the East Coast was deferred to spring 1849. In early April 1849, a Columbus paper commented of the gold rush: "Almost every village furnishes its company, and some two or three." Athens was no exception.

The Buckeye Rovers, as the party from Athens called itself, had a nucleus of thirteen men, mostly from Athens village, Albany, and Hebbardsville. Starting from Albany in early April and joined by ten men from Meigs County, they caught a riverboat at Pomeroy and changed at Cincinnati for a vessel bound for St. Louis, where they embarked on a vessel headed for St. Joseph, Missouri. Low water forced them ashore at Lexington, seventy miles short of St. Joseph. Here they purchased the equipment and provisions necessary for the four- to five-month trek to the Pacific. Three days later under the leadership of their captain, Dr. Joseph D. Dixon, they set off—three wagons, eleven yoke of oxen, a pair of cows, and stocks of food.

Two of the party, J. Elza Armstrong and John Banks, kept diaries of the experience. Armstrong's diary is spare, almost laconic; Banks, by contrast, filled three small books with nearly daily comment on the sights and smells. Banks was full of wonder at the prairie landscape, noted the ever-present wind, was painfully conscious of the potential peril from the Pawnee. Although the Buckeye Rovers moved rapidly, passing dozens of others along the way, the Meigs men thought the pace too slow, and they separated from the others on the Sweetwater, in eastern Wyoming.

Once in California, the Rovers divided. Banks and the majority, after prospecting from Bear River south to the American River, made winter camp near Coloma. Armstrong and two others wintered farther west near the junction of the Feather and Sacramento rivers.

During 1850, some of those who worked the Yuba found enough gold to satisfy their desire and returned home. Those who stayed on the American River fared less well. At the start of the wet season, eleven of the men held a reunion. Few were rich but all had gained a few hundred dollars.

In 1851, James and Joshua Gardner, Harvey Graham, Seth Paine, and two or three others found rich deposits at Gold Hill. In spring 1852, Banks, Armstrong, Barnes, and Ferrill bought into the nearby Ophir mine. By the end of May, most of the Rovers were ready to return home. Six weeks later, having traveled by steamer, they were back in Athens, richer in memories and experiences than in purse. The two Dixons had died in California. William Stone Steadman remained in California for eleven years before returning to Athens, where in later years he and his wife operated the Steadman House at Washington and Congress.

California continued to lure Athenians. In 1851, Joseph Herrold, the miller, set off for California in the company of C. H. Armitage, Isaac Deshler, and Isaiah Baker to start a store. Herrold returned within the year. Three others had storybook experiences. In December 1851, Samuel McCune joined a party of eleven others at Pleasanton, south of Athens. The Ohio River being frozen over, they took a train to New York City where they departed for California by ship. Within three days, the ship's engines failed, and they drifted seventy-two days before reaching Kingston, Jamaica. Two of the group, Harry Finsterwald and John Hull, both of Canaan Township, turned back. Catching another ship, McCune and party sailed to Panama, which they crossed on foot. Once in California, Hamilton Carr made enough money to satisfy him, and he, too, returned home. McCune stayed on, earning considerable money as a storekeeper but losing most of it staking other miners. In returning home via Panama, McCune was charged by local authorities with illegal mining, convicted, and sentenced to be shot. He escaped. Thereafter, the record of his life is obscure—and bizarre— including capture by Indians and six years of captivity, and, in 1864, a stint of school teaching in Salt Lake City. Twenty-five years later, he was living in Idaho, had a family of five sons and five daughters, and was known as George M. Horace.

The experience of Hiram Bingham and his wife was equally bizarre. One of the twelve children of Silas Bingham, Hiram set off for California with his wife on an odyssey that lasted eleven years. Their ship, the *Independence,* was wrecked off Jamaica in a hurricane. In the month-long crossing of Panama, the one other woman in the party died of cholera; four others contracted smallpox. The Binghams spent three years in the gold fields before turning to dairy farming in the Sacramento Valley. In a sudden flood, they lost their entire herd of a hundred cows. Subsequently, they traveled to Oregon, spent some time in the Idaho gold fields, and operated a restaurant in Walla Walla, Washington. In spring 1867, they returned to Athens richer by $4,000.

And then there was John Cornwell, who had set up a business as a clock repairer and daguerreotypist in 1832. Twenty years later, at age forty, he took off for California for four years. Returning in 1856, he resumed his business, a business that is still conducted by his descendants.

When, in 1859, the gold fields of Nevada and Pikes Peak beckoned, the response from Athens was negligible. The experiences of the Buckeye Rovers and their emulators seemed excitement enough for a generation.

ORDINARY TIMES

While the press provided the residents of Athens with an insight into the world at large, it did not see fit to systematically chronicle the many informal domestic activities of the citizenry. For that, the reminiscences of Maria Foster Brown are suggestive of the unmomentous occurrences that marked the daily lives of the residents. There were times for fun—picnics and dances, singing school, and campaign rallies. The torchlight processions and campaign songs proved exciting. Another pastime was hunting wildflowers. Maria Foster Brown recalled springtime, the hillsides covered with dogwood blossoms. "We'd take along things to eat, things like pickled string beans and pickled peaches." But her favorite amusement was singing. Maria danced, too, starting when she was barely twelve. The dances began in late afternoon—at four or five—and broke up before dark. Alternatively, in the absence of streetlights, the dances started before sundown and lasted all night, the dancers going home after daybreak; one stayed off the street after dark.

In 1850, Athens village was a full-blown country village, the center of the political and legal life of the county, the center of trade and of professional services for those within a half-day's wagon trip, an intellectual center by virtue of the presence of the university and newspaper. Yet in 1850, Athens remained largely insulated from the economic forces that the Industrial Revolution had produced in New England and from the commercial forces that were transforming eastern cities. The reality was that the completion of the Baltimore and Ohio Railroad to Parkersburg and of the Marietta and Cincinnati Railroad across southern Ohio would fundamentally alter the relationship of Athens to the rest of the country. The country village would have to adjust to national forces it had thus far escaped.

5

Between the Wars: The 1850s

As ATHENS ENTERED the second half of the nineteenth century, the village contained 882 people. The Mexican War was over; the Buckeye Rovers drifted home. Athenians resumed their everyday routines. During the 1850s, the village added 434 souls, an increase of not quite 50 percent. The community experienced its first really devastating Court Street fire. In 1857 the village's hopes were fulfilled with the completion of the east-west Marietta and Cincinnati Railroad, and major changes would affect the village's economy. Having revived under the leadership of Alfred Ryors, Ohio University enjoyed an extended period of administrative stability under Solomon Howard. A public school system was launched. While Athens had hitherto been physically and economically isolated, there were increasing indications that it would shortly become caught up in political issues beyond its control. Without Athenians knowing it, the decade of the 1850s was a period of calm between wars.

THE SLAVERY CONTROVERSY RESUMES

Athens had a brush with slavery and colonization in the person of Armistead Miller, who led the largest single group of Ohio blacks to Liberia. A native of Greensboro, North Carolina, Miller first appeared in Athens in September 1850 with his whole family. By way of preparing to become a Presbyterian minister and to establish a mission in Liberia, Miller studied privately with the Reverend Aaron Williams, a professor of ancient languages at Ohio University. Miller was both bright and opportunistic, a man variously described as "truly pious" and as exhibiting "forwardness and self-importance." Miller soon won Williams's confidence, and the latter helped raise the funds needed for Miller to leave for Liberia

May 1, 1852. Subsequently, Miller was in and out of Athens as he developed his plan to take about thirty persons, including the family he had left behind in Athens, to Liberia. Arrangements were made to depart in December 1854, but by sailing time there were accommodations for only nine persons, chiefly family members. Miller achieved his goal of being ordained, and he founded a mission at the foot of Mt. Coffee, some thirty miles or so east of Monrovia, Liberia. His school of thirty students was considered decidedly successful. A prudent manager, he repaid, with interest, the money the Presbyterians and the Colonization Society had invested in him. His success lasted only briefly, for he died January 18, 1865, at age thirty-five, of dysentery, at Mt. Coffee. Miller, like Templeton, Roye, and Corbin, merely passed through Athens, but the fact remains that Athenians assisted all four in their quest and that at least some of the community continued to follow their careers.

Although only a handful of Athenians had participated in the Mexican War, the war's political fallout unsettled the entire nation. In annexing Texas, then acquiring from Mexico an area that would include the future states of Utah, New Mexico, Arizona, Nevada, and California, the nation was plunged into a nightmare of issues relating to slavery. The controversy came to a head in Henry Clay's Compromise of 1850. Nelson Van Vorhes, editor of the *Messenger* and soon-to-be congressman, took aim at Clay's proposal, denouncing it as "objectionable to an unbearable degree." In particular, Van Vorhes objected to continuing the slave trade in the District of Columbia—a "traffic which has disgraced us as a nation in the eyes of the civilized world." The *Messenger*, in fact, did not like any part of Clay's proposal. It objected to provisions by which the Federal Government would assume the Texas national debt; it objected to the absence of a ban on slavery in Utah and New Mexico territory. Opposed to opening any additional territory to slavery, Van Vorhes strongly rejected the principle of popular sovereignty.

Clearly not all Athenians agreed with Van Vorhes. In 1854, when the Kansas-Nebraska Bill was under debate, a bill that would let the residents of a territory decide for themselves whether to permit slavery within their state, Samuel B. Pruden stated an alternative position. Although he rejected slavery as "one of the greatest, if not the greatest evils, in our country," he also rejected the abolitionist tactics of Salmon P. Chase, Benjamin F. Wade, and Joshua Giddings as no more than "appeals to the prejudices and passions of the People." A Democrat, Pruden stood for popular sovereignty. The village leadership, however, objecting vehemently to the extension of slave territory, held meetings at the courthouse to denounce the Kansas-Nebraska measure and those who supported it.

In 1856 Athens became the scene of an incident that foreshadowed the Dred Scott case of a year later. In the local incident, a white gentleman named Brown, with a Negro child four or five years of age he claimed as his chattel, stopped overnight in town while en route from Missouri to Virginia. At this point Charles Grimes, a colored citizen of the village, challenged Brown's ownership of the child, alleging that by voluntarily bringing the child into a free state, he had forfeited legal possession. John Welch and Leonidas Jewett prepared the requisite petition for a writ of habeas corpus, which the probate court promptly issued. Brown declined to defend his ownership and the child was freed. The *Messenger* does not reveal the child's fate thereafter. Athenians were developing strong views on issues relating to slavery long before talk of secession and disunion came to the fore.

THE COMMUNITY: SOCIAL CONCERNS

There was a lighter side to life in the village. Periodically, circuses made their way to town. They still limited themselves to a single day with a matinee and evening performance. The July 1853 circus offered a street parade in the morning, the standard two performances, and 150 living, wild animals. A highlight of the Fourth of July 1851 was a balloon ascension scheduled for dusk in front of the courthouse, featuring a hot-air balloon eleven feet long and seven feet in diameter. The 1853 celebration of the Fourth, equally exciting, turned deadly when, in an effort to fire a cannon on the College Green, the piece exploded, horribly mangling one man and fatally wounding another. Other entertainments were tamer. A concert or a visiting elocutionist could relieve the tedium of a winter evening. In the winter of 1859, a newly organized brass band emerged in Athens. Eager to exhibit its skills, the band presented several public concerts. So, too, university faculty, on occasion, offered public lectures. As in earlier years, there were the periodic public "exhibitions" of the student literary societies. The Young Men's Lyceum placed substance ahead of entertainment when it scheduled an evening debate on the state constitutional convention and a series of discussions on Clay's Compromise of 1850. In the 1850s, interest in promoting agriculture by means of agricultural fairs was nationwide. Spurred by a new state law, a county agricultural society was organized in 1851 and with it an annual county fair. At the end of the decade, the fair added a new feature—trotting races. Twelve thousand persons packed the fairgrounds. New Year's Eve could require a party—a "large and fashionable crowd of special friends"—joining in dancing, supper, and hilarity. Midnight was marked with the singing of "Auld Lang Syne." In many parts of the village, juveniles celebrated the occasion by shooting firecrackers or by informal parties of their own and games such as blindman's buff. New Year's Day was made special by dinner parties. The annual exchange of valentines in mid-February provided pleasant diversions for the balance of the month.

Villagers experienced many diversions, some vicariously. Jenny Lind, the "Swedish Nightingale," attracted attention, though Athenians had to imagine what her voice sounded like, for she came no closer than Cincinnati. So, too, Athenians were left to their imaginations with respect to the bloomer craze. Editor Van Vorhes reported he had not less than one hundred notices of the appearance of the bloomer costume. Lancaster, he reported, was the latest place where "the epidemic has broken out." He had not the least doubt that the costume would become universal. He was wrong. At other levels, the *Messenger* also alerted Athenians to the appeal of Harriet Beecher Stowe's *Uncle Tom's Cabin* and to the successive issues of *Godey's*, "doubtless the best Lady's Magazine in the country." How many townsmen were moved to secure a copy of either *Uncle Tom* or *Godey's* is unknown.

By the end of the decade of the fifties, the community gave evidence of its growth in the appearance of a new fraternal organization—the Independent Order of Odd Fellows. Its officers included several of Athens leading citizens—J. F. Mahon, Ezra Walker, and Leonidas Jewett. Its treasurer, Charles Grosvenor, was a young man who would make his mark.

A number of Athens women participated in the Female Benevolent Society—an organization that went back to 1825. The group was dedicated to the support of "the missionary enterprise in the wilds." One significant aspect of the group was that it cut across denominational lines, bringing Presbyterians and Methodists together in a common cause. Likewise, the county Bible Society was active, with a strong sense of mission. In 1859, it was concerned with securing a local agent for each township and with stabilizing its long-term support by soliciting annual pledges of funds. It, too, was non-denominational.

TRANSPORTATION AND COMMUNICATION

While Athenians knew how to lighten-up, to enjoy, they were well aware that man lived by the sweat of his brow and of the ever-present need to broaden the Athens economic base through improved transportation services. In an essentially informative piece, the *Messenger* explained that a plank road—one of the fashionable super roads of the day—could cost $1500 to $4500 a mile. Such a road, if built to Rutland, had the advantage of intersecting a similar road to Pomeroy. While Athenians might daydream of what might be, stagecoach service was reality. There were two routes: Athens to Pomeroy, a six-hour run, and Athens to Lancaster, which took ten hours. In 1854—by which time Lancaster had train service to such exotic places as Chillicothe, Columbus, Newark, and Zanesville—the stage schedule was adjusted to make train connections. This necessitated leaving Athens at noon, laying over in Logan overnight, and arriving at Lancaster the next day. On returning, one left Lancaster at 4 P.M., spent the night at Logan, and reached Athens at noon. Beginning in 1852, a stage line opened between Marietta and Chillicothe, featuring a four-horse coach with service projected for eight months a year. The *Messenger* welcomed the innovation.

As from the first days of settlement, bulk goods destined for Cincinnati and river ports downstream had to reach the Ohio via the Hocking River. In spring 1851, the *Messenger* detailed the experience. The Hocking was up. Andrew Kessinger, now the owner of the East Mill, had shipped 1,500 barrels of flour—"a dangerous and tedious voyage." From Ames some $7,000 to $10,000 in goods had been shipped. To the *Messenger's* knowledge 15 to 20 boats had reached the Ohio; 4 or 5 had sunk en route. Ezra Stewart and a Mr. Brown of Millfield had lost 2,500 bushels of wheat when the flat boat carrying their goods ran on a snag near Skunk Creek. This was not a one-time experience. In 1852, the *Messenger's* reports reflect the anxiety of the merchants awaiting the river's rise. Stewart and Currier—two of the chief merchants of Athens—had a vessel loaded with a cargo valued at $9,000, said to be the most valuable cargo ever to be shipped from the Hocking Valley. As of February 21, the river lacked one foot of being high enough to make navigation safe. Not until Sunday, the first of March, did the Hocking rise high enough. The waiting vessels departed and this time all succeeded in clearing the Hocking. It requires little imagination to understand the degree of anxiety that merchants in particular and townsmen generally felt regarding the need for an all-weather rail connection with eastern markets.

A Railroad for Athens

The decade of the 1850s began with great expectations. Construction of the long-anticipated Belpre and Cincinnati Railroad was about to begin. Athens was abuzz with excitement; meetings—"a dozen or so"—were held nightly to drum up support. The central committees of the Whig, Democratic, and Free Soil parties jointly urged Athens County voters to support a proposal authorizing the county commissioners to subscribe $100,000 in the stock of the B & C Railroad. A local committee assured the electorate that the railroad would produce "liberal dividends" on the investment as well as providing "the cheapest and most expeditious transportation to market and superior accommodations for the traveller."

While the proposed railroad had great potential, Athenians overlooked the diverse, often conflicting, interests of the various constituencies involved. A conflict over whether the B & C should be routed through Greenfield or Hillsboro delayed the start. The nub of the difficulty was that Baltimore, Philadelphia, and New York City were locked in a fierce contest for the exports of Cincinnati. New York City got its foot in the door first thanks to the Erie Canal and the network of canals drawing goods from southwestern Ohio to Lake Erie. In 1853, Philadelphia, seeking to tap this source of goods, joined with Wheeling to fund a rail line from Cincinnati to Wheeling and, reflecting "boundless optimism," expected to complete the line within a year. In this jockeying for access to the Cincinnati trade, the Baltimore and Ohio Railroad was blocked from running its line due west from the crest of the Alleghenies toward either Marietta or Parkersburg. By default, the B & O built toward Wheeling and reached Cincinnati via a connection with the Ohio Central, leaving the Belpre and Cincinnati Railroad without the expected connection to Baltimore.

Angered at being jilted by the B & O, William P. Cutler, the chief engineer for the B & C, turned to the Pennsylvania Railroad for a link to the East Coast. This move was fateful, for it resulted in a frantic effort by the B & C to construct a line north from Marietta to a point where it could link up with the Pennsylvania Railroad. Marietta and Washington County voters overwhelmingly subscribed to municipal and county bond issues to fund the line northward. The two leaders of the Belpre and Cincinnati Railroad—Noah Wilson and W. P. Cutler—then went east to negotiate a bond sale of their own to raise additional construction funds.

The shift in orientation—from Baltimore via Belpre to Philadelphia via Marietta and Wheeling—resulted in the renaming of the railroad. The B & C became the Marietta and Cincinnati Railroad, the M & C, the "great central route for the Valley of the Ohio." In Athens there was some grumbling over the prominence this change accorded Marietta. This was outweighed by relief that construction could begin. From Cincinnati, building progressed eastward, and as each section was completed, it was placed in operation. Simultaneously, preliminary work on the Marietta to Wheeling line was started. This was a major enterprise, occupying twelve hundred workmen and two steam-powered excavators. By early October 1854, the M & C was open to Chillicothe. Jubilation at this accomplishment was tempered by the dawning realization that the costs for the Marietta to Wheeling section, initially projected at $804,180, would run close to $1.7 million—"a formidable error." Furthermore, the M & C was experiencing a serious cash flow problem. For 1855, interest on M & C bonds came to $373,815; operating revenues were but $119,568. To raise additional funds, the M & C mortgaged its rolling stock, its equipment.

With a Marietta-Wheeling line in prospect, the Virginia Legislature which had hitherto prohibited the construction of a rail line to Parkersburg relented and authorized a connecting line, the Northwest Virginia Railroad, between Grafton and Parkersburg, thus reopening the possibility of M & C linkage to the east coast through Athens and Belpre. But the B & O leadership—especially its chief engineer, Benjamin Latrobe—was not anxious to renew a relationship with the M & C. Rather Latrobe alarmed Cutler by proposing that the B & O build its own line from Belpre to Athens, thus bypassing Marietta and rendering the Marietta-Wheeling extension unnecessary. At this point, some Athenians who felt the interests of their community had been overshadowed by those of Chillicothe and Marietta, expressed their displeasure with the M & C.

Strapped for funds, Noah Wilson turned in 1855 to the European bond market to raise the funds needed to complete the M & C east from Chillicothe through Athens to Marietta. By this time, the nation's railroads had saturated the bond market; Wilson's efforts were unsuccessful. However, while in Europe, he met Peter Zaleski, a Polish banker, who, in order to acquire the railroad's coal properties in Vinton County, bought a million dollars in second mortgage bonds. The blast furnace he subsequently built at Zaleski proved defective; the ores, unremunerative. But the M & C acquired the wherewithal to complete its line.

The M & C reached Athens in April 1857 and then pushed as quickly and as straight as possible for Marietta. This meant a series of very expensive trestles and tunnels over the rugged terrain. By mid-April 1857, the line reached Harmar, across the Muskingum from Marietta, completing the line from Cincinnati to Marietta. The firm offered twice-a-day service. Passengers leaving Athens at 1:35 P.M. could expect to arrive in Marietta at 4:45; those leaving Athens on the westbound at 9:35 A.M. were promised an arrival time of 5:20 P.M. in Cincinnati. In early May, passenger and freight service to Baltimore, Philadelphia, and New York commenced. Adams Express, a package service, was also available on a daily basis.

Surprisingly, neither the long-awaited arrival of the M & C at Athens nor the completion of the line to Marietta occasioned the kind of celebration enjoyed by the arrival of the first canal boat in 1843. Rather, the celebration focused on Marietta and Chillicothe, reflecting the controlling position of those two communities. Governor Salmon P. Chase and Lewis Cass led the luminaries at Marietta, and a special train carried the railroad's directors and other celebrants to Chillicothe for a second round. Editor Van Vorhes termed the "Grand Celebration" a disappointment in that no provision was made to let Athens share in the festivities, and he took a degree of delight in describing to fellow Athenians how in the course of the Chillicothe celebration, Cass had been drenched by some exuberant Chillicothe firemen and had lost an expensive silk top hat he had bought just for the occasion.

The fact is that as the M & C reached Marietta, it was in grave financial trouble. There was not enough traffic to support either the Ohio Central or the M & C, much less both. That the B & O had been able to reach Parkersburg belatedly while the M & C had gone to Marietta was financially disastrous. The linkage with Wheeling never materialized, yet a quarter of a million dollars had been expended on "trackless cuts, barren embankments, and masonry for bridges never built." In May 1857, the M & C defaulted on the interest on its bonds. Speculative investments in railroads and bank failures in Philadelphia, Baltimore, Pittsburgh, and Wheeling led to a drying-up of credit. By mid-December 1857, Cutler recognized that the M & C was not earning enough to meet its operating expenses. Unpaid, workers walked out; creditors took possession of twelve locomotives and several cars. Cutler acknowledged: "Everybody who can swear profanely curses the road, upgrade and down grade, around the curves, across the trestles, and through the tunnels."

By this date, Athens had a love-hate relationship with the M & C. Within a few weeks of the completion of the line to Marietta, there were indications that it was not well built. Early in July, the night mail train tumbled off a 50- to 60-foot-high trestle near Vincent, 12 miles west of Marietta. The *Messenger* reported six dead and another twenty passengers injured. Slippages and derailments became a common event. Much of the trackage was unballasted, an invitation to slippage in wet weather. Furthermore, there was evidence of fare discrimination; residents of Marietta bound for Cincinnati paid $4.00 one way, $9.50 round trip. Athenians, forty miles closer, were charged $4.75 one-way, $9.50 round-trip. Fighting for its economic solvency, the M & C had lobbied in Columbus to protect itself from competition—to wit, to prevent construction of a rail line from Belpre to Athens. Enraged, editor Van Vorhes denounced the M & C as a "soulless corporation," seeking "to crush out" the interests of the Hocking Valley "in order to sustain its schemes of monopoly and in its acts of tyranny and domination."

While some of the problems of the M & C were of its own making, it came to grief in the context of the national financial panic of 1857. Much of the eastbound traffic out of Cincinnati that the M & C had counted on securing was moving on the Little Miami, an older line, to the Atlantic and Great Western, while the B & O routed its westbound traffic to Cincinnati via the Central Ohio. The panic led even the B & O to suspend dividend payments in 1857. The more immediate problem was the inability of the M & C to meet its own debts. Saddled with three mortgages totaling $6 million, the M & C defaulted on successive interest payments. By the end of 1859, the road was in default by over $1,120,000. The M & C faced bankruptcy.

An undaunted optimist, W. P. Cutler denounced the English creditors of the M & C, who were pressing for immediate payment, as "hungry adventurers." His solution was forbearance by the creditors to keep the M & C operational and rapprochement with the B & O. With the B & O facing analogous financial problems and still seeking a direct route to Cincinnati, Cutler organized a short line to connect Marietta with Belpre, thus making the M & C more functional. With the cooperation of the B & O, he reasoned, the M & C might then earn enough to carry its debt. Working through an independent corporation, the Union Railroad Company, financed in part by the B & O and the Baltimore City Council, Cutler built a connecting line from Scott's Landing to Belpre. Finished in March 1860, this connecting line permitted rail cars to be transferred by ferry across the Ohio River between Belpre and Parkersburg without the delay or expense of unloading and reloading.

Athenians remained of two minds about the M & C. Supporters of the M & C succeeded once again in persuading the county commissioners to subscribe to the stock of the M & C in mid-1859. At the same time the commissioners declined to pay the interest due on an earlier issue of county bonds floated to subscribe to the stock of the M & C or to levy a tax to meet this interest. This latter action prompted a taxpayers' revolt. Voters of Carthage Township met in September to oppose "the unjust and oppressive" proposed railroad tax and discussed nominating a slate of candidates for the county commission pledged to oppose the tax. The Carthage group also solicited support in neighboring Troy and Lodi townships. A week later John Dew of York Township announced as an independent candidate pledged to "steadfastly oppose the present policy of truckling in slavish subserviency to the demands of the M & C RR Company." Before the 1859 election campaign was over, dissidents from Athens, Alexander, Dover, and Rome townships—Republicans and Democrats alike—joined the movement. The outcome, however, was a draw. John Dew won handily by a 3–2 margin; in turn, R. A. Constable of Athens, the other independent candidate, lost just as handily.

During the whole of 1859, the M & C was in court over its impending bankruptcy. Early in the year, creditors foreclosed on the rolling stock and placed the equipment in the hands of a receiver. By the end of 1859 a reorganization plan for the M & C had been completed, one which placed the interest of the bond holders, the railroad's creditors, ahead of those of the stockholders, that is, the owners who had borrowed the funds. Nelson Van Vorhes, a stockholder, stormed that the plan "bodes no good to the enterprise itself or to the masses of its creditors." It was, he charged, "conceived in bad faith." The evil genius of the reorganization plan, in Van Vorhes' mind, was Noah Wilson, the M & C's president. Calmer voices responded. At a public meeting at the Athens courthouse in early February 1860, Charles H. Grosvenor cautioned that $100,000,000 was invested in Ohio railroads that were in as much trouble as the M & C. He counseled against hasty action. To this, John Welch added his conclusion: the reorganization plan for the M & C was "the best deal we can get." The Ohio Legislature concurred, allowing the charter of the M & C to pass to the new owners. Thus, the investors' high hopes of 1850 were replaced by disillusionment and despair in 1860. At the same time, the users —passengers and shippers—enjoyed rail service both east to the Ohio River and west to Cincinnati.

A Hocking Valley Railroad

In the early 1850s, Columbus interests began to speak of the desirability of a rail line down the Hocking Valley to tap the iron ore in the Sunday and Monday Creek Valleys. And in October 1852, A. B. Walker, a director of the M & C, called for a rail line linking Chicago, Columbus, Athens, Parkersburg, and Baltimore. Northern Athens County possessed "the finest mineral region in Ohio," he asserted. Among those interested were the aging Thomas Ewing of Lancaster, who still had important investments in Athens County, Lorenzo Dow Poston, a Nelsonville coal operator, and Eliakim H. Moore, Athens politician and land speculator. A meeting at the Neil House, Columbus, in August 1853, convened by William Dennison and attended by R. W. Carley and Nelson Van Vorhes of Athens, was especially expansive in its thinking, envisaging a rail line extending from Chicago to

Columbus and Athens. The rewards a rail project could engender were revealed in a letter to the *Messenger* in September 1853. Landowners whose property lay within a mile of the proposed road could expect the value of their land to increase immediately by $8.00 per acre. The townships along the right-of-way would reap a windfall in the form of enhanced tax revenues. Fearing that a north-south line could siphon off much needed freight traffic of their own yet-to-be-completed venture, stockholders of the M & C blocked the Columbus and Hocking Valley proposal for the moment.

Talk of a Hocking Valley Railroad remained insistent. With a public investment of $200,000 in the M & C, Athenians wanted that yet-to-be-finished road to succeed, but they were beguiled by the prospect of a north-south line as well. For Athenians, the attraction was the profits from producing the coal and iron. In May 1857, the *Messenger* took note of a flurry in the buying and selling of coal lands and the increasing value of mineral lands—some land going for $100 per acre. Columbus interests concerned with promoting their own city's growth as a manufacturing center insisted a Hocking Valley railroad was indispensable to gaining access to "the great mineral storehouse of Ohio." Otherwise, they declared, "We [Columbus] must sink into hopeless decay." Following this up, Nelson Van Vorhes commented editorially in the *Messenger* that the Hocking Valley's coal far exceeded that of England's coal regions. J. G. Blair, professor of natural sciences at Ohio University who had studied the extent of the coal field, reported that the most workable deposit of coal was 6 ½ to 9 feet in thickness, extending over an area of 10 miles by 2 miles, and was worth $50 million. In addition, he reported, the valley contained "an inexhaustible supply of iron and salt."

Columbus interests, then, went ahead and incorporated the Columbus and Hocking Valley Railroad. In May 1857, four directors of the new railroad met in Athens in a public meeting at the courthouse. These included S. B. Pruden and Daniel B. Stewart along with Charles Borland of Lancaster, the president, and Benjamin Latrobe, the chief engineer and long-time prime mover of the Baltimore and Ohio. Given the hostility the *Messenger* had expressed toward the M & C RR, the Hocking Valley people had a receptive audience. Significantly, A. B. Walker, a long-time director of the M & C, was also a leader in the promotion of the Columbus & Hocking Valley Railroad. Eighteen-fifty-seven, however, was not a propitious year for financing a new railroad. The project was put on hold.

While Athens was acquiring rail service that would reduce travel time to Cincinnati to one day's train ride, it also added telegraph service. A line from Pomeroy opened in 1859 and with it the possibility of receiving news as rapidly as a telegrapher could tap it out. At a practical level, one could send an inquiry to any point in the United States on a telegraph line and receive a same-day response. To Athens and Pomeroy telegraphers the device was a toy. They amused themselves by playing chess via telegraph.

ECONOMY IN FLUX

Like the sea, the village economy was always in flux. In offering hats for sale—otter and beaver were fashionable in 1850—W. H. Webb also indicated he desired to buy two thousand beaver pelts with bones of the tails, two thousand 'coon skins, and one thousand muskrat pelts. J. F. Crether, wholesaler and retailer, had supplies from the south, that is, he had Havana and New Orleans sugar, coffee, teas, and spices. Reflecting the barter character of the village economy, the 1850 advertisements of local merchants indicated a willingness to accept wool in payment. Pickering and Carley, however, also indicated that taking goods in payment for their merchandise posed a problem for them. They would take "such goods as will demand CASH." Athens still lacked a cash economy.

As the construction of the B & C began, the long arm of the railroad reached Athens in the sense that Noah L. Wilson, a major figure in the financing of the road, joined John Ballard and A. B. Walker as directors of the Athens branch of the Bank of Ohio. Then in spring 1853, Ballard and Sons, A. B. Walker, and E. Stimson acquired the Brice farm west of the village, land through which the B & C would pass en route to town. There was hopeful talk of laying off house lots on the land. Editor Van Vorhes expressed hope that capitalists would also develop industries utilizing local coal deposits. Certainly, there was a sense of optimism abroad. A steam-powered flouring mill, an impressive five-story structure, was going up in the canal basin. It marked one of the earlier uses of steam power in the village. How long the mill operated is uncertain, for it is not referred to again. A. R. Glazier, then of Amesville, announced he was coming to Athens to manufacture all varieties of soap and candles, products that in previous generations had been made at home. With this expectation of growth, Van Vorhes speaks of the need for fifty new houses, saying that most houses in the village are owner-occupied and there is a dearth of affordable housing for mechanics.

The expansive mood of Athenians took another turn. In June 1853, the *Messenger* disclosed that a number of Athenians—W. H. Bartlett, John Ballard, J. M. Dana, E. H. Moore, Professor J. G. Blair, J. L. Currier, and Joseph Jewett—had founded a syndicate capitalized at $40,000 to build the Big Sand Furnace in eastern Vinton County. With shares set at $7,500 each, it was clear that there was no desire to create a broad base of shareholders.

At the end of the decade, the Pickering Brothers opened the Athens Furnace, a blast furnace with a daily output of fourteen tons a day. Editor Van Vorhes was enthusiastic. The furnace was deemed "very productive." At another level Frank Cornell indicated he had become an agent for the Cincinnati Mutual Life Insurance Company, turning into a business an activity that hitherto had been an aspect of fraternal membership. The physical appearance of Court Street was subject to change. Still a street of private residences interspersed with business houses, in the 1850s Court Street would from time to time lose a private home. In 1859, the Hoyt House, where the Worstell building now stands on North Court Street, was refurbished as a hotel, with a Mrs. Mallernee as proprietress.

TEMPERANCE FEVER

Just as businessmen, especially, were excited by the railroad mania, so many church people were gripped by temperance fever. Indeed, in 1850, much of the nation was stricken. Neal Dow, the country's leading temperance promoter, had persuaded the state of Maine to solve the liquor problem once and for all by statute. The "Maine Law" prohibited the manufacture and sale of intoxicating liquors.

The friends of temperance sought to secure a provision in the proposed Ohio state constitution prohibiting the state legislature from enacting laws making it lawful to sell drinks or to make the liquor traffic legal. The constitutional convention was in a difficult position on the liquor issue, for its delegates had not been selected on the basis of their position on prohibition. In particular, they did not want the public's attitude toward the state constitution affected by the alcohol issue. So, they provided for a separate vote on the licensing of liquor establishments. When the constitution squeaked by narrowly in a state-wide vote, the licensing referendum passed by 113,239 votes to 104,255, the margin of victory so small as to assure the debate would continue to be agitated.

Locally, the Sons of Temperance endorsed the Maine Law and editor Van Vorhes, a determined opponent of drink, printed petitions asking the Ohio General Assembly to enact it. A state-wide petition drive produced an enormous Temperance Convention in Columbus in 1852, one at which Athens, unexplainably, was not represented. Petitions bearing the signatures of some 50,000 persons were presented to the legislature praying for legislative action. Mindful that there was also a formidable constituency favoring access to alcoholic beverages, the legislature submitted the issue to another state-wide referendum.

Finally, in February 1853, the village council adopted its version of the Maine Law. The *Messenger* expressed its "unfeigned gratification and delight." The liquor traffic had been "a blasting, deadening curse" to the village. Editor Van Vorhes was sensible of the need for two additional steps—employment of "efficient and energetic officers . . . who *will* execute the law" and the need of citizen support of the officers. Within six weeks, to its pleasure, the *Messenger* reported that the law was being enforced.

At the end of the decade, liquor was again flowing in the village, to the distress of the temperance forces. Some Irish newcomers allegedly were selling liquor from shanties on the edge of town. A Mr. Carley—probably R. W. Carley, the merchant—charged that some of the temperance men had failed to keep their pledges, while some of those who dispensed liquor rented their premises from members of the temperance committee. At this point, the committee charged Charles H. Grosvenor and A. G. Brown with examining village ordinances respecting the sale of ale and lager beer. Clearly, the liquor problem was destined to continue.

FIRE AND FLOODS

In late July 1854, Athens suffered its first "great conflagration," a fire that destroyed Isaac Taylor's Eagle Hotel at the southwest corner of Court and Union Streets. The fire began in the hotel's stable and within minutes enveloped the adjacent barns of S. S. Knowles and O. W. Brown. Soon the hotel, too, was afire along with the kitchen of S. S. Knowles, the building which currently quarters the Baron Men's Shop. Filled with hay and feed, the three barns spewed sparks that showered the area to the north and east of the hotel, setting a dozen small fires on South Court and College Streets.

Lacking a public water system, the village had no effective way to put out the fire in the hotel, which was completely consumed. By posting men on the buildings downwind, bucket brigades succeeded in putting those fires out before they caused serious damage. Taylor's loss was estimated at $5,000 to $8,000 of which $2,000 was covered by insurance. He was ruined. Within days, the land was for sale and the *Messenger* was expressing hope that someone would acquire the land and erect a modern hotel on the property. No one did. Some nondescript structures eventually popped up, but the corner was deemed an eyesore for the next sixty years.

Periodically, the Hocking flooded. The "great spring freshet" of 1832 sent the Hocking over its banks, covering the bottoms east of the village, and water rose "half way up the [Mill Street] hill." It wiped out crops in the bottom lands. Again, in 1847, a "great flood" cost farmers thousands of dollars in the loss of crops. Once more in 1858, a "great and disastrous flood swept down the valley." The primary loss in all these floods was to the farmer who lost his crops; the secondary loss accrued to the merchants who had extended credit to such farmers and to those millers whose dams or mills were damaged. Still a village on a hill, the residents of Athens stayed dry and damage-free.

HEALTH

Nowhere was the helplessness of Athenians to control their own destiny more apparent than in matters of health. Families, of course, continued to rely on hand-me-down recipes for teas, salves, decoctions, and concoctions as a first measure to treat ailing family members. When these remedies failed, the family doctor-apothecary might try his favorite medications. Undoubtedly Maria Foster Brown was not alone in rejecting the dosages of calomel, the bleedings, and the opiates that were the mainstays of country doctors. Quinine was generously dispensed for malarial-type fevers.

Athenians who needed help beyond home remedies and doctor's prescriptions could turn to the nationally distributed patent medicines. Advertisements for these products certainly added to the revenues of the local paper; whether the medicines restored the ailing to health is less certain. Brant's Indian Purifying Extract was strong in its claims—it had saved "Hundreds—Thousands." It had the additional merit of being able to deal with cancers, liver complaint, female weaknesses and complaints, and change of life. If Brant's invoked the efficacy of Indian herbal medicine, H. G. Farbell's Liniment drew on the medical wisdom of the Arabs. Users of this "celebrated Arabian Liniment" had the further benefit of a set of testimonials of its miracle cures to peruse while awaiting evidence of their own cure. There was another choice—Dr. Townshend's Sarsparilla, "the most extraordinary medicine in the world." All three remedies were available from the village's leading druggist, John Perkins. Not to be left out, Ezra Stewart, merchant, offered McAlister's "All Healing Ointment."

The availability of Dr. Cheesman's Pills offers another insight into the state of

Athens society and the practice of medicine. The pills were touted as having been around for twenty-five years, an assurance of their efficacy and acceptance. Nominally, they were sold on the premise that "no woman can enjoy good health unless she is regular." The advertisement went on, however, to explicitly warn that "ladies who are pregnant must not use them, as they will invariably produce a miscarriage." The pills, in fact, were an abortifacient.

As in earlier decades, Athenians were troubled by reports of epidemics. In 1850, as during several summers before, cholera was abroad. It was reported to be in Ohio River towns, was of epidemic proportions in Columbus, and Circleville was in panic. Without understanding the cause of disease, the *Messenger's* editor passed on some commonsense suggestions. As cholera "loves filth, and dreads cleanliness," editor Van Vorhes urged a thorough cleansing of "all cellars, drains, vaults, slop holes, and everything of the kind." He prescribed generous doses of quicklime. Once again, Athens escaped the scourge. Cleanliness was a preventive measure; but the community undoubtedly owed much to being off the beaten track.

ENTER THE PUBLIC SCHOOL

One of the major achievements of the 1850s was the beginning of a public school system. A tax-supported school system for Athens became possible under an 1849 amendment to the Akron Law, an amendment that made Athens lease lands subject to school taxes. The law also introduced the graded school and the "higher grades," that is, grades nine through twelve. Acting promptly, the village electors met New Year's Day 1850, approved a set of regulations for its schools, and elected its first board of education. Within the year, the board voted taxes in support of a village school that began in the winter term, 1850–51, using one room over the Market House (8 North Court) and one in the basement of the Methodist Church for male students. Female students were taught in a room in Brown's Row, on Washington Street. The school term was three months long.

Education was in high repute in Athens and the development of the public system received solid support. In 1853, the school board adopted a nine-month school year, a move that necessitated a substantial increase in taxes. The board called a public meeting of all legal voters to convene at the courthouse on September 17 to vote on the construction of a schoolhouse and on the millage to support it. A unanimous vote directed the board to construct a good, substantial, and convenient schoolhouse. The meeting also approved a tax to raise the needed $8,000.

Proceeding with all deliberate speed, the board engaged its first superintendent of schools, hired teachers, including one teacher for grades nine through twelve as well as a school librarian. The board also appointed a committee to plan a graded curriculum for grades one through twelve.

Finally, the board purchased property at the corner of Lancaster and Dean (West Washington) and contracted for construction of a three-story brick building. Almost square, the new building had four rooms each on the first and second floors; the third floor, named the Atheneum, was left open with an eighteen-foot ceiling and was used both as the high school classroom and as a town meeting hall. A well and "necessaries" were built nearby. The building opened for classes in fall 1857. Graded instruction began also. As high school classes had begun in 1855, the first high school class graduated in 1859—nine students, all women. The town was proud. The absence of male students was hardly surprising; the males were, as they had been for four decades, enrolled in the University's Academy.

OHIO UNIVERSITY—ENTER SOLOMON HOWARD

Little did the university trustees realize in 1852 when they appointed Solomon Howard president that he would lead the university for the next two decades. In fact, when Alfred Ryors stepped down in August 1852, the trustees chose the Reverend Joseph Tomlinson, "a brilliant Methodist preacher and teacher" at Augusta College, Kentucky, as president, while Solomon Howard was hired to teach natural sciences. To the chagrin of the trustees, Tomlinson declined the appointment, and the board turned by default to Howard.

The appointments of Tomlinson and Howard signified the fact that the Methodists had gained a majority on the board of trustees. And the Presbyterians who had hitherto run the university were not happy. Dr. James Hoge, a Presbyterian and a twenty-nine-year member of the board of trustees, quit forthwith; A. G. Brown, also a Presbyterian, refused to serve further as board secretary, and within the next three years Presbyterians who were on the faculty, Addison Ballard and Aaron Williams, left the school, being replaced by Methodist clergy, James G. Blair in natural science and John M. Leavitt in ancient languages.

By 1855 Methodists had displaced Presbyterians both on the University Board and on the faculty. For their part, the new trustees sought to recruit students through agents of both churches. In other respects the trustees pursued a narrow sectarian course. They requested the bishops of the Cincinnati and the Ohio conferences of the Methodist Church to reassign to Ohio University those faculty members who were Methodist clergy subject to their bishop's orders. In effect, faculty appointments at Ohio University required the joint support of the trustees and the requisite Methodist bishop. Ohio University had become de facto a Methodist-controlled institution. From a demographic point of view, this turn of events greatly broadened the appeal of the school, for, by the 1850s, the Methodists enjoyed far and away the largest church membership in Ohio. At the same time, Ohio already had a surfeit of Methodist colleges—Ohio Wesleyan, Mt. Union, Cincinnati Wesleyan Female, and Baldwin (now Baldwin-Wallace)—all competing for the same students.

A man in his early forties, Solomon Howard brought a wealth of academic experience to the presidency. He had attended Miami University and had graduated from Augusta College. Although a clergyman, he had teaching experience at St. Charles (Missouri) College, had helped found Ohio Wesleyan College at Delaware, and had been principal of a Methodist school at Springfield, Ohio.

Yet all was not well with the university as Howard took over. The *Messenger* noted the irony of a campus with beautiful buildings and grounds but few students. The first problem was the "want of easy access." Athens remained isolated from other parts of the state, a problem that a railroad could solve. Second was the "want of extended publicity." The school was not sufficiently known. Finally, the editor pointed to a "want of sympathy" for the college on the part of townsmen. "The prosperity of the village and the surrounding country is closely identified with the prosperity of the College," editor Van Vorhes lectured his readers. What the good editor failed to note was that while the population of Ohio was growing, most of that growth was in the northern and western portions of the state where a plethora of colleges served that population.

Howard approached his presidency as an educator rather than as a clergyman. In the first instance this meant curriculum changes designed to broaden the appeal of the college. He saw a "large class of young men whose time, means, or other circumstances do not admit of pursuing a regular college course but who desire to qualify themselves for teaching or for business pursuits." Accordingly, Howard introduced a two-year curriculum—an extensive course of math, natural science, and belles lettres. By 1862 this had become a three-year program. The math included surveying and navigation; the sciences sampled the field—chemistry, physics, physiology, mineralogy, and geology. The social sciences, still new as academic disciplines, included political science and political economy (economics). In addition, the students studied rhetoric, English literature, and moral philosophy.

A second venture was the establishing of a teachers' institute in collaboration with Marietta College, the institute to begin in 1853. This was a timely innovation: under the impetus of Horace Mann and Henry Barnard in New England, there was an enormous growth of interest in elementary education and in teacher training. Six years later, it was transmuted into the Southeastern Normal Institute offering a four-week-long program.

In casting about to identify programs that would expand the student population, Howard explored the creation of a medical department to be located at Zanesville; a year later he entered discussions over the founding of a law department. In both cases the inquiries came to nought: no funds, insufficient public interest.

The same mind set that led Howard to explore curricula and innovations calculated to expand the student base resulted in a more understanding policy with respect to student behavior. Howard was no less pious than his stern Presbyterian predecessors, but he took a more easygoing approach to student discipline. No longer did the university record books catalog incidents of student delinquency. Students were no longer asked to testify against one another. When students misbehaved, the punishments were milder. The tensions between students and administration that had kept the university on the edge of revolt in earlier years now abated.

Between the university's "marriage" to the Methodists and Howard's leadership, the university prospered in the fifties. Total enrollments, 102 in 1852, soared to 192 in 1857–58, then settled back to 158 at the end of the decade. As in earlier years, in the absence of an effective area-wide public secondary school system, the university's academy overshadowed the college program. The increased enrollments reflected the impact of two programs. First, the trustees again offered cut-rate scholarships—five terms or three years at $15, good until August 1860. Between 1852 and 1857 this program accounted for an average of forty students a year—one-fifth to one-fourth of the total enrollment. Secondly, to show the flag, the trustees again offered free scholarships to one outstanding student from each county. From ten to thirteen students a year were added to the student population on this basis. While these programs filled the classrooms and gave the school a renewed vitality, they added only modestly to the school's operating income. On the other hand, as the students boarded in Athens, they swelled the demand for room and board.

Howard was especially successful in dealing with the university's indebtedness. In January 1853, that debt—utterly insignificant by standards of the 1990s—was a troubling $8,248.83. Through astute management, Howard cut it to less than $6,000 by the start of 1856, then in exchange for instituting the county scholarship program, the state legislature forgave a $5,000 loan. By the start of 1858, the university had a positive balance for the first time in years.

Despite this good fortune, the university continued to be haunted by its role as the community landlord. The same state legislature that avoided appropriating operating funds for the college continued to tinker with the university's leaseholders. In April 1852, the general assembly provided for the assessment and taxation of all property "according to its true value in money." It expressly provided that lands such as those held on leasehold from Ohio University were subject to taxation. Accordingly, the county treasurer assessed the "leasehold estates" a total of $1,100. Given the character of Athens agriculture, local leaseholders viewed the taxes as exorbitant. The new law meant that leasehold properties would now be taxed on the current value of the property rather than on their value at the time the land had first been leased from the university—an enormous increase.

The community was instantly aroused. John Matheny and 770 lessees of Athens and Alexander townships promptly sued to prevent collection of the taxes, employing Samuel F. Vinton, a trustee of the university, to represent them. In November, Judge Simeon Nash, Athens Common Pleas Court, issued injunctive relief to the plaintiffs. The *Messenger*, usually strongly pro-university, sided with the community.

Thwarted in its efforts to tax the college lands, the general assembly, in 1854, authorized the leaseholders to convert their titles to fee simple, absolute ownership. To do so, they were to pay the state treasurer a sum 16.66 times the yearly rent set in the original leasehold. This sum would become part of the State's irreducible debt, and Ohio University would thereafter draw 6 percent per year forever. The offer had few advantages to the leaseholders, for while it would remove the university as their landlord, it exposed them to annual property tax payments already far higher than the annual rents otherwise due the university.

On appeal in December 1856, Judge John Brinkerhoff, ruling on the 1856 suit, held for the plaintiffs, arguing that the lessees had accepted freedom from taxation forever as an inducement for enduring the risks and hardships of settling the college lands. The community won. But a legislature that could raise no revenue from the college lands was not disposed to appropriate state funds in support of the college.

In the wake of the Brinkerhoff decision, the university cast about to find a mechanism that would generate a source of public funds to meet its operating costs. In June 1860, it petitioned the general assembly for relief from the 1843 legislation that blocked reevaluation of the college lands. The legislature, meeting in 1861 and distracted by the Civil War, did nothing.

For the next four years, 1861–65, Athens was preoccupied with the War between the States.

6

The War between the States

No WAR AMERICANS have fought has been more traumatic, more bloody than the War between the States. For a decade the voting record of Athenians indicated that a majority strongly opposed the further expansion of slave territory. The county had supported Lincoln by a margin of 3–2 in November 1860. Lincoln's call for volunteers in mid-April 1861 prompted an immediate response—a community rally on April 20 on the College Green. The Ohio State Guards of Athens appeared in full uniform. Patriotic oratory and the unfurling of a flag from the upper windows of the College Edifice added to the excitement. A fund of $2,000 was raised to assist the families of the soldiers-to-be. Another response was the creation of a local military committee to whip up zeal, to sustain patriotic fervor, and to promote the recruiting of troops. Finally, Robert A. Constable, a general in the Ohio militia, called for ten companies from Athens and nearby counties for three months' service.

Athenians' response was immediate. A place to the west of the village, the present-day site of West Elementary School, was made into a training center. First called Camp Jewett, it was later renamed Camp Wool after General John Ellis Wool. Athenians enlisted.

The Ohio State Guards—reorganized as Company C, 3d Regiment, Ohio Volunteer Infantry (OVI), under Captain Joseph M. Dana—claimed the honor of being the first Athens unit to leave on three months' service. Shortly after, a second company from the village under the command of Captain E. A. Guthrie left for Camp Dennison. This unit became Co. B, 22d OVI, again for three months' service, for at the time the expectation was that the hostilities would not last long. The stunning defeat of General Irvin McDowell at Bull Run in July 1861 made clear that the war would not end quickly.

In July 1861 Governor Dennison called for two full regiments from the Athens district for three years' service. The 92d OVI, Nelson Van Vorhes commanding, was fully recruited on the 15th of August and off to Point Pleasant, Virginia. Recruiting for the 116th OVI began immediately. Companies I & K were from Athens, as was the regiment's second in command, Lt. Colonel Thomas F. Wildes. By August Athens County had raised 1,000 men, and eight companies had left for Camp Dennison. Still more Athenians entered service in 1862. Recruiting of replacements and raising additional regiments continued to the end of the war. And for a time in 1863 Camp Wool had 6,000 men encamped. With no more than one or two companies to a regiment, Athenians served in a wide variety of regiments that saw service in every major theater.

LEONARD COOLEY'S WAR

The wartime service of Leonard J. Cooley reflects many of the experiences of Athens-area men in the Union Army. A carpenter and farmer from near Coolville, Cooley was married and the father of four children. An abolitionist and Unionist, in midsummer 1862 Cooley enlisted in Company B, 116th Regiment, OVI. At age forty-one, he left his wife, Frances, behind to care for their children and to manage their farm in the Hocking River bottoms as best she could.

Much of Cooley's duty was quite prosaic. His company's first assignment was guarding the railway bridges and trestles near Athens. Army food was plain— bread and meat, coffee with sugar, and apples. Civilian "neighbors" supplied milk, apples, and tomatoes to supplement their diet. The company had nightly religious services, Captain Edwin Keys reading a chapter from the Bible, followed by prayers. Cooley noted that prayers were also offered at meals. By the end of September 1862 the company had moved to the Gallipolis area.

Together with the 40th OVI at nearby Point Pleasant, the 2d Virginia Cavalry and two companies of the 92d OVI and the 116th OVI guarded a possible crossing point of the Ohio River. In November, the 116th shifted to the upper Potomac, moving in turn from New Creek Station on the Potomac to Burlington, some eleven miles from Romney, [West] Virginia, to Petersburg on the South Branch of the Potomac. At this point one-fourth of the regiment was ravaged by the measles. In mid-January 1863 Cooley was at Romney. Much of his remaining active service was spent either along the upper Potomac or in the Shenandoah Valley of Virginia, especially in the neighborhood of Winchester.

Service in rebel territory had a different character than had guard duty on Ohio soil. Cooley had utter contempt for the "Sesesh," as he called the Confederates, and although he was a deeply religious man, he accepted the practice of fellow soldiers who appropriated—stole—corn, chickens, and cattle for food and fence posts for fuel. "The boys," he told Fanny, had got "eighteen chickens and two calves" in one exploit. On another occasion, in the absence of good timber, they had used rail fencing for kindling. While Cooley rationalized stealing from the enemy, he made fine distinctions. Romney he thought "the worst town I've ever seen," though in part this was because Union troops had abused rebel homes, sometimes stabling their horses in what had been private homes. By contrast, while Winchester was desolate, Cooley recognized that it had had "nice yards and gardens with all kinds of trees and shrubs and flowers of all kinds."

The dull dreariness of guard and picket duty was broken briefly at the end of December 1862 and in early 1863. At this point, he was at Moorefield—surrounded by "Sesesh." The latter had captured thirteen teams and drivers, a fact that underscored the risk he faced. And here he participated in his first battle. "The shells made quite a screeching," he confided to his wife.

The war quickly took its toll on Cooley's health as it did for so many soldiers. Cooley was in Winchester little more than two months before he complained of "a sort of direah" [sic] and that his digestion was not good. He was sufficiently indisposed that he shifted from picket duty to driving a horse-drawn ambulance, an assignment he regarded as both less taxing and less risky. Ironically, when his unit came under attack in mid-June 1863, he was captured while transporting sick and wounded soldiers to hospital in town, while most of his unit escaped capture.

After a relatively brief period of confinement at the notorious Libby Prison in Richmond and on Belle Island, his captors sent him to Camp Parole, Annapolis, Maryland. While he welcomed being "rid of old Jeff's [Davis] filth" in his confinement, his morale was sorely put to the test as numbers of his fellow soldiers deserted, returning to Athens County without leave. Lt. Colonel Wildes writes of this period as the lowest point of the war. The men were agreed on holding the Union together, but many utterly rejected putting their lives at risk in support of emancipating the slaves. And so they deserted. Some of the officers resigned. Although terribly homesick for his wife and children, Cooley steadfastly refused to go home without authorization. His situation was made worse as his wife confessed her "heartsickness" and "heart loneliness" was aggravated as friends and neighbors inquired as to when L. J. was returning. In mid-August 1863, Fanny Cooley noted that Coolville was "nearly full of paroled prisoners" and that some of the returned soldiers had doffed their uniforms for civilian dress. Some of these soldiers explained away their position by averring that their officers had encouraged them to return home. Cooley, however, explained to his wife that these men were AWOL, absent without leave, and that to come home they had to avoid the trains and main highways where they were subject to arrest by the provost guard, and indeed, he cited persons who had been taken into custody and returned to camp under guard.

By early September 1863, Cooley was in hospital with intermittent fever and chills—probably malaria. His condition was sufficiently severe that a friend had to write in his behalf. A month later, he was exchanged, that is, released from the status of a paroled captive, and was transferred back to active duty with the 116th. Despite his capture and illness, he did not succeed in securing a furlough until December 1863.

Returning to his unit before Christmas, Cooley's remaining service was marked by intermittent ill health. At Back Creek, Virginia, in early February 1864, he reported, he was again bothered by diarrhea from which he never completely recovered. Moving to Martinsburg in April, he again experienced an attack of malaria, the doctor dosing him with quinine. Shortly afterward, he was hospitalized, first at Martinsburg, then at Frederick and finally at Camp Parole, Annapolis, Maryland, and while he shook the chills, the diarrhea persisted. A nephew, George Bumgardner, who was with him, observed that Martinsburg was "a poor place for a sick man." Thereafter his condition varied. At times he was "tolerably comfortable," could sit up and walk around; at other times he felt "weaker" as the malaria recurred. When the malarial fevers and chills abated, he helped nurse in a forty-patient ward.

Through the late summer and fall of 1864, Cooley gained experience as a nurse, learning to bandage wounds, especially the stumps of amputees. Conscientiously he performed his duty, always homesick, thankful for the letters from his wife and his daughter, Sarah. He longed for a chance to gather with them at "the family hearth." He lamented: "Oh how I wish that this cruel war was over." Then without warning on Wednesday, November 4, 1864, he became ill again, bilious; four days later Leonard Cooley died.

The military action in which L. J. Cooley became a prisoner of war in June 1863 was part of a major operation in which the Confederates pushed northward through the Shenandoah Valley. On June 12, 1863, Union scouts had alerted General Robert Milroy that a large rebel force was advancing northward from Front Royal and Strasburg toward Winchester. Milroy conducted an ambuscade of the rebels south of Winchester that captured forty or so rebels. As General Milroy, greatly outnumbered, sought to evacuate Winchester, General James Longstreet, the Confederate commander, turned the tables on Milroy's forces and with combined infantry, artillery, and cavalry succeeded in ambushing him three miles north of Winchester. The result, as Colonel T. F. Wildes, now regimental commander of the 116th, reported to the *Messenger*, was a "grand skedaddle." It was at this point that Companies I and A of the 116th lost half their personnel, killed or captured, and the readers of the *Messenger* were subsequently told that their action contributed to blocking Lee's troops for three days, allowing General George Meade's troops time to intercept Lee's army at Gettysburg. L. J. Cooley was one of some 150 members of the 116th to be captured. All told, between 4,000 and 5,000 Union troops were captured—a sizable portion of Milroy's forces. Routed, the 116th was left to its own devices. Crossing the mountains and the Potomac, it found sanctuary at Sharpsburg, Maryland, not far from Antietam.

While Cooley was in prison and in hospital, the 116th was posted along the rail line linking Cumberland, Maryland, to Harpers Ferry—"arduous duty" holding off "despicable guerillas" who preyed on the B & O. In late spring and early summer 1864, the 116th, beginning near Strasburg, conducted a 433-mile expedition through rebel territory, skirmishing nearly every day, burning bridges, factories, mills, furnaces and foundries, and public buildings. At Piedmont, near Staunton, Virginia, the regiment came under hostile fire and lost 176 officers and men, killed or wounded.

APPALACHIA AND THE VALLEY OF VIRGINIA

While Athenians who served in the Union armies shared many of the experiences of Leonard Cooley, the war was fought in dozens of places Leonard Cooley never saw. At the war's outset, Governor Dennison was fearful that either rebel military forces or guerrillas would cross into Ohio. It was with this in mind that the three-months' men were rushed to patrol along the Ohio River and that as a preemptive measure Ohio asked to take responsibility for guarding western Virginia.

In 1861, the companies of three-months' men were assigned to guard the rail lines and the Ohio River from guerrilla attacks, and as the first regiments enlisted for three years' service were organized, they often spent the first weeks on such duty. The 92d OVI under Nelson Van Vorhes would spend fall 1862 cleaning the rebels out of the Kanawha Valley; the 116th went first to Parkersburg, then to Gallipolis. The 4th Virginia Volunteers, an Ohio regiment despite its name, with one company from Athens, was actually mustered into the federal service at Point Pleasant and the 7th Ohio Volunteer Cavalry (OVC), known for a time as the River Regiment, rendezvoused at Ripley in October 1862 at a time the rebels threatened Cincinnati.

Although some troops would always be posted along the Ohio River, other concerns arose over securing the rail lines linking the Ohio Valley with the East, and suppressing bushwhackers who disrupted rail lines in western Virginia. In the spring of 1862 the First Virginia Cavalry, of which Company E was drawn largely from Athens County, served at Clarksburg, Virginia, then Philippi. From early 1862, the 73d and 75th OVI were sent to Grafton, Romney, and Moorefield. For the 73d, an eighty-mile forced march over "wretched mountain roads in stormy weather" was a painful introduction to soldiering. Within weeks, the new regiment was paralyzed by an epidemic of measles and camp fever that put three hundred men in hospital and cost thirty men their lives. In spring 1863, the 75th OVI reported itself comfortably quartered in log huts covered with shelter tents in which the men spent many a pleasant evening around the firesides swapping stories of home.

At times, military exigency required these troops to cross into the Shenandoah Valley. The valley was an important source of food to the Confederates and a potential invasion route for an end run around the Union forces defending Washington that could lead to an invasion of Pennsylvania or an attack on the Union capital from the rear. Less dramatic, perhaps, than the front between Washington and Richmond, the Shenandoah Valley was the scene of repeated encounters and costly losses.

Winchester, in the center of the valley, changed hands eighty-four times during the war. There were major battles in and about Winchester in May 1862, June 1863, and in July and September of 1864. As noted earlier, Cooley and the 116th OVI took a beating in the June 1863 action, when they stood in the path of Confederate forces moving north toward Gettysburg. In July 1864, the 36th OVI, which had Ohio University Professor William H. G. Adney as its second in command and Professor J. G. Blair as its chaplain, found itself in the Valley. Defeated, it fled in disorder, having lost 150 men killed and wounded. Athens men also took part in the July 1864 raid on Lexington, Virginia, that burned the town and destroyed both Washington College and the Virginia Military Institute. In August, General Philip Sheridan, of Somerset, Ohio, took command. As the 36th regiment pulled itself together, General Grant ordered Sheridan to conduct a scorched earth campaign—to so devastate the Shenandoah Valley that "a crow, in passing over it, would be compelled to carry his rations with him." At the time of the September 1864 attack on Winchester, the 36th to the south at Opequon routed the rebels. Then, on the morning of October 19, the 36th was, in its turn, surprised and overwhelmed by the forces of General Jubal Early. General Sheridan, returning from Washington when the attack occurred, arrived on the scene in the early afternoon and promptly rallied the troops; the 36th had the pleasure of utterly routing the rebels before nightfall, finally ending the rebel presence in the valley.

The 4th VVI, too, found itself in the Shenandoah Valley in summer 1864. At Snicker's Ferry in July, Early's force killed or wounded one-third of the regiment; four days later the 4th VVI sustained further heavy losses at Winchester and joined in the flight to Maryland to regroup. Yet in September the 4th VVI was back in the valley and helped deal the rebels a defeat at Opequon.

In spring 1864, in order to release as many veterans as possible for service with General Grant, the army called for the enlistment of a large number of men for 100-day service. Accordingly, some 420 Athens Countians enlisted in the 114th OVI, which was headquartered at Barboursville, West Virginia, and assigned to patrol the area from Guyandotte to Charleston, an area "infested" with "bush-whackers."

These "one-hundred day men" provoked bitter denunciation, some of it from the regulars. From the vantage of those who had enlisted back in 1861 and 1862, these johnnies-come-lately had sat out three years of war, earning peacetime wages while the three-year volunteers received $13 per month and no allowances. Now, late in the war, these hundred-day men were to receive their regular wages from their employers, their wives got $13 a month from the army, and the men were loaded with gifts. One embittered veteran, Frank Rashleigh, suggested that if these hundred-day men were so wonderful, they ought to be sent to confront either Lee or Johnston.

As their term of service neared its end, members of Companies L and K became further embroiled in controversy. As they had not been sworn into service immediately on reporting for duty, their hundred days of federal service extended longer than they had anticipated. To one observer these boys were "more homesick than patriotic." "Special," the 141st's correspondent to the *Messenger*, looked forward to returning to "the soot-covered roofs of Athens" and its "familiar, badly-paved streets."

THE EASTERN THEATER

Several regiments with men from Athens—the 30th, 36th, 61st, and 75th—saw significant service in the Eastern theater. In August 1862, the 75th OVI led by R. A. Constable took heavy losses at Freeman's Ford, when it was in the way of Stonewall Jackson's forces, moving northward toward Antietam. Again on the 28th of August, a day before the second battle of Bull Run, the 75th was involved in "severe" fighting when attacked near that battlefield. The 36th and 61st OVI were at Second Bull Run, but both escaped the battle itself. The 36th was in reserve during the battle but afterwards kept the "stragglers and fugitives" from stampeding into Washington. The 61st was sent to Washington to guard the Chain Bridge. Subsequently, the 30th and the 36th OVI moved to South Mountain. On the 14th of September, as the target of a forty-five-minute artillery barrage, the 30th lost 18 men dead and 48 wounded; meanwhile, the 36th had a brush with Jeb Stuart's cavalry at Frederick, Maryland, on September 12 and engaged in "a memorable bayonet charge" against the rebels at South Mountain two days later.

On the eve of the battle at Antietam, the bloodiest single day of the entire war, the 30th OVI charged five hundred yards across a newly plowed field near the Antietam bridge, an action that cost it over forty casualties. For its part, the 36th lost its colonel, killed by a ten-pound shell, but otherwise sustained few casualties.

In summer 1863 the 61st and the 75th OVIs were still in the East. Both were at Chancellorsville, the battle in which "Fighting Joe" Hooker's effort to encircle Lee's army miscarried, although it cost Stonewall Jackson his life. In this battle, lasting May 1–4, the 75th, on the extreme right flank of the Army of the Potomac, was surprised by the rebels and lost 150 men killed and wounded. The 61st fared somewhat better, losing but 5 officers wounded and 5 men killed. The Union Army was stunned, and General Hooker was replaced with General George C. Meade. General Lee headed north to Gettysburg.

At Gettysburg, the 61st OVI was in battle on the first day, July 1, and was "roughly handled," losing heavily in men killed, wounded, and taken prisoner. Of its 16 officers, only 4 emerged unscathed; of 292 enlisted men, 169 were either killed or wounded and another 34 taken prisoner. It was at Gettysburg that William D. McVay of Athens, a nineteen-year-old who had enlisted in his brother-in-law's company, was wounded; he died in hospital four days later. The 61st pursued the rebels after the battle and skirmished with them at Hagerstown. In the aftermath, both the 61st and 75th were transferred elsewhere. Not until the closing months of the war were Athens-area regiments again conspicuous in the Eastern theater.

THE WESTERN THEATER

A major portion of the militia units from the Athens area served in the campaigns along the Mississippi, Cumberland, and Tennessee Rivers, and in Sherman's march to the sea. The Union campaign to gain control of the Mississippi River from

Cairo, Illinois, to the Gulf of Mexico was designed to divide the Confederacy, separating Texas, Louisiana, and Arkansas from contact with the rest of the Confederacy. As a means of facilitating this action, General Grant moved armies up the Tennessee and Cumberland rivers to Fort Donelson and Fort Henry, depriving the Confederates of bases from which they might reinforce Vicksburg and other strongholds on the Mississippi River. Control of the Tennessee River and of Chattanooga provided a gateway to the Lower South, and gaining Chattanooga, the Yankees were poised to stage a drive toward Atlanta and Savannah, splitting Alabama and Mississippi from Virginia and the Carolinas. Athenians in this Western theater saw some of the bloodiest action of the war.

One of the earliest units, the 18th OVI, one-third of whom were from Athens County, got off on the wrong foot. Stationed at Camp Jefferson, Bacon Creek, Kentucky, in early 1862, nearly one-third of its personnel fell sick and four died. Twenty of the men reported hospitalized lay shoulder-to-shoulder in a room 18 by 20 feet. A reporter thought the term "miserable pen" more accurately described the facility. The condition of this unit moved T. F. Wildes, the editor of the *Messenger,* to call for the creation of a Soldiers' Aid Society, such as other communities had long since organized. "Let us do our duty," he urged Athens, "our whole duty, to our friends." As the regiment secured new tents, stoves, clothes, and arms and moved to a drier camp site, physical conditions improved, but not before more men died. The problem, as their brigade commander, General John B. Turchin told them: "You are no soldiers. You are farmers with guns in your hands." The whole brigade was subjected to drill. But creating a self-disciplined brigade was no easy task.

As General Grant moved on Fort Henry on the Tennessee River and Fort Donelson on the Cumberland, the 18th OVI, under Colonel Timothy R. Stanley, followed in his wake, marching cross-country, passing through Elizabethtown, to the Green River, Bowling Green, and crossing the Barren River. Duncan Huling of A Company refers to pillaging, a problem that would plague the entire brigade of which the 18th was a part. At Bowling Green members of the 19th Illinois Regiment looted the stores, provoking Colonel Stanley to post a provost guard "at every corner" to stop the pillaging. Subsequently, the 19th and 24th Illinois regiments were moved to the far side of the river because of their "thieving propensities." Huling was proud that his own unit had "molested nothing." Yet, as the army moved into Tennessee and Alabama, even Huling could not refrain from appropriating wood for fuel or to fashion a makeshift bunk or from augmenting his army rations with peaches, apples, roasting ears of corn and, on occasion, a chicken or hog belonging to a rebel farmer. In fact, pillaging was such an embarrassment to the command that General Buell made an example of Colonel Stanley by placing him under arrest for his failure to stem petty pillaging by his troops. The move backfired, for when Stanley was released from arrest, the men of the 18th gathered before his tent to cheer "the good colonel," while the commanding officers of other units came to congratulate him.

The service of the 18th OVI, like that of the 116th, was generally unexciting. In spring 1862, while General Buell took most of his army to Pittsburg Landing, the inexperienced 18th was assigned to guard the rail lines south from Louisville, especially bridge crossings and trestles. Where the rebels had destroyed a bridge, the men of the 18th were detailed to replace it. When the troops did move, they frequently got so far ahead of their wagon train that they were forced to camp without tents, food, or utensils. At times, they were on half-rations—a half loaf of bread for a day's food. When the line of march was halted for a day or two, there was drill—the manual of arms, company drill, and brigade drill. And on Sunday, a dress parade.

Like the older Private Leonard Cooley, young Huling was homesick. He "[wished] to God this war was at an end." When not on the move, he was bored; even more, the lack of mail from home distressed him, though he carried on an extensive correspondence. What hurt most was that while his "dear Emmie" had confided through a mutual friend that she wanted to hear from him, she waited for months before answering his letters. The fellows played pranks on one another. On April Fool's Day, two of the fellows were sent off on wild goose chases to the delight of the tricksters.

While the 18th missed out on the bloody battle at Pittsburg Landing, the 53d OVI, of which Companies B and G came from Athens County, were in the thick of the fighting. Although made up of still raw recruits, the 53d was ordered to Pittsburg Landing on the middle Tennessee. The men of the 53d received arms en route at Paducah; when they arrived at Pittsburg Landing, many of them had never fired their muskets. On April 6, 1862, the Union forces were attacked by Confederates under General Albert Sidney Johnston, catching senior Union officers completely off guard. The men of the 53d suddenly found themselves at the focal point of ten rebel regiments—and with two companies away on picket duty, the 53d had but 450 effective men. In the accounts that reached Athens, the rebels were a scant twenty-five steps away before the 53d was even aware of the attacking forces. In the ensuing confusion, Colonel Jesse J. Appler succeeded in forming his men into a line in time to fire two volleys, after which he ordered a retreat, which he led, not stopping himself until he reached the nearby Tennessee River. The second in command, Lt. Colonel Robert A. Fulton of Athens, rallied the men and stood his ground. Appler returned briefly two days later and found Fulton leading the men of the 53d in a bayonet charge, whereupon Appler again absented himself. The attack was the opening of a two-day battle, now generally referred to as Shiloh, in which the Union held firm on the first day, Sunday, April 6, then went on to force the Confederates to abandon their attack on the second day. At the time the battle was heralded as "the greatest battle ever seen on this continent." It involved in excess of 100,000 men. Surprisingly, the 53d sustained but 17 killed, though 51 were wounded. Colonel Appler was promptly cashiered for his behavior and new officers appointed.

By the end of April 1862, Grant was near Corinth, a major rail center in northeast Mississippi. In the wake of the Confederate defeat at Pittsburg Landing, the 18th moved into northern Alabama; by the 10th of May it was busy pursuing the rebels in the area of Huntsville, Decatur, and Tuscumbia. While there were no pitched battles, each night the pickets were attacked—"an exciting time." But, then, as General Buell drove the main force of the rebels away from the Corinth area, the 18th OVI found itself in the path of this much larger Confederate force and scrambled to get out of the way. "Dunc" Huling thought his officers "unnecessarily" scared. On occasion, while on picket duty Huling got a chance to take a shot at a civilian slipping along. While daytime picket duty afforded time to fish, to look for curiosities, and to write letters, there was risk. In early May, twenty-nine members of his company were captured by the rebels. Often he was dog-tired from the extensive moving from place to place. In June Huling's unit covered 412 miles.

In July 1862, the 18th OVI was again ordered back to Tennessee because of the pillaging by the two Illinois units with which it was brigaded. Again it was detailed to guard the rail lines, and Huling complained: ". . . this camp is full of lice and fleas, dirty, dirty, dirty." He found sleep almost impossible because of the fleas. To this was added the annoyance of "mosquitos and gnats." Nor was this a brief flare up. The 13th of December 1862, he wrote, was "the day we got cabbage [lice] in our soup."

Ironically, banishment to Tennessee pushed the 18th OVI into combat. Still moving frequently, the unit was variously posted at Tullahoma, Manchester, and Nashville during the late summer and the early fall. Experiencing chills and fever, possibly malaria, Huling was hospitalized for a time in Nashville. Then in November, as General William S. Rosecrans relieved General Buell, the 18th was posted to guard the southern approaches to Nashville. Following a big oyster supper on Christmas night, the oysters being purchased for the occasion, the unit moved out at 7 A.M. the next day—without knapsacks, tents, or rations. The overcast sky shortly gave way to a heavy, prolonged rain. After three days on the march, the 18th OVI neared Murfreesboro, where it entered its first major battle, Stone's River. The 3d OVI, having been reorganized for three years' service and having spent a half year in West Virginia, likewise found itself at Stone's River. At stake was control of the rail line between Nashville and Chattanooga. While General Rosecrans was searching for General Braxton Bragg, it was Bragg who launched "a series of furious assaults" on the Union forces.

Huling sensed that a battle of import was imminent. His diary entry for December 29, 1862, is headed "Camp on battlefield before Murfreesboro." He had been deployed as a skirmisher during the day and had fired at rebel pickets; the Union artillery had "throwed a few shells" at the rebels which had caused them to "skedaddle"; and he had got in "a shot now and then." But the battle was still ahead. The next morning he found himself under fire; the men to his right and left fell. "The bullets whistled around." Taking shelter behind some rails, he loaded his rifle while lying on his back, rolling over and "firing while lying on my belly." Relieved after several hours, he had "a supper of crackers, coffee and broiled bacon." The next day, December 31st, he saw "something of what soldiering is as regards the fighting part." The 18th was under fire for six hours, fighting "as hard as troops could fight." At day's end, Huling thought the Union forces had "fought one of the hardest fights probably of the campaign." The 18th had sustained 15 or 20 killed and wounded, "a sad day." "Tired and hungry," he ended the day but noted, "we will go into it [battle] again if needed tomorrow."

In fact, for the Union, the day had been a failure. Only on the insistence of Generals Thomas and Sheridan did the Union not break off and abandon the field to the rebels. On Friday, January 2, the battle was resumed, and T. R. Stanley, now in command of the 29th Brigade, led his men in orderly, deliberate fashion across Stone's River, took position, and awaited a charge by the forces of the Confederate general, John Breckinridge. Stanley's men withstood the rebel charge, then took the offensive and forced Breckinridge's forces to flee, "panic stricken." This was a far bloodier affair than the assault of the 31st. The 18th OVI lost 4 officers and 32 enlisted men killed and 147 officers and men wounded, including Johnson Welch and A. W. S. Minear. As the Confederates retreated towards Chattanooga, General Rosecrans telegraphed President Lincoln: "We have fought the greatest battle of the war and are victorious." Rosecrans overstated the case, but, for the moment, the battle ended the Confederate threat to Union control of the middle Tennessee and the Cumberland Plateau. Although far fewer troops were involved than at Pittsburg Landing, the casualties were comparable.

In 1863 several Athens units were involved in search and destroy raids. During the time when John Hunt Morgan's Confederate raiders were terrorizing Ohio, the

7th OVC, a party of 900, conducted an extensive search and destroy raid in the Cumberland and Tennessee valleys of eastern Tennessee. At one point, it set fire to a 1,200-foot-long railroad bridge. As it burned, "the whole heavens seemed a glow of fire and the river beneath seemed gold." Passing through New Market had different rewards, for the town was "abounding with pretty girls, who were for the Union." The raid was exhausting, the men falling asleep at times in their saddles. Half the horses died. The men ran out of rations, and as their shoes wore out, many either went barefooted or wrapped their feet in strips of blanket. Later in the year, near Jonesboro, Tennessee, they were attacked at daybreak, and almost surrounded; they engaged in "the most disastrous" fight they had been in, losing everything—their "teams, blankets, arms, and one battery of artillery."

The men of the 3d OVI also enjoyed the excitement of a search and destroy raid that led them from Murfreesboro, Tennessee, across northern Alabama toward the Confederate arsenal at Rome, Georgia. This operation, which included men from four regiments, began in early April 1863 and ended disastrously in early May. Although "poorly mounted on unbroken and unshod mules," the early stages of the campaign went well as the men went cross-country "recruiting" mules and livestock in behalf of Fort Henry. At the end of April, rebels under Confederate General Roddy began to engage the Union forces. At this point, some forty miles from Rome, an elite group of fifty men from each of the four regiments was detatched "to make all possible speed" to Rome where it was to destroy the Rome Mountain Iron Works. Challenged by Confederate guards at the Coosa River crossing, the men conned the guards into ferrying them across the river whereupon they took the guards prisoners, then in a night march covered the remaining twenty miles to Rome. There they destroyed "an extensive manufactory of shot, shell, and cannon, also a cassion factory." On May 3, their luck ran out as General Nathan Forrest's forces checkmated the daring raiders and forced all four regiments to surrender. In the aftermath, the regimental correspondent complained bitterly that the Confederates had reneged on the surrender terms and had seized "all our blankets, haversacks, canteens, cups and watches, and even money from some of the men." As prisoners, he wrote, "we were treated cruelly and suffered much." By August 1863, a reconstituted 3d OVI was back in business, but it saw no more hard combat, and when its three years' service was up in 1864, it went home to be discharged.

While the Athenians in the 7th OVC were engaged in guerrilla raids in northern Alabama, northwest Georgia, eastern Tennessee, and Kentucky, Athenians in the 4th VVI and 30th OVI were slugging it out at Vicksburg, a vital position indispensable to the control of the Mississippi, a campaign that extended from

March 29 to July 4, 1863. The 4th VVI was involved in two assaults on the Confederate entrenchments. In the assault of May 19, the regiment lost 192 men killed and wounded; in the second assault, three days later, it lost another 31 men killed and wounded. In the same action Captain John L. Mallanee of the 4th VVI was wounded, while T. W. Brewer, the unit's correspondent to the *Messenger,* and Major Arza M. Goodspeed, another senior regimental officer, were killed. Goodspeed, the *Messenger* reported, fell "amid the thunders that rocked" Vicksburg while "gallantly cheering the men on" in a charge. The 30th OVI, after recouping from its adventure at South Mountain and the Antietam bridge, moved to the vicinity of Vicksburg. On the 19th of May, it was in the rear of Vicksburg, and in the battle on the 22d, three of its companies took serious losses. When all his superior officers were killed or wounded, Sergeant "Si" Allen, Co. C, 30th OVI, took command of the remnant of his company and led them in a desperate attack until he, too, was wounded, a wound that cost him his left arm. Before the Confederate capitulation in July, the 30th lost another 61 men and officers.

With General Lee forced to abandon his invasion of Pennsylvania after Gettysburg and the Union in control of the Mississippi River after the fall of Vicksburg, Union attention shifted to the area of Chattanooga, Tennessee. General Rosecrans occupied the city, then moved eastward in pursuit of Bragg's Confederate forces. They clashed September 19 and 20, 1863, on Chickamauga Creek. The 92d OVI found itself in the "white heat" of the fight and the 36th OVI, which had lost one colonel at Antietam, lost another, W. G. Jones, on the field at Chickamauga, one of the 70 members of the regiment killed in action. On the second day of the battle, the 18th OVI made several "brilliant charges" and Captain Charles Grosvenor was recognized for "gallantry and coolness" under fire. However gallant, the rebels smashed the Union's right flank, forcing half of Rosecrans's army to flee the field of battle. Overall each side sustained losses of 28 percent.

Following his victory at Chickamauga Creek, General Bragg began a siege of the Union forces at Chattanooga. In late November General Grant and reinforcements arrived. Again the fighting, particularly at nearby Lookout Mountain and Missionary Ridge, was costly. The 73d OVI, having been transferred to the Army of the Cumberland after Gettysburg, lost 65 men out of 200 at Lookout Mountain. In a twenty-minute period, the 92d OVI lost one-third of its officers and a tenth of its enlisted personnel. The 36th, in tackling Missionary Ridge, lost 83 killed and wounded. Bragg's siege broken, his troops fled in disorder to Dalton, Georgia. The 4th VVI, despite heavy losses at Chattanooga, formed part of the pursuing party.

At the end of 1863, while General Sherman was moving the greater part of his forces to Chattanooga, the 53d OVI was assigned to rebuilding the rail lines and bridges between Columbia, Tennessee, and Huntsville, Alabama, to expedite the flow of supplies to his forces.

As spring came in 1864, William T. Sherman, who had command of the Union forces, set in motion a four-month-long campaign to take Atlanta. The 18th, 30th, 53d, 61st, 73d, and 92d all had a role. The campaign entailed a series of battles, including Dalton, Reasca, Kennesaw Mountain, and Peachtree Creek. The 30th was under fire at Kennesaw Mountain; the 61st engaged in a series of skirmishes and minor engagements, but found Peachtree Creek to be "one of the most desperate" of the war. So, too, the 73d found Peachtree Creek the first battle in which it was faced with repelling an enemy in an open field; the 73d charged. By the time the 30th OVI reached Atlanta in September, it had been under fire 103 of the previous 120 days. Finally, the 92d rejoined Sherman's army in time to participate in the taking of Atlanta. At this point, as experienced soldiers, their morale restored, Sherman's forces moved without tents or shelters of any kind, and were seldom "out of sound of artillery or musketry."

Charles Townsend of the 30th Regiment, writing to the *Messenger* from Marietta, Georgia, in mid-August 1864, before Atlanta fell, commented that no campaign "has been so laborious, exhausting, and perilous. With hard bread, side meat, coffee and sugar unvaried; untented and only bedded with a blanket, we have found this campaign to be the work of *men*. Yet all these privations have [been] only the stern seasoning of battle. Men go sternly in, when ordered, but it is only in obedience to the call of country and duty. The veteran is satiated with glory. It must now cover so many; it is but a thin robe, scarcely a veil, a tender fabric soon worn out." He went on to note that the Army of the Tennessee had been repulsed at Dallas, had made the charge at Kennesaw Mountain, and now was on the eve of another battle. The sick and wounded had been evacuated from the field hospitals. It was within a stone's throw of the rebels.

The war weariness that marked the comments of Charles Townsend's report from the 30th OVI at Marietta, Georgia, was echoed, albeit briefly, by John H. Lair, surgeon of the 53d OVI. This regiment, which had sustained the initial attack at Pittsburg Landing, had subsequently been at Chickamauga and Chattanooga and now was at Kennesaw Mountain. The 53d had just engaged in a hard-fought, hand-to-hand battle in which there had been no time to reload or to fix bayonets. Rather it had clubbed its attackers. Jonathan Cross of Athens was among the casualties. Lair characterized the men as "watch-worn and weary."

The campaign for Atlanta cost the Union over 30,000 dead, wounded, and missing. By contrast, for the Union, the "March to the Sea" was a romp. The 73d

OVI fired nary a shot between Atlanta and Savannah. The 92d OVI was at Milledgeville on Thanksgiving Day and in Savannah on Christmas. Sherman's march brought devastation to the rebels as the Union forces lived off the land.

Toward the end of 1864 and during early 1865, there was a break of sorts in the war. The three-year enlistment periods for several regiments were up. Many troops re-enlisted, regiments were reorganized, and the veterans got a month's furlough. The Ohio 18th, which was reorganized in November 1864, emerged with Charles Grosvenor, now a lieutenant colonel, as its commander, and it consolidated detachments of the 1st, 2d, 18th, 24th, and 35th regiments. The 73d OVI, while in Athens in early 1864, filled its ranks with new recruits to return with a regiment of 318 men total. The 30th OVI on reorganizing as a veteran regiment claimed 315 men.

At the end of 1864, as Sherman's forces were marching toward Savannah, General John Hood, with a force of 22,000 men, threatened the Union's hold on Nashville in north central Tennessee. In the early stages of Hood's operation, the 92d OVI had been part of a force pursuing Hood, but it was recalled and dispatched to Atlanta and the march to the sea. Charles Grosvenor and the Ohio 18th, however, were participants in the battle of Nashville in December. In a skirmish in early December, his brother, Edward Grosvenor, was killed. In the major battle on the 16th of December, the 18th OVI lost 4 of its 7 officers and a total of 75 killed and wounded from a force of less than 200. Subsequently, the 18th pursued General Hood to Huntsville and then assisted in the capture of Decatur and Tuscumbia. Returning to Chattanooga, Grosvenor was given the temporary rank of brigadier general.

Sherman's forces devoted much of January 1865 to recouping and re-equipping. In early February, the various regiments turned north, crossing into South Carolina and continuing their campaign of destruction—tearing up the railroads, "utterly destroying everything valuable to the enemy." The march took the 92d through storms and floods, through swamps and pine barrens. April found several of the regiments in the vicinity of Goldsboro, North Carolina, where they halted as the war ended.

ATHENS COLORED TROOPS

Less well known than the two black regiments from Massachusetts, the 5th U.S. Colored Regiment from Ohio made its mark. Company C hailed from Athens and Ross counties, recruited for the most part by Milton M. Holland, its sergeant major. The company received its colors on the Athens courthouse steps in 1863. The prospects for colored troops at the time were grim. Many in the North doubted the wisdom of using blacks in combat; the rebels reportedly threatened colored troops with death, if captured. For its part, the *Messenger* rejoiced at the policy of recruiting blacks: "the hard hand of prejudice has been forced open by the brave deeds and suffering nobly borne."

Sergeant Major Holland was one of the more remarkable Athenians in the Civil War. Born in slavery in Texas, he was sent to Ohio in the late 1850s when still in his teens. He attended the public colored school in Albany, and for a time was a servant in Nelson Van Vorhes' household. Although Holland had attempted to enlist in the Union Army in 1861, he was rejected because of his race. In 1863, the Army reversed itself and admitted Negro troops into the enlisted ranks. On his own, Holland recruited some 149 blacks, intending to lead them into one of the Massachusetts regiments. However, he finally yielded to the persuasion of John Mercer Langston, the recruiter for the 5th USCT.

During the winter of 1863–64, the 5th USCT conducted raids through Virginia and North Carolina, "liberating slaves of both loyal and disloyal masters" and confiscating the property of those who "neglected" to take an oath of loyalty to the Union. The regiment endured fatiguing marches and incessant rain, the men "sleeping" while marching. In April 1864, the 5th was transported up the James River to within a dozen miles of Richmond, then shifted to Petersburg. Its moment of glory, Holland's moment of distinction, came September 29, 1864, in the Battle of Chaffin's Farm. Holland's regiment was part of the unique 18th Army Corps, a unit with both white and colored troops. When, in an assault on Fort Gibson, the white troops faltered, panicked, and ran, Holland rallied Company C. With all of the commissioned officers dead or disabled, Holland took command and "alone and unsupported continued in hand-to-hand combat." His men captured two Confederate forts that day. Subsequently, Holland received the Congressional Medal of Honor.

The war over, Holland returned to Athens and worked for a time as a shoemaker. At the same time, John Mercer Langston, having gone to Washington, D. C., became head of the Howard University Law School. This time, Langston bid Holland to come to Washington, where he enrolled in the new law school. He went on to a distinguished career as an attorney and businessman in the nation's capital.

APPOMATTOX COURT HOUSE

For the 116th Regiment, the end of the war had a story-book ending. After over two years of alternately parrying with bushwhackers in West Virginia and sparring with rebel forces in the Shenandoah Valley, the 116th was transferred to the Army of the James. April 1, 1865, found the regiment storming an outpost of the rebel defenses at Petersburg. In a bayonet charge and hand-to-hand combat with clubbed muskets, the 116th lost 15 men killed and 33 wounded. This was only the first of nine grueling days of soldiering. While on picket the night of April 2, it discovered Fort Lee deserted and occupied it; on the next day, General Lee abandoned Petersburg, and the 116th was one of the Union regiments under General Sheridan sent in hot pursuit to intercept him. A series of day-long marches, part of the time in steady rain, followed. On April 8, the men were on the line of march from 3 A.M. to 11 P.M., covering 38 miles and stopping at Appomattox Court House. On the fateful 9th, the 116th was up and in line of battle at 4 A.M. At this point, George Armstrong Custer's cavalry, equally tired, had interposed itself across Lee's escape route, and the 116th was among the infantry units called on to relieve the cavalry. With Lee's men dispersed in a woods on its front, the left wing of the 116th, under fire by the rebels, began advancing across the open field that separated the two armies. At this point, as T. F. Wildes tells it, "out of the enemy's line, comes a rider, bound on bound, bearing a white flag of truce, to ask time to consummate the surrender." The firing stopped; the advance stopped. Shortly the meaning became clear. The war was over.

Athens celebrated Lee's surrender. Thanks to the telegraph, the news came immediately and, on April 14, the town celebrated. The next day, with the news of Lincoln's assassination, the town was "sunken in gloom." The troops did not return immediately. Most were on three years' service, and they had to await release first from federal service, then by Ohio authorities. Unit by unit they drifted back during the summer and fall. Finally in August 1866, the county tendered a great barbecue on the College Green for the returned veterans. Fifteen thousand persons attended.

In after years when recalling Athens County's war record, even thirty and forty years later, local historians remembered "the terrible four years." They recalled with pride "the promptness and the zeal" of the 2,600 Athens County men who volunteered, their effort to preserve the Union, to suppress the rebellion. But no word was uttered as to the cost in dead and wounded. One figure lists 1,000 dead and wounded, 40 percent of the men who served. At most, the community could acknowledge the individual who lost an arm, who spent time at Libby Prison, who returned home broken in health. But in 1865 the community was traumatized by its losses; it remained traumatized.

ON THE HOME FRONT

If the war had traumatized the soldiers in the field, so it affected the men and women left at home. Throughout the war, there was the problem of supporting the boys in the service, especially those who were sick or injured. There were problems of filling in for those who were away. And in the middle of everything else, the intrusion of General John Hunt Morgan and his Confederate raiders brought the war into Athens County. So, too, those who supported the Union had to come to grips with the Peace Democrats, the Copperheads, and Butternuts. And finally, there was the impact of the war on the university.

Soldiers' Aid Society

As the war dragged into the last months of its first year, T. F. Wildes, editor of the *Messenger*, called for the formation of a Soldiers' Aid Society (SAS) to supply bandages and other medical supplies that the Union Army seemed unable to provide. Such organizations had sprung up in the neighboring townships during the fall of 1861. Indeed the first Soldiers' Aid Society had been organized in Cleveland the day that Lincoln first called for volunteers.

Athenians responded promptly enough to editor Wildes's plea. On January 29, 1862, an organizational meeting at the Presbyterian Church chose the editor's wife, Mrs. L. M. Wildes, as president, while other women of the local establishment were named to other offices and committees. Within a few days, the SAS had packed and shipped two boxes, one of fruit and wines to the hospitalized; the other, a carton of sheets, shirts, and hospital goods. In sending the supplies, the SAS made clear that the goods were for the use of all regiments, not just those companies from Athens.

The SAS was well received. For its part, Coolville made it loud and clear that it had beaten Athens to the punch, having organized its SAS in October 1861, and as a token of its good feeling, it remitted the residue of its funds, $3.00, to be used by the Athens group. Mr. Bennett, a "daguerreian artist," [*sic*] agreed to donate to the Athens SAS ten cents for each thirty-five-cent picture ordered from him. And, in a burst of enthusiasm, the ladies set about hosting a Washington's Birthday Festival—a supper featuring tableaux, music, and performers in costume—for fifty cents per head. The response was enthusiastic; between 400 and 500 persons attended, and the SAS netted $108. In a society isolated from the bright lights of urban centers such as Cincinnati, the festival gave village women the chance to indulge in dressing up in costumes, including Swiss toy girls, Little Red Riding Hood, a "Gypsey," Polish and Turkish ladies. One woman even donned a bloomer costume.

Thereafter, the SAS settled into a routine. Meetings were held weekly at the homes of members. The women generally rolled bandages, packed lint (for surgical use), and made shirts or other clothing. In a notice of June 12, 1862, the women were told that nearly 100 yards of material was on hand to make up into clothes. A notice of August 27, 1863, indicated a need for shirts and drawers for the sick and wounded. Women were needed to cut and baste for a sewing machine operator who would be on hand. As the work became routine and the war dragged on, attendance dropped off, and in December 1863, editor Jesse Van Law complained that the work of the SAS had fallen too much in the hands of a "limited number."

Stimulated by the examples of the Great Western Sanitary Fair of Chicago and a similar fair in Cincinnati, SAS activities soared to a new high. An Athens fair, scheduled for the Christmas season of 1863, was pitched to "minister to the comfort" of soldiers "with no mother's or sisters' hand to smooth their pillows nor sympathizing hearts to cheer and comfort them in their hours of anguish and sorrow." The fair called forth a wide variety of contributions and skills. While some women made twenty large and beautiful cakes "tastefully ornamented" and each named for a prominent American, others contributed canned fruit, dried fruits and berries, pickles, catsup, and apple butter. Still others produced shirts, socks, drawers, quilts, and pillows. The several townships held their own fairs. Goods that could be used by the soldiers were shipped to them; other goods were auctioned. The county's effort produced $868.64 in cash and $1,026.80 in goods, slightly more than half coming from the village.

By midsummer 1864, the fourth summer of the war, enthusiasm had again waned. While Governor Brough was calling for more hospital supplies, Jesse Van Law expressed his fears that the women were burned out. Continuing to provide support, the *Messenger* noted that clean linen, cotton rags, and lint were needed. It also called for yarn for a pair of socks or linen for a towel, as well as packages of dried fruit. Dried blackberries were especially sought for their presumed medicinal value. In September, Mrs. E. D. Stewart, while acknowledging the receipt of valuable hospital supplies, urged: "Let no one withhold her mite." She asked for good reading materials, "Something cheerful and cultivated to occupy the weary hours in hospital."

Despite the goodwill with which folks at home participated in the Soldiers' Aid Society, the work generated some complaints in the field. The first shipment of goods by the Athens SAS was sent via Columbus, where it was diverted from the 18th OVI, whose plight had prompted the formation of the SAS. Bad feeling developed between members of the 73d and the 75th OVI over whether they had received their fair share of clothing sent by the Albany SAS. In time, the SAS and the units in the field worked out a routine for the delivery of supplies, but complaints never completely disappeared. Writing in July 1864, A. B. Monahan, surgeon to the 63d OVI, attributed the problems to dishonest agents of the SAS in the North. But, he assured the people at home, "on every battlefield, and at every Hospital," the supplies were there and the supplies were "honestly dealt out to the wounded and sick."

MORGAN'S RAID

In July 1863, John Hunt Morgan, a Confederate cavalry man, brought the war to Athens County. To Athenians who read the *Messenger* closely, Morgan was already well known. In spring 1862, Morgan had captured 115 members of the 18th OVI at Pulaski, Tennessee, and in July of that year Athenians in the 74th OVI spent five days on a wild goose chase pursuing Morgan and his troopers across northern Tennessee and into Kentucky, never coming closer than thirty miles of its quarry. In late winter 1862–63, Morgan was again raiding Union-occupied areas of Tennessee. Always in need of replacements for his unit, he was dubbed "the great horse thief."

In July 1863, Morgan and his men crossed the Ohio River below New Albany, Indiana, and on reaching the railroad at Salem, Indiana, tore up tracks and burned railroad buildings before turning eastward. By July 14, Morgan's force had entered Ohio, cutting the Miami Railroad below Loveland. Proceeding eastward, Morgan skipped recrossing the Ohio to Maysville, Kentucky, raising the possibility of his recrossing the Ohio at Gallipolis, Guyandotte, or Pomeroy. At this time Morgan's force split into several detachments.

Alarmed, Athens men still at home mobilized on July 17; 250 volunteer militiamen assembled and were transported by wagon to Albany en route to Wilkesville, where it was assumed that Morgan was encamped. The officers, Athens respectability, included Major de Steiguer, Major E. A. Guthrie, Captain J. M. Dana, and

Captain J. G. Stedman. At Hebbardsville, one wagon train stopped briefly to borrow quilts for the "college-bred gentlemen" to protect them from the night air. Two miles beyond Albany, the Athens contingent detrained, and began its march toward Wilkesville "in the dim starlight" to the accompaniment of the "measured tramp," an occasional clink of bayonets, and the sound of barking dogs. By 10 A.M., it halted at Harrisonville, awaiting the arrival of Colonel Gilmore's force of Chillicothe volunteers. At this point, reports reached the party that Morgan was at Rutland, six miles or so to the south.

As it turned out, Colonel Gilmore had never been ordered to Wilkesville. By 1 P.M., the Athens unit again took the road southward, then was halted, ordered to about face and march toward Athens. The men were furious and were mollified only when their officers reported to them that the latest intelligence indicated that Morgan was not at Wilkesville but on the far side of Athens and that they were needed to defend their homes.

In fact, the elusive Morgan was many places. On July 18, he was reported both at Rutland and in Jackson County. On Sunday the nineteenth, he showed up at Portland and Buffington Island and was halfway across the Ohio River when federal gunboats appeared. This same day another party of Morgan's men sought to cross to the West Virginia side of the Ohio River at Bellville; dispersed, it then approached Hockingport. Here the locals fell out armed with "muskets, shotguns, rifles, revolvers, and old pistols," "determined to halt the robbers." While a crossing of the Ohio was interdicted, Morgan escaped, having lost forty men and sixty horses.

As Morgan's men headed for Hockingport, Fanny Cooley hid her horses in the woods, and as Morgan's party passed nearby, she reported, his men seized horses, looted houses, broke dishes, and turned animals out into the fields of rye. From dark to ten P.M., she heard their "tramp, crash, thunder." She escaped without loss, but venting her anger, she expressed hope that Morgan and his men would be "put in some prison like Libby"; then she added, "I needn't wish that for there's no such dirty lousey hole as that in these United States."

A few of Morgan's men reached the West Virginia shore, but 800 of his force surrendered, while the remaining group made good its escape. Morgan made his way to Harrisonville, then turned south to Cheshire, where again a federal "gunboat" on the Ohio blocked his crossing, and another 1,020 of his men surrendered. Now desperate, the guerrilla leader headed first for Gallipolis on Monday evening, July 20, but on Wednesday the twenty-second he crossed the M & C railroad in Vinton County and by noon was in Nelsonville. The people of Nelsonville seemed unaware of Morgan's presence in the area until his troops were within a mile of the village. The populace was "in wild confusion." Shortly some 660 to 800 troopers poured into the village from all directions. Hungry, the men demanded to be fed. "Never," the *Messenger* reported, was "a meal given more grudgingly." While Morgan's men, "dirty and ragged," seemed "the hardest set of people we ever looked upon," the unwelcome guests "behaved very civilly," which is to say their depredations were directed at property, not people.

As Morgan departed Nelsonville two hours later, time was running out. He remained elusive, but his men and horses were exhausted. Although the Nelsonville raid occurred mid-week, at the end of the week he was north of Steubenville where at last a Michigan cavalry unit intercepted his party, killing 20 to 30 of his men, wounding another 50, and taking 200 prisoners. Shortly afterward, General J. H. Schackford captured Morgan and the remaining 400 men of his command. Subsequently Morgan was incarcerated in the Ohio State penitentiary.

Neither Morgan nor any other Confederate ever again threatened the tranquility of Athens. Yet in a sense, Morgan had the last word. On November 26, 1863, "the notorious rebel," "the great horse thief," escaped the Ohio penitentiary together with six of his companions.

COPPERHEADS AND BUTTERNUTS

The war had much impact on the political scene. Regardless of what candidates sought office, debate centered on the future role of Negro Americans and controversy swirled about those opposed to the war, the Copperheads and Butternuts.

Athenians' attitudes toward Negro Americans were ambivalent. While a number of Athenians had been active in the abolition movement and had participated in the Underground Railroad, few blacks had made their homes in Athens village. Rather clearly, Athenians were not of one mind. T. F. Wildes, the Canadian-born editor of the *Messenger*, was a committed Republican who as early as March 1862 called for the compensated, gradual emancipation of slaves and expressed his belief that "a large majority" would approve. A month later, Congressman William P. Cutler, speaking in Athens, argued that it was "the right and duty of Congress to destroy slavery." Pointing to the constitutional provision that no person shall be "deprived of liberty without due process of law," he went on to argue that when states adopted legislation providing that the legal status of the child follows the condition of the mother, to make slaves of the children born of slave mothers, the states were negating a constitutional guarantee. Cutler ardently supported the Confiscation Bill authorizing the president to free those slaves liberated by federal forces. Through 1862, the opposition to slavery was abstract.

The arguments gradually took on a utilitarian character. In an item termed: "What Generals Say on the Negro Question," editor Wildes quoted General Dumont, who pointed out that planters could go off to war without imposing a great economic burden on their wives because the slaves whom they left behind continued to produce crops. Similarly, General Lew Wallace added his testimony that slaves kept southern fields in cultivation, bolstering the economy of the Confederates. Taking a different tack, Jesse Van Law, who took over the *Messenger* in 1862, refuted the conventional wisdom that Negroes were "a cowardly race and fit only for slaves." In a long editorial he pointed to the examples of slaves who had stood up to be counted: Toussaint L'Ouverture, the liberator of Haiti; the anonymous slaves who joined John Brown at Harpers Ferry; and Nat Turner, who led the uprising of 1831. Presumably, slaves could assist the Union in defeating the Confederacy and in freeing themselves from bondage. After Lincoln's Emancipation Proclamation, "A Soldier Boy," a member of the 114th OVI, wrote the *Messenger* endorsing the Proclamation as "a necessity, a war policy, one that is endorsed almost unanimously by the soldier boys."

Support of Negro emancipation was not unanimous, however. A. W. and E. A. Bratton, Democrats and publishers of the nearby *Vinton Democrat,* were distressed by the influx of Negroes into eastern Vinton County, that is, the area adjacent to Albany. Further evidence of hostility was manifested by an Ohio militia officer who, contrary to regulations, sold a free colored servant of his organization into slavery, a practice that was apparently not unprecedented. Found out, the officer was discharged with loss of pay and allowances.

Most forthright in objecting to the emancipation of the blacks was Colonel R. E. Constable, a Maryland-born Democrat and a perennial officeholder of Athens. Constable was willing enough to support the war to preserve the Union, but he drew the line at using the war to free the slaves. He dreaded the social and economic consequences of emancipation. Speaking at a Fourth of July celebration at Amesville in 1862, Constable drew "a vivid picture of turning the 'dirty, NASTY, BLACK NIGGERS' *loose* (!!!) *amongst us.*" They would "come in contact with our laborers" and "*marry our daughters.*" A determined racist, Constable suggested that if the blacks were freed, South Carolina should be fenced in and once all the blacks were assembled there, one should "sink it to hell." A year later, Nathan Elliott, then in the Union army at La Grange, Tennessee, wrote home protesting the Emancipation Proclamation. He "didn't enlist to fight to free the Niggers." Elliott and Constable were not isolated individuals. Lieutenant Colonel Wildes attributed the high level of desertion by members of the 116th OVI to the unwillingness of the men to fight in support of emancipation of the slaves.

At the political level, the Republicans used the war to further their own ends. Athens supported Lincoln in the 1860 election. Reflecting his Republican affiliation, editor Wildes avoided criticism of the Lincoln administration, but he did battle with the editors of the Democratic press at McArthur, Logan, and Marietta. His attacks were often personal. The editor of the *Vinton Democrat*, Wildes charged, was "an ignoramus of the most contemptible pattern" and his paper was a "dirty squally ungrammatical sheet."

The political climate in Athens favored the Republicans who, wrapping themselves in the Union flag, attempted to draw everyone into the ranks in the name of patriotism. To do so, they put party labels aside in favor of a non-partisan Union Party. So long as they could represent the war as an "effort to preserve the Union," they were tolerably successful. In July 1862, they scheduled a "Grand Rally for the Union" with speeches by the most eloquent of the party faithful—Judge Whitman, Samuel Galloway, Thomas Ewing, and William P. Cutler. Significantly, the Committee of Arrangements included both Thomas F. Wildes, a committed Republican, along with William Reed Golden, an equally committed Democrat. The thrust of the rally was that: "The Country you love is in danger of destruction at traitor's hands and foreign foes to freedom and Republics."

The adversaries were the "Copperheads" and "Butternuts." Named for one of the two poisonous snakes of the state, the Copperheads were charged with fomenting "disention [*sic*] and dissatisfaction in the army and rebellion against the law at the North." They put the soldiers' lives at additional risk. In editor Van Law's judgment, those Copperheads in the military ought to be shot or drummed out of the service, their heads shaved and then branded on the cheek with a "D." Certainly, by this time, numerous militiamen, tired of the service, had deserted. The "Butternuts," an alternative label for the Copperheads, were described as "pestilent traitors" who raised the "Sesesh" flag of Jefferson Davis, threatening to murder Union men and resist the draft.

As the war ground on, patience with the Copperheads at home wore thin. Back on active duty, Leonard Cooley told his wife the Copperheads ought to behave, for "their time is short," and when Union soldiers get home, the Copperheads "will have to keep dark and low, to [*sic*]." The Cooley correspondence is replete with snide asides about relatives and neighbors thought to harbor "sesesh" sentiments or to favor Clement Vallandigham, the most prominent Copperhead in the nation. Fanny pointed to a neighbor's son who, having enlisted, refused to visit his father who was "sesesh." She approved the dismissal of local schoolteachers who espoused secessionist sympathies. She noted, too, that members of the 116th OVI had sent valentines in 1864 to local Copperheads with "a great picture of a copperhead with a man's head." While Athenians ultimately took great pride that the county had never had to resort to the draft to raise its quota of men, some Athens-area people, like Fanny Cooley, hoped the draft would be employed, to force the Peace Democrats and especially the Copperheads and Butternuts into the military service. Indeed, much of the animus directed at the Copperheads and Peace Democrats was due to the fact that they were staying at home out of harm's way and enjoying a degree of prosperity, while the Unionists put their lives and fortunes at risk.

For their part, the local Democrats, with an inner circle consisting of William Reed Golden, R. A. Constable, W. M. Hastings, A. Lewis, J. C. Wheeler, D. Walker, and B. B. Sheffield, stuck to their principles. While they renounced secession as "a miserable heresy" and gave thanks to the volunteer soldiers, they objected to converting the war into a crusade to free the slaves. They pledged themselves to "the Constitution as it is, and the Union as it was. . . ." Supporting the writ of habeas corpus, they objected to the arrest of Vallandigham without a warrant issued on probable cause. A "great Democratic Meeting" in Athens in September 1863 provoked a confrontation. First, local abolitionists sought to prevent the Democrats from speaking, then a scuffle developed over the use of a "splendid silk flag." Originally purchased by ladies of Athens for use by a state militia unit, the flag had become a subject of controversy when its use at a funeral service for Captain Columbus Golden, the first Athenian killed in combat, had been denied, but now was used in a street parade by the Vallandigham group. Feelings ran high, and in October 1863, editor Van Law reported that "boys" had hoisted the signs of "Golden" and "Constable" up a tree, having painted the word "traitor" under their names. In many ways, it was this bitter hostility between Unionist and Peace Democrat, between Unionist and Copperhead or Butternut that divided friends and families at home that constituted the civil war, not the military War between the States.

Ultimately the Unionists prevailed. In 1864 in a face-off between John Brough, the Union candidate for governor, and Clement Vallandigham, the Democrat, Brough easily outpaced his opponent by a margin of better than 2.5 to 1. Indeed, Vallandigham carried but one township in the county, York, by 181 to 169. In Athens, the vote was 424 to 76, a 6 to 1 margin for the Union candidate.

In the course of the war, the Unionists formed the Union League, a secret society whose members were sworn "to support the Constitution and the Government of the United States against its foes, either domestic or foreign, to bear true faith and allegiance and fealty to the same."

There was hostility of another kind. In spring 1865, the M & C ran into an embarrassing problem that called for the intervention of the Ohio militia and contributed to Athens lore: the Affair Currier. At issue was a "shoo-fly," a temporary bypass around the hill on which the town sits, a rail line that was to be replaced by a tunnel under the West State Street Cemetery. The railroad, however, failed to reckon with the irate women of the Currier family who took exception to the road crossing their farm near the present-day site of Morton Math Building. When the railroad began condemnation proceedings, the women, all five of them, blocked the track, piling up rails, ties, and brush. Failing to get the women to desist, Sheriff J. M. Johnson turned for help to General Hooker of the Ohio Department of the Army, who sent his provost marshal to Athens on a special train.

When the train carrying the provost marshal approached, Mrs. Adaline Currier Brown planted herself on the track, the national flag wrapped around her, and defied the engineer to run her down. The train, of course, stopped in time, but the soldiers aboard the train were no help. When they caught sight of Mrs. Brown wrapped in the flag, they began to sing "We'll Rally Round the Flag Boys." A workman seized a rail to remove it, but Mrs. Brown grabbed the other end and clung to it—"an altogether ridiculous scene." Ultimately, the provost marshal had to dispatch a detachment of soldiers to keep the track clear. The shoo-fly remained. The tunnel under West State Cemetery hill was never dug, but the approaches along Brown Avenue and to the east of the cemetery were. As late as the 1890s, the village was filling in the cut east of the cemetery. There was a fine irony in the protest of the Currier women, collectively the richest family in town. The family patriarch, Judge Ebenezer Currier, had been one of the earliest, strongest advocates of a railroad for Athens.

OHIO UNIVERSITY AT WAR

The War between the States proved a time of trial for the university. On April 20, 1861, only five days after Lincoln's call for volunteers, a mass meeting assembled on the campus with speeches by local citizens and military leaders aiming to spur enlistments as well as to raise funds in aid of those who joined. Caught up in the excitement of the moment, students brought forward a resolution declaring: "In this hour of treason and impending anarchy, there is no neutral ground."

Of the university's younger graduates, three of the five seniors of 1860 enlisted, all completing their service as officers, while six of the eleven graduates of 1861 entered the military, two of whom lost their lives—Hugh Townsend at Missionary Ridge and William Wirt Cooper at the Wilderness. As the war heated up, enthusiasm waned so that only one of the nine graduates of 1862 entered the service. As news of the demise of alumni filtered back to Athens, the Athenian and Philomathean societies took note and adopted resolutions commemorating the passing of their fallen friends.

Certainly, the war had a severe impact on college enrollments. Prep school enrollments of youths too young for general military service held up, but college enrollments dropped off to fewer than fifty in 1862–63. The difficulty in maintaining a stable student base was matched by the problems of retaining faculty. Only President Howard remained at his post through the war. William H. Young took leave for military service, returning briefly before leaving to become the U.S. Consul at Karlsruhe, Germany. Both J. G. Blair, the vice president, and R. A. Arthur, a math professor, had a falling out with President Howard in which Blair quit and Arthur was dismissed. William H. Scott left to teach at Indiana University, and E. I. Tappan quit to accept the presidency of Kenyon College.

To stabilize enrollment, President Howard and the trustees urged the state legislature to establish a military department at the university to train students. Despite favorable recommendations by Governors Dennison and Tod, the legislature demurred. Nor was President Howard any more successful in gaining for the university a share of the largess created by the Morrill Act, by which Congress authorized the Land Grant Colleges. A committee of trustees was appointed to collaborate with a similar committee at Miami University. At stake was access to the income that might be derived from a federal grant of 630,000 acres to Ohio for the support of a school of "agriculture and mechanical arts." On the advice of the state auditor that such a school would be a burden to the state, the state legislature rejected the grant in 1863. A year later in response to the urgings of the State Board of Agriculture, the general assembly reversed itself and began thinking in terms of creating a separate college of agriculture and the mechanical arts. The long and short of the matter was that the general assembly did not take Ohio University seriously as a state institution. In part, the university's public identification with the Ohio Conference of the Methodist Church undermined the university's claim to tax support. Ultimately, the legislature founded Ohio State College of Agriculture at Columbus. The question of providing regular support for the operating expenses of Ohio and Miami universities was put off.

As an increasing number of militiamen finished their enlistments, both the university trustees and the general assembly began to ponder this pool of potential college students. In 1863, with underutilized facilities, the university's trustees offered free tuition to wounded veterans. Then, early in 1864, the general assembly directed both Ohio and Miami universities to admit tuition-free those honorably discharged veterans who had enlisted as minors. They were to receive one month of free tuition for each month of service prior to their 21st birthday. The program worked to the extent that in 1865–66, Ohio enrolled 70 veterans. On the other hand, the total of 243 students filled all available housing and provoked much discontent. And, of course, while the veterans generated income for room rentals and filled classrooms, the veterans—30 percent of the total student population—generated not a cent of operating income for the university. Only in 1866 did the legislature reimburse the colleges for the tuition of such veterans and then only for those attending in 1866 and 1867.

At war's end, the university had survived. The classrooms were again filled but in circumstances that created "customer" discontent. Basic problems, the lack of a stable faculty and the ongoing search for a stable financial base, continued. Solomon Howard had his work cut out for what would be his last years at Ohio.

7

Postwar Athens to 1870

As THE SOLDIERS returned home, the village adjusted to peacetime routines. The war had propelled a handful of men into public roles. The university faced a surge of veteran enrollments, then settled into the familiar rhythms of academe. The Black community found itself much changed by the war, while the church scene was altered more by the coming of the railroads than by the war per se. The community's way of earning a living in 1870 provides a measure of the ways in which the village had changed in the course of two decades.

PUBLIC FIGURES

The war years made public figures of several Athens men. One of those was "rough, tough" John Brough, one-time compositor for the Athens *Mirror* and a graduate of Ohio University. Although he had left Athens for Cleveland and later Columbus, Brough had retained ties with the village, having married Achsah Pruden (sister of Samuel B. Pruden), and serving as a trustee of Ohio University. Republicans found a speech he made in June 1863 in support of the Union so moving that they picked him as their gubernatorial candidate for the fall 1863 election. Brough defeated his opponent, Clement Vallandigham, by 100,000 votes, a margin not surpassed for forty years.

Military service itself brought fame to a number of Athenians. The war lasted long enough that even those who entered as buck privates or as junior officers might, through demonstrated competence and some luck, emerge as captains, majors, and colonels, or, in a few cases, as generals, titles they would savor the rest of their lives. General Grosvenor resumed the practice of law. Captain Townsend and General Van Vorhes went off to law school and then, having been admitted to the bar, began the practice of law. Major Jewett read law with his father, then entered legal practice with Rudolph de Steiguer. The affable Josiah "Si" Allen—a disabled veteran, a hero at Vicksburg, and among the longest-lived survivors of the Civil War—held a series of public sector jobs in the course of a long career..

In the political turmoil that marked Andrew Johnson's presidency, Athenians with long memories could find a local connection. On taking office, President Johnson had fired Attorney General Edwin Stanton and replaced him with Henry Stanbery, one of the circuit-riding attorneys who in the mid-1820s had argued his first case in Athens. When Johnson was impeached and brought to trial before the United States Senate, Stanbery, having resigned as attorney general, was Johnson's personal attorney.

CHANGING TIMES

As the decade of the 1860s wound down, there were several signs of the shape of things to come. On the domestic front, the sewing machine made its appearance. Henry Pollard, agent for the Singer machine, claimed: "I can learn any lady to sew successfully in 30 minutes." He offered a hand-powered Singer for the same price as in Cincinnati. In March 1869 Singer beguiled the public with a treadle machine, freeing both hands to guide the material while the feet provided the motive power. In midsummer 1868, Luther Wedge introduced home delivery of milk and cream, while William H. Potter offered home delivery of ice.

The turnover of businesses on Court Street continued. A. L. Roach (grocer) and James Ballard (dry goods) bought out Topky and Child's hardware, announcing that they would continue the business. John and James D. Brown's Bank of Athens took over the building at the northwest corner of Court and Washington vacated by Topky and Childs. Jesse A. Van Law, wartime publisher of the *Messenger,* and his brother T. W. Van Law sold their book and stationery business to Charles Norris and William Kurtz. William Reed Golden, an attorney and two-term state senator, announced his decision to relocate in Columbus, a place where he anticipated greater professional opportunity and perhaps a more friendly acceptance of a Democrat. Olive W. Atkinson put up a building on East State near Court, to house a grocery operated by her son, G. W. Atkinson. In some cases, these changes represented the failure of an enterprise and a decision to try something different. More often, change represented growth. In April 1869, the *Messenger* was almost boastful in listing the business and professional men relocating from Albany to engage in business in Athens: W. W. Kurtz, Dr. C. L. Wilson, Colonel W. S. Wilson, John and James D. Brown, and Leonard Brown and the list went on.

THE UNIVERSITY: HOWARD'S LAST YEARS

During the war, college enrollments had dropped to the same dismal level that existed when Solomon Howard had come to the presidency. In fall 1865 they shot up. A total of 243 students filled all available rooms to the point of crowding and dissatisfaction with living conditions. Twenty of the seventy veterans who enrolled in 1865–66 reflected the feeling evidently shared by many students that it was more important to have attended college than to have completed a degree; few students stayed more than one year. Enrollments plummeted in 1867 to 176 from the previous year's 243. As Ohio began to forge a public secondary school system, enrollments in the prep school also tailed off.

President Howard was fully aware of the university's plight. "Ohio University must get more money or she will not be able to maintain her position among the sister institutions of the state. The State [of Ohio] is our patron, to her we must look," Howard advised the trustees. To Howard the university had potential. Only Ohio University and Marietta College operated in the area south of the National Road, east of the Little Miami River, and north of the Ohio River. "With suitable accommodations such as buildings, libraries, and endowment of professorships, we might have five hundred students."

While Howard saw clearly enough, the Ohio Legislature had its eyes turned elsewhere. The usually cheerful Howard became discouraged. "The income of the institution is not enough to carry on," he reported. A select committee consisting of trustees Bellamy Storer, Eliakim H. Moore, and the president got nowhere with the general assembly. Help from the State of Ohio, he concluded, was remote. The legislature was thoroughly absorbed with the creation of the Ohio State Agricultural and Mechanical College. When the board of trustees of the new agricultural school first met, it elected as its president Valentine B. Horton. An Ohio University trustee since 1844, Horton had chaired the committee lobbying the general assembly in behalf of Ohio University's claim to a share in Ohio's proceeds from the Morrill Act. To some Athenians it seemed that Horton "had been riding two horses."

The university, however, had also been "riding two horses." It was both a state school and Methodist-controlled, ties that enabled both church and state to look the other way when university trustees came seeking funds. Avowedly Methodist colleges such as Baldwin, Ohio Wesleyan, and Mount Union enjoyed substantial increases in their endowments. So, too, did other private schools such as Oberlin, Marietta, and Otterbein. At most Howard might take comfort that Ohio University was not the only school with problems. Kenyon, Denison, Western Reserve, and Miami, among others, were also experiencing declining enrollments.

In a move to broaden its enrollment base, the university trustees in 1870 voted to admit women students. The move had its origin with the faculty, who recognized that yielding to the trend of the times would generate much-needed additional tuition income. Indeed, at the time the trustees acted, Margaret Boyd, an Athens woman, was already enrolled.

As the university entered the 1870s, Howard was ill and requested a three-month leave to go to Europe to recover his health. The leave produced only a temporary recovery. On returning to Athens, Howard made his final report to the trustees in June 1872. His despair was manifest. "The poverty of the institution," he told the trustees, "is such as to prevent making the improvements which are absolutely necessary and unless means are devised to increase the income of the University, it cannot any longer hold its position among the colleges of the State." Having said this, Howard resigned the presidency. Moving to San Jose, California, he died the following year.

Solomon Howard had fought the good fight. The ablest of the university's presidents thus far, he brought enlightened leadership to the university in broadening the curriculum and ending the antagonism that had permeated student-administration relations. He saw clearly the university's need to induce the State of Ohio to accept its responsibility to fund the institution adequately. He was hindered in his efforts, for the Methodist connection, like the Presbyterian connection before it, "limited the public support and appeal of the University." The Athens community continued to resent the university's legal position as landlord, yet the university was without authority to end this relationship. As neither Athens village nor the Hocking Valley was growing at a rate to stimulate the growth or support of the university, so the university failed to attract outside resources that in stimulating the growth of the college would trickle down to the community.

THE ATHENS BLACK COMMUNITY

The War between the States transformed the village's black community. In 1850, the "community" consisted of two black households, the Morgans and the Flowers who accounted for fifteen persons, and one unattached individual, a total of sixteen persons. While for years slaves had been crossing the Ohio River to seek freedom, Athens was much too close to Virginia to afford a safe sanctuary; the runaways did not linger. With one exception, the members of the Athens black community of 1850 were free-born Ohioans.

In the course of the eighteen-fifties, the black population grew; in 1860 it numbered twenty-six. The Morgan family no longer resided in the village, nor did several of the Flowers clan, though it had added five new members during the decade. Three additional families were present, all three of which represented mixed marriages. In addition, there were nine single blacks. One was Charles Valentine, a fifty-three-year-old laborer. Born in slavery as Daniel Walden, he had fled Virginia and taken a new name on coming to Athens. He had prospered to the degree that he reported $75 in real property and another $50 in personal property. He lived alone. Seven young women, presumably all single, lived in separate households headed by whites and acted as domestic servants for the likes of President Howard, Eliakim Moore, R. H. Stewart, the Widow Currier, and S. S. Knowles. The black community was still fragile, tentative. Of the four adult males, two were laborers, one a barber, and one a bricklayer. Only two had property and their combined assets totaled only $225, not a very promising base.

The overwhelming majority of the Athens black community of 1870 were newcomers to the village, if not to Ohio. The 1870 census reported 24 black households, containing 140 persons, and another 47 unattached blacks living in other households. In light of latter-day concern about the structure of black families, it is worth noting that of the 24 black households, 21 consisted of a husband and wife. Only two were headed by a woman. Sixty percent of the unattached black males lived in a household headed by a black, while 70 percent of the unattached black women lived in homes headed by a white.

The black community in 1870 had several notable characteristics. First, a sizable proportion of the adults were mulattos; one black male householder had a white wife as did three mulatto male householders. Second, by a three-to-one margin the black adults had been born outside Ohio—chiefly in Virginia (which would include present-day West Virginia) with lesser numbers having been born in the Carolinas, Tennessee, or Kentucky. Third, as one examines the dates and places of birth of their children, it is apparent that most of the blacks living in Athens in 1870 had migrated to the village after the end of the war.

In a community where nearly all adult whites were literate, the black community operated at a serious disadvantage. Fewer than half of the blacks age nineteen and over could both read and write. This limited the kinds of employment available to them, diminished the ability of the males to support themselves and their families, and reduced their ability to acquire personal or real property. The pervasive illiteracy of black parents severely limited their ability to aid their children in the pursuit of formal schooling or to free themselves of superstition and folk myths.

While black children would enjoy less parental support than white children as they pursued their education, 84 percent of the black children attended elementary school. The next generation of blacks would be literate. At the same time, because no black child was enrolled in the high school, the next generation of blacks would find it difficult to reach the upper levels of the workplace.

Finally, the black community faced a serious demographic problem. At every age from twenty to fifty, there was a serious imbalance of the sexes—a ratio of 62 women per 100 males. Given the prevailing community attitudes regarding interracial marriage, this imbalance effectively precluded the possibility of marriage and family life for 38 percent of the adult black male population of Athens, a problem for the spouseless male and a potential problem for the community as a whole.

In terms of employment the blacks were vulnerable. While all 53 adult black males reported holding a job, the range of jobs they occupied was narrowly proscribed. Thirty-nine were laborers of one sort or another. Most of the remainder worked in service occupations—as hostlers, hotel porter, cook, and barber—all honorable work, but generally not rewarding financially. Three had established themselves as craftsmen. Not surprisingly, barely one-half of the black householders claimed any property. Only seven had claims to as much as $500 in combined real and personal property. John West and William N. Harris, barbers, and Matthew Patrick, clerk of probate court, were moderately well off. The most affluent of the black community was Charles Valentine, now a prosperous blacksmith reporting a tidy $5,500 in property and better off than many of the whites.

Black women who were in the labor force, 24 women in a total of 45, without exception worked as domestic servants. For black women, employment as a domestic was clearly a prelude to the adult woman's life. Coming from a slave background and at best semiliterate, the black girl was likely to have quite different views about how to prepare meals and to care for children than her white, middle-class employer. At the same time, as a live-in servant the young black woman had ample opportunity to observe the lifestyle of the white middle class and was under pressure while at work to emulate the ways of the white middle class, an opportunity few black males would have.

The question in 1870 was whether the Athens economy would generate a broader range of employment in the future that would enable the black community to thrive and attract still others to their community.

Herrold's Mill and Dam. Built by Silas Bingham in 1816; burned 1912. *(Courtesy of James Anastas.)*

Herrold Place and West Bridge, 1875. *(Courtesy of James Anastas.)*

Woolen factory and
flour mill of D. B. Stew-
art and East Bridge,
c. 1875. *(Reprinted from* Atlas
of Athens County, Ohio,
1875.)

Daniel Bertine Stewart,
entrepreneur. *(Reprinted from the*
History of the Hocking Valley,
Ohio, *1883.)*

Otto Barth's Mill and Dam, c. 1907. On the site of the Gregory and Havner Mill of 1806. Barth
lost his life in the 1907 flood for which he posthumously received the Carnegie Hero Medal.
(Courtesy of Margene Bush.)

South Bridge, steel span of 1908, which served Athens until 1932 when it was replaced with the present concrete bridge. *(Courtesy of the* Athens Messenger.*)*

South Bridge, covered bridge of 1876 with steel span over railroad. The covered bridge trapped "filth" and "reeked with disease germs." *(Courtesy of James Anastas.)*

East-bound Baltimore and Ohio Engine No. 172 with old South Bridge in background, 1878. *(Courtesy of James Anastas.)*

Bishop David Hastings Moore. *(Reprinted from* The Athens Home Coming.*)*

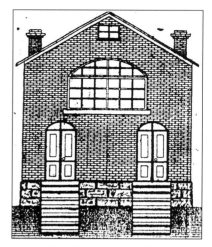

Methodist Church of 1812, South Congress Street. This view was drawn from memory by Sarah Steenrod. *(Courtesy of ACHS&M.)*

Methodist Church of 1908, College Street, was positioned slightly to the south of its predecessors so as to be centered on Washington Street. *(Courtesy of Margene Bush.)*

Methodist Church of 1837, College and Washington streets. The building underwent several remodelings. *(Courtesy of ACHS&M.)*

St. Paul's Catholic Church, North Congress Street, as pictured by the *Athens Journal*, 1892. *(Reprinted from Steiner and Steiner,* Faith and Family, *ACHS&M, 1995.)*

St. Paul's Catholic Church, North College Street, 1895. The entire town rejoiced in its completion and dedication. *(Courtesy of Margene Bush.)*

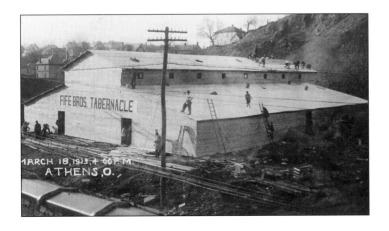

Fife Brothers' Tabernacle, Carpenter and Court streets, 1913. The tabernacle, seating 2000 persons, was completed in less than three days. *(Courtesy of The Dairy Barn, and Archives and Special Collections, Ohio University Libraries.)*

Booker T. Washington literary club, Mt. Zion Baptist Church, 1909. *(Courtesy of Michel Perdreau, and Archives and Special Collections, Ohio University Libraries.)*

Reverend Joseph Wilson, pastor, Mt. Zion Baptist Church. *(Courtesy of Archives and Special Collections, Ohio University Libraries.)*

Presbyterian Church as remodeled in 1865. The vestibule, tower, and meeting room were added to the original 1828 structure. *(Reproduced with permission from the First Presbyterian Church, Athens.)*

Presbyterian Church of 1903. *(Reproduced with permission from the First Presbyterian Church, Athens.)*

East Side School, 1911, Wallace Drive at Ohio Avenue. *(Courtesy of James Anastas.)*

Athens High School, 1906. *(Courtesy of James Anastas.)*

Athens County Children's Home, c. 1900, marked an awareness of public responsibility for the care of the vulnerable and helpless. *(Courtesy of The Dairy Barn, and Archives and Special Collections, Ohio University Libraries.)*

Athens State Hospital, c. 1900. The hospital was famed for the beauty of its grounds. *(Courtesy of Margene Bush.)*

Nurses of Athens State Hospital. The hospital operated its own nurses training program. *(Courtesy of The Dairy Barn, and Archives and Special Collections, Ohio University Libraries.)*

Women patients of the Athens State Hospital gather by one of the hospital's lakes, 1893.
(Courtesy of The Dairy Barn, and Archives and Special Collections, Ohio University Libraries.)

Men's Wing, Athens State Hospital, 1893. *(Courtesy of The Dairy Barn, and Archives and Special Collections, Ohio University Libraries.)*

Athens Mirror Building, West Union Street, built 1824 by John Walder. The building was demolished in 1910 to make way for the new U.S. post office. *(Courtesy of the* Athens Messenger.*)*

Archibald Green Brown, founder of the *Athens Mirror and Literary Register*, 1825-30. Taking up the law, Brown went on to be a judge and banker. *(Reprinted from* The Athens Home Coming.*)*

Charles E. M. Jennings, editor-publisher of the *Athens Messenger*, 1868-96. An ardent Republican, Jennings promoted industrialization for Athens. *(Reprinted from* The Athens Home Coming.*)*

Frederick W. Bush, publisher of the *Athens Messenger*, 1896-1929. Bush converted the *Messenger* into a modern daily newspaper. *(Courtesy of the* Athens Messenger.*)*

University Terrace home of Nelson Van Vorhes, 1850s-1870s. *(Reprinted from* Atlas of Athens County, Ohio, *1875.)*

Nelson Van Vorhes. *(Reprinted from* The Athens Home Coming.*)*

Judge J. Perry Wood, president of the Spanish Treaty Claims Commission, 1900-1910. *(Courtesy of the* Athens Messenger.*)*

Joseph M. Dana. Early Ohio University graduate, county official, attorney, and mayor of Athens. His home stands next to Gordy Hall. *(Courtesy of the* Athens Messenger.*)*

Ebenezer Currier home, "Flat Iron Square," Athens showplace of the 1840s and 1850s. Currier was a leading merchant and promoter of a rail connection to the East coast for Athens. *(Reprinted from* Atlas of Athens County, Ohio, 1875.*)*

George Falloon home, c. 1904. East Union and College Streets. A member of the Ohio Senate, Falloon had extensive out-of-state business interests. *(Reprinted from* Athens County Illustrated, 1897.*)*

Clinton L. Poston home, 1899, Park Place, a home befitting the town's only millionaire and owner of the Sunday Creek Coal Co. *(Reprinted from* The Centennial Atlas of Athens County Ohio, 1905.*)*

Bernhard Fauser, Jr., home, c. 1900. College and Washington Streets. The Fausers lived upstairs while they rented the first floor offices to local doctors. *(Courtesy of the* Athens Messenger.*)*

The Charles Grosvenor house of the late 1860s to 1902, West State and Court Street. In summertime the sideyard was the scene of ice cream socials. *(Reprinted from* Atlas of Athens County, Ohio, *1875.)*

General Grosvenor hosts President Taft and Lawrence G. Worstell at his University Terrace home, 1916. *(Courtesy of James Anastas.)*

The Charles Grosvenor home on University Terrace, 1902, designed by his cousin, Bertram Grosvenor Goodhue. *(Courtesy of James Anastas.)*

East Union Street, c. 1915. The three residences from left to right are those of T. D. M. Pilcher, Henry O'Bleness, and Wallace McVay. The Masonic Temple (next to the McVay home) replaced the Falloon home in 1910. *(Courtesy of the Athens Messenger.)*

Members of the 27th Regiment, U.S. Army confront the Provost Guard of the 5th regiment, ONG, West Washington Street next to the sheriff's house, August 1904. One guardsman was killed, four wounded.

Co. K, 1st ONG, on summer maneuvers, north and west of Athens, August 1904. (*Courtesy of Margene Bush.*)

The 1907 flood, looking down Morris Avenue. *(Courtesy of The Dairy Barn, and Archives and Special Collections, Ohio University Libraries.)*

The 1907 flood. Citizens surveying the chaos along Richland Avenue. *(Courtesy of The Dairy Barn, and Archives and Special Collections, Ohio University Libraries.)*

U.S. postal employees preparing to deliver mail, Christmas Day, 1910. *(Courtesy of The Dairy Barn, and Archives and Special Collections, Ohio University Libraries.)*

World War I barracks for Student Army Training Corps on the College Green, 1918. *(Courtesy of the Athens Messenger.)*

ATHENS CHURCHES

The church scene in Athens changed markedly between 1850 and 1870. A Catholic congregation was organized and a church built, while the Presbyterians gave way to the Methodists as the pre-eminent church in the village.

The organization of St. Paul's Catholic Church in Athens was the product of the Irish migration to America and the coming of the railroad to the village. The arrival in the Athens area of Peter Fagan in 1834 and Edward Sheridan about 1838 provided a nucleus of Catholic laymen. The Irish famine shortly forced others—John Brown, John Fagan (reputedly Peter's brother), James Walsh, and Patrick Mulligan—to leave Ireland and come to Athens to be near Peter Fagan. Hard-working, they all prospered as farmers, their real estate holdings in 1860 placing them in the ranks of "solid citizen status." Living along the Athens-Canaan township border, they were too isolated and too few to command regular access to a priest.

The building of the M & C Railroad eastward from Chillicothe brought several hundred construction workers, chiefly Irish, into the area and the beginning of a Catholic ministry to the workmen's camps. Not until 1856 or early 1857 were there Irish construction workers in the immediate vicinity of Athens village. The tradition at St. Paul's has Father John C. H. Albrinck of Pomeroy as the first priest to make regular once-a-month visits in the area. Even so the Paris-educated Father, only twenty-four years old, officiated in the railroad camps, not the village itself. When the railroad was completed in 1857, the Irish construction gangs moved on and were succeeded by a smaller, but permanent, force of maintenance workers.

By 1860, there were at least twenty-one Irish Catholic households in the village or in nearby Athens and Canaan townships who could routinely assemble for worship. At this point, Fr. Philip McMahon, residing at Zaleski, came to Athens in early 1860 "to arrange about purchasing some Church property." By the middle of February, a church site had been purchased and the good Father asked Bishop Purcell for permission to build. The lot was at 7 North Congress, that is, on the west side of Congress just north of its intersection with Washington Street. Before the end of the year Father McMahon was gone; Father Timothy J. Tierney succeeded him. Before construction could begin, Richard and Ellen Hennessey bought the lot immediately to the south of the church lot. They promptly built a two-story dwelling, used as a boardinghouse for rail hands. Until a church structure was in place, it was in the Hennesseys' boardinghouse that successive priests said Mass.

The researches of Catherine and Bruce Steiner point to 1865 or 1866 as the date by which construction of the church building had progressed far enough to allow the congregation to assemble in it for Mass. The building—"a simple wooden box, without steeple or belfry"—was approximately 30 feet wide by 50 feet long. The nave featured two tiers of pews. The chancel space was so "small and hampered up" that the priest could scarcely turn around.

Throughout the 1860s, the congregation depended on priests based elsewhere who came and went via the M & C. These railway priests said Mass at different places every day from Harmar (now part of Marietta) to Londonderry and down the Portsmouth branch of the Scioto and Hocking Valley Railroad as far south as Washington Furnace. In the best of circumstances, the priest visited Athens once a month. An insight into the pressure under which the priest performed his duties is seen in the baptismal record of one of the Ferriter children. His note, pinned to the baptismal record, reads: "The Train on which I was to leave Athens arrived before I had time to find out when the child was born, names of sponsors, etc." As the Steiners observe of this time period, "the ministrations of an in-and-out priest . . . left much to be desired."

For the Presbyterians, the 1850s and 1860s were an era of prolonged stability. The second departure from Athens of Alfred Ryors marked the end of an era in which the Presbyterians controlled the university and enjoyed a favored position in the community. After a brief interregnum, the church in 1854 called the Reverend Mr. John H. Pratt, Athens-born and an 1840 graduate of the university, to be its pastor. Pratt remained fourteen years, seeing the parish through the Civil War, "a notable and profitable" pastorate.

Making use of the revival, Pratt stirred interest in the church and attracted nearly 200 new church members. He also changed the basis for support of the church, ending the practice of renting pews, and, in 1868, the session voted that all pews should be rent-free. Pratt also saw to completion a major remodeling of the thirty-year-old church building. A lecture room was added, along with a belltower and bell. The latter was used not only to summon members to church, but as a public alarm for fires. One other innovation of Pratt's ministry was the founding of a Sunday School for primary-school children, with Augusta Walker as superintendent, a post she filled for thirty-five years.

The progress of the Methodists is hard to track with accuracy since their records were destroyed by fire in the 1950s. What is certain is that they had gained control of the university's board of trustees and became the premier church of the village. The Reverend Solomon Howard, the new university president, although a Methodist minister, made no effort to pastor the Methodist Church. By this date the Methodists had full-time clergy. In 1861, their building on College Street was remodeled.

The 1850s were the years that Charles C. McCabe, Earl Cranston, and David H. Moore were growing up, going to church, attending Athens schools and completing their studies at Ohio University. McCabe and Moore entered the Methodist ministry in 1860; Cranston, in 1867. All three men served in the Union Army during the war. McCabe served first as chaplain of the 126th OVI and later with the Christian Commission. Cranston recruited a company of men into the 60th OVI whom he led as a captain in the siege of Petersburg. Moore volunteered as a private but was elected captain of A Company, 87th OVI. Later, he was assigned as lieutenant colonel of the 125th OVI, which he led through most of the Atlanta campaign. The war over, these men, now experienced in leadership, turned back to the church and to careers that would carry all three to leadership roles in the national church.

During these same years, the local church benefited especially from the support of three laymen—Calvary Morris, Daniel B. Stewart, and Eliakim H. Moore, the father of D. H. Moore. A five-time member of the Ohio General Assembly and a three-term Congressmen, Morris was one of the community's chief pillars. Stewart was one of the foremost businessmen of the era; E. H. Moore, a one-term Congressman, was the town's banker.

THE ATHENS ECONOMY

Economics is not everything, yet what Athens had become by 1870 was in many ways indicated by the character of its economy. What was so telling was not just the number of jobs, but the character of the jobs—the mix of the skilled and unskilled, the changing proportions of professional and managerial employments, of the commercial and industrial, the place of service and unskilled work in society, and, of course, who did the work.

Women in the Labor Force

Despite the rise of a woman's movement in the late 1840s, a woman's place was still in the home in 1870. From age seven to fourteen, girls and boys were in school. As girls finished school, the great majority remained at home, helping their mothers, until they married; thereafter they kept house. Among women, the world of paid work was for the minority, and most such work had a strong domestic aspect to it. All of the 138 women in the village labor force in 1870 drew on some aspect of the homemaker's craft. Ninety women, the great majority, were employed as domestic servants. Many were children, some as young as twelve; only 13 were as much as thirty years old, reflecting that domestic service was not a career. Most of the other working women were engaged in some specialized aspect of domesticity— as cook, dressmaker, seamstress, milliner, coat maker, or laundress. All of these were jobs likely to be performed within the confines of the home, either the employer's or the employee's. Most of the 90 domestic servants lived in the home of their employer. The matter is not discussed in the press, but the practice attests to a value system that "protected" adult women from rubbing shoulders daily with a wide range of non-family members.

Perhaps 20 of the 138 women worked outside the confines of a home. Milliners were among the few women likely to operate shops of their own, usually located on the less-expensive second floors of the business district. So, too, hotel waitresses were in an ambiguous position, for while they did not live in a private, family home, they were likely to live at the hotel under the eye of their employer. The fifteen women teachers of the village, daughters of Athens merchants and professionals, seem to have lived at home and worked with children. The three women who toiled in the local woolen mill all lived at home.

While only a minority of all adult women worked for pay in 1870, a slight majority of young women got at least a brief introduction to the labor force. Just over half of the seventeen- and eighteen-year-old women of the village were employed. They had completed their formal education but had not yet married. Thereafter, as they married and had children, their labor force participation rate dropped off. Even so, for women from age 20 to 24, the labor force rate was 35 percent, and for those 25 to 29, the rate was 25 percent. Although work and marriage were supposedly incompatible, even among women between ages 35 and 44, ages at which most women were married and had children, one woman in eight was employed. Beyond age 50 women were seldom employed.

If roughly half the young women of Athens were getting a brief exposure to the labor force, the range of jobs available to them was far more restricted than for males. Almost the only white-collar employment open to them was teaching. No woman, of any age, was employed in the traditional professions—law, medicine, or clergy. Nor were any employed in clerical or sales work. They were also excluded from the crafts. The available occupations were in the service sector—cooking, cleaning, laundering, ironing in somebody else's home.

Men in the Marketplace

While difficult to document with precision, the male role as worker was in flux. In 1800, at least nine out of ten adult, white males in the United States were farmers of one sort or another. By 1870, farmers were still in the majority; that is, there were more farmers than persons employed in any other single occupation. The number of farms in the nation exceeded 2.6 million and was still growing. But non-agricultural employments were increasing even more rapidly. What cannot be measured with certainty is the number and proportion of adult, village males who had grown up on a farm, men whose fathers had been farmers rather than urban dwellers who had supported their families as merchants or craftsmen, salaried white-collar employees or day-wage laborers. Certainly, the number of village males whose fathers had been farmers must have been considerable, and the biographical sketches of Athenians of the midcentury refer to the farm backgrounds of men such as Calvary Morris and Charles Grosvenor. Some, like Wallace McVay, moved back and forth between farm and village. The point is important, for the farmer personified the man who set his own work schedule, who was the self-reliant generalist. Until the midcentury, the urban worker, in contrast, had been a self-employed professional, merchant or craftsmen, or aspired to be. The urban employee, in contrast to the farmer, was a specialist, often working at tasks and on schedules set by his employer.

Athens in 1870 had just under 500 males in its labor force. There were 70 to 80 different categories of jobs. This compares with 235 jobs and 64 job categories in 1850. To the youth who regarded farm work as unmitigated, unrewarding drudgery, the village offered choices of jobs, cash remuneration, and presumably a higher level of job satisfaction. The number of jobs in each job category varied widely— 1 cigar maker, 1 broom maker, 1 dentist. At the other end of the spectrum there were 61 general laborers, 56 railroad laborers, and 44 farm laborers. The village had need of 41 clerks, 27 carpenters, and 20 teamsters. Most job classifications, however, employed fewer than ten persons each. Obviously there were wide differences in the skill levels and responsibilities entailed in the various employments as job classifications increasingly connoted a degree of specialization that had not existed at earlier times.

The Professionals

Reflecting the position of Athens as county seat, market town, and college town, serving a region extending miles beyond the village limits, its economy had a place for many professionals, proprietors and managers, and clerical and sales personnel, people now termed white-collar workers. The professional ranks were top-heavy with lawyers and judges, since much legal business could be conducted only at the county courthouse. In fact, one-third of the 46 professionals were employed in the legal system. Although the village was also a health-care center, doctors, dentists, and druggist-apothecaries had less need than lawyers to locate in the county seat. And there were three clergy. With the university enrollment still small, so was its teaching staff. Otherwise the professionals included two artists (photographers), the editor of the *Messenger,* and a pair of engineers. These professionals bulked large among the village leaders—its respectability. They were likely to be heads of households and to possess a modest amount of property. Half of the professionals reported at least $4,000 in property; one-fourth claimed $10,000 or more. As a group they were moderately young, men in their mid-thirties to late forties.

Proprietors and Managers

Economic leadership was far more forthcoming from the 58 proprietors and managers and 115 craftsmen than from the professional people. Especially impressive is that 60 to 70 persons were required to distribute food and clothing to the community. Fewer and fewer townsmen fed themselves from kitchen gardens. The raising of cattle, pigs, and sheep in town was discouraged. Ready-made clothing and shoes increasingly appeared on merchants' shelves. And to these changes, the coming of the Marietta and Cincinnati Railroad contributed. David Zenner, Bavarian-born merchant, had moved to Athens in 1852 from Cincinnati in the expectation that daily railroad service would offer a retailer a much larger field of opportunity than had existed hitherto. In 1870 Zenner was fifty-six, well-established and worth some $30,000, and still on the rise. Zenner's was a family affair, but as of 1870, the junior member was John Friday, who would become Zenner's son-in-law. The great merchant was James Ballard, long established at the northeast corner of Court and Union, the corner originally occupied by the Perkinses, father and son. Now this was Ballard's Corner. The elder Ballard, John, was worth $50,000. Ballard's, too, was a family business that included Fred, James, and Frank. The third dry-goods merchant was the youthful Isaac Half, associated with Leopold Selig, who had commercial ties with Philadelphia much as Zenner had ties with Cincinnati. Both men were Alsatian by birth, both Jewish, both in their mid-to-late twenties, and just putting down roots as merchants.

The community's dozen retail grocers were independent operators. The grocery business required a smaller investment in inventory than the dry-goods business and so was open to men with less capital at their disposal than was the case with the dry-goods moguls. The reigning grocers of 1870 included Isaac Silvus, Rufus Crippen, Alonzo Roach, and Abner Cooley, all respectable merchants but with only a fraction of the resources of a James Ballard or David Zenner. Grocers still accepted country goods in "payment" for merchandise, and the *Messenger* obliged by printing a list of market prices for wheat, corn, beef, pork, butter and eggs and the like, a guide to the prices merchants would pay for the products. Grocery prices were not advertised; customers and merchants negotiated the price. Many of the transactions, especially with rural customers, were on credit.

Ranking along with the grocers were the five village hardware merchants: Ezra Walker, Henry Topky, William Bartlett, Nelson Van Vorhes, and Oliver Childs. Whereas in 1850, a Court Street merchant was likely to stock groceries, dry goods, and hardware, by 1870 these had become separate specialties. The hardware business, like the grocery business, was volatile. Men moved in and out of business. Partnerships were formed, dissolved, and new partnerships formed. There was much moving from store site to store site, a feature of business life that applied to the dry-goods business as well.

One of the signs of a new age was the appearance of the self-proclaimed capitalist and land speculator. There were only three such men, but they stand out. The land speculator was Johnson M. Welch, son of John Welch, the town's foremost attorney. Johnson Welch had property interests at least as far afield as Chillicothe. At thirty-eight and with claims to $30,000 in property, he was already well established and in a position to be a leading player in the village's business affairs in the years to come. The two avowed capitalists were Louis W. Brown and the long-established, still formidable Daniel Bertine Stewart, one of the town's wealthiest citizens. Namesake and son of a veteran of the American Revolution who had migrated to Athens County, Daniel B. is the one who laid out Stewart, Ohio, acquired the East Mill, and extended the variety of manufacturing carried on there. In calling themselves capitalists, Brown and Stewart were reflecting their role as investors in various business ventures managed by others rather than as hands-on managers themselves.

The term capitalist might also have been applied to George T. Gould and Joseph Herrold, two of the wealthier men in the village. Both described themselves as manufacturers of salt. Gould had taken over the salt operations at Salina, operations that had passed from Fuller and Walker to Milbury M. Greene. When Greene became preoccupied with the Hocking Valley Railroad, he passed the Salina complex on to Gould, his half-brother, who continued to live in Athens.

Joseph Herrold, having returned to Athens after his flirtation with the California gold fields, continued to own the mill originally built by Silas Bingham, but his new, major interest was the saltworks at Armitage.

The Bankers

Eliakim H. Moore and John and James D. Brown, father and son, were the town's bankers. Banking in Athens was still new in 1850, the Athens branch of the Ohio State Bank having been in operation for only a year and a half. The bank operated under its own directors, for the most part local business and professional men. Throughout its existence the chief operating officer was the cashier; John R. Crawford and L. H. Stewart divided the duties.

The year 1863 brought a major change in banking. With the South out of the Union for the time being, the Republicans pushed through Congress the National Bank Act of 1863. In August, the leadership of the Athens branch of the Ohio State Bank secured a federal charter, incorporating as the First National Bank, which then took over the assets of what had been the local branch of the Ohio State Bank. The capital was set at $50,000. John Welch and John Ballard, who had been directors of the old bank, became directors of the new. A. G. Brown became cashier of the new and remained so until his death in 1882. The president was Eliakim H. Moore, who would guide the bank's loans and investments. The new bank continued to operate at the southeast corner of Court and Washington.

In 1868, Athens got another bank, the Bank of Athens. Whereas the First National was incorporated under a federal charter, the Bank of Athens was a merchant bank, the creation of its owners. John Brown and his son, James D., had engaged in the banking business in Albany. In 1868, they moved their operation to Athens, taking over the northwest corner of Court and Washington. As a private bank, the security of deposits depended wholly on the financial stability and soundness of the two Browns. The capital structure of their bank was $100,000. In 1870, it was just getting under way.

That two banks could operate profitably in Athens underscores that the village economy was increasingly a market economy involving financial transactions of a magnitude and complexity requiring specialized financial services that individuals could no longer easily manage on their own.

Officials and Clerks

Another sign of the times was the emergence of an officialdom, persons holding public office at a level that made their position their primary occupation. There were eight of these functionaries in 1870: the village postmaster, a federal employee; the mayor and the constable, employees of the village corporation; the remainder formed part of the county's administrative bureaucracy. Some county officials drew modest salaries set by the state in accordance with the county's population. But in general these public servants were still compensated on a fee basis. The mayor's compensation derived principally from fines he levied in his role as judge in the mayor's court.

The village economy required roughly as many clerical and sales people (56) as it did managers and proprietors (58). Few businesses had more than one or two hired employees. The clerical people were essentially support personnel, the teller and cashier at the local bank who handled routine transactions, for example. Of the town's 41 clerks, only seven were as much as thirty years old. All but a handful were nominally salespersons, most likely also sweeping and dusting, as well as replenishing the stock. The elite among the clerks were those few with administrative responsibilities in the probate court, the county recorder's office, and at the state asylum.

Craftsmen

While the village gained an impressive number of proprietors and salespeople between 1850 and 1870, in relative terms the role of craftsmen declined. Reflecting the nearby farm economy were 20 craftsmen who served the horse and farm: the blacksmiths, tanners and saddlers, carriage and wagon makers. In terms of other basics—food, shelter, and clothing—a few village craftsmen baked, but otherwise food supplies came through the grocers. The village had a lingering self-sufficiency in clothing. Custom women's clothing came from village dressmakers, seamstresses, and milliners; men's custom clothing, from tailors. Less attuned to individualized apparel than were women, Athens men provided employment to only four tailors for their clothing as opposed to seventeen women who fabricated dresses, coats, and hats. The proliferation of dry-goods stores, though, attests to the increase in the use of ready-made clothing. Boot- and shoemakers fabricated footwear for both men and women, although Fanny Cooley's Civil War letters

a hard-pressed wife and mother might undertake to repair shoes

ing trades employed 62 persons, accounting for over half of the vil-
n. Houses and stores were built on site, to order, one-by-one. Bricks,
be imported economically, were made locally, but in a brickyard now,
on site; they were laid by masons. Increasingly, solid masonry con-
as giving way to balloon-construction, framing using two-by-fours and
covered either by brick veneer or wood siding. The town employed 27
rs. Special inside trim used the skills of cabinetmakers and turners. A tin-
oricated the roof covering. At a time when the kerosene lamp provided light
indoor plumbing was only dreamed of, there were no plumbers or electricians.
Craftsmen provided their own tools; they were often self-employed and likely to
possess a few hundred to a thousand dollars or so in property. Athens carpenters,
the most numerous group of craftsmen, were generally at least forty years of age,
heads of households, and property owners.

Industrial Operatives and Unskilled Laborers

That Athens had remained more mercantile than industrial is reflected in the small
numbers of operatives and the character of its unskilled labor force. There were,
perhaps, 12 persons who, as the census classified workers, were operatives, and 117
non-farm laborers. Of the latter, 56 held jobs created by the presence of the
Marietta and Cincinnati and the Hocking Valley Railroad, far more employees
than the Hocking Canal had ever required.

Some of the 61 common laborers did general labor (15); a far larger number (27)
were employed in the local brickyard, usually men under thirty years of age, few of
whom claimed any property, real or personal. Five laborers worked in the local
woolen mill, four of whom were under twenty years of age. The other 19 laborers
found employment in the local foundry, furniture factory, shoe shops, and wagon
shop. Surprisingly, 28 of the common laborers were heads of households, men
with families to support, the nucleus of an industrial proletariat. They reflected
the fact that the modes of production had changed to the degree that some males
would spend the bulk of their working years as unskilled laborers. Only seven of
these laborers reported owning any real property; sixteen claimed some personal
property. In no case did any laborer's combined real and personal property reach
$1,000. That younger men far out-numbered older men as laborers suggests that
the occupation was a transient one, pursued until a skill was mastered and a better

opportunity came along. A few men, obviously, hung on, acquiring experience and a wage that permitted acquisition of property. It is possible, too, that some of these older laborers had acquired their property in connection with some other kind of employment they had given up to become laborers.

Service Workers

Along with the 117 non-farm laborers were 37 males involved in service work. Here, in particular, the contrast between male and female workers stands out sharply. The female labor force was overwhelmingly involved in service work, chiefly young women, often girls, in domestic service; in the far larger male labor force, less than eight percent pursued service work. The personal service of males was limited to four barbers, a cook, and a hotel porter. All the rest of the male service workers managed horses in one capacity or another as hostlers, draymen, stage coach drivers, or teamsters. The porter, hostlers, draymen, and stage coach drivers were young, without families or property. By contrast, all four barbers and the cook were family men with some property. Because horses and wagons were essential to their work, the teamsters more often than not possessed a few hundred to a thousand or fifteen hundred dollars in property and most were householders. Far better to be a teamster in Athens than a railroad laborer in terms of opportunity to acquire property and to provide a family with a modicum of economic security.

Finally, the village had not altogether shed its agricultural past. In the village's bottom lands there were still functioning farms. None of the village's four farmers was rich, but their property claims did place them on a par with the village grocers. More significantly, 44 farm laborers lived in the village, surely an anomaly. Thirty of these, however, were less than twenty-five years of age; several were fifteen or younger. For the great majority of them, farm labor afforded an introduction to the labor force, a job for a season or so until they found a job with a future. There were, of course, farms beyond the Hocking, within easy walking distance of the village, and most of the farm laborers who were twenty-five years old or over attempted to support families from their labor. A few had acquired property.

In 1800, when the village was platted by Rufus Putnam, the attraction of the Hocking Valley had been the opportunity to acquire land and in the context of a village the chance to "grow up" with the community. A village economy, however, stressed ways of making a living that emphasized personal property, cash, and other liquid assets. In 1870, 22 of the village's nearly 500 male workers had amassed at least $10,000 in either real or personal property. In the year in which John D.

Rockefeller incorporated the Standard Oil Company, a million-dollar corporation, nine Athenians admitted to possessing $50,000 or more in real and personal property. At the peak of the pyramid stood Joseph Herrold, manufacturer of salt with $126,000; next in order came Daniel B. Stewart, $95,000; George T. Gould, $92,000; and Eliakim H. Moore, $83,000. William Vorhes, John Brown (banker), John Welch, Eber Carpenter, and James Ballard completed the list. In most cases these claims to wealth rested on real property. It was John Brown, the merchant banker, and James Ballard and David Zenner, dry-goods merchants, who were conspicuous for having claims to more personal property than real property. In 1870 the village economy still had more ties to the land than to commerce and industry.

SOCIAL AND CULTURAL AMENITIES

Athenians felt a need for social and cultural entertainment. In the late 1860s, the Athens Musical Club, a group of eighteen to twenty local musicians, presented a series of concerts and expressed the wish that young boys be accompanied by their parents. Past experience indicated that unaccompanied lads were "accustomed to shriek, whistle, and stamp," distracting audience and musicians alike. Toward the end of 1868 a plan was afoot to present the "Opera of the Gipsey Girl" [sic] at the Atheneum, as announced in the *Athens Messenger* late that year. Another ambitious venture was the presentation of "Cinderella," but there were hints that the Musical Club was in financial trouble, and attendance at a June 1869 performance was disappointing. Now that travel by train was possible, an occasional traveling troupe would come to Athens.

By this time baseball was beginning to claim attention. In a free-hitting contest in June 1868, a group of Ohio University students took on the Energetics of Marietta, losing 58 to 44. At another level, the community took a stab at organizing a YMCA. Both sexes were invited to join in this effort "to promote the cause of good morals." Good intentions did not suffice. A permanent YMCA would await a later time.

Another evidence of change was the way the community observed Christmas. While the day had been ignored early in the century, it was now established as a family day. Leonard Cooley, encamped in a wheat field near Petersburg with the 116th OVI and very homesick, wrote his wife Fanny on Christmas Day 1862 wishing her "a Merry Christmas and a Very Happy New Year." It was clearly a special day, warranting the cancellation of drill. For one of the Cooleys' mutual friends, Christmas meant a short vacation and a chance to go to Coolville for the day. For

Athenians in the 18th OVI, camped five miles south of Nashville, Christmas, 1862, was honored as the cooks "got up" a very good dinner, but the day did not merit cancellation of drill. Duncan Huling commented: "No rest for the soldiers, no special day set apart for him to rest." Clearly, he regarded Christmas as a special day, measuring Christmas, 1862, by earlier Christmases he remembered and looking forward to Christmas 1863 at home with his family. The newspapers, the letters of the Cooleys, and the diary of Duncan Huling make no reference to Santa Claus, to presents, to Christmas trees, or to special celebrations.

As the decade ended, there was a sense that an era was also drawing to a close. The last of Athens' fourteen veterans of the American Revolution, in whose interest the Ohio Company had been organized, had died in 1852. Now, their children and the children of the other first families were passing on. At what would become a ritual among the oldsters, a dinner was tendered Judge Isaac Barker, Jr., at the Steadman House. At ninety, Barker was toasted by fellow citizens, and A. B. Walker, himself one of the town's elder citizens, proposed founding a Pioneer Society. Walker would devote much time in his remaining years to keeping alive an awareness of the village's past.

Beyond 1870, the United States would push into the second industrial revolution, agriculture would become mechanized, and urban areas would grow enormously. Athens faced a quite different milieu.

8

The Maturing Village: 1870–1900

As the Civil War began to fade into history, Athens village began to mature. Politically, the village fathers struggled for three decades with the problems of fashioning an infrastructure. Economically, the village moved into a cash economy and became caught up in the forces of a national market. Socially, culturally, and intellectually the village mirrored national trends, fashions, and interests. Evidences of an emerging cosmopolitanism surfaced.

FASHIONING AN INFRASTRUCTURE

In the three decades between 1870 and 1900, Athenians sought to extricate themselves from the mud—literally. A homesick volunteer during the Civil War stated as his fondest wish: to get home to muddy Athens. Successive editors of the *Messenger* spoke for both farmers of the surrounding area and merchants of Court Street when they pronounced the need for improved roads and streets. Indeed, improved rural roads were as essential to Court Street merchants as to the farmers. For years a solution seemed beyond the means either of private property owners or of the municipality.

In an extravagant moment in October 1873 editor Jennings boasted that Athens had more first-class sidewalks than any other town of its size in Ohio. His boast must surely have been a libel on other communities. For the seventies, at least, the solution lay with the property owners. When the village hall, now the City Building, was completed in 1874, it boasted a fine brick walk. Court Street merchants, to make their places attractive and accessible, were left to their own devices, and when the Phoenix Building (28 South Court Street) was completed in 1878, its owners included a "fine pavement" as part of the project. Jennings expressed hope that other merchants would be moved to emulate that work. Yet, as of the end of the decade, only a scattering of brick sidewalks had displaced boardwalks and dirt paths.

Roadways posed greater problems because of their greater width, the weight of the wagons they had to bear, and the narrow iron wheels that cut into the roadbeds. At most, one might hope for a roadbed featuring a solid base of rocks and gravel with a covering of finer stones. The crown needed to be high enough that rain would drain promptly to the sides, while ditches would carry the runoff away. To construct such roadbeds was beyond the skill of a township commissioner who had at his disposal only local property owners obligated by law to devote two days' labor a year to working on the township roads or else to pay $3.00 in cash. As a result, through most of the winter until late spring, the rural roads were impassable. Nor did the village fathers act to improve the streets within the village. Patience remained the order of the day throughout the seventies.

On the other hand, improved access to the village was addressed. To the delight of the community, the South Bridge was replaced in 1876 with a new covered bridge located more or less at the south end of Court Street.

The Seventies

Some problems lent themselves to partial solutions. As early as 1873, the lighting of streets, stores, and homes with gas was feasible, and Athens moved ahead. To this time, Court Street, at least, was lit by oil lamps. In the spring of 1873, construction of an artificial gas plant commenced. Work moved ahead quickly. By August, homes were being made ready "tubularly" for gaslight fixtures. By November 3, the oil lamps on Court Street had been converted to gas, and the first illumination occurred. Not everything ran smoothly. Boys, all too often, gave into the temptation to tamper with the lights. Another annoyance was that a thrifty town council had contracted for limited service: the lights were to run from a half hour after sundown to 9:00 P.M., and, on nights with a relatively full moon, the lights were not turned on at all, even if a dense cloud cover obscured the moon. Presumably, the citizenry was expected to practice the old saw about "early to bed, early to rise . . . ." As the years went by, the area of gaslighted streets was extended. Indeed, almost from the start, gaslights began to appear along East State. By fall 1878, West Washington Street, then the principal route to the rail depot, was lighted in the area south of the school grounds.

Unquestionably, the source of greatest pride was construction of the village hall. The village fathers thought big. The structure was to be multipurpose—to house the village government, to generate an income from rental of space to local businessmen, and to provide the community with an opera house seating six hundred. A clock tower with four faces would keep Athenians on time; a bell would strike the hour but could also sound an alarm in the event of fire, riot, or other crisis. The contractor was young Henry O'Bleness. Completion of the village hall in 1874 occasioned a major community celebration. Thereafter, high school and college commencements as well as various home-made and commercial entertainments were held at the opera house.

Always alive to what was up-to-date and desirable, editor Jennings was not one to be satisfied with one or two improvements when others seemed equally urgent. A public waterworks was "indispensible." He estimated one could be put in operation for $30,000. His primary concern was protection against fire and secondarily the "great convenience" to householders whose wells and cisterns were prone to run dry in late summer. In an age still devoid of knowledge of bacteria and microbes, much less of viruses, Jennings made no claim that pure water would cut illness. The fact is, Athenians were still dependent on well water—wells increasingly susceptible to contamination as the population increased and outhouses proliferated. Indeed, the first well to serve the village, dug in 1805 on what became Judge Barker's lot at College and Mill, was still in use, a balance pole being used to lift the water to the surface. Another much-used community well was located on Vine Street (University Terrace). Still another was just behind the College Edifice. Jennings's appeal for a community water system fell on deaf ears.

The Eighties

The infrastructure fashioned for the village in the seventies was a start, but only a start. Many projects seemed too costly. Within the village, brick or stone sidewalks seemed affordable. When citizens failed to acknowledge a responsibility, the village council could speak the will of the community. It could and did order property owners in particular places to construct a brick or flagstone walk and specified the width and grade. At times, the council interceded to cut into hillsides to permit the laying of a sidewalk with a user-friendly grade. Over time, the sidewalk problem was reduced; serviceable all-weather roads continued to be a problem.

Each January and February, the *Messenger* lamented the impassable roads that brought business in the village to a standstill. From editor Jennings's perspective, a major aspect of the rural road problem was the mode of managing the community's resources. Too few people performed the two days' service, and such money as was available was generally wasted by incompetent, if well-meaning, self-appointed supervisors. The roads could be turnpiked and macadamized in short order, he argued, if the supervisory mechanism were overhauled. This meant centralizing the supervision as a means of securing efficient and competent leadership. Jennings also proposed a unified bridge and culvert fund for the whole county.

Through the early eighties, little progress was made on township roads. Yet, there were hints of change. As early as April 1881, that part of East State Street in the vicinity of the Children's Home, now Children Services, was rerouted to run to the south of the home and was scheduled to be piked. A costly and time-consuming job, the improvement of this road to Canaanville dragged on, a few hundred feet a year. The most hopeful signs of change came in 1887, as several village council members visited Charleston, West Virginia, to explore the feasibility of brick pavement, its cost and durability. A few months earlier, Emmett Tompkins, the county's representative in the Ohio General Assembly, pushed through the state legislature a measure authorizing the village to issue bonds for the purpose of improving its streets and alleys. A bond issue required popular approval by a two-thirds majority. Acting quickly, in April 1887, council scheduled a referendum which carried by a 6–1 margin, and in May, the council authorized issuance of $25,000 in bonds. What promised to offer a solution soon collapsed. A legal challenge to the law established that the state's legislation was defective and the bonds were of questionable validity.

As in the seventies, the "bridge problem" resurfaced. This time it was the East Bridge. At the foot of Mill Street, it was the oldest important bridge in the county, a double, covered bridge that linked D. B. Stewart's mills to the village as well as serving persons living along Harmony Road, Rock Riffle, and in the Clark's Chapel area. A county matter, a replacement bridge was not completed until 1887.

WASTE DISPOSAL

Provision for sewage disposal was increasingly urgent. Athens practices were often repugnant. Operating as much on hunches as on firm knowledge, editor Jennings repeatedly urged fellow citizens to take care, to use quicklime in their privies and to have the vaults emptied periodically. For their part, county commissioners had a sewer line constructed along Court Street from the courthouse to the Hocking River. Further, they allowed several private connections to be made. Unfortunately, during dry spells, the sewage was trapped in the backwaters of the Hocking, creating what had to have been a serious health problem, although at the time perceived chiefly as an odoriferous nuisance.

The first village-built sewer lines were as troublesome. A line from the Phoenix block on Court Street extended eastward to a pond at the base of Union Street hill, creating a giant, open cesspool. Editor Jennings protested at the health problem, motivated undoubtedly by the fact that he lived at the top of Union Street hill. Further, in the summer of 1883, the town was plagued with dysentery, a product of faulty sewage disposal and the lack of a pure water supply. When the pond was drained in mid-July, the town doctors pointed out that, as it had long been the receptacle for "fluid filth from domiciles and outhouses," draining it exposed the community to the even more sickening conglomeration at its bottom. Cart loads of disinfectants needed to be dumped on it. The doctors also testified that all the wells in town were contaminated.

The situation was no better in July 1884, when the sewer at the intersection of College and Washington became plugged and discharged "poisonous gases." At this point, a proposal emerged to provide a sewer for College Street from Mill to Union. The *Messenger*, however, does not report any follow-up. Here was a problem that in a municipal setting was beyond the capacity of the most civic-spirited individuals to resolve. Like streets and schools, a sewage system required corporate action by the village government, an expansion of government services, and higher levels of taxes.

VOLUNTEERISM

Volunteerism could and did address several problems bearing on the quality of life in the village. One was the perennial question of a library. Interest, which was prone to wax and wane, waxed, and the "People's Library" was moved to the office of A. G. Brown & L. A. Koons. As the library was open to the public only on Wednesday afternoons from 2 to 4 P.M., patrons had to be very intentional about its use. This arrangement was awkward at best, and in January 1884, the reading room moved to the Village Hall, open Tuesday, Thursday, and Saturday afternoons.

A second concern bore on the aesthetics of the village. The once wooded hilltop had been denuded of trees. To the pioneer generation, trees occupied prime sites for homes, barns, streets, and fields. As they afforded an inexpensive, at-hand source of building materials and fuel, they had been cut down. In the 1840s William Holmes McGuffey had enhanced the landscaping of the College Green by planting a line of elms along what was then the northern edge of the campus.

Now, in the post-war era, editor Jennings annually urged fellow townsmen to plant shade trees by their homes, and, in April 1882, he took satisfaction in noting the first official Arbor Day. Jennings also appreciated plants, and he went out of his way to call attention to townsmen who demonstrated that flowers, indoors or out, added a pleasant dimension to life.

Finally, on a practical level, volunteers, largely ad hoc, took care of the village's fire protection, although the volunteers always enjoyed some official standing. By unspoken consensus, townsmen, especially merchants and professionals with valuable property in the old town, fell out whenever the village bell sounded an alarm. This response was hardly adequate. And the town failed to learn from the great fire of December 1877 that ravaged the east side of Court Street from Union to the first alley to the north and east from Court towards College Street. Even so, the "Citizen" who, in January 1886, urged Athens to prepare against future disasters by acquiring a fire engine, remained a voice crying in the wilderness.

PUBLIC UTILITIES

As early as 1881, the village explored the use of the telephone. In March 1881, a Hocking Valley Railroad telegraph line was used experimentally to communicate between Columbus and Athens. When the line worked satisfactorily, the *Messenger* advised Athenians to expect a long-distance line to be installed between the village and Columbus before long. A month later, Harry A. Crippen, the telegraph manager in Athens, tried his own experiment, connecting a telephone to a telegraph line to communicate with the telegrapher at Gallipolis. His co-experimenter in Gallipolis entertained Crippen with harp music. Columbus interests saw utility in running telephone lines to various Hocking Valley coal mines. Within Athens, at most several private lines were run between businessmen's offices and their homes. By contrast, Nelsonville, which was booming, authorized the creation of a telephone exchange, that is, a switchboard allowing any one subscriber to be connected to any other subscriber. Athenians waited.

Gaslit streets continued to increase in number. Indeed, the Athens Gas Light Company offered to extend its service pipes free of charge, although the village government had to buy the lamps and pay a monthly service fee. The home-owned firm had as its directors representatives of what may fairly be called the Athens establishment: Johnson M. Welch, Daniel B. Stewart, Andrew Ullom, Emmett Tompkins, and William D. Bartlett. The chief problem continued to lie in the niggardliness of the village council in limiting the time the lights were operative. Jennings claimed that complaints were "loud and deep" over the extinguishing of the lights at 9 P.M. and urged that they be kept lit until 11 P.M. and that discretion be exercised when clouds obscured a full moon. A petition, citing the practices of other Ohio communities that kept their lights on all night or at least until midnight, circulated in support of Jennings's argument. The discussion went on to midsummer when at last the council accepted a proposal roughly the same as that of editor Jennings. Even so, not everyone was pleased; "Goosetown residents," that is, those persons living along East State between modern Carpenter Street and Morris Avenue, complained that the lamps were too far apart.

Two other developments merit notice. Athenians still received their mail at general delivery. They had to go fetch it, and nearly every issue of the *Messenger* or the *Journal* listed persons who had mail awaiting them. The interest of the village was piqued in 1885 when the Post Office Department announced a new service, special delivery. For a ten-cent surcharge, in towns of four thousand persons or more, mail would be delivered directly to the homes of addressees who lived within a mile of the post office. Letting the optimist in him dominate, Jennings thought Athens might already have the requisite population to qualify. It did not.

Finally, Athenians got themselves in a snit over time. So long as people traveled either afoot or by horse, each community could easily operate on "sun time," that is, noon was the time the sun rose highest above the horizon. The greater speed of railroads (and by the 1880s passenger trains traveled seven to fifteen times faster than a man on foot) required that for safe operation all trains in a given area must operate on standard time. The railroads, then, took the initiative in establishing time zones fifteen degrees of longitude in width. Athens fell on the eastern side of the Central Time zone and its sun time was roughly thirty minutes "fast" of Central Standard Time. The village fathers promptly agreed to adopt Central Standard Time and had the town hall clock set accordingly. Some citizens grumbled at this "unnatural" time. The village clock, apparently with a mind of its own, refused to work on the new schedule, and, after a brief trial, council voted to revert to sun time, meaning of course that local businesses operated nearly a half hour out of phase with the trains serving the community or with those persons making phone calls from towns on standard time.

The Nineties

If innovations in the infrastructure had moved ahead arithmetically in the seventies and eighties, they leaped ahead geometrically in the nineties. Old business continued to dictate the village agenda—street paving, a working sewer system, the creation of a telephone system. New business focused on a public water system

195

and the introduction of electric lights. By 1890, the town was talked out. It was prepared to act.

GOOD ROADS

Editor Jennings continued his campaign for all-weather roads. He recognized that the chief opponents of rural road improvement were the very farmers such roads would benefit. Area farmers perceived that if macadamized roads were built, they would have to pay taxes in cash rather than give the two-days-a-year service. Jennings tried to overcome the farmers' objections by pointing out the experience of New Jersey farmers who had discovered that macadamized roads, by cutting transportation costs, had increased farm profits by 25 percent while farm property values soared 85 percent.

For the village, the value of hard-surfaced roads was not questioned; the problem was securing the requisite financing and prioritizing the streets to be paved. At the start of the decade, the emphasis was on macadamizing the roads. The road north over Courtney Hill (North Lancaster-Columbus Road), deemed the worst road in the area, was chosen for immediate improvement. The county commissioners assumed responsibility for the approach to the village while the village council took care of the paving within its limits.

In 1891, to finance street improvements, Representative Joseph L. Kessinger pushed a bill through the Ohio Legislature allowing the village to issue $100,000 in bonds, half for street work, half for sewers. Village voters approved a bond issue in a special election, 440 for, 63 against—a 7–1 margin. Thereafter, the council was steadily engaged in setting the grade for new sidewalks and streets. Reflecting the exploratory trip it had made sometime earlier to Charleston, council resolved to rely on brick streets, and, in October 1893, it authorized the paving of Union Street from Congress to Court with brick—the first bricked street in Athens. The decision to use brick was anticipated by an earlier action of council which provided start-up money for the Athens Brick Company, to be repaid at a later time with bricks.

In May 1896, Court Street landowners, led by A. L. Roach, came before council asking that Court Street be paved. For its part, Ohio University pledged to pay its share for paving all the streets adjacent to the College Green whenever the other property owners were ready. The next year council scheduled pavement on Washington Street, Mill and State streets, Morris Avenue, and College Street. In each case, the work was to be completed in ninety days. Once again, progress brought new problems; property owners along the newly paved streets made no effort to clean accumulated debris, and, in the age of horse-drawn conveyances, there was indeed debris. Nor was the village council yet ready to accept the responsibility, although a periodic cleanup of village streets at the end of winter had long been a regular municipal undertaking. Fred Bush, the new editor of the *Messenger*, pointedly inquired what the village street commissioner did for his pay.

Once more the bridge problem popped up. A new iron bridge was thrown across the Hocking River near Herrold's Mill. It was scarcely in place when a twenty-foot section of the East Bridge collapsed under the weight of a horse and wagon. The roadbed of this relatively new bridge had been constructed of hemlock, a wood highly subject to dry rot. Although repaired, the bridge again became a problem when another twenty-foot section dropped into the river, this time because the load exceeded the capacity of the bridge.

WATER AND SEWERS

A need for a village-wide public water and sanitary sewer system went hand-in-hand. An adequate water supply was needed to flush the sewer lines, which drained by gravity, while the existence of a water distribution system made water available in quantities that cesspools could no longer accommodate. As with roads and sidewalks, the goodwill of townsmen did not not suffice to take care of their own water requirements adequately, nor could village wells any longer be counted on to provide the necessary quality or quantity of water. While a private firm might offer to build and operate a water-supply system or a sewer system or both, only the municipality could compel all householders to cease reliance on privies in favor of a community-wide sanitary sewer, thereby expanding the role of government and forcing the development of a bureaucracy adequate to manage the expanded activities. Like other communities, Athens proceeded by trial and error.

As the town fathers pondered the problems of creating a municipal water system, they faced the fact that the village government lacked the requisite skilled personnel to build its own plant. By default, the system would be built by a private contractor. The question would then be whether to franchise the system to a private firm or whether the village should operate the system itself. When the C. E. Coon Company of Sandusky proposed to furnish the wells, standpipe, pumping station, water lines, and fire hydrants for $45,000, *Messenger* editor Jennings, having taken time to look into other water systems in the state, declared that Coon's bid was much too high; $30,000 was a far more reasonable figure. Furthermore, he insisted that once built, the system be municipally owned and operated. He especially opposed any franchise that would allow a private firm to set its own fees.

Pushing ahead, the council submitted Coon's proposal to a public vote. It was approved by a 2–1 margin. Drawing on his business experience, Daniel B. Stewart promptly charged publicly that the contract with Coon was deeply flawed. It failed, among other things, to specify which streets should get water and the size of the water lines. Surprisingly, within two weeks, council rescinded its contract with Coon, alleging that the firm had failed to meet the terms of the offer.

In the end, a new contract was drafted, and, with Daniel Stewart's objections addressed, voters approved the new proposal by a whopping 17–1 margin. This proposal reserved the construction jobs for local laborers. When the water system was completed and tested, the village exercised its right to buy the system. The test of the new system brought out the "little boy" in Athens officials. The adequacy of the water pressure was demonstrated when a firehose, connected to a hydrant at Court and Washington, shot a stream of water to the height of the clock tower on the courthouse. The cost of the system, $38,000, was midway between Jennings's estimate and the original bid.

With the water system in operation, the village proceeded to spend another $20,000 developing a sanitary sewer. In May 1894, a Columbus firm invited Athenians to explore the convenience of modern bathtubs, washstands, and water closets. Hot water, as well as cold, would be available. Although the community had given nearly unanimous approval to water and sewer construction, few citizens availed themselves of the sanitary sewer. In August 1896, after nearly two and a half years, only 47 households in a total of 750 had connected to the sanitary sewer. At times there were "stagnant cesspools" on Court Street when private vaults overflowed. Nor did the newly built lines always suffice. In July 1897, the sewer line on Mill Street failed. Village crews were unable to clear it, and sewage backed up. In the interest of public health, and perhaps with an eye to operating costs, the Board of Health ordered property owners adjacent to sanitary sewer lines to connect "all water closets, privies, cesspools, urinals, sinks, laundries and waste water" to the lines. Thus, individual interest was made to yield to the community welfare.

GAS AND ELECTRIC POWER

As public water and sewer systems were interrelated, so, too, were systems for the production and distribution of gas and electricity. At the start of the 1890s, the gas company began promoting use of gas stoves for cooking, claiming that fifteen to twenty of the town's homes already were using such stoves. Certainly, the gas stove represented a giant leap forward from the old wood cookstove. It freed women from the necessity of chopping wood. The coal or wood stove took time to start and, once started, heated the entire room whether one wanted that heat or not. In generating unneeded heat, it wasted much fuel. The gas stove concentrated its heat on the pan or oven as needed, a point the local gas company emphasized in a half-page advertisement of July 1893: "Keep Cool in Hot Weather by Using Gas for Cooking."

The introduction of electricity was related to the development of new technology. George Westinghouse's alternating-current generators and transformers provided a cost-efficient means for producing and distributing electric power over a wide area. Furthermore, Edison's electric light bulb, announced in 1889, was so superior to candles, oil lamps, gaslights, and even electric arc lights that it immediately increased the demand for access to electric power for street, institutional, and home lighting.

Ohio University took the lead in 1890 by building an electric power plant of its own and introducing electric lights in its buildings. The following year, it installed incandescent lights along its walkways. For its part, the village replaced gaslights with electric arc lamps. Such lights produced an intense white light that was much steadier than the gaslights then in use. More importantly, the streets were better illuminated. While arc lights were suited to street and institutional lighting, they were inferior to incandescent light bulbs for residential use. By 1900, the superiority of incandescent lighting was sufficiently evident that the Athens Gas Company, now renamed the Athens Gas and Electric Company, built a new electric plant with a 60-kilowatt generator, a capacity adequate to power incandescent lights for homes as well as arc lights for streets. The firm did so with some misgivings, for at the moment gaslight was so much cheaper than electric lights that it inhibited the introduction of incandescent lights. Nonetheless, the village fathers marked the end of the nineteenth century by installing incandescent lights in lieu of gaslights in the opera house, largely as a safety measure, but affirming that the future lay with incandescent lamps.

TELEPHONE SERVICE

Oddly, Athens secured long-distance telephone service and private lines well before it acquired a central office to create a local telephone system. To some degree, a community phone system was delayed by the bitter rivalry between Alexander Graham Bell and Elisha Gray. A community exchange did not appear in Athens until Bell's original patent rights expired, making his technology available royalty-free. Then, Athens became involved in a three-way contest for control of the local phone market.

In 1894 Central Union Telephone Company secured a franchise to erect telephone poles within the village. It offered local phone service at $36 a year, terribly expensive in view of the fact that few Athenians had annual cash incomes of as much as $500. By January 1895, a central office was in operation. There were forty-nine customers of whom only seven were residential, the rest mostly merchants. A year later local grocers, grumbling that the business rates of $36 a year were too high, had their phones disconnected. In short order, they recanted, but an undercurrent of discontent continued, and in May 1899 Mayor Davis was entertaining a franchise proposal from a second firm. The proposal was tainted, however, for Davis had been employed by the firm to promote its interest.

At this point, the Chillicothe, McArthur, and Athens Telephone Co., a long-lines firm, announced it had signed up a hundred subscribers and would have a switchboard installed in Athens within a month, giving Athens its second local phone company. The plot thickened as a third group, terming itself the Home Telephone Company, all Athens businessmen, bid for a franchise. Editor Bush called for a halt, an appeal to reason. The village, he thought, might sustain two hundred phones, sufficient to permit one firm to prosper, but split three ways, there could only be uneconomical duplication of services. As with gas, electric, water, and sewer services, economic considerations required a single, unified service, a natural monopoly either owned by the community or franchised and regulated by the village. The Athens Home Telephone Company, with the local dentist Clarence L. Jones as its driving force, offered good terms—$1.00 a month for residential service, $2.00 for business customers. In spite of editor Bush, the Home Telephone Company got its franchise. In practice, business firms and professional men had to subscribe to the services of both Central Union and Home Telephone to be reachable by customers and clients.

At the century's end, Athens had ceased to be a hamlet of individuals who by and large took care of their own needs—had their own wells and privies, made do with such sidewalks as they or their neighbors saw fit to install in front of their homes and businesses, relied on kerosene lamps for nighttime illumination, cooked and baked on wood or coal stoves, and heated their homes by coal grates installed in their fireplaces.

By 1900, Athens was becoming a village in which the community's well-being increasingly demanded standards that individuals had to abide by. In exchange for this restriction of personal autonomy, there was a prospect of pure water, a more efficient, certainly less odoriferous and far healthier mode of waste disposal, more convenient means for cooking meals and for heating and lighting homes. The new amenities required investments in water lines, plumbing facilities, gas lines, electric and phone lines, and appliances. The *Messenger* did take notice when a resident installed steam heat in his home, when a new house included a bathroom, or when an older home was remodeled to provide a modern kitchen. At the time, these innovations and amenities were limited to the elite and the more prosperous middle class. The residents of West End, the black community, the railroad workers, the day laborers remained without.

THE MONEY ECONOMY

In the last three decades of the nineteenth century, the United States in many ways became a nation as it had never been before the war. The completion of the transcontinental railroad, the double-tracking of eastern railroads, and the creation of regional rail systems such as the New York Central, the Pennsylvania, and the Baltimore and Ohio not only spurred development of the steel industry but generated national markets for many products. Industrialization promoted the growth of cities whose populations were measured in hundreds of thousands of people. Agriculture became mechanized as well as commercialized. Craftsmen found their handcraft methods increasingly outmoded by machine production so that semi-skilled and unskilled laborers began to displace the skilled craftsmen. The nation's economy expanded, driven especially by the growth in metals, coal and oil, and electric power. Inevitably, Athens felt these forces, but often unevenly.

Banks

As a money economy displaced a barter economy, Athens developed its banking structure. During much of the last three decades of the century Athenians were served by two banks: The First National Bank and the Bank of Athens.

The First National Bank, the older institution, increased its capital in 1883 to $75,000. More telling, its resources had reached $600,000 by 1905. At its inception the First National had ties to the Marietta and Cincinnati Railroad in that the bank's trustees included Noah L. Wilson, president of the M & C, while John Ballard and E. H. Moore were also trustees of the railroad. Eliakim H. Moore, the founding president, retained his presidency until 1879. David H. Moore, his nephew, became the cashier in 1882, continuing in that position into the present century. After the M & C was absorbed by the B & O, the railroad's influence on the bank waned. The First National could handle the day-to-day credit needs of Court Street merchants, village craftsmen and manufacturers, and area farmers; it was not prepared to underwrite any but the most modest venture-capital investments.

The other bank, the Bank of Athens, continued as a private venture of John Brown and his son James Dickey Brown. A man in his late sixties when he moved his bank from Albany to Athens, John Brown was regarded as a man with "clear perception and great caution," a man who merited public confidence and patronage. By the time he died in 1875, his transplanted bank was well founded. To twenty-three-year-old James fell the responsibility of guiding the bank for the balance of the century. Pictures of James D. Brown suggest a spare, austere man.

The Bank of Athens was unique. It accepted only demand deposits, that is, checking accounts. Lizzie (Mrs. James D.) Brown, educated at the Female Seminary in Oxford, served as assistant cashier and was noted for her practical business judgment. When Brown ordered a new building for his bank in 1883, the new structure combined the bank with a new home for himself and his wife. The front door of the bank featured a bell pull connected to a bell in the family kitchen. There were no formal banking hours, so the Browns were available to customers from sunup to sundown, except on Sunday. The bank did well. Through the hard times of the 1870s, the bank never failed to earn less than 10 percent on its capital. The bottom line, however, was that the stability of the bank depended on the judgment of its owner. James Brown met the test, taking his bank into the twentieth century without loss to any depositor or even delay in meeting its obligations.

The First National Bank and the Bank of Athens were designed chiefly to serve area merchants and farmers who needed short-term business loans. In 1880, a group of local men organized a third financial institution, the Athens Home Building Association, to help finance the purchase of homes, transactions requiring long-term credit. Charles L. Kurtz, David H. Moore, and John P. Dana were principals in this. This institution seems not to have fared especially well, and, in January 1883, the Peoples Building and Loan was organized by a different coalition: W. H. Brown, E. B. Clarke, and F. O. Pickering among others, largely Court Street merchants. A year and a half later, a third building and loan was announced. Implicit in the building and loan firms is the fact that a significant portion of the community lived in rented houses. A major, but hidden, economic activity of local merchants and professional men was the building of houses for resale or rental.

Economy in Transition

In 1870, Athenians made a living much as their parents' generation had done. Few persons were rich, upper-class citizens; relatively few were poor, working-class laborers. Yet, there were new elements in the economic equation. A cash economy rapidly replaced the barter economy of earlier years. The M & C and the B & O railroads provided outlets for bulk produce either at Cincinnati or eastward in Baltimore. Athens craftsmen increasingly faced competition with manufacturers on the East Coast. The newly completed Columbus and Hocking Valley Railroad opened the market for area coal in Columbus and the Great Lakes. The isolation and self-sufficiency that had characterized the economic milieu of the past was gone.

Agriculture

The ties to agriculture were loosening. Thomas Ewing, son of the Ohio University graduate of 1815, spelled it out clearly in June 1872. With a sense of history, he pointed out how the Hocking Valley had afforded enough rich bottom lands for the small-scale husbandry possible in 1800. But the quantity of such land was limited; so was the possibility of agricultural growth in Southeast Ohio. Ewing might have added, that while five-, ten-, and fifteen-acre "farms" could produce an adequate living by the standards of 1800, or even of 1850, these lands were not well adapted to the commercial agriculture made possible with Oliver's chilled plow, McCormick's reaper, the steam-powered tractor, or the combine.

Athens County farmers in the 1870s were in search of a crop or crops that would produce yields that would enable them to support their families in comfort. One such effort was directed at producing wool. In the early 1870s, Athens County was a leading wool producer. Sheep could graze on land that mechanized equipment could not till. Wool production in 1872 was 180,000 pounds. The amount of land in pasture, in fact, exceeded the amount under cultivation by twenty percent. In 1879, the county exported 300,000 pounds of wool and was still thought to be under-producing the crop. Wool was regarded as the most profitable product for the farmer.

Wool had to be processed and marketed, and hence it provided business opportunities for local merchants and processors. The merchants might change from decade to decade, but Colonel T. R. Stanley in 1879 shipped out over 100,000 pounds of wool, a third of the county's production. Alex Ewing, who leased the Herrold woolen mills, bought wool and produced yarn, blankets, jeans, and flannels. The Stewart mills likewise provided a market for raw wool which it carded and spun. And on Court Street, William B. Vorhes and Son exchanged raw wool for woolen fabrics. For the time being, this was a profitable enterprise for farmers, mill operators, and merchants, a culmination of the old ways.

The major crops remained corn and wheat. Corn, which flourished in bottom lands, was the mainstay of many Athens County farmers, generating 624,000 bushels from 23,408 acres in 1878, a yield approaching 30 bushels an acre. Traditional as it was, wheat disappointed. The yield in 1878, for example, was but eight to nine bushels per acre, no path to prosperity when yields elsewhere were double or triple for the same effort. Nehemiah Warren's farm near Stewart gained county-wide acclaim as the "champion local wheat producer" for a wheat yield of 40 bushels to the acre. The *Messenger* cautioned that such yields could not be sustained. Nonetheless, Warren, clearly into commercial agriculture, threshed in excess of 3,000 bushels of wheat in 1879.

Even in 1870, few Athens County farmers could put as much as 100 acres into cultivation. To find a profitable use for their land, some Athenians experimented. Land in the eastern part of the county lent itself to tobacco. Others tried sweet potatoes, tomatoes, apples, and peaches. Still others made butter and cheese, or, in season, maple syrup. Most of these were auxiliary enterprises and invariably small-scale operations. There were but 145 acres devoted to tobacco in the entire county, only 33 acres to sweet potatoes. Joseph Higgins's experiment with potatoes— 70,000 sweet potato plants alone, plus Irish potatoes—failed as potato bugs destroyed much of his crop. For a rare individual, specialty crops paid; for the conventional farmer, no.

Fruit production worked well for those with hilly land where the slopes faced southward. The upper sides of such hills afforded protection against freezing when crops at lower elevations and in the bottom lands became victims of temperature inversion. But even here, fruit crops provided no easy path to wealth. The Rome apple, which some local enthusiasts claim took its name from Rome township of Athens County, was more certain to produce steady yields in Rome Township, Lawrence County, a more likely place of origin. Peaches, which could be converted into brandy, did well for a time. North Hill and Peach Ridge was one vast orchard. But peach trees seldom produced two years in a row, a serious limitation to farmers accustomed to eating year-round.

And then there were hogs and cattle. The county offered ample pasturage, and, fattened on corn just prior to marketing, hogs might pay handsomely. Cattle and hogs had a market in Athens. Many Court Street merchants still functioned as produce merchants, buying country produce to accommodate country customers, consolidating the goods, and shipping them to a larger market. Merchant-craftsmen such as Cyrus Rose processed hides to manufacture saddles, harnesses, and whips for the local market. In season—that is, in fall and winter—John Farrell and John Ring operated meat markets. These were part-time operations: Monday, Wednesday, Friday and Saturday from 4 P.M. to 7 P.M. However, the community was not enchanted with in-town slaughterhouses. They were "unhealthy and offensive." As early as June 1874, the village council ordered them to move outside the village limits or be sued, an assertion of expanded public authority in the interest of the community's health.

The roles of the stock raiser, butcher, and leather worker were old ones, but Athens village could never consume more than a fraction of the beef, pork, and hides area farmers produced. They had to find a market for their animals, whether on the hoof or slaughtered, elsewhere. Yet the times were out of joint. The railroad, the refrigerator car, and the steamship put both American beef and pork in competition with expanding output from Canada and Argentina, depressing prices. In 1878, unusually low hog prices caused the *Messenger* to comment that farmers would have fared better had they knocked their swine in the head early in the fall and marketed their corn as such.

Agriculture and stock raising could not fuel an expanding local economy. Most of the productive land was in use by 1870; expanded production would depend on new technology, new plant species. Higher farm prices would depend on an urban population that grew at a faster rate than farm output.

The Commercial Scene

Although Court Street was the business center for the village in 1870, few of the business structures of 1870 survive. Between State Street and Union Street, only the buildings housing Perk's coffeehouse at Court and Union, Cornwell Jewelers and its neighbors to the north and south, and the Crippen building, housing Zachary's and the C. I., remain. In fact, in 1870, Court Street ended at State-Mill Street, and still boasted a number of private homes, some elegant, interspersed with open lots and business houses.

The major figures in the commercial world were the Ballards—John, Fred, and James—occupying the northeast corner of Court and Union. Their building still embodied within it the log courthouse Eliphaz Perkins had reconstructed on the site early in the century. The McGuffey house was adjacent to it on Union Street; the Ballard house was on Court Street. Advanced in age, John Ballard turned the enterprise over to son James, but the dominance of the Ballards on Court Street was checked by the devastating fire of December 1877. The Ballards lost not only their building, but much of their merchandise, some by fire, much by looting. They would resume business, but they faced new competitors. Fred Ballard departed for Philadelphia where, in the late 1880s, his daughter Margaret became one of the first women tennis stars in the United States.

Up Court Street, adjacent to the courthouse, was the venerable John Perkins, son of Eliphaz Perkins. John Perkins was still the town druggist. His handsome brick residence housed his drugstore in the corner next the courthouse. Directly across the street, the old Pickering and Carley building housed several stores, in one of which, starting in 1832, John Cornwell had off-and-on functioned as a daguerreotypist in the second-floor "sky-room" and repaired watches when not occupied with his photography. The building itself may date back to the days of Charles Shipman in the 1820s and thus be the oldest structure on Court Street. Athough John Cornwell's presence was not continuous, he invariably returned to this building, and in the early 1870s, his son D. C. Cornwell settled in, moved to the first floor, and eventually acquired ownership of the building. In time, Cornwells would be able to claim the status of being the oldest family-firm in Athens. The other merchant prince was David Zenner. In early 1875, his firm well established, David Zenner retired to Cincinnati, relinquishing the business to his son-in-law, John Friday. In short, the village greeted a new generation of businessmen and enterprises in the 1870s.

The commercial enterprises of Court Street in 1870 were diverse. The Misses Harker and Dunnington, among the first female milliners to operate their own store, offered home-made millinery. After taking over from his father, D. C. Cornwell specialized in clocks, watches, books, stationery, and jewelry. Next door, Pickering and Sons sold groceries. For the most part, such goods were staple products, sold in bulk. A. L. Roach, a grocer, was one of the first Court Street merchants to advertise prices—sugar at 10 cents a pound; salt, $1.50 a barrel; a gallon of canned apples or peaches, 50 cents. In late fall and winter, John Ring, a stock raiser, offered fresh meat. His place of operation was the village-owned Market House, now 8 North Court Street.

Reflecting the growing propensity for merchants to specialize and the proliferation of the kinds of goods available, Thomas D. M. Pilcher opened a furniture store on Court Street and operated his own factory off West Union Street. Both his store and warehouse, located behind Ballard's store, went up in flames in the

1877 fire. S. G. Wright offered pianos, organs, and sewing machines. While he did not list prices, Wright was specific about payments. Organs were $15.00 down, $10.00 a month until paid. Pianos required $50.00 down and $20.00 a month. Wright operated from a place on South Congress next to today's Baker Building. Nelson Van Vorhes and William B. Bartlett, hardware merchants, sold cookstoves—saving fuel, reducing dust, and cheap. They also sold the Studebaker wagon, "the best farm wagon manufactured," pitting their merchandise against wagons manufactured by local craftsmen. So, too, the merchants offering factory-made shoes competed with the local craftsmen who made shoes to order, just as the purveyors of ready-made clothes increasingly competed with the village's custom tailors.

As the 1880s moved along, the range of goods widened and the degree of retail specialization increased. Among the innovations were the marble-topped soda fountain of Carpenter and Henderson. In the early 1880s E. C. Berry began to make his own ice cream for his confectionery. Later he shifted directions and established himself as a restaurateur and caterer. James Farrell installed a "cooling room," a walk-in refrigerator, at his Union Street store. In 1887, Court Street got a combination confectionery and fruit store. Still another innovation was A. O. Sloane's 5-, 10-, and 25-cent counter and the "5- and 10-cent tables" of A. and L. Gilley, forerunners of the five- and ten-cent stores made famous by F. W. Woolworth.

The 1890s saw the introduction of merchants specializing in farm equipment and builder's hardware, in paints, in rubber overshoes, and in celluloid collars and cuffs. A. B. Laurie operated one of the first restaurants as such, featuring oysters. He also sold oysters over the counter as well as fish and celery. However, Laurie did not have the field to himself. The Elmer Van Pelts, husband and wife, operated a confectionery and restaurant in the new Phoenix Block, then passed it on to the C. L. Phillipses. In 1890, ever seeking to find just the right niche in the business community, E. C. Berry discontinued his restaurant to concentrate on catering and a carry-out trade in baked goods, ice cream, oysters in season, and fresh bread. Reflecting the rural character of the township, J. E. Spicer specialized in a full line of feed and grain as well as fertilizer for spring and fall crops. He also sold low sulfur coal.

Along with new lines of merchandise, Athens acquired a bowling alley that featured Ladies' Night on Fridays, and a pool and billiard room in the Phoenix Block. Yet another new service was the Athens Steam Laundry, which claimed a capacity to process the laundry of 50 families a day plus 2,000 shirts and 800 dozen cuffs and collars. Butterick patterns became available at Zenner's in 1894.

New times brought new modes of doing business, modes that would push the community toward the ways of the twentieth century. One innovation was the employment of female clerks. Young women such as Maria Foster had worked in family-operated businesses prior to the Civil War, and Mrs. Mallarme managed a Court Street hotel at the threshold of the Civil War. Post–Civil War hotels were often husband-wife enterprises, the unique skills and personalities of the couples dictating the division of work. In the old Brown House, facing the College Green, as General John Brown aged, the management devolved on his daughter. Before being demolished to make way for what became Howard Hall, the Brown House passed to a husband-wife team. At the Warren House, a Mrs. Barrow presided as hostess. Similarly, the Alex Ewings took over the Central Hotel, later named the Palmer House, occupying what today is (in part) the Baker Building.

The most important innovation lay in the employment of women not related to their employer. The first such women were anonymous so far as the *Messenger* was concerned. Yet, they were celebrities of a sort, so that their presence as pioneers was noted after the fact. Emma Geren, one of the first, was a telegrapher as well as a cashier at Zenner's. Such women were most likely to be employed by dry goods stores, selling merchandise to women. As factory-made hats became common, women were employed as trimmers to individualize the hats for customers. In the 1890s, Lilian (Mrs. Henry) Zenner, wife of David Zenner's son, took charge of purchasing hats in the wholesale houses of the East and overseeing the trimming and sale of hats in Athens. By 1900, salesladies were commonplace figures in the Court Street department stores. However, many of the the milliners and probably all of the twenty-four dressmakers of 1900 were self-employed. The business community gradually included women stenographers and bookkeepers.

To escape the limitations of the local market, several enterprising merchants expanded their businesses either by opening retail outlets in other communities or by developing a wholesale business that supplied outlying country stores. W. H. Brown was among the first to switch from retail to wholesale, distributing "staple and fancy groceries" to retailers in Athens and southern Ohio. Hiram Bingham's grocery operated both at the retail and wholesale levels. What worked in the grocery business was tried in other lines of selling. F. E. Waterman Company, druggists, catered to "country dealers." While Kurtz & Moore supplied school books to Athens and adjacent townships, Zenner's opened a branch in Logan. This establishment of branches could work in reverse, too. Thus, F. L. Preston's department store had its origin as a branch of the parent store in Nelsonville, as did the Carpenter hardware store.

The most significant change was the move toward the cash system. In the wake of the 1873 depression grocer A. L. Roach announced he was adopting "*a cash system —NO CREDIT.*" He went on to explain that by doing so he could offer goods for ten to fifteen percent less than charged by his competitors who extended credit. Others would spell out that credit sales inflated the merchant's costs when the inevitable deadbeat skipped out, both from the expenses of bringing delinquents to court and from the loss to the merchant of the use of his money while he waited for the purchaser to pay up.

In 1876, M. Selig's department store moved to the "One Price System," cautioning customers, "no more bargaining over price." A. L. Roach and M. Selig were in the vanguard. Most grocers and dry-goods merchants continued the old ways, a factor that explains the absence of specific prices attached to goods in advertisements. As Henry Zenner explained, the prices were coded on tags, enabling the salesperson to know the asking price and the margin he had to work with in bargaining over prices with individual customers. In 1891, D. Zenner & Co. joined the "one price system."

Although Athens was relatively isolated from the 1873 panic, the same was not true of 1893. For the first time a number of merchants suffered serious cash-flow problems when they were unable to sell their merchandise quickly enough to pay their suppliers. In August 1893, the *Messenger* noted that tax delinquencies were at a high level, although the local banks were doing fine. For the businesses of L. O. Tullis, "a small dealer in clothing and furnishings," and F. O. Foley, who now operated a meat market at 8 North Court, the situation was fatal. Both had to make an assignment of their goods for the benefit of creditors. A third party was charged with liquidating as much property as needed to pay off the outstanding obligations. In both cases, the *Messenger* explained that the merchants' problems stemmed from their difficulty in collecting from their credit customers. In October 1893, James A. Palmer went bankrupt, sued by the First National Bank for recovery of the $7,000 he owed the bank. Early in November, a half-page advertisement in the *Messenger* announced "the Great Bankrupt Sale." Editor Jennings sought to ease Palmer's pain, praising him as an "active and enterprising citizen." The economic situation became worse in 1894, and it lingered. As late as 1897, A. O. Sloane was forced to join the ranks of the bankrupt.

With the upturn in business in the late 1890s, a number of firms took heart and announced a switch to a cash-only system. Fred Stalder, whose grocery was reputedly the oldest in the village, promised customers lower prices. The Cotton Brothers, also grocers, announced that beginning with the new year, 1899, all transactions would be for cash, assuring lower prices, as paying customers would no longer have to make up the losses merchants incurred from bad debts. Finally, Kern and Foster joined the cash-only parade. The public repetition of explanations and rationales for "cash-only" transactions underscored that the merchants feared an adverse reaction from customers. And, in fact, a number of merchants continued to sell on credit.

Court Street, in 1900, looked far different than in 1870. Over time, a number of business houses occupied premises originally built as private dwellings. Two kinds of renovations were made. First, the floors were lowered to street level, giving customers easier access to the stores. Secondly, the facades were redone, the fronts extended to the sidewalk and "French glass" windows installed; broad plate glass facilitated window displays while flooding the store with daylight. Among the first to upgrade his place of business was Edward Berry, who, in 1880, engaged Frank Towsley, a local builder-architect, to provide his establishment with plate glass windows 6' by 10'. Later in the year, Towsley remodeled the grocery store of C. R. Sheldon, also installing French glass windows while extending the store to the rear. The changes proved contagious. Joseph Norton had his floor lowered to sidewalk level. So, too, the John Perkins house-drugstore was remodeled. The floor was lowered to street level and the facade redone with French glass windows. The structure was also extended, making it ninety feet deep.

While cosmetic changes extended the life of already old structures and updated the appearance of Court Street, new structures made an even bigger difference. Construction of the Masonic Hall, still standing on the west side of Court Street, was a major event. As built, the first floor held two storerooms, the second floor was available for offices, and the third housed the lodge rooms of the village's various Masonic organizations. A tin awning extended from the building over the sidewalk. A source of community pride, the dedication occasioned a grand celebration with band, parade, and delegations from many parts of Ohio. Almost immediately, William Nelson constructed the Nelson Block across the street. It gave Nelson a modern storeroom for his own business and rental income from the other spaces in the building. Literally out of the ashes of the 1877 fire came the Phoenix Building and shortly the Moore-Russell Building, both on South Court Street.

In the next block to the north and on the west side of Court Street, Nehemiah Warren built the town's most impressive hotel, the multi-story Warren House. Having first located on South Court, in 1872 D. Zenner built his own store—a three-story structure, with ample display windows and recessed entrances—on the west side of North Court, the structure last used by Belk Simpson. The W. H.

Potter building at Court and West State, then a two-story structure, which accommodated two stores at ground level and had a large, high-ceilinged room on the second, dates from 1875. And in 1883, J. D. Brown razed the building his Bank of Athens had occupied ever since it located in Athens, a house reputed to have been built in 1812, and erected a combination bank building and home on the corner of Washington and Court Street. These new structures of the 1870s and early 1880s, along with the new Village Hall (1874) and the new Athens County Courthouse (1880), gave evidence of a level of prosperity and a spirit of optimism, and provided room for growth.

The end of the century saw another spurt of building at the north end of Court Street. The Potter Building, having become the property of O. B. Sloane, and the other buildings that stood north of the Warren House were given a facelift to create a uniform facade. In the early 1890s Edward Berry began a twenty-room hotel across from the Warren House, a structure he would expand periodically. Not to be overlooked were a number of smaller structures constructed by merchant-builder David Dyson and builder-architects Frank Towsley and George W. Towsley. Typical of these are the store Dyson did for Peter Kern, a shoe merchant (now occupied by the Mountain Leather shop); the tiny structure wedged between the former Masonic Hall and the Courthouse Annex (now the law office of Robert Stewart and the Night Court); and the structure to the north of the Peoples Bank, one-time headquarters for the Home Telephone Company.

Industry

Athens had scarcely reached the threshold of the industrial revolution in 1870. The village contained ten enterprises that could be termed industrial, eight of which were tied to agriculture. Four of the enterprises were mills, two woolen mills, two gristmills. Another four firms processed leather, one of them producing saddles and harnesses, the other three making boots and shoes. And finally, there were two metal-working firms, one making tinware, the other, the foundry of W. W. Love.

Daniel B. Stewart's woolen mill, the successor to Jehiel Gregory's mill, was the largest enterprise. Representing a capital investment of $25,000, the woolen mill had five employees with an annual payroll of $3,000. Stewart's mill produced a variety of fabrics—jeans, satine, and checkered flannel as well as blankets and stocking yarn. The mill was equipped with six narrow looms, a broad loom, and 744 spindles. Stewart competed with Joseph Herrold, whose mill upstream represented a far smaller investment, $10,000, with three employees. Working in both cotton and wool, Herrold produced jeans and cashmere, blankets and yarns. These same two entrepreneurs each owned gristmills. Stewart's gristmill, which required 6.5 employees, produced both flour and meal, but its specialty was animal feed. Herrold's gristmill, operating at one-third the scale, produced a nominal quantity of buckwheat flour, some ordinary flour, and also concentrated on animal feed. Oddly enough, Herrold's millwheel was rated at 60 horsepower, Stewart's at 40.

The boot and shoe and the harness and saddle enterprises provided local farmers and cattle raisers with a modest market for their hides. Davis Brothers and Alexander Cochran, the leading boot makers, each turned out 1,200 pairs of boots a year as well as from 500 to 600 pairs of shoes. Alonzo J. McCune produced a total of 700 pairs of boots and shoes. In the aggregate the three boot- and shoe-making enterprises represented $5,000 in capital and employed a total of nine persons who shared a payroll of $4,600. The saddle and harness maker, J. Higgins, had one employee and turned out 30 saddles and 100 sets of harness a year.

The two metalworking firms were as different as night and day. Jacob Groins, with one employee, produced tinware. His was a handcraft operation, requiring a minimum of capital—$600—and no power equipment. At the other end of the continuum was W. W. Love's agricultural implement business and foundry. His agricultural implement business, using a 20-horsepower steam engine, made some 2,000 plows a year. The foundry, which produced stoves and grates as well as miscellaneous castings, utilized a 5-horsepower engine. The foundry was the only steam-powered plant in the community.

In the early 1870s, Love's firm developed a new product, a turbine water wheel. Designed by John Case and patented in 1872, Case's turbine seemed superior to other wheels. The firm quickly found itself with orders for more wheels than it could produce. However, its scale of operation was such that even after expanding, it still produced no more than four to six wheels a week, hardly a production level capable of propelling Athens into a major industrial center. To expand further, Love and Case required additional capital. Always enthusiastic, editor Jennings thought the firm, if adequately capitalized, could become a firm with 200 employees and an annual payroll of $100,000, Yet, when a public meeting convened to organize a joint-stock company to raise the necessary funds, few people attended. By December 1872, however, a dozen or so Athenians pooled $40,000 to incorporate the Athens Water Wheel and Machine Shop. Daniel B. Stewart was elected president, H. K. Blackstone secretary-treasurer and superintendent. The directors included George T. Gould, the salt magnate of Salina, James Ballard, and Isaac

Silvus, Court Street merchants, Henry O'Bleness, building contractor, Joseph Herrold, miller, and J. M. Case, the designer of the water wheel. Eliakim Moore, Charles Grosvenor, and S. W. Pickering were among the stockholders.

For a decade, the firm did well enough, so that in 1883 it constructed three brick buildings, a foundry, a machine shop, and a boiler plant, in the approximate area of today's Athens Lumber Company. Additional expansion followed for a time. The mid-nineties, which brought Athens face-to-face with its first depression, did the firm in. In May 1896, the sheriff auctioned the property off. The property was appraised at $14,333, roughly one third of the original investment.

J. C. Campbell, a Court Street merchant turned investor, and John Brannan, the new owners, imported new managers and recruited a new labor force. A year later, the firm had 25 to 30 employees and was operating a twelve-hour day, six and sometimes seven days a week. Satisfied with their resuscitation of the enterprise, Campbell and Brannan sold the business to E. S. Jennings of Pataskala, an experienced mechanic who had just reorganized a foundry in Nelsonville. As the century ended, Jennings was planning to invest further capital and increase the labor force to fifty men.

The thirty years 1870–1900 saw a variety of manufacturing enterprises appear in Athens. Some succeeded; some failed. One of the new industries, beginning in 1873, was the Athens Gas Company, which "cooked" coal to produce manufactured gas and, as a by-product, coke. The firm offered consumers 30 bushels of coke for $2.00. Coke was cheaper than coal but required a tighter, more expensive stove, so the market was limited. During the seventies, gas was manufactured primarily for street and home lighting, replacing the coal-oil or kerosene lamps that had proliferated during the 1860s. In the 1880s, gas was increasingly used for home heating and, in the 1890s, for cooking. In the 1890s the firm began producing electric power and changed its name to Athens Gas and Electric Company.

Despite the growing market for its services, the management of Athens Gas and Electric faced difficult choices. Their initial plant had produced artificial gas, relying on the easy availability of low-cost coal. But the Athens area also produced natural gas, and much time and money was invested by a variety of local and outside interests in trying to develop a large, dependable flow of natural gas. The question then became: Should Athens continue to rely on artificial gas or should it switch to natural gas? The answer seemed simple as natural gas at the time cost only one-fifth as much as artificial gas. At this point, Johnson M. Welch and Major Leonidas M. Jewett, major holders of Athens Gas and Electric stock, sold their shares to the Logan Natural Gas and Fuel Company, and Welch's son Charles H.

Welch became president of Athens Gas and Electric Company, now a subsidiary of the Logan firm. The village was caught by surprise. The decision to sell, however, was hardly capricious. Welch and Jewett recognized that natural gas could easily undercut artificial gas, but they were leery that the Athens area would ever be able to supply the local demand for natural gas. Hence, they turned to the Logan firm, which seemed able to assure an ample supply from its field at Sugar Grove. While Charles Welch was an Athenian and would gain a national reputation as an expert in the field, future management decisions would rest with the out-of-town owners. For Athens, the cost of progress entailed a diminution of local autonomy.

Several Athenians manufactured wagons to supply the local agricultural economy. The wagonmaking business of Alonzo Laird fared none too well, and in the business downturn of 1884–85, his debts exceeded his assets to the extent that the sheriff closed him down. Editor Jennings praised him as "a worthy and square dealing businessman." That Laird was both a dealer in wagons manufactured elsewhere and a wagonmaker reflects a problem faced by craftsmen of all kinds in the late nineteenth century. Individual local craftsmen were frequently forced to abandon their craft and become salesmen of other people's manufactures. Where Laird failed, John and Henry Crippen ventured in, taking the precaution of incorporating their firm and thereby limiting their personal financial liability. They were joined in the business by James D. Brown, Fred Stalder, and Thomas Craig, who shared as stockholders. At the heart of the business was a wagon brake invented by Henry M. Crippen. The brake had a broad market potential, for it could be installed on wagons already in use, wagons made by others. They also manufactured wagons, locating off West Union near the new depot.

Yet another enterprise geared to the land, though not to the farm per se, was the Athens Lumber Company. Timber the county had in abundance. All along, individuals had operated small-scale sawmills to process timber for barns and houses. Now in 1896, five local men, Stacy Wolfe, Henry O'Bleness, W. N. Alderman, J. W. Bryson, and Harry Allen, incorporated the Athens Lumber Company, a firm that would process timber in the requisite lengths and dimensions of a variety of woods to keep in stock for local contractors, one of whom was Henry O'Bleness.

The grand coup of those who saw industry as the force that would drive the Athens economy was inducing Wilfred and Samuel Hudson in 1893 to relocate their school furniture firm to Athens. From the first, the possibilities were irresistible to a village still shy of 3,000 persons. The firm promised 100 to 125 employees and a weekly payroll of between $900 and $1,100. Since a number of these employees would have to be imported into Athens, there was a prospect of attracting several hundred additional residents to the village. The spin-off would include drawing other industries to the village and possibly doubling the value of building lots within a year because of the demand for new housing. After examining the books of the Hudson Brothers, Henry O'Bleness, Andrew W. Ullom, and Stacy Wolfe attested that the firm was financially sound. In ecstasy, editor Jennings foresaw "a new and promising industrial life" for the village.

Already experienced in the production of school furniture, the Hudson brothers proposed to share the prosperity generated by their enterprise in an unusual way. The Hudsons bought a considerable block of land east of May Avenue and south of East State Street, locating their plant adjacent to the railroad. The brothers proposed to own the plant. To the townsmen they offered building lots on what are now Hudson and Lorene streets, lots on which townsmen were invited to construct affordable housing for the workmen who would move to Athens to take jobs. The Hudsons would profit from the production and sale of school furniture; townsmen would profit from the sale and rental of housing. As the firm completed their new plant and commenced production, they began with forty employees. Covering 40,000 square feet, the plant claimed to be the largest of its kind in the United States. Workers' wages ran from $3.00 to $4.00 a day, at least double the average for the community. From the beginning the firm reported a ready market for its product.

The Hudson School Furniture Company was the sort of business Athens had longed for. It turned out a product that permitted relatively high wages, and, in finding a market elsewhere, it brought money into the community. The trade-off was that the prosperity of the village now depended on the demand for the product in other parts of the country. This was a world apart from the pre–Civil War economy in which village craftsmen produced goods for fellow townsmen, a market that was steady, although lacking a potential for rapid growth.

When the Athens Lunatic Asylum was under construction in the late 1860s and early 1870s, the bricks, millions of them, were manufactured on site from clay dug nearby. Athenians had ordinarily produced bricks as an adjunct to building, not as a business per se. Robert Arscott changed that. In the 1870s, Arscott created a brickyard. Employing blacks paid $1.50 a day, he made bricks in a central spot and burned them in permanent kilns. Brickmaking was seasonal, limited to that part of the year when clay could be easily extracted from the ground and when builders were busy. Low tech and entailing only a modest capital, the business invited competition. In 1880, Lute Walker and Charles Gabriel set up a kiln on the site of Camp Wool. With a head start, Arscott expanded his enterprise to manufacture drain tile as well as brick. Even so, builders repeatedly complained that Arscott could not meet the demand in timely fashion. In 1885, Fred Fenzel entered the business, with "a fresh brick kiln of large capacity." By 1890, Fenzel was in position to secure a contract for 500,000 bricks for a new school building in Logan.

In the 1890s, paving bricks came on the scene. At a time when an affluent urban middle class was taking to the bicycle and strenuously objecting to streets filthy and dusty in summer and quagmires after each downpour, there was the prospect of a steady, long-term demand for paving brick. In 1891 Fred Stalder, local inventor and business man, joined D. H. Doan and James Dew, both of Nelsonville, in organizing a brick works for Athens. Short on capital of their own, they proposed that the village advance the firm $20,000, to be repaid in the form of paving bricks. The firm would raise the other $30,000, giving the company a capitalization of $50,000. The plant would begin with a capability of turning out 40,000 paving bricks a day. The town council saw the proposal as mutually advantageous and promptly advanced the $20,000.

The Athens Brick Company, as it styled itself, located along what is now Stimson Avenue, securing shale from the area long occupied by the armory building and the hill to its rear. At the start, the firm bettered its original proposal by producing 50,000 paving bricks a day, and with a labor force of 75 to 100 men, it quickly became a major economic force in the community.

The demand for both conventional building brick and paving brick was highly affected by the cyclical character of a market economy. The 1893 depression quickly halted house building and George Fenzel, who had succeeded Fred Fenzel as a brickmaker, went under. Municipal governments, unable to persuade taxpayers to approve the requisite bond and tax levies, halted street paving. The Athens Brick Company closed down in November 1894, not reopening until May 1896. Even a year later, the firm was uncertain whether it would ever be able to operate at full scale with 75 employees. If the immediate future for paving bricks seemed uncertain in the late 1890s, the long-term prospects were bright, for the automobile was making its presence felt elsewhere and automobile owners would generate an insistent demand for paved streets.

Though the enterprise seemed promising enough, the Star Match Company apparently took fire, then flickered, sputtered, and died out. Organized in October 1880, the Star Match Company had as directors a number of leading businessmen, including Johnson Welch, Augustus Norton, John Friday, James D. Brown, and Henry O'Bleness. It built a plant off West Union Street and proposed to employ as many as 140 persons and produce up to 200 cases of matches a day. As it began production, it advertised for 30 girls, ages 13 to 17. A half year later the firm installed new machinery to increase production. For reasons not clear, the enterprise did not thrive. A cryptic note in the *Messenger* of August 1886 informs that the company's property had been sold at auction by the sheriff for $3,375, underscoring the risk entrepreneurs take in undertaking a new enterprise.

Occupancy of the building erected for the match factory passed briefly to Isaac Half, a merchant with some experience with furniture. By 1883 he had left Selig & Company, the Court Street department store, to undertake on his own the sale of furniture and reupholstering, filling what the *Messenger* termed a local need. Half moved first into the recently vacated Masonic Hall and later into the now empty match factory. Evidently in no position to buy the building, Half shortly found himself forced out when it sold. Unable to find suitable quarters in Athens, he moved his enterprise, which had developed into a manufacturing operation, to Marysville, Ohio. Editor Jennings, predictably, commiserated with Half. "Zealous and intelligent," he pontificated, Half had not received the support he deserved from fellow Athenians.

The new tenant of the match factory, a building with rail service near at hand, was George Peters, who in 1887 commenced a produce-exporting business. Peters concentrated on buying the surpluses of farmers, consolidating them, and shipping them to market. His specialty was the export of area turkeys. In the days immediately preceding Thanksgiving 1887, he exported ten tons of birds.

The Labor Force

The social and economic changes Athens experienced in the last three decades of the nineteenth century are reflected in the composition of its labor force in 1900—the way Athenians earned a living. The whole thrust of development since the first days of settlement had been a shift away from agriculture toward trade and industry, from generalized commerce and craft production to specialization.

The total labor force for the village grew from 486 in 1870 to 865 in 1900, an increase of 78 percent. In terms of the community's professionals, the three decades brought a near doubling in numbers—more clergy, more teachers and professors, more doctors. But it also brought new kinds of professional services—the first nurse, the first veterinarian, the first librarian, the first electrical engineer.

Changes in the character of the business community are reflected in the 1900 labor force. Although the number of craftsmen increased from 115 to 149, the proportion of all workers employed in the crafts declined. The craftsmen of 1900 still included members of the building trades, for houses and stores are built on site. With the appearance of gaslight and heat as well as a municipal water and sewer system, plumbers arrived—four of them—since it was plumbers who installed the gas lines as well as water lines and sewers. The coming of electricity produced seven electricians. Enjoying a greater ease of life, homeowners could have their walls decorated by a professional paperhanger. The 12 operatives of 1870 had become 77 by 1900, as classified by the census, including teamsters, linemen, and wire stringers; Athens had not rushed into factory production on a big scale. Underscoring that the railroads passed through Athens and that the coal area was north of the village, only a token number of railroad or mine workers lived within the village.

With the national trend to machine production of goods—textiles, clothing, and household goods—the number of merchants and their clerical help doubled during these decades. Here, too, change was marked by the proliferation of specialized enterprises. In 1900, Athens had merchants who specialized in selling music, pianos, fish, candy, coal, and fruit. The clerical help reveals fifty-six generic clerks, mostly salespersons, to match forty-seven merchants and grocers. With few exceptions, the merchants were small-scale entrepreneurs who required a minimum of managerial support. The entire village afforded employment to but seven bookkeepers and two stenographers. Presumably most businessmen kept their own books and wrote their own letters. There were no "typewriters," as typists were then called. The coming of the railroad is evident in the presence of eight traveling salesmen, as suppliers increasingly sent their representatives to the customer. The traveling salesmen recorded in the Athens census were Athenians employed to canvass the hamlets away from the village on behalf of those Athens firms that sought to expand business by wholesale trade.

As one might expect, the population Athens gained between 1870 and 1900 prompted a proliferation of services. The village continued to exploit its position as a market town and county seat. The services available in 1870 had focused on the horse—hostelers, livery stables, teamsters, stage drivers, and draymen. Aside from this, the town had offered the public the services of four barbers and a cook, although the saloons and hotels also served meals. By 1900, however, the town boasted a number of restaurants, several hotels, and a lunch counter. A number of persons worked as waiters or cooks. Business places were tidied up by porters and janitors. Men had the services of a bootblack and a shoeshiner. For recreation, aside from the saloons, there was a billiard parlor. As business property often required protection beyond that provided by the one or two village policemen who were on duty at any one time, the first private watchmen were on the job.

Finally, the three decades brought a doubling of the non-farm laborers. Almost none of these were unskilled factory employees. Close to 50 of these laborers worked in jobs related to horses; another 39 were brickyard workers, largely manual laborers. Only 15 were railroad employees. The largest number, 104, were described simply as "laborers" or as "general laborers." A third of these were black men. In age, Athens laborers ranged from fifteen to seventy-six. Most of those who were in their mid-thirties or older were householders and had family responsibilities.

The blacks in the labor force numbered ninety-six. They did not come close to replicating the job experience of their white townsmen. Only one, Andrew Davidson, enjoyed professional employment. Only Edward Berry and James West were proprietors. Nearly all were employed either in menial service jobs or as laborers. Athens schools might be open to black youngsters, but employment opportunities were distinctly restricted.

The Athens female labor force, likewise, had a distinctive profile. Altogether 231 women claimed an occupation in 1900. The numbers were larger than in 1870, and the character of employment differed significantly. By 1900 the consensus that children should remain in school until age sixteen resulted in the exclusion of children from the labor force. This meant a sharp decline in the use of young girls as live-in domestic servants. Growing affluence permitted middle-class men to support their families without the need of pushing teenaged daughters into the labor force, while modest changes in the ways of housekeeping increasingly freed daughters from domestic duties at home. In practice in 1900 more Athens women attended school than entered the labor force until age 21. The labor force rate for girls aged 15 to 19, which had been 44.8 in 1870, dropped to 17.7 in 1900. For young women 20 to 24 years old, it dipped from 35.1 in 1870 to 31.0 in 1900.

Although Athens women, particularly the unmarried ones were increasingly joining the labor force, the range of jobs available to them remained distinctly limited. No woman in 1900 held an old-line professional job—doctor, lawyer, or clergy. Edna Thompson joined her older brother, Claud, in the practice of dentistry. A few women professionals were nurses; the majority were teachers. An uncertain number conducted businesses, Retta Munn as hotelier and Alice Goldsberry as merchant. Several others were in business as milliners or dressmakers, and still others took in boarders or contracted to do laundry. But none was a leading Court Street entrepreneur.

Generally, the village turned to women to provide stenographic and bookkeeping services and to serve as telephone operators. A handful were printers, but those in the crafts were limited to traditional skills in making hats and clothes. Nearly half of all employed women were in personal service occupations, hired for their home-making skills. It is likely that then, as now, many of these employments were part-time or part-year or both.

Railroads, 1870–1900

After the war Athens' place in the sun depended heavily on the railroads that served it. Of first importance was their presence in providing transportation for goods and people. Whereas a horse and wagon were limited to moving a ton or so of goods twenty or twenty-five miles a day and the Hocking Canal several tons but no faster than by wagon, the railroad could move ten or twelve cars, each carrying, perhaps, fifteen tons at an average speed of twenty-five miles an hour. Further-more, a railroad, unlike a canal, could function in times of drought as well as in below-freezing weather.

In post-war years, the Hocking Canal's limitations became especially obvious. It could not move coal during peak wintertime demand for home heating or indus-try. While earlier floods had temporarily interrupted canal service, the flood of 1884 damaged the canal to the degree that the Athens-Nelsonville segment was abandoned. Subsequent flood damage caused the canal north of Nelsonville to be abandoned also, leaving an unused right-of-way.

By the end of the Civil War, it was abundantly clear that the M & C's original line from Athens to Marietta was both ill-designed and ill-advised—too many tunnels, too many trestles, turns that were too tight, grades that were too steep. It also ended at the wrong place, Marietta. But then it had reflected the interests of William P. Cutler, the chief engineer, who represented Marietta interests. Econ-omy of operation required a line that ran from Athens to Belpre and, via a bridge across the Ohio, to Parkersburg, making a direct connection with the Baltimore and Ohio. Such a line was built as the B & O Short Line, the last track being laid in October 1874. The original Athens-Marietta route was limited to twelve loaded cars at a time, but the new route could take thirty. For passengers the travel time from Athens to Parkersburg was cut by one hour; for freight, by three hours. The new B & O Short Line gave Athens connections to Guysville, Stewart, Coolville, Torch, and Little Hocking.

As the B & O pulled itself together after the Civil War so that it could operate from Baltimore to St. Louis, it felt constrained to control the M & C, even to the point of acquiring ownership. The details of the takeover are not relevant to this account, but the end result was that Athens lost whatever management influence it originally had, and the B & O, however well or badly managed it was, became a giant, faceless corporation.

As the M & C was straightening out its affairs after the war, Milbury M. Greene, one-time resident of Congress Street, and Eliakim H. Moore, bank president, promoted a rail connection between Athens and Columbus. Sensing perhaps that Athens County salt had far less growth potential than a Hocking Valley railroad, Greene moved to Columbus, leaving the salt business to his half-brother and erstwhile business associate, George T. Gould. Reviving interest in such a road in Columbus seemed easy enough, and Greene, who had prior experience as a railroad contractor, quickly emerged as the engineer for the Hocking Valley Railroad and, in time, its president. Greene's prior experience as a railroad contractor enabled him to avoid the trial-and-error mistakes that flawed W. P. Cutler's work on the M & C. Greene's cost estimates were realistic, his income-projections, conservative. Well-built, the road produced profits from the start. Its profitability rested on the transportation of a single item, coal.

The Hocking Valley Railroad reached Athens in 1870 and gave Athens a passenger and freight outlet to Columbus. Within two years, Toledo interests, to hold their own with Cleveland as a lake port, sought access to Athens County coal and began exploration of a rail connection through Columbus to tap Hocking Valley fuel. As president of the Hocking Valley Railroad, Greene encouraged them, for to assure Hocking Valley coal an optimal market, it needed to reach the Great Lakes. This access would also serve the interests of the Hocking Valley Railroad. It took Toledo interests four years to reach Columbus. The community of interests of the two roads resulted in their merger in 1881 as the Columbus, Hocking Valley, and Toledo Railroad (C, HV & T), a $20 million corporation. An eminently sensible marriage of convenience from a financial standpoint, at the very least the merger diluted the potential for Athens to exert influence on the management of the road.

Railroading changed greatly during the period from the end of the Civil War to 1900. The trains of the late 1860s were relatively primitive, and passengers and employees were at risk. Accidents were common. In 1872, under the weight of a coal train, a trestle on the Columbus and Hocking Valley Railroad northwest of Lancaster gave way, producing "a general smash up." Less than three weeks later, La Rue's Tunnel on the Marietta and Cincinnati caught fire from the sparks of a passing locomotive. Two weeks later, three cars, loaded with 150 barrels of oil, caught fire four miles west of Athens. Within a week, an M & C express train hit a standing freight train, causing considerable damage to the engine. If, in the early 1870s, the M & C was "an unlucky corporation," so was the Hocking Valley Railroad.

In the course of the next three decades, much progress was made in terms of safety and efficiency. In the improvement of rail service and operations, Athens shared with other communities. One of the innovations of the mid-1870s was the airbrake, which gave the engineer of passenger trains almost "absolute control of the train." By the mid-1870s, the M & C had corrected its defects and began making a name for itself as a safe road, "the ever reliable M & C." The Hocking Valley, too, was praised as "this excellently manned railroad." The Boyden Automatic Brake of 1890 allowed either engineer or conductor to halt the train, and it set the brakes automatically should a car become disconnected from the train. A specific improvement by the Hocking Valley was the rebuilding of the tracks, ballasting the roadbed and replacing the original iron rails with new 85-pound steel rails, rails that permitted both heavier loads and higher speeds while enhancing safety and making it one of the first all-steel railroads in the nation. Other innovations or improvements related to the coupling devices. The use of a speedometer in the caboose kept the conductor informed of his train's progress.

The B & O made changes, too. Some were cosmetic, the repainting of passenger coaches and the upgrading of devices for lighting, heating, and ventilation. The use of through cars made long-distance travel more convenient. Other changes were substantive, the introduction of coal cars 35 feet long and capable of handling 25 tons each. As the century ended, the B & O was installing 85-pounds-per-yard steel rails and had built a union depot located on Union Street. In May 1900 the *Messenger* could report the longest train ever passing through Athens—seventy cars in length, half of them loaded. The whole length was a half mile.

The village immediately felt the impact of several aspects of railroading. First, the cars, standing or moving, proved irresistible to town youngsters. And a few were maimed or even killed in the course of their play. So, too, rail employees lost fingers, arms, and legs while working about the cars. As Major Johnson M. Welch was boarding a train, it lurched, and he lost his balance and a foot. Second, the original depot area, at Cemetery Street and Dean Street (now Shafer and West Washington), became infamous for its rowdy saloons, street violence, and prostitution. Third, the aborted wartime effort of the M & C to tunnel under the old cemetery had left a deep gulch east of the cemetery that was both a nuisance and unsightly.

As a "coal" road, the Hocking Valley focused on serving coal mines along the

Hocking River and in the Monday Creek Valley. It needed only to run spurs or switches relatively short distances to mines along the Hocking. In 1880, by way of expansion, it created a loop that ran eastward from Nelsonville with a spur that passed through Buchtel and dead-ended at Murray City. Before reaching Buchtel, the loop itself turned northward from Snow Fork junction and passed through Monday and Longstreth to Carbon Hill to intersect with a line that had been built from Logan through Winona and Gore to New Straitsville.

The promise of the coal fields in Athens, Hocking, and Perry counties attracted other entrepreneurs, capitalists bent on exploiting the coal and those bent on building the necessary railroads. By 1900, two other railroads had entered Athens County: The Kanawha and Michigan (K & M) in 1880–81 and the Toledo and Ohio Central (T & OC) in 1881. The K & M, briefly the Kanawha and Ohio, linked Athens to Pomeroy and Charleston, West Virginia, while its ties with the Chesapeake and Ohio gave it access to Newport News and Norfolk on the Atlantic. In the long run, it provided a means to bring West Virginia coal through Athens to be marketed in Toledo in competition with Hocking Valley coal. The T & OC was the work of a second group of Toledo investors who believed there were profitable opportunities in the Hocking Valley, particularly along Sunday Creek, that the C, HV & T was missing. It took years before the T & OC was able to enter Athens County.

Beginning in the early 1880s, the C, HV & T, facing potential competition from the T & OC and the K & M, moved to protect its coal-carrying business by acquiring coal properties of its own. By the same token, Hocking Valley coal operators who envisioned markets that could be served only with expanded rail service sought control of the railroads. This was especially true of the coal operators in the valley of the Hocking River as well as those downstream on Monday and Sunday creeks. There were three players—the railroads, coal land owners, and coal mine operators. Their machinations were byzantine. The pressure for all of them was to protect their investment by diversification: acquire several coal properties, operate multiple mines, and tie their fortunes to a railroad. If possible, acquire the railroad. For the moment, the T & OC was unable to compete aggressively, for, in late 1883, it was in the throes of receivership, and it remained in financial trouble off and on for several years. In the mid-1880s, M. M. Greene surrendered management of the Hocking Valley to his son William. In 1888, a lawsuit by the C, HV & T against the former Columbus and Toledo president disclosed that the merger of the Columbus and Toledo with the C, HV & T had been accompanied by a series of transactions, legally permissible, that gave the original owners of the Columbus and Toledo handsome windfall profits and left the new management with a shaky enterprise.

During the 1880s, the T & OC began to open up the Sunday Creek coal areas, a far more expensive venture than the Hocking Valley Railroad's expansion up Monday Creek. As the T & OC came southward from New Lexington, it, too, acquired coal lands of its own, most notably in the Rendville-Corning area just north of Athens County. The competition in Toledo was as much between Hocking Valley –Monday Creek coal and Sunday Creek coal as it was between the C, HV & T Railroad and the T & OC Railroad.

In the course of the 1890s, the financial stakes got still higher. The contest was no longer played out in the Hocking Valley. Coal land owners and coal mine operators became subordinate to the railroads that hauled their product. Increasingly, there was an overlap of ownership between the railroads, the mine operators, and the coal owners.

One of the ironies in the emergence of Athens as a junction point of the B & O, the Hocking Valley, the Toledo and Ohio Central, and the Kanawha and Michigan was that it never became a major rail center. Momentarily, in 1874, Athens bid to become such a center. The M & C car shop at Zaleski had burned, and, knowing that the car shop was to be relocated, a delegation of Athenians went to Baltimore to lobby the B & O management. To underscore their earnestness, Athenians raised a subscription to facilitate its relocation to Athens. The shops were moved to Chillicothe.

Nor did Athens fare any better with the Hocking Valley Railroad. The coal market was in Columbus and Toledo, and the multiple spurs that led from the coal banks to the main line funneled the traffic northward toward Logan. And while Nelsonville secured an enormous railroad marshaling yard, Logan got the rail shops. The impact is seen in the census figures. In 1870 Nelsonville counted 1,080 people; Logan claimed 1,827; Athens reported 1,696. In 1900, Nelsonville reported 5,421 residents; Logan, 3,480; Athens 3,066. In 1900, Athens had only a handful of railroad employees, and four persons with work expressly related to mining. There was another dimension. In terms of transportation, Athenians, whether as passengers or shippers, had easy rail access to Washington and Baltimore to the east, to Columbus, Toledo, and Chicago to the north, and to Cincinnati and St. Louis to the west. It also had rail connections to Pomeroy, Amesville, and the communities of the Sunday Creek Valley, as well as to those astride the B & O. If the railroads had not directly caused Athens village to grow, they had stimulated the growth of York, Trimble, and Dover townships, with an indirect effect on Athens village as the county seat. By 1900 the property of the various railroads operating in the county had added on the order of one million dollars to the county's tax base.

Coal and Iron

In 1870, coal was being extracted on a modest scale in and about Nelsonville, particularly the coal adjacent to the Hocking Canal, which for nearly three decades had carried the coal northward to Columbus. In the earlier years the ownership of coal lands had been local; the scale of mining, limited. Production of coal in Athens County in 1870 was 131,000 tons. Production surpassed 550,000 tons in 1872, surged to 835,000 tons in 1880, passed 1,000,000 tons in 1887, approached 1,500,000 tons three years later, and reached 2,594,000 tons in 1900. The growing awareness of the magnitude of the coal deposits in the Athens-Hocking-Perry area generated both optimism and frustration. Although the demand for coal in producing steel was unprecedented, Hocking Valley coal was not suited to the industry's needs. Even so, the possibilities of personal fortunes in Hocking Valley coal seemed unlimited. To Athenians, the likelihood of rapid expansion of the area's population and general prosperity seemed strong. The potentials that stirred local enthusiasm attracted outside interests and thrust the Hocking Valley into a national industrial economy that linked coal, iron, and railroads. There was also the possibility of developing oil and gas.

The Athens Township plat of 1875 shows the land north of Athens village along the Hocking River and Sugar Creek still to be held in tracts of eighty acres or so, none of it in the name of a coal company, although three to four hundred acres were claimed by the Hocking Valley Oil Company. By contrast, the lands in and about Nelsonville frequently bore such names as L. D. Poston, the Bessemer Coal & Furnace Co., T. Longstreth, and W. B. Brooks. Rail spurs snaked out to coal banks along Monday Creek and the hills back from the Hocking River. At this point, a few Athenians busied themselves buying and selling coal lands north of the village. S. W. Pickering bought eighty acres at $9,000. This was speculative buying and selling. The New York and Ohio Coal Company, organized by outside interests in 1871, invested at least a half million dollars, its stockholders in New York and Europe and Nathan Doan its superintendent. Having secured twelve hundred acres, it broke ground in 1877, laid one and a half miles of track to link up with the Hocking Valley Railroad, and laid out the hamlet of Doanville to start with a hundred houses the first season of operation. It projected an output of fifty cars a day. Athenians might dream, but none possessed the financial resources to become a major player. Coal would have a major impact on Nelsonville and the hamlets along Sunday and Monday creeks. It had a major impact on Athens County. But to 1900, Athens village was strictly on the sidelines.

The impact of the burgeoning coal fields to the north was selective. First, it was the need of Columbus industrial interests for access to Hocking Valley coal that brought the Hocking Valley Railroad to Athens as its southern terminus. By the same token Thaddeus Longstreth, William Brooks, and Peter Hayden, Columbus businessmen, came into the area to exploit the coal, and in their wake, consortia of Boston and New York investors. The result was that the development of the area's coal depended on decisions made by men and corporations from outside and in terms of their other investments. During these years, Johnson M. Welch, as a lawyer, employed his legal skills to manage the 1,400-acre Lick Run mines on behalf of their absentee owners.

Second, the development of the mines required a labor force far greater than could be recruited locally. As a result mine owners recruited immigrants, Poles and Hungarians, and, at times, Negroes. The ethnic mix of Athens County's population was altered, while the population grew. Decade by decade, to the chagrin of Athens, Nelsonville outpaced Athens village in population growth.

Third, the miners organized to protect their incomes and to gain some measure of control over their working conditions. The Hocking Valley was the home base of the United Mine Workers. As John Mitchell and William Green came to the fore, they spoke occasionally in Athens. As labor-management relations in the mines turned sour, the county developed a labor force with a tradition of militancy that would affect the village for decades to come.

Finally, while out-of-state firms jockeyed for dominance, Clinton L. Poston of Nelsonville quietly acquired effective control of an impressive amount of acreage of coal lands. Poston's father Lorenzo Dow Poston had been a pioneer in the Hocking Valley coal business. Retiring in 1873, L. D. Poston left his interests to his sons Clinton L. and William and his son-in-law E. P. Pendleton. Clinton Poston was the managing director; then in 1880 William Poston and E. P. Pendleton sold their interests to two Chillicothe men, and the firm reorganized as C. L. Poston & Company. The firm was producing 150,000 tons of coal per year. In 1889, C. L. Poston bought out his partners.

At the end of the century John Pierpont Morgan, the New York investment banker, intruded into the steel business, first merging a number of steel firms, including Carnegie Steel, to form the United States Steel Company in 1901. As part of this consolidation, Morgan, operating through the Continental Coal Company, bought out C. L. Poston under conditions by which Poston sold his mines but retained the ownership of the coal properties, collecting a royalty on his coal. In the late 1890s, Poston, having married an Athens woman, Delia Kessinger, made Athens his home and became its leading businessman.

When all was said and done, by 1900 Athens County was a major producer of coal, but the economics of the business placed ownership, Poston excepted, in the hands of outsiders. As of 1900 the mines were sufficiently distant from Athens village that few economic benefits came directly to the village. But between the proliferation of the railroads and the development of the coal industry, by 1900 Athens was thoroughly enmeshed in a national, money economy.

9

A Maturing Social Order: 1870–1900

As the village developed its infrastructure and as its money economy evolved, its social, cultural, and intellectual life matured. More and more the individual found himself or herself relying on social institutions apart from the family.

THE ASYLUM

A major spur to the growth of Athens in the period from 1870 to 1900 was the establishment of the Athens Lunatic Asylum, as it was originally called. In the wake of the Civil War, the State of Ohio concluded that the care of the mentally ill was a public responsibility. In April 1867 the Ohio General Assembly enacted legislation, sponsored by Athens representative Dr. William Parker Johnson, providing for the creation of an asylum in Southeast Ohio. Eliakim H. Moore, who combined political experience in Congress with broad business experience, used his influence as a member of the site-selection board to secure the institution for Athens. That a group of Athenians raised money locally to buy the Arthur Coates farm to be given to the state as the site for the hospital helped assure the location of the institution in Athens. In August 1867 the Athens site was approved, and in November 1868 the cornerstone was laid.

Athens sensed the importance of the project and celebrated the cornerstone laying, which was directed by the officers of the Grand Lodge of Free and Accepted Masons of Ohio. The local Masons, augmented by upwards of a thousand visiting brethren, the Athens Brass Band, and the choirs of the Methodist and Presbyterian churches, judges, the mayor, and the village council, led hundreds of townsmen across the South Bridge to the ridge overlooking the Hocking River where the institution would be located.

The economic impact of the hospital on the village was immediate. Construction of the hospital was a major project. The original building would be 853 feet long when completed—if not the largest such building in the nation, then close to it. Several Athenians won major construction contracts. The contract for making and laying three million bricks was taken over by Henry O'Bleness, thus also laying the beginning of the O'Bleness fortune. As the building was completed, other Athenians secured contracts to furnish it. A. S. Troup won the contract for bedsteads, washstands, and bureaus. Merchants James and F. L. Ballard and Issac Half divided the contracts for the bedding. Once open, the institution became a major consumer of goods and services. C. A. Snow & Sons secured a contract to supply 150 gallons of milk a day. Still other Athenians secured year-round employment. The professional staff generally came from outside the community, but from time to time Athenians like Josiah (Si) Allen secured managerial posts. Even before the hospital registered its first patient, the *Messenger* commented that after twenty-five years of the doldrums, the village was humming. There were new buildings on "every knob and patch." The Asylum opened January 1, 1874. Soon there were over five hundred patients.

The patient count increased steadily—633 in 1880 and 771 in 1886. The growing patient population required additional buildings. The rubble and brick kilns from the original construction work were pushed forward, packed down, and covered over to make a broad terrace in front of the main building. A network of ponds was constructed at the base of the ridge on which the hospital sat. The ponds provided ice for the institution as well as ice-skating for townspeople. The combination of the hilltop site and the subsequent landscaping designed by Herman Haerlin, a student of Frederick Law Olmstead, and executed by George Link, brought the hospital grounds acclaim for unparalleled beauty.

In the mid-1880s, a decision to separate "the quiet and convalescent" from patients subject "to fits of passion and violence" necessitated construction of additional wings. Henry O'Bleness won the general building contract, advancing his career as a general contractor. The patient load grew steadily; by 1900 there were 961 patients. The implications for the village economy were significant. In 1893, for example, the State's operating support for the hospital was $96,800; by contrast the Ohio University subsidy was $12,750.

The administration of the Asylum was uneven. Its first superintendent, Dr. Richard Gundry, was first-rate, and Dr. H. C. Rutter also served well, but the appointment of the superintendent soon became subject to the pressures of political patronage. The competent Dr. A. B. Richardson (1881–89), dismissed as a result of a change in administrations in Columbus, went on to a distinguished career nationally. Insistence in Columbus on treating the superintendency as a political reward proved disastrous. In the judgment of the *Messenger,* Dr. P. H. Clarke was incompetent, and Clarke was denounced as an alcoholic addicted to opium. A subsequent investigation by a legislative committee found the hospital's finances in disarray. The institution's steward was dismissed, and Dr. Rutter was brought back briefly to reorganize the staff. Politics could not be eliminated. Four years later the institution's trustees dismissed three of the professional staff to create jobs for Democrats after that party won back the state house.

Operating a mental hospital in the late nineteenth century was frustrating. There was little the doctors or staff could do beyond making patients comfortable and keeping them physically healthy. Freud's pioneering works on the mind were not available in English until well after 1900. The hospital's records indicate that in any given year on the order of 20 percent of the patients were discharged as recovered. The number of former patients who had to be readmitted to the hospital in a given year was on the order of 20 percent of the number discharged. For the most part, once admitted, a patient remained until death.

THE CHILDREN'S HOME

As the State of Ohio undertook to care for the mentally ill, Athens County moved to care for its orphaned children. Prior to the 1880s, township trustees either placed orphaned children in private homes or else sent them to the county infirmary to be housed with the aged, the indigent, and the widowed. In the mid-1870s, John S. Fowler, a Quaker, appalled at the treatment accorded the children, conceived the project of a county home for children. At the time, Athens County was reeling from the damage inflicted by the 1873 and 1875 floods of the Hocking River, the costs of a new courthouse, and the need for major repairs to the county infirmary. Recognizing that the county was unlikely to create a children's home from the general tax fund, Fowler spent four years going house-to-house, township-by-township soliciting pledges to raise $13,000 for the construction of a children's home. Finally, in 1880, the state legislature approved the project and directed the Athens County Commissioners to collect the pledges solicited by Fowler and to begin construction.

A 125-acre site was chosen a mile to the east of the village, a place once occupied by Indians and today traversed by the east bypass. Under the supervision of the Reverend and Mrs. J. M. Nourse, the institution got underway. In 1883, the Nourses departed. Later that year, Elza Armstrong, one of the Buckeye Rovers, and his wife, Lydia Carpenter Armstrong, began their superintendency, which lasted into the present century. By the end of the century on the order of six hundred children had been cared for by the institution, children ranging in age from a few weeks to fifteen years. The facility grew in size so that by early in the present century it had thirteen buildings, its own water system, gas heat, and light. Isolated as it was from the village, the Children's Home operated its own school, built in 1883. In keeping with the prevailing approach to social welfare, the children were dressed in hand-me-downs. The children were not coddled.

OHIO UNIVERSITY: THE AGE OF SCOTT AND SUPER

William Henry Scott and Charles W. Super, two strong but quite different personalities, dominated Ohio University from 1872 to 1902. Between them, they gave the university a social mission: the training of public school teachers.

William Henry Scott was local. Born in Chauncey in 1840, he attended Ohio University, graduating in 1862. For brief intervals, he had been superintendent of the Athens school system and principal of the university's Academy. Before returning to the university as a professor of Greek, he had been ordained as a Methodist minister. He brought to the presidency of the university a thorough understanding of the school, its problems, and a sense of where it must go in the future.

By contrast, Charles W. Super was a cosmopolitan. Two years younger than Scott, he was born in Pottsville, Pennsylvania, took his baccalaureate at Dickinson College, and pursued graduate studies in Germany at Tuebingen. He was the first academic scholar and non-clergyman to head the university. Like Scott, he was a specialist in Greek, but his mastery of languages extended from French, Spanish, and Italian to Arabic, Hebrew, and Sanskrit. He was well versed in music. A tall, slender man, he came to the university as a self-assured scholar who tended to set the agenda for the university trustees.

Eighteen seventy-two was not the best of times for the university. Although the trustees had known for a year that Solomon Howard intended to retire in June 1872, they procrastinated about finding his successor. At the last minute, they turned to William Henry Scott, making him acting president for 1872–73 and, appointing him president a year later. As Scott began his tenure, the college enrollment was 55; the preparatory school, the new term for the old Academy, had 54

pupils. The graduating class in June 1873 numbered seven students. The low enrollment meant a limited tuition income for the school. Further, the country was
dropping into a prolonged depression. With corn selling at 22¢ a bushel and wheat
at 89¢, area farmers were not in a position to send their youngsters to college. The
economy of the coal and iron region was in chaos. Half of the iron furnaces of
the state closed. Ironically, this was a depression marked by high prices for consumer goods and by low wages. Furthermore, there were needs on campus that required attention. The buildings were not "all that could be desired." In Scott's
judgment, they were "insufficient," slowly falling into decay. No additions to the
equipment had been made for years; the only regular additions to the library were
Patent Office reports and issues of the *Congressional Globe.*

Depression or not, Scott recognized that the school's financial problem was immediate and had two components: a need for capital funds and a need for augmented, dependable operating funds. Almost immediately, he sought to raise
private funds for building. He sought $100,000; he secured some $5,000 in pledges,
which, given the depression, produced less than $4,000 in cash. In an effort to be
helpful the state legislature enacted a law directing the trustees to collect the rent
on the College Lands. This had a potential of generating $3,000 a year. Promptly,
J. R. Cable and 277 other lessees filed suit to contest the university's right to collect the fees. In the lawsuit that followed, the university prevailed in the Ohio
Supreme Court, but before the case could be heard on appeal by the United States
Supreme Court, the lessees agreed to an out-of-court settlement acknowledging
the university's right to collect leasehold fees. This was a Pyrrhic victory for the
university, since the fees were capped at six percent of the initial valuation.

Leasehold tenure was no more popular in the 1870s than it had been in
McGuffey's time. The *Athens Journal,* the village's Democratic paper, suggested that
some disgruntled Athenians regarded the university as "the Lord of the Manor
and the lessees the vassals" who owe it allegiance. To the *Messenger,* aside from the
rental fee, the rights of those holding ninety-year leases were the same as those
who owned land in fee simple.

Several other strategies to generate income were developed. In 1877 a bill authorizing state funds for Ohio University, Miami University, and The Ohio State
University met overwhelming defeat, the opposition being mobilized by Ohio's
private colleges. Next, in 1880, Charles Townsend, Athens County's representative
in the Ohio House, introduced a bill creating an irreducible fund of $250,000
from which the university would receive six percent a year—$15,000. The Ohio
State University lobbied the measure to death. Finally, in 1881, Scott asked $20,000
of the Ohio General Assembly to pay for a list of specific repairs. The legislature

agreed, although before the university got one cent, it had to secure a writ of mandamus directing the state auditor to pay the money. The court's decision in awarding the writ was important, for it expressly affirmed that the university was a ward of the state and had legitimate claims to public funds. The funds went for a comprehensive overhaul of the College Edifice (Cutler Hall) and construction of a university chapel. Having succeeded in getting capital funds for the school in 1881, Scott returned to the legislature in 1883 with a list of items to be funded. This time he secured $10,000, chiefly for reoutfitting the recently refurbished College Edifice and for furnishing the chapel. He remained frustrated in his effort to secure adequate operating funds.

Scott also ran into a roadblock in solving the problem of the Commons. Still used for hitching horses, as well as for piling rubbish and accommodating itinerant tent shows, it was unsightly and unhealthy—"an offense against taste and wholly at variance with the proper association of a place to study." For a short time the local chapter of the GAR (Grand Army of the Republic) seemed inclined to lease the land, fence it, and erect a monument to the Civil War veterans. Then it backed down. When the university began to fence the land, the town marshal promptly tore the fence down. While control over the parade grounds was less critical than the school's financial support, Scott was again checked.

While financial concerns had the highest priority, Scott, having been both student and faculty member at OU, understood the school's academic limitations. He succeeded in getting a revised written entrance examination designed to rid the entering class of "the few dull or ignorant students" who were incapable of doing college work and were "a dead weight on both the class and the teacher." He was not successful, however, in reviving the use of outside examining committees such as had been employed before the war. Nor did he succeed in instituting competitive examinations for the county scholarship students.

In the effort to upgrade the quality of the curriculum, Scott scored some gains. What he sought was "an education which will be at once thorough and liberal." Reflecting his roots in the classical curriculum of the pre-Civil War, Scott added a year of Latin to the curriculum of the preparatory school. A command of Latin and Greek was required for admission to the baccalaureate program. To make certain that the scientific curriculum should be "comparable in time and work to the classical course," more courses in the sciences were added to the requirements, as were modern languages.

Scott's most significant innovation was the introduction of a teacher-training course in spring 1879. With more and more youngsters completing elementary school, the demand for trained teachers exceeded the supply. The university's new teacher-training program began with ten students, then increased to between twenty-two and twenty-five. While Scott realized the need for a specially trained instructor for these students, the trustees demurred. In fact, the facilities that the University offered these first students "precluded instruction equal to that of good normal schools." Even so, Scott made a start in curriculum reform, especially in the area of the sciences and teacher training.

Throughout Scott's presidency there were efforts to merge Ohio University, Miami University, and The Ohio State University. President Edward Orton of Ohio State brought the issue to a head when, in 1880, he floated a proposal to combine the three universities into a single institution. The state legislature did not act on the requisite legislation, but Scott, despairing of ever getting adequate operating funds for Ohio University, was taken with Orton's idea. As things then were, Scott told his trustees: "The cause of higher education in Ohio demands a concentration of means and effort. The attempt to sustain so many institutions of learning of this rank would fail in any state. . . . It is possible to create one strong institution. . . . But to create more than one is impossible." Confessing to the trustees that his position as Ohio University's president had become "in some respects uncongenial," Scott offered his resignation; the trustees put off accepting it. However, when President Orton left Ohio State in 1883, he proposed Scott as his successor. And when Ohio State summoned him, Scott readily accepted. Once in place at Ohio State, Scott continued to advocate a merger of the three institutions. The Ohio University trustees waited until Scott left Athens before taking a public stand, but when they did speak, they were clear and to the point. They committed themselves "to resist and oppose any and all schemes of consolidation that in any way would curtail or restrict the course of study in Ohio University, or in any way impair its position as a university or favor its removal from Athens." The trustees tendered no testimonial dinner for Scott on his departure. The *Messenger*, however, bade him a cordial good-bye, noting his "constant and arduous labors to build up the University," and declared that he left with the "well wishes of the best citizens of Athens." For Scott, Athens had brought twelve years of frustration.

Charles W. Super backed into the presidency when the trustees' first choice, the Reverend Hugh Boyd, a former Methodist pastor in Athens and the current president of Cornell College (Iowa), rejected the offer. At the start of the fall term 1883 Super was appointed president pro tempore. The first impressions were positive, and almost impulsively the *Messenger* urged the trustees to call him "permanently to the head of it [the university]." In the course of the school year, Super demonstrated "a surprising capacity" for administration, and in 1884 he received the appointment.

Establishing a solid financial footing remained the school's top priority. Super's problem was made more difficult by the fact that Scott, now president of Ohio State, kept insisting that the State of Ohio needed but one university. Yet Super succeeded in gaining the legislature's support to a degree only dreamed of by his predecessors. Following Scott's example, he asked for funds for specific items and got what he requested. Thus encouraged, when he next asked for equipment funds, he appended a request for a token sum for salaries—$500. Again, he secured the entire amount. In 1887 he sought $3,000 for salaries; in 1896 he received $77,000!

In 1885 the state legislature authorized the Athens County treasurer to collect state taxes on all land in Athens and Alexander townships, the college lands, whether held on leasehold or in fee simple, and then to transfer the funds collected to the university. This directive should have simplified the tax collecting. But the lessees retaliated by refusing to pay their rents. At one point, the university had such a severe cash-flow problem that it had to borrow $1,500 to tide it over. President Super suggested that the trustees impose a penalty on delinquent rents; despite the university's distress the trustees declined to act. Although pressed to draw up a list of the delinquent leaseholders and to formulate a program for the collection of the funds, Eliakim Moore, the treasurer, did nothing. In fact, Super came to see Moore's "haphazard records, inefficient collecting program, and delayed annual reports" as the cause of the financial problem. He asked the trustees to engage an auditor to examine Moore's books. The trustees not only failed to hire an auditor, they reelected Moore as treasurer for another eight years. The records suggest that although the local trustees were able to lobby the legislature aggressively, they were almost paralyzed when their actions might offend friends and neighbors.

The solution to the university's financial problem came with enactment of the Sleeper Bill in 1896. David L. Sleeper, one-time publisher of the *Athens Herald* and speaker of the Ohio House, drafted a measure levying a statewide property tax in the amount of .05 mill to be divided between Ohio University and Miami University. Charles Townsend promoted the bill in the Ohio House, and George Falloon of Athens and member of the Ohio Senate promoted it in the senate. Lobbying for the Sleeper Bill was intense. Friends of the university induced the Senate Finance Committee to come to Athens. Here they were entertained at a sumptuous banquet at the Berry Hotel. Major Leonidas M. Jewett, university trustee and secretary, serving as toastmaster, shamelessly stroked their egos. The bill passed. As adopted, the measure funneled $33,000 to Ohio University. Equally important, it put future operating subsidies on a permanent basis, independent of the legislature.

Fully understanding the import of the Sleeper Bill, villagers, on learning of the bill's enactment, were plunged into a "state of enjoyment bordering on hilarity." Shouting and cheering, the citizens gathered around a huge bonfire. The community staged a grand rally for Sleeper and Falloon on their return from Columbus. The town's bells pealed. In enacting the Sleeper Bill, the state finally acknowledged its responsibility for support of its public colleges.

Enactment of the Sleeper Bill transformed the university. In Manasseh Cutler's vision, the rents from the College Lands were to provide the operating funds. Had this worked out the university would have been autonomous. Following the enactment of the Sleeper Bill, the University trustees might still propose programs and draft budgets, but the state legislature had the final say.

President Super, again building on Scott's foundations, pushed curriculum reform along. William S. Matthews, a university alumnus and member of the state legislature, suggested to the university trustees that they organize a normal department for teacher education. Scott's innovations had been "a gesture," not a solution. The trustees responded favorably and the Ohio University "gang" in Columbus—Charles S. Welch in the Ohio Senate, Emmett Tompkins and Matthews in the House, "Si" Allen, the Sergeant-at-Arms, and LeRoy Brown, State School Commissioner—pushed the bill through in June 1886, getting $5,000 in start-up funds. The normal department got underway promptly, led by Professor John P. Gordy. As prescribed by Gordy, the curriculum featured only two courses relating to education, both emphasizing the history of education. Even if the graduates of the normal department did not acquire much insight into the problems of classroom instruction, they entered the classroom far better educated than any of their predecessors.

Super initiated significant changes in the university in other ways. The classical course was modified to give students a thorough introduction to the life sciences —physiology and botany—as well as to the physical sciences—physics, chemistry, astronomy, and geology. The philosophical course was amended by substituting French and German for Greek, and the language requirement was reduced to two years. A start was made on a music program. Music courses had been introduced in 1886–87, relying on local musicians Eva Norris and Myrtle Stimson. In 1894 a program offering instruction in chorus, voice, piano, and theory was organized, and in 1896 the program was elevated to a department. The shift in status brought changes in personnel, but the development of the department was directed, for the most part, by James P. McVey. An attempt to create a School of Mines miscarried, largely because Ohio State, with such a program already in place, did not want a competitor.

The contest between the university and the village over title to the Commons continued. In December 1887, Judge Hiram L. Sibley found for the village. Nonetheless, persistent and angry, university officials appealed Judge Sibley's decision and lost again. Then, almost overnight, the controversy was settled. Led by General Grosvenor, a group of Civil War veterans proposed to erect a monument on the Commons. The group incorporated for the purpose of raising the necessary money and purchasing the monument. The village council then released the Commons as a site for the monument, and the University took responsibility for the care of the land. End of controversy. The monument was dedicated in 1893.

Super added a new building to the campus with funds secured in the mid-1890s from the state legislature for a general classroom and administration building. Ewing Hall featured an auditorium seating 1,200 persons, nine classrooms each with an adjacent office, and offices for the university president. To make room for the new building, the chapel was moved to a place south of the College Edifice, and Ewing then was erected on the site vacated by the chapel.

Super's presidency saw both an increase and turnover in the faculty. One notable change was the employment of women. Cynthia Weld, the first woman faculty member, had been employed by Scott in 1881 to teach history, rhetoric, and English literature. Super hired nearly a dozen women, especially for the modern languages, the normal school, and drawing and music. Given the long period of financial problems, the university's salaries were so low that faculty were forever moving to other schools, the women included. Weld stayed but two years before being lured to Ohio State University. Over the years, the faculty changed in other respects. Before 1872 most of the senior faculty—Scott, Adney, Hatfield, and Blair —were alumni. As the school grew, the new members came from a wide variety of universities, some from Europe. Although few faculty by 1900 had an earned doctorate, most held at least a master's degree in their academic specialty. The university had become academic and secular. With twenty faculty, the university was an important employer in the village, and the faculty constituted a significant segment of the village's professional population.

Slowly the university developed a bureaucracy of its own. In 1872 the Alumni Association, which had existed informally for several years, incorporated. For its part, the board of trustees employed a part-time secretary-auditor and a part-time treasurer. By the turn of the century, the school had two deans, one to manage the normal department, the other to direct the College of Liberal Arts. The president had a secretary, and there was a janitor and assistant janitor.

One of the most significant events of the post–Civil War era was the admission in 1868 of Margaret Boyd to the university. The faculty had recommended the admission of women, and Boyd's entrance caused nary a ripple, but it betokened a world of change. While much has been written about the fact that her name appeared in the university catalog as M. Boyd, the use of initials rather than full first names was common in the 1860s and 1870s. Once enrolled, she attracted little attention, probably because some of her college classmates had been public school classmates before. The Philomathean Society elected her to membership by acclamation, and she participated actively, reading an essay before the society and its guests early in 1871. When Boyd graduated in 1873, the *Messenger* acknowledged her graduation as "a novel feature" of commencement, adding that her graduation essay had been well received. President Scott told the commencement gathering that he found it "gratifying" that Boyd had enjoyed the opportunity of becoming thoroughly educated. "College doors ought to be thrown open for the reception of every worthy candidate without distinction of sex," he declared. "The Cause of Woman is gradually gaining ground. I rejoice in it."

Other women did not rush in where Margaret Boyd had dared to tread. But in the course of the 1870s, they did trickle in, first to the preparatory school, then the college. In 1882, women students had lead roles in the competitions of the literary societies. Nina Schwefel, daughter of the late Presbyterian minister, went head-to-head with a man in an essay contest, besting her male rival as did Jennie Kurtz, also of Athens, in the oratorical competition. In the years that followed, women students were invariably visible and in active competition. In 1883 the Philomathean Society elected Nina Schwefel its president and Addie Coe, vice-president, and in 1892 the Athenian Literary Society elected Anna Pearl McVay, "easily the outstanding member of her organization" to be their president.

By fall 1893, one-third of the university's students were women. The *Messenger* observed that a women's dormitory was needed. Given the university's past difficulties in getting financial support from the State of Ohio, a dormitory had to be a private venture. As organization of a normal department began to draw still more women to campus, the need for women's housing escalated. Construction of a Ladies' Hall was undertaken by a corporation organized by several of the Athens members of the board of trustees and businessmen, who, following its completion, leased it to the university. Located at College and Union on the site of the old Brown House, it opened early in 1896 and lodged thirty women.

The growth of the female student population led to the organization in 1876 of a female fraternity (as it was then called), Kappa Alpha Theta, and in the course of the next decade it had initiated thirty-five members. At that point, it lost its national charter. Three years later, December 1889, Pi Beta Phi organized at the home of President Super, his daughter Corinne being one of the five charter members.

The Pi Phis, primarily from Athens, met weekly, usually in private homes. By the end of the 1890s, the graduation banquets of the Pi Phis and of the two male fraternities, Phi Delta Theta and Beta Theta Pi, became highlights of commencement week and began to overshadow the competitions of the two college literary societies.

More important to the university than to the community was the Isaac Crook episode. In 1896, profoundly tired by his dozen years of administrative duties, Super asked to be relieved as president and to return to the faculty. The trustees, in this instance, acted promptly and chose the Reverend Isaac Crook, the candidate of the Methodist trustees. Crook's administration, as Professor Hoover puts it, "was not a happy one." He had been elected by a 10–8 vote of the trustees, not an unqualified vote of confidence; more importantly, Crook was overshadowed by the ex-president who had remained on the faculty. In 1898 Crook resigned; Super took over direction of the university as Dean of Faculty for a year, then resumed the title of president.

To the end of the century, college enrollment remained an activity of a small, elite group, but it was coed. Of those who enrolled, only a fraction completed their degrees. Thus, in 1899, the university graduated but eleven students, seven men, four women. Total student enrollment was eighty-two; the faculty numbered twenty. Both the president and faculty were laymen with academic degrees. There were baccalaureate programs in liberal arts and the sciences and a nucleus of programs in music, commerce, and education. In Ewing Hall the university had a modern classroom building. Finally, it had secured a regular subsidy from the state legislature, and during the late 1890s its operating subsidy began to match the funds brought into the community by the Asylum.

CONSERVATION AND PUBLIC HEALTH

The growth of Athens village, slow as it was, continued to make its impact felt on the physical environment. The community crept northward along the Lancaster Road, eastward along East State through what was termed "Goosetown" to what is now Morris Avenue, and westward along Dean Street (West Washington) and West Union and along Cemetery (South Shafer Street). Trees were cleared to make way for houses, sidewalks, and roadways. Streets were graded to even out the irregular local terrain. The village's first solution to sewage disposal, dumping raw sewage into the river, polluted the Hocking. As the University secured possession of the disputed area between the line of McGuffey elms and Union Street, the north end of the campus was regraded, soil being added and grass planted. The stately sycamores that originally had lined the Hocking, however, were knocked down by the "hurricane" of 1860 rather than felled by timber-hungry settlers. Most of the heavy forests that still surrounded the village in 1870 had disappeared before the end of the century. In some of the rural areas, aggressive timbering supplemented the income of area farmers and greatly reduced the amount of forested land. On the edges of the county, the *Messenger* reported, Canadian timbermen were harvesting oak timber for export to England. While some of these activities opened land to pasture and even cultivation, they also speeded the runoff of rainstorms and increased the propensity of local streams to rise quickly and flood.

A callous attitude toward native animals also continued. The pelts of wild animals remained a source of income. Otter pelts fetched $3.00 each, and when, by chance, Matt Porter spotted an otter on an August day in 1880, he pursued it, kicking it to death. Otter were on their way to becoming extinct. On another occasion, a local farmer demonstrated his expertise as a marksman by shooting some thirty squirrels while walking to town. The sighting of an exotic bird or one of unusual size aroused an irresistible urge to shoot it by way of documenting its existence and the hunter's prowess. Thus, the shooting of a blue heron with a six-foot wingspread brought short-term fame to the individual who killed it; so, too, Master Willie Brown gained fleeting fame for winging an eagle, the only one seen locally in a number of years. "Of huge dimensions," the wounded bird subsequently died. The habitat for birds that nested on the ground dwindled as mowing machines cut closer to the ground than the scythes they replaced and as wire fences displaced split-rail fences that zigzagged along the margins of fields, providing a belt of land around every field safe from plow or mowing machine. English sparrows were regarded as a nuisance, and the Ohio General Assembly marked them for eradication, offering a bounty of one cent a sparrow delivered to the county clerk twenty-five at a time. Deer and wild turkeys became virtually extinct; quail became increasingly scarce.

Conservation

The harsh impact of human occupation on the terrain produced a growing sense of loss. There was an increased sensitivity to the social value of song birds, which were hunted commercially to be displayed on the hats of fashionable women. Robins, blue birds, orioles, thrushes, and meadow larks began to be valued for the

pleasure they gave as well as for their appetite for insect pests. Editor Jennings supported efforts to limit the season during which quail might be hunted or to ban
their hunting altogether.

From the first national mention of the subject, editor Jennings, whose home
looked out on the McGuffey elms, urged townspeople to take note of Arbor Day
and to plant a tree; Athens schools promptly joined the movement. The handful of
Athenians who had formed a gun club reorganized in the spring of 1889 as the
Athens Sportsmen's Club actively advocating rigid enforcement of the new state
fish and game laws that set seasons for fishing and hunting. Other evidences of
a growing sensitivity to animals came in 1890 as the Society for the Prevention
of Cruelty to Animals sought to identify and prosecute the person who had
killed "Old George," a black Newfoundland dog, for its hide. A few months later
Athenians gathered at the Presbyterian church to organize their own chapter of the
Ohio Humane Society. Slowly an ethic emerged that sought to define the community's interest in the natural environment. The state would restock lakes and rivers
with fish, but it established bounds within which individuals might fish; it would
protect specific animals and birds from exploitative hunting in the interest of the
general welfare.

Public Health

The August 1872 notice in the *Messenger* that the infant daughter of John Friday had
died of cholera infantum was the kind of notice Athenians were well acquainted
with. To the end of the century, life in Athens village remained risky. But increasingly there was a sense that with a combination of private measures and village intervention, some of the risks could be reduced. There was a vague awareness that
the concentration of people in an urban milieu intensified the need for the community to take measures beyond the capability of individuals to undertake.

Wives and mothers were still the primary health-care providers, doctoring and
nursing family members. They combined varying degrees of tender-loving-care
with a mix of traditional home-made teas, herbs, and salves along with a growing
array of proprietary medicines and the concoctions prepared by local druggists. If
the wife-mother's diagnosis was correct, some of the herbal medicines undoubtedly provided the patient with relief.

Athens doctors of this period studied medicine with a general practitioner before attending a medical college for a year or two, and then practiced for a time

with an older, experienced physician before setting out on their own. The training of Dr. E. G. Dorr, born and educated in Athens, illustrates the sequence. Dorr studied medicine with Doctors William P. Johnson and C. L. Wilson, then attended the Medical College of Ohio at Cincinnati, graduating in 1868. He located first in Logan before moving to Athens in 1871.

The profession, as such, lacked a comprehensive view of the nature of illness and of effective treatment for most diseases. A few practitioners, like Dr. C. E. Ward, were homeopathic physicians, essentially herbalists. Patients convinced of the merits of mineral waters went to various spas, entrusting their health to the care of hydropaths. Those requiring specialized care depended on specialists who came to Athens for a day or two, meeting patients at a local hotel. Dr. C. C. Knapp, an out-of-town optician, met patients at the Palmer House, while during the mid-1880s a Columbus specialist, J. J. McClellan, made monthly visits to treat his patients at the Warren House. All too many doctors, however, still relied on calomel, opiates, quinine, and bleeding to treat patients, treatments that might aggravate an already serious condition and interfere with the body's ability to heal itself. Indeed, many doctors compounded some of their own medicines, thus functioning, according to circumstances, as physician, surgeon, pharmacist, and even as nurse.

Until the 1890s, any appraisal of the village's state of health is imprecise and impressionistic. One knows, for example, that Lizzie Hawk, a public school teacher, was down with malaria and that the *Messenger* noted an active local trade in quinine, evidence of the general presence of the ague and malaria. There were repeated reports over the years of typhoid, which was usually debilitating and sometimes fatal. Thomas Hoover, the historian of Ohio University, reports that every fall brought the return of low-grade typhoid to the village. Scarlet fever and diphtheria repeatedly plagued the community. At best, local doctors could cite the threat of these diseases, warning that "filthy cellars and yards are the primary cause in engendering diphtheria and other epidemic diseases."

Certainly, typhoid and diphtheria were democratic in that sons and daughters, husbands and wives of the elite were not exempt. Gertrude Half, daughter of merchant Isaac Half, the aging Judge John Welch, and the merchant Henry Nelson contracted them. The heartbreak was the inability of doctors either to prevent these diseases or to cure them. The tragedy was the failure of so many persons, more in the rural areas of the county, to secure vaccinations against smallpox, a preventable disease. When smallpox was abroad in early 1889, editor Jennings sounded the alarm and urged Athens school officials to make vaccination mandatory.

School officials did not act, but, in November 1893, the Ohio State Board of Health issued orders requiring evidence of successful vaccination as a precondition of enrolling in any school, public, private, or parochial. While this measure extended the coercive powers of the state in behalf of the public welfare, it was a major step toward eradicating this dread disease. To the end of the century Athenians periodically experienced malaria, typhoid, and diphtheria just as had the first settlers of the village.

Like most American communities of the time, Athens had a pollution problem. Wood and coal stoves for heating and cooking polluted the air and produced quantities of ashes to be disposed of. The preparation of food generated a residue of garbage. Inadequately maintained privies contaminated the village's well water, and casually kept stables nurtured a seasonal fly problem. Dependent as the town was on horses for transportation, its streets abounded "with reeking accumulations of filth" made worse by the absence of any program for the systematic removal of animal droppings. In law, the responsibility for cleaning gutters belonged to the owners of the adjacent property. Those who neglected to clean up were periodically threatened with having the city contract to have it done for them and then bill them, but there was little, if any, enforcement of these ordinances.

The 1890s hinted at possible solutions. First, the work of Louis Pasteur, in particular, began to confirm what had hitherto been more hunch than knowledge, that cleanliness promoted health. Individuals began to put screens on their windows and doors. At this point, town fathers acknowledged the need for community-wide measures that only the local government could implement. The village council in 1890 adopted a set of sanitary regulations. Henceforth, the slaughtering of animals within the village was prohibited. Pens, stables, and yards for hogs, horses, and cows were to be kept clean. Drainpipes must have traps to prevent the escape of sewer gas. Privies, henceforth, were to be at least six feet deep or of the "dry earth" type. Finally, in the emptying of privy vaults, the contents were not to be hauled except between midnight and four A.M.

The nineties brought a burgeoning of data on public health. Statistics for age at death document the extreme risks encountered in infancy. In 1893, for example, fully one-fifth of the year's deaths were of children less than a year old. In fact, twice as many youngsters died before reaching their fifth birthday as during the next fifteen years. Overall, pneumonia, tuberculosis, and diphtheria were the most frequent killers, accounting for nearly one death in four. Typhoid and scarlet fever trailed.

Relatively simple measures focusing on cleanliness, combined with the beginnings of a municipal water supply and the few sewer lines, worked miracles. In 1900, the village counted forty-six deaths. TB, contagious and deadly and for which no effective medical cure yet existed, claimed eight of those forty-six lives; accidents another seven; pneumonia and heart disease six each. Four deaths were attributable to premature and stillborn babies. On the other hand, the village counted but one case each of diphtheria and scarlet fever. No one had died of typhoid. A new era in public health seemed to be underway.

ORGANIZED RELIGION

Without doubt, churches remained the foremost organizations in the lives of many Athenians. Following the well-worn paths of tradition by way of providing a focus to spiritual life, parents introduced their children to the church as infants, often to be baptized, later to attend Sunday school and church. The minister married them and at the end buried them. Yet, the religious scene continued to change.

First of all, the Presbyterians and Methodists put aside much of the denominational rivalry of the pre-war years. A major factor in nurturing an atmosphere of cooperation was the Sunday School movement. While each church operated its own Sunday School, the leadership was bound together in a county-wide, inter-denominational union that sought to train teachers and offer programming support; county-wide meetings were held in summers, bringing together the superintendents and teachers. Secondly, as congregations recognized that pastors required vacations, the Methodists and Presbyterians arranged summer schedules by which the two congregations met together when either of their ministers was away. In the hottest weather, they also combined their Sunday evening services and met on the courthouse steps or on the College Green. A third factor was that President William Henry Scott, an ordained Methodist minister, was equally prone to preach at the Presbyterian or the Methodist Church when a guest clergyman was required. A fourth, and especially important, factor was the common interest of the two churches in their support of the temperance movement, a non-denominational effort that brought together women of the Methodist and Presbyterian churches, and, in time, of the Christian Church–Disciples of Christ. Cooperation rather than rivalry among the denominations characterized the religious scene in the final three decades of the nineteenth century.

The Presbyterians

The Presbyterians entered the post-war period in good shape, a memorable revival of 1869 having added some forty-seven members to their congregation. But shortly after, they were struck by tragedy when their Prussian-born minister, E. W. Schwefel, much admired as "a vigorous and logical thinker," died as a result of an accidental gunshot wound. His successor, James M. Nourse, came with a decade's experience with the Presbyterian Board of Home Missions. And for a time the congregation thrived. The Women's Missionary Society enjoyed as its leaders several of the village's first ladies—Laura (Mrs. James) Ballard, Lizzie (Mrs. James D.) Brown, and Emma McVay. Dreary January and February evenings were occupied with annual revivals, "protracted meetings" in the parlance of the day. In 1877 the Presbyterians and Methodists joined in a "Week of Prayer," holding meetings alternately at the Presbyterian and Methodist churches.

Yet all was not right. Nourse's pastorate proved rocky enough that the Presbytery, a regional body, appointed a committee to look into the difficulties. "The Spiritual condition" of the church, it concluded, was "deplorable." After the committee voiced its approval of Nourse, the Ohio Synod, the statewide organization of the church, elected him its Moderator (presiding officer) at its October 1880 meeting. Nonetheless, relations between pastor and congregation remained cool. On the sabbath Nourse was often away preaching elsewhere, a visiting minister taking his place in Athens. Indeed, on Easter Day 1881 there were no services as Nourse was in Gallipolis that day. In 1882 Nourse left the Athens church to become the first manager of the newly organized Athens County Children's Home. He subsequently returned to the East.

In the last decade of the century, the Presbyterians were more active than ever. On one hand, there was a renewed concern with communicants' personal behavior. A number of members, several of them among the town's leading citizens, were censured for excessive drinking or for failure to attend church. On the other hand, the church, acting as its brother's keeper, dispensed funds to the poor. In 1895, at the height of great economic distress among area miners, the session petitioned the mayor of Athens to convene a citizens' meeting "to devise plans for helping to relieve the distress" among the miners. On another occasion, the session joined other churches in an effort to invoke the power of the state to enforce Sunday blue laws designed to keep most business houses closed on the sabbath.

In the course of the nineties, the Presbyterians once more began to consider ways of improving their facilities. One concern centered on the "propriety" of securing a new organ. A decision was deferred while the congregation reviewed the church's music program. Session minutes are often cryptic, but it is clear that on occasion a choir member received payment for her services. By 1897 the forces in favor of acquiring a pipe organ were in the ascendancy. Another concern centered on the building itself. Whatever was done to fix up the 1828 building seemed out of step with the spate of new buildings which had sprung up on Court Street. By 1900, a new building was only a matter of time.

The Methodists

The experiences of the Methodist Episcopal Church, a block away, roughly paralleled those of the Presbyterians. Although the Reverend William Henry Scott never tried to combine the role of college president and minister, his activities added to the Methodists' visibility and influence in the community.

The spiritual calm of the Methodists was disturbed in the early 1880s as Scott was charged with heresy by the Ohio Conference of the Methodist Episcopal Church. He faced three charges. First, he was accused of denying the trinity; questioning the divinity of Christ; denying the "vicarious atonement" of Christ; denying the doctrine of original sin; and denying the reality of Christ's resurrection. Second, he was charged with conduct unbecoming a minister and a Christian in that he had accepted ordination as a Methodist clergyman when he already had articulated views contrary to those of the Methodist Church. Third, he had sowed discord in the Church. In this regard, early in 1882, while preaching in Athens, he had denounced the national Methodist Episcopal Church for expelling from the church one Dr. Thomas, declaring the action to be "of a piece with the rack and thumbscrew of the Inquisition." Nor did he support the use of revivals, which he regarded as "an abomination." In a unanimous decision, a church court found him innocent on every charge and specification. The court's judgment was then confirmed by the Ohio Conference. Almost certainly, Scott's "heresy" generated enormous comment in the village. But editor Jennings limited reportage to a straightforward report of the court's verdict.

An especially distinctive aspect of the Methodist practice was its willingness during the 1880s to license women evangelists. Mrs. R. J. Trego, an evangelist and temperance advocate, led the "protracted meeting" during the winter of 1886–87. She made a positive impact and was back in Athens in September 1887 to preside at a Sunday service in which her converts were received into full membership. She also spoke the preceding evening on temperance, attracting a full house as she hammered home the personal consequences of intemperance.

247

As the new century dawned, the Methodists, with much the largest congregation in the village, were contemplating a new church edifice.

The Christian Church (Disciples of Christ)

The Christian Church was "the new kid in town." In the years immediately after the Civil War, the Reverend Mr. A. P. Frost periodically did evangelical work in the village, but no permanent organization materialized. Subsequently, the Reverend Benjamin Franklin located in the village and gathered some eighty converts, but failed to create a church organization.

In the spring of 1886, the Reverend Mr. J. L. Parsons, "a learned, instructive, and eloquent speaker," succeeded in pulling together the nucleus of a local congregation. The fledgling congregation reportedly numbered seventy persons and scheduled regular services: Sunday morning at the Village Hall, Sunday afternoon at Mechanicsburg. As Mr. Parsons bowed out, the Reverend George Van Pelt supplanted him. The summer of 1886 saw a series of exceptionally successful "tent meetings," and in the fall the group moved to the Phoenix Building. For months at a time the congregation met regularly for Sunday services and midweek prayer meeting, relying on lay leadership.

By November 1887 the group was sufficiently cohesive that it called the Reverend A. P. Frost back to be its first pastor. A one-time resident of Lodi, Frost had worked with Disciples in Nelsonville. Like the Presbyterians and Methodists, the Disciples emphasized the spoken word, the sermon; they were promptly accepted into the village's community of faith, the Disciples' pastors participating alongside their Presbyterian and Methodist counterparts in community affairs.

In 1893, led by the evangelist H. F. McLane, the Disciples secured a property at the southwest corner of Congress and Washington and during the summer and fall of 1893 built a house of worship. At this point the church boasted a membership of 125 persons; its Sunday School claimed 100 members.

The Black Churches: The AME and Mount Zion Baptist

Underscoring the importance of the church in the lives of individuals, Black Athenians made concerted efforts to establish churches of their own. In January 1877, the *Messenger* took note of the presence of a colored, female missionary who sought to found an AME (African Methodist Episcopal) Church in the village.

Her sermons were marked with "fervor, eloquence, and ability." The group succeeded in founding a Sunday School which met at Potter's Hall. Like other Athens
churches, the AME was partial to "protracted meetings," which were held at the
county fairgrounds in June. "Impressive and orderly," the meetings consisted of
prayer, singing, addresses by out-of-town clergy, and a grand march about the
campsite as a finale. In 1881, the group put up a modest church building near the
Hocking Valley depot and engaged a pastor, the Reverend McClellan, although
it lost him to a lung ailment later that year. His successor, the Reverend Mr. E.
Cumberland, reported a year later that the church was on a solid financial base and
had in hand funds to finish the interior of the building, to make it comfortable
to use. The church hosted the Reverend Annie Auty, a veteran evangelist of the
Wesleyan Church of England. She led a program of "soul inspiring jubilee
singing." Beyond this point, the AME church fades from view.

The greater proportion of the Athens black community organized a church
affiliated with the Union Baptist Association. In fall 1872, members acquired property to the west of the public school on which to construct a church building.
Terming the project "a laudable object," editor Jennings urged the white community to pitch in and help. By November 1873, the foundation was nearly complete.
Taking Jennings at his word, the Baptists held a series of community suppers to
augment their building fund. Jennings publicized these affairs and urged fellow
Athenians to partake of the wonderful food offered. By the same token, the Baptists reached out to the whole community. Their services on the College Green in
the summer of 1879 were attended by a cross-section of Athens—men, women,
and children, whites and blacks. Their camp meeting at the fairgrounds in 1880 featured a group of "Jubilee Singers" who attracted whites as well as blacks to their
performances. By November 1882, the church building was completed and paid
for. The dedication, calling for much celebration, came in June 1883 with a variety
of visiting Baptist dignitaries participating. As willing as the white community was
to help the black churches raise money, they did not invite the black clergy to join
in various community events.

An Episcopal Mission

In the mid-1870s, the Protestant Episcopal Church made a bid to establish its
presence in Athens. The creation of the Diocese of Southern Ohio in 1875
prompted the newly ordained Bishop Augustus Jaggar to send a series of missioners to the Hocking Valley to test the waters. His interest was matched by several

249

Athenians with Episcopal backgrounds, particularly Adalina (Mrs. Johnson M.) Welch, Elizabeth (Mrs. R. E.) Constable, and Elizabeth (Mrs. John) Welch. They had organized a Sunday school in July 1875, followed shortly by founding an Episcopal Mite Society. In the fall, they held a "social" at the Constable home. In December 1875, the bishop came to Athens to see for himself the efforts of the "zealously engaged" ladies.

Pleased with what he saw and heard, the bishop assigned the Reverend J. N. Lee to work the Hocking Valley, making Athens his home base. Services were held on the second floor of the newly opened Potter Building at the southwest corner of Court and State Street. Lee found six communicants on his arrival, yet within a few weeks he reported forty Sunday school pupils served by eight teachers, and an average attendance at Sunday evening service of fifty persons. Outgoing and with a sense of the role of publicity, he participated in the community's Centennial Fourth of July celebration, giving both the invocation and benediction. After two years Lee was promoted to a larger parish.

Lee's successor, the Reverend Mr. Charles D. Barbour, a single man, arrived in September 1878. Barbour evidently recognized that although the "pillars" of the mission were community leaders, they were also community elders. To thrive, the church needed young families. An energetic advocate of temperance, Barbour gave the Episcopalians high visibility through his role in the local temperance movement. While he drew full houses to his temperance rallies, there was no carryover from temperance to membership in the Episcopal church. Furthermore, some of the original church members moved away from Athens, offsetting gains from new converts. Not only was talk of securing a building of their own premature, but the group was much too small to sustain a clergyman, even one shared with the booming communities of Nelsonville and Logan. In June 1880, Barbour indicated that thereafter services in Athens would be on alternate Sundays; by early 1881, Barbour, too, had moved on, being replaced by a veteran missionary, the Reverend Mr. Jacob Rambo. A man in his late sixties, Rambo chose Logan as his base, and he conducted services on alternate Sundays. This was no formula for growth. And in December 1881, the *Messenger* carried a cryptic notice that Episcopal services in Athens were suspended.

The mid-1890s witnessed another attempt at forming an Episcopal congregation in Athens. The College Chapel provided the venue. The services were conducted variously by Archdeacon Edwards, who commuted from Cincinnati, and the Suffragan Bishop Boyd Vincent. But to little avail. Beyond July 1897, this effort was abandoned.

St. Paul's Catholic Church

In 1870, the Roman Catholics made do in a small, box-like building, served by a "railroad priest." Based at Zaleski, the "railway priests" moved back and forth on the Marietta and Cincinnati Railroad, providing limited service to any one mission. The aim was to be in Athens one Sunday a month, but the reality was, as one parishioner put it, "often, very, very often, not once in two months." The frail, scholarly Fr. Francis J. Campbell remains memorable as the first resident priest. In 1875 the mission took the name St. Paul's. A succession of priests, serving a few weeks to several years at a time, held on.

Of the priests, Martin M. A. Hartnedy, a man of "seemingly inexhaustible energy, out-going and genial" was "the key figure" among the nineteenth-century priests. It was he who bought the Hennessey boarding house next to the church for use as a rectory. As the mission at Chauncey declined, he salvaged its church building and used the materials to expand St. Paul's. The latter was altered by the addition of a two-stage tower with a slender spire topped by a gold-leafed cross. The bell acquired for the church was less successful. Editor Jennings complained that it "does not tintinabulate very mellifluously." On the other hand, Father Hartnedy succeeded in securing "a very good organ." A vestibule with double doors was added to the building. Thanks to a three-day "Grand Fair and Festival" at the Village Hall, a thousand dollars was raised to finance an extension of the building. Bishop Sylvester Rosecrans came in mid-November 1876, first confirming 144 persons, then dedicating the structure.

Relations between Athens Protestants, the overwhelming majority of villagers, and the Catholic minority seem to have been remarkably cordial. Their Catholic neighbors impressed the Protestants as "peaceable, exemplary people." The predominantly Irish and Irish-American parishioners, many of whom were railroad hands, lived hard lives; indeed, Protestant patronage of the "grand fair and festival" had been instrumental in raising the needed funds for the church building, help the Catholics graciously acknowledged: "Our Protestant neighbors helped us nobly."

While the stereotypical Irishman of late–nineteenth-century America was notorious for his abuse of alcohol, only one Athens saloonkeeper in 1876 was Irish and a member of St. Paul's. In truth, Father Hartnedy organized a Holy Name Temperance Society in 1875, reinforcing the village's Protestant temperance crusaders. When the village sent a delegation to Columbus to lobby for a Sunday-closing law, Thomas Walsh, a young merchant-tailor and member of St. Paul's, was one of the delegation. Although the Temperance Society probably lasted no more than a decade, St. Paul's leadership remained a strong force for temperance until the end of the century.

The character of the parish gradually changed. While many, if not most, of the Irish-born founders were illiterate, their American-born children attended the local schools. The founders had been limited to working as railroad section hands, but their sons became members of the train crews and railroad telegraphers; their daughters took jobs as schoolmarms or at the Asylum. The ethnic base of church membership broadened to include persons of German as well as old-American ancestry. But St. Paul's would also include the Norwegian convert, Martin Rasmussen, a stone mason, and his Scottish-born wife; George Link, who laid out the ponds and gardens at the Asylum; and Conrad Josten, the first Catholic to serve on the village council.

As Athens grew, so did St. Paul's. In 1883, Father J. C. Madden acquired property on North Lancaster for use as Mt. Calvary cemetery, and Kate (Dunn) Ferriter, a victim of TB, was the first to be buried there. In 1890 the parish held its first Sunday-to-Sunday mission, a revival program analogous to the "protracted meetings" of the various Protestant churches.

By the 1890s St. Paul's had outgrown the building on Congress Street, a fact forcibly impressed on the congregation by Bishop Watterson. At a parish function in 1893, without forewarning the bishop informed the congregation that they should build a new rectory and plan a new church building, or he (the bishop) would "withdraw the priest from the pastorate here" (in Athens). As Nelsonville was at this point twice the size of Athens, the choice was to comply promptly with the bishop's directive or allow St. Paul's to become a mission of St. Andrew's, Nelsonville.

In December 1893 Father Jerome B. Mattingly came to the parish. A builder, within weeks Mattingly had purchased the northeast corner of Mill and College streets. Plans for a building—46' by 94' with a 110' steeple—were drawn. Again the parish resorted to a two-day fair to raise money. With the support of the Protestant community, the fair netted over $2,100, a fifth of the estimated cost of the new building. On May 12, 1895, in the presence of a crowd estimated at from 3,000 to 5,000 persons, Bishop Watterson laid the cornerstone. Mass was offered for the first time July 26, 1896, the nave outfitted with pews and altar furniture from the Congress Street building. To raise additional money, the old building was sold for $800 to Company B, ONG, for use as its armory. With money tight, completion of the church interior was a drawn-out process.

On May 14, 1899, St. Paul's was dedicated, a civic affair as well as a parish event.

Special trains brought hundreds of people to town. To assure the occasion would not be marred, the saloons were closed. Church officials conducted the dedicatory service. St. Paul's choir, augmented by members of other church choirs, including Jane Ryan, soloist at the Methodist church, provided special music. A parade that wound up and down Congress, Court, and College streets was led by mounted horsemen and headed by banker D. H. Moore. St. Paul's, its steeple rising above Athens, was a structure the entire village took pride in.

LODGES AND CLUBS

While church membership was traditional, affiliation with fraternal orders reflected the growing secular temper of society. In the post-war era as males felt an increasing compulsion to seek out male companionship, the number of fraternal orders increased.

The Masonic order, of course, was not new, but it had experienced much growth and emulation. York Rite bodies appeared in Athens as early as 1849, followed by the Athens Chapter, No. 34, Royal Arch Masons (1849), Athens Council, No. 15, Royal and Select Masters (1850), and the Athens Commandery, No. 15, Knights Templar (1857). With several branches of the Masons in the village, in 1878 they constructed the Masonic Hall on South Court Street. The handsomest structure on the street at the time, its dedication called for a major community celebration, featuring the 18th Regimental Band, the Athens Light Guards, bands from Zaleski and Nelsonville, a parade, and speeches. Masons took their lodge work seriously, and for some like Major J. M. Goodspeed, membership brought an extra measure of personal distinction when they were elected to an office in the state organization. By 1900, membership approached 150 in the Paramuthia Lodge alone, a significant portion of the village's adult males.

But the fraternal societies proliferated. The Serno Lodge, No 479, of the IOOF—the Independent Order of Odd Fellows—came to Athens in 1871. During the decade, they organized a women's auxiliary, the Rebeccas, which conducted its own programs, and on special occasions the two organizations combined forces. One such function in 1890 drew from 250 to 300 persons. Not to be outdone was the Athenian Lodge, No. 104, Knights of Pythias, which had been chartered in 1877. With close to 150 members at the end of the 1890s, it was comparable in size to the Paramuthian Lodge of the Masons. In fact, there was a modest degree of overlap in membership. As Athens grew, other lodges appeared. In 1897,

Mohawk Lodge No. 174, Improved Order of Red Men, organized with fifty charter members. In short order, its membership roll passed one hundred. The fraternal scene also included the Athens Lodge, No, 973, of the Benevolent and Protective Order of Elks, the now defunct Athens Conclave No. 9, Seven Wise Men, the Athens Hive No. 272 of the Knights of the Maccabees, and the Athens Aerie, No. 529, Fraternal Order of Eagles.

Once post-war life settled into a routine, veterans joined the GAR (Grand Army of the Republic) and made time to attend their annual regimental reunions. By the turn of the century, the ranks of the veterans were thinning. The privations endured while in the army, the lingering effects of dysentery, typhoid, and malaria, along with the impact of battle wounds had shortened lives. While in terms of their fortunes and family obligations, the veterans may have been freer to attend the regimental reunions as they aged, the aging process increasingly restricted the distances they could comfortably stray from home. Thus, Athens County veterans began turning to county-wide reunions of their companies and welcomed attendance by any and all veterans from other organizations. The "boys of '61" had become "senior citizens."

Ladies of the Clubs

Women, too, sought sisterly fellowship outside the home. To be sure, prior to the Civil War women had worked together in church-related and temperance organizations, and they had associated on an even larger scale in the Soldiers' Aid Society during the war. These were all activities in which Christian conscience had spurred the woman to step out of her traditional domestic routines to address a specific community problem but without a sense that she was taking on a new role in society. In the 1870s, Athens women resumed their pre-war activities.

Membership in the traditional missionary societies had first priority. The columns of the *Messenger* are replete with notices of the election of officers, of the monthly programs, and of the occasional appearances of an out-of-town speaker. In the early 1870s a revived temperance crusade pulled dozens of Athens women, especially church women, into the WCTU, the Woman's Christian Temperance Union. Before long, Athens had not only the original chapter, consisting of the wives and widows of the community leaders, but a second one consisting of younger women. By the end of the century, the national WCTU was the largest women's organization in the country. In Athens as elsewhere the WCTU dealt with the problems of alcohol while sensitizing women to a variety of civic issues relating to women's place in society.

In the 1880s, wives of Union veterans joined the Women's Relief Corps, the auxiliary of the GAR, an activity justified by patriotism. Not terribly demanding of their time, it also drew them out of the home and into the public arena.

Ultimately Athens women became involved in the women's club movement. Village women had a running start, for in 1871 women and men from the village's leading families joined the Athens Reading Club. The organization met twice monthly from September to May. Each meeting focused on a particular reading or readings presented by a man and a woman. A second pair, a man and a woman, conducted a critique of the reading. Under club rules, husbands and wives were never paired, so, in fact, from 1871 on many Athens women became thoroughly accustomed to discussing public affairs in mixed company.

In 1895, the women organized the Pallas Club, a women-only literary club. Although the Reading Club proceeded in an ad hoc manner in choosing its topics, the Pallas Club was decidedly more intentional. It chose a topic of study for an extended period of time, often a year, then subdivided it and proceeded to explore it systematically. In 1897, having completed a review of American history, the Pallas Club began a study of American literature. It was still exploring literature two years later when C. Augusta Morse, speaking on *The House of Seven Gables*, analyzed Hawthorne's style, use of language, and method of work.

During the 1890s another notable club appeared, the Woman Suffrage Club. In 1894, the Ohio General Assembly accorded women the right to vote in school board elections and to be elected members of village and city school boards. One response, the Woman Suffrage Club, brought together wives of community leaders— Laura (Mrs. James) Ballard, Mary (Mrs. Rudolph) de Steiguer, Mrs. John P. Gordy, and Jennie (Mrs. A. J.) Frame. In short order they recruited two women to run for Athens Village School Board: Ella Osborne, daughter of a leading merchant, and the college-trained Mary Drake Means. Both were experienced teachers. The Suffrage Club counseled women on the mechanics of the voting process, campaigned for their two candidates, and succeeded in getting them elected. In winning, Osborne and Means unseated the incumbents, two of the village's leading attorneys. When their terms expired, Means stood for reelection and Anna Hobson replaced Osborne; they ran unopposed. As of 1900, Athens women's clubs had prepared women for active participation in civic affairs.

THE ATHENS BLACK COMMUNITY

The Civil War decade gave black Americans a new lease on life. For the first time all blacks were free persons, entitled to the equal protection of the law, to vote, and to hold public office. In short, they were American citizens. In Athens, as elsewhere, both the majority white community and the minority black community would have to work out their relationship to one another.

In 1870 the most distinctive characteristic of the Athens black community was its lack of roots. Close to 70 percent of the adults had been born outside Ohio. Of those, the overwhelming majority had been born in Virginia. Those blacks who had grown up in Athens were simply swamped by the newcomers. The Athens-born had no status or traditions that would enable them to direct the course of the evolution of the black community. And, if things did not work out for them, the newcomers had no compelling reason to remain in the village. Second, while there had been a black presence in the village before the war, the numbers had been so small as to cast doubts on whether they possessed a sense of community. In 1870, the village had 143 blacks living in one or another of forty-four households, the great majority in husband-wife households. All but two of the black households were headed by a male.

The black community of 1870 was young. Of the 143 persons, 48 were youngsters under 15 years of age; another 23 were between 15 and 24, youths on the threshold of entering the labor market and functioning fully in adult society. At the other extreme, there were but two persons who had reached their sixties. This meant, then, that the active adults—the 70 persons between ages 20 and 59—had virtually no old persons to care for, though a modest number of children to support.

In terms of gender, the population was skewed: 42 males, 28 females in the age range 20 to 59. While the adult females had a high likelihood of finding a husband and enjoying family life, a third of the males would have to find much of their social life outside a family of their own and who, unable to establish roots in a family of their own in Athens, would be tempted to move elsewhere. The burden of support of the community's children was concentrated on twenty to twenty-five families.

It is difficult to assess the economic standing of the village's blacks with any degree of assurance. For the large group that had been born in slavery, there was gain in that they were now free to seek kinds of work that were agreeable to them and to reject kinds of work that were repugnant. They could negotiate for a wage, but they were responsible for securing their own food, shelter, and clothing. In migrating to Athens, these persons were the avant-garde of the migration of southern blacks to northern cities. Slavery had never prepared blacks for roles as professionals, managers, or merchants. At most, a small minority had been trained as craftsmen. Not surprisingly, then, those blacks who were heads of households in 1870 generally held menial jobs. Nonetheless, just over half of these black heads of households reported owning some property in 1870. Three of them claimed at least $1,000 in real property; thirteen claimed a modest amount of personal property, typically in the amount of $100 to $200—not much, but far better than slavery.

Of the twenty blacks who in 1870 did not live within the framework of a black household, a pattern of menial labor also existed. The twelve females, chiefly in their teens and twenties, were engaged as live-in domestic servants. The eight males were either laborers or hotel employees. Overall, the blacks were neither equipped to provide one another with goods and services nor to provide the larger community with leadership.

One final measure of the black community in 1870 was their children's access to education. Of the nineteen black youths ages seven through fourteen for whom there are data, fifteen were in school. Of the four not in school, one had not yet enrolled at age seven, two others had left school at age fourteen. While it seems fair to conclude that black children had access to elementary education, none was enrolled in high school. In 1870 it remained to be seen what the often illiterate or marginally literate adult blacks would achieve in their new homes in Athens or what the young people would make of their education in the years ahead.

The blacks did develop a sense of community. The first evidence was the annual celebration in September of Emancipation Day, a commemoration of the British West Indian Emancipation and of Lincoln's preliminary Emancipation Proclamation. In 1876 the day was honored by inviting the Honorable John M. Langston, the "noted colored orator," to come to Athens to speak, and he would return in other years. By the 1880s Emancipation Day had become an area-wide function, delegations coming from Parkersburg, Belpre, and Marietta to join Athens County blacks at the fairgrounds. Several of the leading local white orators were invited to address these meetings, Emmett Tompkins and Charles Townsend. These were major meetings drawing at times 2,500 persons.

A sense of community was also forged by the creation of black institutions. One evidence was the Haitian Ball held on January 1. In 1879, blacks organized their own Odd Fellows lodge, and this organization participated in the Emancipation

Day celebrations. As the temperance movement was revived in the 1870s, Athens blacks organized their own lodge of Good Templars. While an occasional black shows up in the records as a member of one of the white churches, most blacks belonged to black churches, the African Methodist Episcopal Church (AME) or the Mount Zion Baptist Church. Without any public debate over the matter, Athens whites and blacks went their separate ways in social and religious matters.

From the *Messenger,* one gets some sense of how the white community experienced its black townsmen. Most black families lived in the West End with one or two black families as neighbors, but white families were seldom more than two or three doors away. Although Athens had no black ghetto per se, a concentration of blacks is suggested in the naming of Africa Alley, now called Depot Street.

West End was lively, even rowdy. It was the locus of a number of saloons and places of prostitution. At worst, the blacks added to the noise and confusion, but on occasion there were incidents that pitted whites and blacks against one another. One such incident, a "lively old rumpus" in which "blacks and whites alike intermingled" in rock throwing and in which "oaths vociferated," occurred along West Washington in the vicinity of a saloon. However noisy the occasion, there were no arrests. On another occasion, a group of whites barged into a Christmas Eve dance held by some blacks in a private home. "Unpleasantries" followed, but when the police were summoned, it was a black man who was arrested. Editor Jennings suggested that the intrusion of the whites into a black dance constituted prima facie evidence of an intent of the whites to commit a disturbance. Occasionally, white and black youths scuffled on Court Street, throwing stones and breaking a plate glass store window or two. White hoodlums, on occasion, provoked a black woman into the utterance of "the vilest epithets" and the "most voluble profanity." But then blacks could quarrel among themselves. Thus, in one instance, Marshal Peter Finsterwald was summoned to break up a street fight between "three feminines of the colored persuasion." Clearly, there was an edginess in the day-to-day relations between black and white.

In reporting the news, editor Jennings felt a need to tag the character of blacks who were newsworthy—underscoring that because of the social distance between the races, the white reader needed a clue as to the black's character. Thus, Henderson Williams was "a well-known and justly highly esteemed colored resident of Athens." Isaac Montfort, the Presbyterian pastor, conducted Williams's funeral. Again, Wade Redus was "a worthy and favorably known colored person." Mattie Berry, Edward Berry's wife, was an admirable person, and when she suffered an "afflicting malady," Jennings repeatedly expressed in print his concern for her health and speedy recovery. Likewise, he pronounced his satisfaction at seeing James Qualls, a colored man, on the street after a long period of illness had kept him homebound. But there were less admirable blacks as well. One he characterized as a person of "well-known vicious proclivities." Another miscreant was "a Buchtel darkey." Two black women who engaged in a fight were "swarthy Amazons." Those blacks who conformed to the norms of middle-class society might be praised; those who deviated would be castigated. No effort, however, was made to recruit blacks into the establishment. And when a bid was made for interracial marriage, the *Messenger* spoke firmly against it. When a white woman from Trimble eloped with a black man, "black as the proverbial ace of spades," the *Messenger* calmly reported that the fascination seemed mutual; the lady, "tolerably attractive." When a judge declined to marry an interracial couple, editor Jennings commended him. He did not sensationalize such events.

The *Messenger* seems to have spoken the prevailing sentiments of the community: blacks were not to be harassed; their children were entitled to attend the public schools. Indeed, it expressed pride that Athens schools were integrated. There is limited evidence that some blacks made the school system work for them. At a time when few white youngsters entered, much less graduated from, high school, even fewer blacks did so. When they did, the *Messenger* rejoiced. Anna Stevens, who was "uniformly . . . highly esteemed," secured a teaching post in a public school to the west of Herrold's mill. In the 1890s, at least two local blacks—Emma Bougher and Wesley Chase—graduated from Athens High School. Unfortunately, the Bougher girl died shortly thereafter of TB; the Chase lad moved out-of-state to take a teaching job.

Despite the social distance between whites and blacks, a few blacks achieved celebrity status. One of the first, Daniel Walden, a runaway slave and known as Charles Valentine, was an unlikely candidate. In the late 1870s, Valentine was in court, pleading guilty to maintaining a public nuisance—that is for selling liquor and maintaining a place of "resort for evil persons of both sexes." Valentine, however, redeemed himself later when, yielding to the pressure of the WCTU, he abandoned the liquor business. In death, he is remembered by an elegant tombstone in the Old Cemetery.

Eliza Brown Davidson, too, acquired a degree of celebrity that prompted Athens school children to collect pennies to erect a bronze plaque for her grave in the Old Cemetery. Born in slavery in the Blue Ridge area of Virginia, she had made her way to General George Custer's camp in 1862, becoming his personal cook. Remaining with Custer through the rest of the war, she became a companion to his young bride, and had a variety of experiences, some hair-raising. In the early 1870s she left Custer's service, met and married Andrew Davidson, and came to Athens when her husband located his law practice here. Her heroics while in Custer's service were publicized by Custer's widow, and some of the Custer luster rubbed off on her. There was genuine affection between Libbie Custer and Eliza Brown Davidson, and on several occasions Mrs. Custer visited Eliza Davidson in Athens. Eliza Davidson died in 1912.

Eliza's husband Andrew Jackson Davidson achieved celebrity status as the first black attorney in Athens. Born in Alabama in 1847, "A. Jay" was taken to Ashtabula County, Ohio, by two Union army officers at the end of the war. Learning to read and write, young Davidson attended school, went on to college, read law, and was admitted to the Ohio bar in 1873. Although Davidson began the practice of law in Albany, Ohio, he soon moved to Athens. In Athens, Davidson identified with the Democrats, and as a Democrat, he solicited rewards for his party service in the form of political appointments in Columbus and Washington, for which editor Jennings denounced him as "this colored political Judas . . . who has at last got his thirty pieces of silver for his mercenary treachery." Nonetheless, Jennings conceded that Davidson was "well read in his profession," "a good lawyer." In later years, Davidson ran for prosecuting attorney of Athens County, challenging Israel Foster, and though he lost, Davidson had Foster running scared. To the present day, Davidson remains the only black to have practiced law in Athens.

Within Athens, Edward C. Berry was the foremost member of the black community from the 1880s until his death four decades later. Making his reputation as a confectioner, restaurateur, and caterer, he was called on by the white community to plan a number of public events held in Athens at the turn of the century. In 1893 he began the Hotel Berry. He had to overcome substantial barriers. Local bankers refused him credit; for a time local businessmen pressured traveling salesmen into boycotting the hotel. Fortuitously, at a crucial moment C. L. Kurtz advanced Berry the funds needed to pay his bills. It is also clear from the record that Berry enjoyed the unflagging support of Charles Grosvenor. Berry prevailed. He made a reputation for the excellence of his service, gaining a solid patronage from commercial travelers. In the 1890s, college and village clubs held their annual banquets at Berry's hotel. From time to time, Berry expanded his hotel until it reached fifty rooms.

Between 1870 and 1890, the Athens black community more than doubled, reaching 317. Then in the 1890s, the population began to drop off, standing at 279 persons in 1900. There were now 79 households with at least one black resident, and of these, 67 had blacks as head of the household. As in 1870, the handful of blacks living in a non-black household were, for the most part, servants. This small group of 15 excepted, Athens blacks lived with their fellow blacks, chiefly in West End.

By 1900 the age distribution of the black community had changed. Children constituted a smaller fraction of the whole; people older than 60 formed a some-what larger fraction than in 1870. Even so, the median age was less than 30 years. The gender profile was more balanced than in 1870. Overall, there were 147 males compared to 132 females. In the age group most concerned about the availability of marriage partners, the 15- to 24-year-old cohort, there were 41 males, 38 females. For those aged 25 through 44, there was some imbalance at specific ages, but absolute balance for the group as a whole.

Certainly, in 1900 the black community was more rooted in Athens than it had been in 1870. For one thing, both the total number and the percentage of blacks born outside Ohio was smaller in 1900 than in 1870. The growth in the commu-nity's black population had come from Ohio-born blacks, not from the migration of those born in other states.

That in 1900 the black community was thriving is doubtful. Those blacks who were heads of households, who had family responsibilities, were still chiefly en-gaged in menial labor. Andrew Davidson was the only black professional. Carr Minor was a railroad conductor. Despite the community's growth, Edward Berry was still the only black Court Street businessman. At most two blacks operated businesses serving their own community, the Frank Hall family which ran a res-taurant and James West who operated a lunch counter. Athens black heads of households supported their families as laborers, barbers, plasterers, cooks, and teamsters. They were blue-collar, not white-collar. Berry excepted, they were not among the movers and shakers. Yet, one cannot dismiss this thirty-year period as one in which the blacks had nothing to show for their efforts. First, these black householders of 1900 did sufficiently well that none of their wives were forced into the labor force. They had done well enough to emulate the white, middle-class ideal that a husband should support his wife from his own labor. Second, the black community had a creditable record in educating their children.

Nonetheless two areas of concern remained. In comparing Athens blacks with those in nearby Albany, it is apparent that the Albany community had offered its blacks far greater opportunities to work as craftsmen, to secure real and personal property than had Athens. Second, the black population in Athens had peaked in 1890 and had declined by one-eighth during the nineties. This was potentially a serious matter.

IN PURSUIT OF CULTURE

Village life was not limited to formulating a program of civic improvement, to earning a living, nor to seeking satisfying social organizations. Athenians took time to relax the body and the mind, to entertain and to be entertained, to express themselves creatively and intellectually.

Although in 1870 such luminaries as Adelina Patti, Julia Rive King, Camilla Urso, and Sarah Bernhardt toured the hinterlands extensively, Athens was seldom on their itinerary. The coming of the railroad simplified the journey to Marietta, Cincinnati, or Columbus to take in such performances. Thus, when Camilla Urso, one of the top violinists of her era, played Marietta in May 1876, Charles L. Kurtz organized a party of Athenians who traveled to Marietta to hear her, a trip requiring an overnight stay. Cincinnati drew successive parties of Athenians to its varied attractions: the "divine Sarah" Bernhardt, who brightened an otherwise dull January 1881; the Cincinnati Opera Festival—a six-day-long offering of a variety of shows; Adelina Patti, who was making her first of many American tours. Returning in February 1882, Patti sang *Aida* and *Il Trovatore*. Over the years, scores of Athenians made their way to Cincinnati's May Festival, hearing at one time or another Theodore Thomas, the nation's premiere conductor; Julia Rive King, "the most eminent lady pianist in the world;" and Lillian Russell, soprano. Though smaller, Columbus offered the likes of Helena Modjeska and the fabulous Lily Langtry.

Culture Comes to Athens

In time the railroad brought a few of the nation's premier performers to Athens. The lives of Athenians were enriched, the gap between the quality of life in the village and that in the great cities of the East narrowed. Among the notables were Urso in 1886 and Edouard Remenyi, a world-class violinist, in 1897. The Mendelssohn Quintette of Boston, en route west, performed, was much appreciated, and returned a year later. The well-regarded Schubert Quartet of Chicago, however, drew a small audience. For the performer there were risks. When O. R. French presented a complimentary concert at the Opera House, the *Messenger*'s reviewer chastised him, reminding him that "the musical cultivation of an Athens audience is not equal to two movements from a Sonata by Beethoven." Musicians in New York City, Boston, and Chicago faced the same criticisms.

Minstrel shows had a far broader appeal. By the 1870s, the format was familiar;

the music, toe-tapping, and a variety of companies were on the road. Three companies especially pleased. The New Orleans Minstrels, who played the village in late January 1873, were praised for their unusually high standard. They came back. The Al Fields' Minstrels also gave a "most gratifying" performance in May 1890, drawing a large audience. But clearly "Hi" Henry's Minstrels were the town favorites. The most important consideration to the *Messenger* was that a show be free of vulgarities.

A musical group of another kind that played Athens was the Fisk College Jubilee Singers of Tennessee, the group that first introduced white Americans to the Negro spiritual. Although their appearance was first announced from the pulpit on a Sunday morning, they filled the Methodist Church that same afternoon despite rainy weather. Over the years Athens welcomed the group's return.

The circus, though, was easily the most popular of the traveling shows. The coming of the railroads eased transportation problems for the peripatetic companies while expanding the area from which they could draw an audience. Sells Brothers, which returned repeatedly, in 1871 featured seven elephants, including a pair of nursing twin elephants, "the only living horned horse of Ethiopia," and a herd of twelve camels. The show met expectations. To sustain interest, circus companies continuously modified their presentations in the interest of the grander and more spectacular. By 1890, having combined with a second company, Sells Brothers boasted that it took sixty rail cars and four engines to move its company. Its special attraction, a "Children's Dream of Fairyland," promised Robinson Crusoe, Old Mother Goose, Cinderella, and several other figures of children's literature.

Not even Sells Brothers could match the appeal of "Buffalo Bill" Cody's Wild West show. Cody had been "an object of attraction" to those who happened to be at the station when his eastbound train had stopped briefly in August 1878. When he returned to perform in summer 1900, Cody came with 1,200 men and horses, or so he claimed. His company featured Roosevelt's Rough Riders, "straight tall Germans," "swarthy Mexicans," and "fierce Cossacks." The early birds began arriving at 6 A.M. At 10 A.M., when the street parade began, standing room on Court Street was at a premium. The parade began with "There'll Be a Hot Time in the Old Town Tonight." In fact, those attending the matinee were drenched in a blinding summer storm. When the evening show ended, Cody reported 17,000 spectators— more than five times the total population of the village—a figure the *Messenger* did not question.

Among the illustrious travelers drawn to Athens was Dorothea Dix, "the well known philanthropist," who came in July 1874 to tour and observe the newly opened asylum. Dozens of others came to speak. John M. Langston, the eloquent acting president of Howard University, spoke at the Village Hall on several occasions, while Bayard Taylor, "distinguished traveller and literateur," spoke on Ancient Egypt, holding his audience in rapt attention. The editor-publisher of the *Louisville Courier*, Colonel Henry Watterson, drew mixed reviews. His address to villagers, editor Jennings thought dull; his chapel talk to university students, delightful. Russell Conwell, who made a career of delivering his "Acres of Diamonds," held the undivided attention of his audience for two and a half hours. Among the most distinguished visitors was Susan B. Anthony who spoke at the Opera House on a Saturday evening in October 1878. Clearly, logically, she argued the case for woman suffrage. Washington Gladden, a leader in the social gospel movement, appeared as a commencement speaker at Athens High School.

Because the Ohio governor was an ex-officio member of the university board of trustees, Rutherford B. Hayes and William McKinley, both of whom eventually became presidents of the United States, visited Athens many times, usually on university business, and, at times, speaking at political rallies. So, too, James A. Garfield was a frequenter of Athens. Hayes's visit of July 1876 was officially as a university trustee, but as a presidential candidate, townsmen serenaded him, and he responded with an accomplished address. Later that fall, Robert Ingersoll, famed for his "eloquent and ringing speeches" came to further the Republican cause. In 1884 the Democrat James G. Blaine drew an estimated 17,000 persons to the College Green, a mark that few speakers have equaled, much less surpassed. The attraction Athens held for eminent persons is balanced by the "visit" of President Benjamin Harrison. When his train stopped briefly in the middle of the night, the sleepy president raised his window, peered out, and inquired of a stranger on the station platform: "What town is this?"

Theater fare varied. Innumerable troupes offered *Uncle Tom's Cabin*. It still drew audiences in June 1891 when it was performed in a tent on the Commons. A presentation in 1898 was topped off with a street parade. Melodrama, too, was favored; *Ten Nights in a Bar Room*, a temperance play, was offered at the Village Hall in December 1891 and *East Lynne* in December 1898.

Theater had an image problem, however. It had not completely lived down its unsavory reputation dating to Elizabethan England. Fanny May's *British Blondes* only confirmed old prejudices. Editor Jennings characterized it as a "mainly vulgar exhibition." The company, he warned, was not welcome to return to Athens. Audiences preferred familiar plays. In these circumstances, Athens saw a variety of Shakespeare: *Romeo and Juliet* by the Julia A. Hunt Company and again by the Josephine Riley Combo. James Owen O'Conner presented a perhaps idiosyncratic interpretation of *Hamlet*. Undoubtedly, the most exciting Shakespeare was Thomas Keene's *Richard III*. That an actor enjoying wide acclaim would play Athens was initially met with disbelief; the first announcement of his coming was dismissed as a hoax. Doubting Thomases speculated that he was failing and no longer able to satisfy discerning audiences. Keene came, he performed, he convinced. The *Messenger* hailed his company as "the most polished and accomplished company of actors to have played Athens. "Keene," the *Messenger* gushed, "was Richard III."

While wary of the theater generally, Athenians did get an introduction to the contemporary theater. The Irene Taylor Company balanced *East Lynne*, an old chestnut, with the far more daring and contemporary *Camille*. But the village was absolutely smitten with Gilbert and Sullivan. Miles Juvenile Opera Company gave Athens its first taste with its *H. M. S. Pinafore* in March 1880. The *Messenger* thought that nothing hitherto presented on the Athens stage had been more gratifying. In 1886 it welcomed *The Mikado*. The fascination with Gilbert and Sullivan was verified by emulation when a local group, to raise funds with which to assist the poor, staged *Pinafore*, a performance that sold out and prompted a second presentation to accommodate the demand.

In a hint of what was to come, as early as September 1890, for five cents one could drop in at a room across from the courthouse and hear Edison's phonograph. An 1893 production, "Limelight and Phonograph," elevated the phonograph from a curious gadget to a cultural medium. Another foreshadowing of the new century came in October 1900 as the Opera House presented a moving picture of the "Passion Play."

Home-made Entertainment

While Athens was graced with a variety of professional entertainers, the day-to-day leisure activities of individual Athenians went largely unrecorded. In August 1890, "Little Annie Rooney" was a tune that could be heard on the streets "almost any time of the day" and "from any direction." In the heat of August, a glass of "cool, sparkling soda" was available at Dorr's drugstore; at home, refreshments included peaches and blackberries in July, watermelon in August.

Much entertainment, even at home, centered on group activities. Although some groups thought card-playing one of the vices that paved the road to hell, many of the Athens elite took delight in card games. That Grace Grosvenor or Mame O'Bleness entertained in such fashion assured others that euchre and whist were socially acceptable; played in a saloon, however, cards might lead to a fight.

For a small number of people, chess was a passion, the jovial Major L. M. Jewett being reputed to be the best player in the Twelfth Congressional District. Taffy-pulls were still another activity, although such an event at Alexander, when combined with hard cider, ended in a drunken brawl. As wool carpets began to be used for floor coverings, some perverse souls derived pleasure in shuffling across thick rugs, then startling unsuspecting partiers by touching their fingers, nose, or lips—"an electric party."

Athenians also enjoyed dancing, a tradition rooted in the pre–Civil War era. Several business houses on Court Street had top floors designed to double as ball-rooms. In August 1882, for example, some Athenians organized the Lotus Club to hold dances at the Warren House. The Opera House was the site for a masked ball on Friday, December 29, 1882. At times a dancing master settled in town for a season to introduce a new generation to the dance. New Year's Eve, Leap Year, the Fourth of July, all provided an excuse for a dance.

At all times and for all ages, birthdays prompted parties. "Bec" Davis, on the occasion of her fourth birthday, partied with her "little girl friends" in "feast and mirth." So, too, Daniel B. Stewart observed his seventy-fifth at his College Street home, hosting some fifty of his gentlemen friends, who presented him with a large easy chair and otherwise amused one another with "mirth provoking anecdotes." A party for Sarah D. Whipple on the occasion of her ninetieth birthday, New Year's night 1884, illustrated how elaborate such parties might be. The guests appeared in period costumes, some ladies in Elizabethan dress, others with Martha Washington caps. Not to be outdone, men dressed in costumes of Sir Walter Raleigh's time: "knee breeches, powdered hair [and] formidably extended ruff. . . ."

Reflecting their rural past, some of the town's most affluent men developed an interest in horses: a pair of half-Clydesdales, in one case, or more commonly, the animals that pulled their carriages and rigs. James D. Brown felt it worth his time to go to Lexington, Kentucky, to secure "a roadster." John Friday, a Zenner in-law, boasted a splendid four-year old. The possession of a fine horse to show off about town was accompanied by a need to test its running ability against other animals. A fling at harness racing usually sufficed. The most common venue was the Athens County Fair, but wanting even more racing, in the 1890s D. H. Moore offered a prize for a season of Friday afternoon harness races, the competition limited to Athens County horses, winners to be determined by the best two out of three half-mile heats. The sponsors included Dr. Biddle, Fred Bush, and the local livery operators.

An uncertain number of Athenians expressed themselves in print. From time to time, the *Messenger* carried verses by local writers, verse that never made it to anthologies of American poetry. Charles M. Walker, son of A. B. Walker, established himself as editor of the Indianapolis *Times* but returned to Athens after the Civil War long enough to publish his *History of Athens County* in 1869. Walker's volume is top-heavy with the founding of the county, verbatim extracts from the early minutes of the county commissioners, long lists of public officials and their terms of office, and biographical sketches of the founders. He gathered substantial quantities of data that otherwise would have vanished.

Two Athens-born women succeeded in getting published nationally. Elizabeth Sampson Hoyt, a one-time student of Sally Foster, wrote children's poems for the *Atlantic Monthly*. In later life some of her short poems were published by the *Springfield* (Massachusetts) *Republican*. For three years, 1887–1890, she lectured on logic and psychology at the University of Wyoming, where she earned her doctorate in psychology. Adna Cornell Lightner, the other writer of note, was an equally prolific author of religious material for Sunday School magazines. In the mid-1880s, she authored three novels. Her first, *Shadow and Sunshine* (1884), enjoyed "a large and steady sale." Her novels relied heavily on mistaken identities and convoluted plots. She "mingled sentiment and piety with a romantic determination to find rich, young husbands for her troubled heroines." At a time when the minstrel show and melodrama reflected popular taste, Lightner satisfied her readers. The great bulk of her writing, however, took form in the short story. Although most of her married life was lived elsewhere, she retained strong ties to Athens as her father, Frank Cornell, was an Athens businessman, and her doctor-husband was for years a trustee of the Asylum.

Judge John Welch, after leaving the Ohio Supreme Court, devoted years to *Welch's Index-Digest* (1887) of Ohio Court decisions. Fascinated with mathematics, he also published a volume of *Mathematical Curiosities* (1883). Charles Grosvenor published a biography of *William McKinley, His Life and Work* (1901) and *The Book of the Presidents* (1902).

The most prolific writer was Charles Jennings, the Canadian-born editor-publisher of the Athens *Messenger* from 1868 to his death in 1896. Writing against weekly deadlines, most of his copy had a transient quality. Yet his journalistic writings were marked by themes intended to influence readers. He was, first, last, and always a partisan Republican. But as a Republican, he was an uncompromising opponent of Charles Grosvenor, whom he viewed as a self-centered politician who put self-interest ahead of party. On the local scene, Jennings was always the enthusiastic advocate of industrialization as the means to economic growth for the village. He acted as the village conscience and encouraged the development of an infrastructure appropriate to a modern community.

Athens' heritage was enriched not only by those visiting dignitaries who spoke in the village—persons as diverse as John Mercer Langston, Susan B. Anthony, Russell Conwell, and James G. Blaine—but by the local orators to whom the community ordinarily turned. For the patriotic celebrations Charles Townsend, Leonidas M. Jewett, Emmett Tompkins, and Charles Grosvenor were the mainstays. Their reputations as effective, entertaining speakers won them bids to speak all over Ohio.

Athenians would have been as familiar with Angie Crippen Davis and "Mother" Eliza Daniel Stewart as with any of the local male orators. Both were active in the temperance movement beyond Athens, Davis speaking on a regional scale, Stewart on an international scale. On temperance themes, Davis and Stewart were the peers of any of the four men.

Travel

Whether in 1870 or 1900, few Athenians had time for travel; work was all-absorbing. Farmers, of course, worked from sunup to sundown, and because most Athens County agriculture was general farming, there were few periods devoid of pressing work. Villagers were little better off. Storekeepers opened as early as 7 A.M. and closed at 9 P.M. in summer, 6 P.M. in winter. The work week was six days. The most common away-from-home respite from work consisted of visiting family or friends. Young, unmarried women were relatively free to visit brothers, sisters, aunts, and uncles who lived at a distance. The illness of a family member, combined with the general lack of hospitals, frequently precipitated a trip to provide nursing care to the ailing family member.

Following the coming of both north-south and east-west railroads, those Athenians with means—the professional men, merchants, and incipient industrialist —found increasing ease in getting away from the village.

The several railroads serving Athens promoted low-fare, overnight excursions that drew hundreds of Athenians to visit such points of interest as Niagara Falls, Cedar Point, Detroit (and nearby Lake St. Clair). Likewise special fares lured the affluent to visit a succession of expositions from Philadelphia's Centennial Exposition in 1876 to Chicago's Columbian Exposition in 1893. Special rates enticed Athenians to visit the Ohio State Fair in Columbus and the May Festival in Cincinnati.

Among those with means, vacations were justified in the pursuit of health. Especially favored were health spas that featured hot springs or mineral waters such as Hot Sulphur Springs, Virginia, and Mountain Lake Park, Maryland. Others sought relief at the mineral springs at Mt. Clemens, Michigan, or at the Kelloggs' sanitarium at Battle Creek, Michigan. For a few, Hot Springs, Arkansas, was the mecca. Closer home was the Magnetic Springs near Urbana.

Others fled town to escape summer heat and pollen or else to avoid winter's cold. Thus, Mrs. W. H. G. Adney and Miss Gould spent the summer of 1872 at the seashore, while John Ballard and his lady retreated to Massachusetts. Lesser trips took Mrs. Rudoph de Steiguer and Mrs. Charles Grosvenor to Put-in-Bay. Henry T. Atkinson took a month's recreation in Canada and diverse northern and eastern cities. The aging D. B. Stewart and his spouse chose to spend December 1888 through mid-April 1889 in the mild climate of Pasadena, California. Obviously, all of these vacationers were from the most affluent segment of the community.

The elite few traveled abroad, an adventure facilitated by the steamship. The European-born merchants—Isaac Selig, Leopold Friday, and David Zenner—returned to visit family and friends left behind. The visit of Leopold Friday ended in tragedy when he was fatally struck by a streetcar in Munich. Charles Grosvenor and his wife repeatedly took leave of politics to visit England and the continent. By chance, banker David H. Moore and his wife toured Cuba in the last days of Spanish rule. Several of the travelers, including Zenner, Grosvenor, and Moore, shared their experiences and observations with the *Messenger*. Athens may have been a small town, but its leading citizens were reasonably cosmopolitan.

Updating the Holidays

Some old holidays were redefined; new ones appeared. While the young "joyously and hilariously" welcomed 1876 with bonfires and explosions of gunpowder, their elders were abandoning the older custom of "calling" on New Year's day. By 1890, the custom was gone.

The February routine was broken by Valentine's Day and Washington's Birthday. Valentines were exchanged by mail. While lovers might exchange valentines in elaborate, sometimes perfumed envelopes, satirical, even savage, valentines designed to hurt were as often sent anonymously. Editor Jennings claimed to have received one such ugly caricature. He passed it off tongue-in-cheek as having "such a suggestive resemblance" to Col. R. W. Jones, publisher of the rival Democratic paper, "as to lead us to think it was missent." In 1885, Jennings condemned the cheap, slanderous valentines then in circulation. Washington's Birthday seldom occasioned special notice in Athens. Banks did not close; the Village Hall and County Courthouse conducted business as usual. At most, school children got the day off, prompting one child to remark: "I'm glad George Washington was born." Except as an excuse for a Republican party get-together by way of preparing for the spring elections, Lincoln's birthday was yet to be discovered. Along the way, the *Messenger* took note of Ground Hog Day—February 2d, and at four-year intervals, the town's young people seized on Leap Year to let young ladies overtly court a male of their choice. Often as not, this resulted in a series of dances, ranging from a formal supper dance to an informal Calico Ball, stretched out over late winter and spring.

Although a most important day in Christianity, Easter had a surprisingly low profile. A major factor was that it was church-centered, each denomination having its own traditions. For St. Paul's, a series of special services preceded Easter, Ash Wednesday marking the start of Lent, a season of somber, prayerful observances and fasting. Holy Week featured Palm Sunday, Maunday Thursday, Good Friday, and finally, Easter Sunday. Protestants, on the other hand, let Lent pass almost unnoticed and focused on Palm Sunday and Easter. Indeed, when the Episcopal mission scheduled a Good Friday service, the *Messenger*'s editor felt it necessary to explain to the community what the occasion signified. As a special day at the threshold of spring, Easter day might prompt a display of one's new spring finery, but there was no Easter Parade. While the Easter Bunny had not yet arrived, editor Jennings noted in April 1881 that Athens children were looking forward to the "versatile hens that lay colored eggs." This was roughly the time when the White House began its annual Easter Egg Hunt for the children of Washington.

Summer was marked by three holidays, Decoration Day, the Fourth of July, and Labor Day. Athenians generally took a detached view of the Fourth. Celebrating an event of a century before, the Fourth was taken for granted and ignored. The notable exception was the Fourth of July 1876. The community sensed the importance of this centenary of the nation's independence and staged an extravaganza, draping homes and stores with bunting, exhibiting the flag, illuminating homes and stores with the new gaslights, and organizing an elaborate parade and a program on the College Green. A grandstand on the College Green bore a banner: "Proclaim Thou Liberty Throughout the World to all the People thereof." The program included a reading of the Declaration of Independence, patriotic music, a speech by Charles Grosvenor, and a sketch of Athens history. When a summer storm scattered the crowd, many "skedaddled" to the Village Hall where Charles Townsend delivered the major address of the day. The storm having passed, the day ended with fireworks and dancing on the Green. An estimated 5,000 out-oftowners shared the celebration with the villagers. A day to remember, the Centennial Fourth was a day by which all subsequent celebrations to the end of the century were measured. And it was a celebration that exhausted villagers were not quick to repeat.

In other years, those villagers who had to have "an old-fashioned Fourth" went to the outlying villages or to the State Hospital or the Children's Home for fireworks. Otherwise, families might picnic on the College Green. In the absence of an official celebration, other groups, especially temperance groups, appropriated the day to promote their own causes. In 1878, for example, "Mother" Eliza Daniel Stewart, who happened to be in town, gave an impromptu temperance address on the College Green. And in 1881, the villagers, stunned by the shooting of President Garfield two days earlier, drafted a resolution of the community's profound "hope and prayers for the President's recovery" and telegraphed it to Mrs. Garfield.

By default, Decoration Day came to outrank the Fourth in importance. Its start in 1868 was inauspicious. General John A. Logan had called for a day on which to place flowers on the graves of deceased Union veterans. Ohio University students were the first to respond when, in 1872, they organized a dignified program on the College Green to be followed by the placing of flowers in the local cemeteries. The day did not catch on immediately. Toward the end of the seventies the veterans' groups took the lead, and with the organization of the GAR that group assumed the responsibility and began to urge local businesses to close from 1 to 4 P.M. as a measure of respect.

Labor Day was, so far as Athens was concerned, a non-day. It was first proposed by the Knights of Labor in 1882, a day for working men. As noted earlier, Athens did not possess a significant number of laborers, and to local merchants and craftsmen organized labor in the Eastern communities seemed turbulent and threatening. To the end of the century Athens continued business as usual, but Nelsonville, with its masses of miners and railroad workers, was quick to recognize the day.

Observed chiefly by young people, Halloween could be marked by bacchanalian celebrations, and in 1882 the *Messenger* condemned the "mob-like character" of sixty or seventy rowdy celebrants. The evening also afforded an excuse to party and to dress up in exotic ways. The young women of Kappa Alpha Omega Society held a memorable party at the Vine Street home of Nellie Van Vorhes, the belle of the day. Miss Van Vorhes dressed as the Queen of the Witches, the other girls as members of her court. Their male guests came as hobgoblins. The record makes no mention of door-to-door begging.

Thanksgiving, although dating to Plymouth and colonial Virginia, did not acquire official status until the Civil War. Always it combined elements of thankfulness for the blessing of God with a family feast, the feast generally overshadowing whatever religious character the day might have. At best the Presbyterians, Methodists, and, in time, the Disciples joined in a union service which rotated from year to year. Widely observed, Thanksgiving was essentially a family occasion.

Christmas, too, was a relatively new celebration for the community. In 1872 the *Messenger* advised that every household with a child should have a Christmas tree and it undertook to advise on a practical way to set it up. Within a short time local churches scheduled Christmas programs for the children. On the Wednesday before Christmas of 1873, a nearby Christian Church held a party replete with a magnificent Christmas tree and the reading of a Santa Claus story. Merchants took notice of Christmas, but to the end of the century they were very restrained. The first notice came little more than three weeks before Christmas. The tailors Grones and Link featured "a Ladies' Day" for shopping. In the 1890s D. Zenner and Company hosted Santa Claus on three evenings just prior to Christmas, allowing children to shake hands with Santa. Advertisements called attention to dolls of all sorts up to $5.00—close to a week's wages for many working men. Toys had become part of the Christmas expectations of children.

TEMPERANCE REVIVED

As memories of the War between the States mellowed, social issues that had been put aside as the bonds of union unraveled in the 1850s reasserted themselves. The foremost was the temperance crusade—a particularly tenacious issue with moral, social, economic, and political overtones. No social issue of this era consumed more time or energy. Since the issues had been fully defined before the war, it took little effort to bring the controversy once more to a boil. A public meeting was called for a Sunday afternoon in June 1872, to voice concern that, except for Mayor William Golden, town officials had neglected to enforce the liquor laws. The mayor, in fact, presided. The chief speakers were town clergymen. For the moment, the approach was to urge village druggists to refuse to sell whiskey, brandy, or wines to persons not known to be consistent temperance men unless they presented a prescription from a regular practicing physician.

As the temperance issue revived, it became increasingly clear that the community was not of a single mind. The core of the anti-drinking party consisted of the church-going Protestants, Methodists, Presbyterians, and Disciples of Christ. The clergy of these churches formed the nucleus of the movement and in many cases had taken vows never to touch liquor. One element, represented by the Reverend E. H. Schwefel, the Presbyterian pastor, rejected temperance, i.e., moderate drinking, and insisted that total abstinence was "the only sure and safe remedy." William H. Scott, now the university president, rhetorically asked: Why keep plugging for reform when the movement had gone on for a generation and spirituous beverages were still on sale? His implied answer was that Christians had a moral imperative to oppose the use of alcoholic beverages.

A second group of Athenians, believing that it would be impossible to eliminate the production and consumption of liquor, felt that the most practical measure was to license its sale and thereby generate a revenue to support the local government. Judge John Welch, Congressman Charles Grosvenor, and Mayor Golden, however, dismissed licensing as ineffectual. Licensing imposed punitive fees intended to reduce the profits of the saloonkeepers and to raise the cost of drinking to the consumer, thereby discouraging the sale and consumption of liquor. In practice, the fees did not deter men from drinking nor did they erase the saloonkeepers' profits. However, the license fees created a dilemma for the temperance group. Property taxes were so low that the liquor-license fees generated a significant income for the village treasury, funds the village could scarcely forgo.

A third element consisted of the drinkers themselves. Members of the Catholic Church used wine in observing the Eucharist and were unlikely to view use of alcohol as evidence of personal depravity. Residents of Irish and German backgrounds, church-goers or not, came out of cultures long accustomed to taking beer or wine with their meals and to a social life for males that centered around the tavern. The most conspicuous drinkers were railroad men and miners, especially the single men who were often at loose ends when off work. What was at issue was a clash of cultures—the puritan inheritance that insisted that the sabbath be given over in its entirety to the worship of God and advocates of a "continental sabbath" that combined attendance at an early Sunday morning church service with the pursuit of worldly pleasures the rest of the day. Be that as it may, successive priests at St. Paul's lined up on the side of temperance. Even so, the temperance group was bent on imposing its values on the drinkers, and neither intended to yield.

As the sides squared off, the temperance forces organized. A woman's temperance society surfaced spontaneously in 1873 in Logan and Hillsboro, Ohio, and shortly thereafter in Athens. This was months before the Woman's Christian Temperance Union (WCTU) was organized. Pursuing "God's Work," temperance forces by early

1874 were full of energy and fight. In January, they organized a second group, the Sons of Temperance, assuring organized support of males. In less than a month, the women launched a campaign to shut down the town's watering holes, led by wives of some of the village's leading merchants. Afternoon meetings convened at the Presbyterian Church; evening meetings, at the Methodist Church. The group had a multi-pronged program: individuals were asked to forswear intoxicating liquor for one year, preferably for life; property owners were to decline renting or leasing space to purveyors of alcoholic beverages; physicians were to abstain from issuing prescriptions with an alcoholic content unless nothing else would work; druggists were to decline to sell alcohol except for medicinal purposes; business-men, generally, were to cease selling intoxicating beverages.

While one group of women remained at the Presbyterian Church for prayer, others sallied forth to confront the known purveyors of alcohol. Many saloonists, when first approached, stalled. They were caught on the horns of a dilemma. If they curtly refused the women a hearing, they offended the spouses of the town's business leaders; if they acceded to their requests, they were out of business. But the women were unrelenting, and, by the end of the first week, a few purveyors began to accede to the women's demands. Some saloonists like George Gittings gave a verbal promise not to sell liquor but refused to sign any document. Others, like druggist Eli R. Lash, signed both a dealer's pledge and a personal pledge, for-swearing both the sale and consumption of liquor. At evening meetings, where such pledges were announced, village leaders such as Fred L. Ballard, W. W. Kurtz, and Charles Townsend spoke to full houses. So, too, did Angie Davis, one of the town's most committed temperance reformers. The *Messenger* unreservedly sup-ported these efforts. While termed the "women's war on whisky," the warriors were not all women, nor were the adversaries all men. Although she averred that she had removed liquor from her storeroom, Olive Atkinson declined categorically to sign a pledge. By early March 1874 only two liquor sellers still held out.

The claims of victory by temperance forces sprang from promises made under duress, and as the women congratulated themselves on their success, the *Messenger* reported rumors that some merchants who had signed the pledge were surrepti-tiously selling once more. The *Messenger* offered to expose such persons on the pre-sentation of "conclusive evidence." In fact, the village mothers did not succeed in permanently closing the saloons.

In May 1876, the village council sought to curtail liquor sales by adopting a 10 P.M. closing hour for weekdays and forbidding any Sunday sales. This measure did not satisfy the confirmed drinker who demanded instant gratification.

In the eighties, the temperance advocates turned to invoking the power of government to solve the liquor problem. First choice was state-wide prohibition. Alternatively, they favored local option to give individual communities the right to abolish the sale and consumption of alcoholic beverages, if a majority of the community agreed. The problem remained the demand for seven-day-a-week access to alcohol by those who drank and the willingness of some saloonists to supply their demand. When, in September 1881, Ezra Rose opened his saloon on Sunday, in violation of local ordinances, he was fined $40 and costs. Nor was Rose alone in selling on Sunday, and the *Messenger* challenged the county grand jury to take on the saloonists who, with "utter nonchalance," open on Sunday and "defiantly desecrate" the sabbath by playing cards.

For the rest of the century, the anti-liquor forces tested a variety of state legislative ploys to control, if not halt, the liquor business. The Pond Act, passed in 1882, levied a license for sellers of liquor and mandated Sunday closing. Saloonists resisted compliance, and, in a court test, the Ohio Supreme Court held the act to be unconstitutional. Next came the Scott Law, imposing a tax on liquor dealers, the first assessment due June 20, 1883. When Athens County Auditor A. J. Frame declined to publish the notice of the impending tax, the state attorney general sued him to force him to do so. Controlled by Democrats, the Ohio Supreme Court wasted little time in holding the Scott Act unconstitutional. Athens County, which had succeeded in collecting some $15,000 in liquor license fees, was now faced with refunding the "illegal" fees, a heavy burden on the county inasmuch as it had already spent the money.

By the mid-1880s, the temperance issue had statewide political overtones. The Democrats, usually a minority in post-war Ohio politics, favored laissez-faire policies in matters alcoholic; the Republicans generally supported state-mandated prohibition, but party interest in winning the governorship and control of the state legislature led them to trim their sails: strong talk about curbing the liquor interests at election time and temporizing measures in practice. A third party, the Prohibitionists, opposed any compromise, and, while unable to have its way, enjoyed enough support to split the Republican vote and to deny the Republicans an electoral majority in close elections.

At this point, still another force operated in Athens— "Mother" Eliza Daniel Stewart, the second wife of Hiram Stewart, a Court Street merchant. During the mid-1840s and 1850s, "Mother" Stewart gained distinction as a temperance leader here in Athens, and after the family removed to Springfield, Ohio, she went on to acquire a national and international reputation. With in-laws in Athens, she periodically visited. Her stature was such that she could—and did—arrange speaking events that filled whatever auditorium was available. She was invariably "movingly eloquent." While never setting the local agenda, she could always be counted on to revive the spirits of Athens prohibitionists, and she had a considerable impact on the direction taken by state temperance advocates. "Mother" Stewart remained a force to the end of the century. She is one of the few Athenians—male or female—to attain an entry in the prestigious *Dictionary of American Biography.*

With the constitutionality of legislative efforts to regulate or prohibit the liquor business checkmated, in 1883, Athens representative in the Ohio General Assembly, Charles L. Kurtz, promoted a constitutional amendment to establish the requisite authority for legislative reform.

For a time in the mid-1880s, the sale of liquor proceeded on terms set by the dealers. The *Messenger* again complained that local police did not enforce the Sunday closing laws. It became especially upset with those taverns that also served as venues for prostitution. When two "very soiled doves" and their "johns" were arrested in February 1885, the girls (they were sisters ages 16 and 18) were jailed, the "johns" sentenced to work on a stone pile behind the village hall. From the point of view of the temperance forces, the West End (Union, Cemetery, and Dean streets) was "honey-combed with low drinking dives." Certainly, the area accounted for a disproportionate share of the disturbances reported by the *Messenger*, although Court Street saloons, too, could be rowdy. Altogether, in fall 1886, the village boasted sixteen liquor establishments, the most numerous of the varied types of retail establishments of the village.

At this time, fall 1886, the village fathers called for a referendum on local option. The ladies were out in full force on election day, and while ineligible to vote on the issue, they actively worked at getting out the vote and offered lunch to the voters. For the moment, the temperance forces secured a decisive 2-1 majority—380 for local option, 175 against. On the announcement of the vote, church bells rang and a meeting gathered at the village hall. The speakers included a variety of Athenians—the Reverend A. B. Riker, Mrs. Rudolph de Steiguer, Superintendent of Schools Bonebreak, and William Kurtz. Reflecting the character of the community in the late nineteenth century, the speakers also included three "respected colored citizens"—Joseph C. Miller, Edward C. Berry, and James Qualls. The *Messenger* used the occasion to remind the village council that it was expected to respond promptly and positively to this mandate. Reflecting fears that the council would vacillate, townsmen organized a Law and Order League with some two hundred members, all persons eligible to vote. The leadership included Ohio University president Charles W. Super and merchant Edward Berry. The strategy worked; the council voted for total prohibition beginning February 1, 1886.

Prohibition failed. Saloonists resisted compliance; the police remained loath to enforce the law. As the *Messenger* put it, the ordinance was "flagitiously and contin- uously violated." In the spring election of 1887, proponents and opponents of pro- hibition faced off once more. The anti-liquor forces won, Dr. Hoit S. Stimson, Winfield Scott, and Andrew Ullom being elected to council. Prohibition contin- ued to be flouted. One technique was to order liquor shipped into town by express. Another dodge was to move one's saloon to the far side of the Hocking, especially along what is now Richland Avenue, and thus beyond the reach of village author- ities. This rankled, especially when one of these "over-the-Rhine" saloonists, Daniel Bottomly, was charged with selling to minors and operating on Sunday. Still another dodge was employed by John Slaughter, who began selling liquor in quantities of one gallon or more, claiming that, as an agent of a distiller, he was a wholesaler and thus exempt from prohibition which was aimed at retail sales. That prohibition did not altogether halt drinking in the village was documented by a hotelier who exhibited a market basket of flasks and bottles left behind in guests' rooms.

Disillusioned and frustrated, editor Jennings wrote in fall 1887 that prohibition was "daily violated . . . in scores of instances." In a sense it produced the worst of two worlds; the drinking continued along with its attendant problems of violence and prostitution, while the community was deprived of the benefit of the taxes on the liquor traffic. Once more, many "professed friends" of temperance proved indifferent to the execution of the new law. For his part, the venerable Daniel B. Stewart, the brother-in-law of Eliza Daniel Stewart, who had lost a bid for a seat on the village council, swore out warrants for the arrest of several saloonkeepers and their "beer jerkers" for violating the state law. When the first defendant, Daniel Bottomly, came to trial, the jury, without leaving its seats, declined to con- vict him. On balance, local option seems to have closed down the open traffic in alcoholic beverages within the village. While a surreptitious trade continued, the incidence of public drunkenness during the Christmas–New Year's holidays was greatly reduced.

In the ongoing effort to banish the demon rum, Athens representative Charles Townsend persuaded the state legislature to prohibit the sale of alcohol within 1,200 yards of the State Hospital, effectively outlawing the "over-the-Rhine" pubs. The saloons closed immediately but within a week reopened in recognition that the police were unlikely to enforce the law. The case against H. K. Dorr proved to be the last straw. Although the prosecution presented thirty-seven witnesses to the violation, the jury found Dorr not guilty. Within a month, the village council re- pealed the local option ordinance 4–2.

By mid-1889, Athens village had eleven saloons, one for every fifty adult males, a ratio that provided patrons with a plenitude of choices but slim patronage for the proprietors. For the village government, repeal of local option made the re-opened saloons subject to taxes under the state's Dow Law, generating a not-to-be-sniffed-at annual income of $6,751.18 for the village. To the extent that some imbibers got out of hand, fines and court costs generated additional income to the city. Anticipating twentieth-century practice, advocates of a "sin" tax on liquor sought to make it palatable to opponents of drinking by earmarking it for support of a socially desired goal, in this case, street construction. For the balance of the century the village endured the taverns and devoted its energies to other issues.

DELINQUENT YOUTHS AND OBSTREPEROUS ADULTS

The conventional wisdom is that country villages and small towns of the past, unlike big cities, were crime-free or almost so. The reality was that Athens village had its share of juvenile delinquents and obstreperous adults. Much objectionable behavior represented an excess of exuberance, the letting off of steam in minor acts of vandalism or in other ways that offended the sensibilities of respectable citizens. The *Messenger* protested "a new phase of deviltry" in November 1872, when some youths broke and carried off the new street lamps. It denounced some youths who had tormented animals by shooting them in the eye with beans and those who had vandalized parked buggies. Other youths played around railroad cars, jumping on and off moving cars at peril to life and limbs. In these activities, Athens youths were no different than youths elsewhere.

The record makes clear that not every parent knew where his youngster was after supper. The *Messenger* complained of youths who hung out on the streets to nine or ten P.M. Letting boys roam the streets after dark "results in ruin," editor Jennings warned, and he urged authorities to make an example of the disorderly boys. Some youth offended townsmen with "their customary profane and obscene language." Other youngsters congregated along West Washington Street, the principal route between Court Street and the depot, "to insult female passers" who had "to run the gauntlet of their indecencies." Exasperated, the *Messenger* named names of the gang of toughs who haunted the area around the depot. "What is the matter with parents?" the *Messenger* inquired. "Have they lost interest in their children or have they lost all authority . . . ?" The antics of delinquent juveniles became so distracting to the Athens Coronet Band that it gave up its outdoor concerts. The *Messenger* protested that the police could not or would not squelch the boisterous youths. The kids were "noisy and brazen." The only solution hit upon, and that after enduring years of aggravation, was adoption of an eight P.M. curfew for youths under fifteen years.

Young women were less likely to be on the street after hours, but a few came to public attention as their mothers found them difficult to control. A teenage girl who was prone to engage in sexual encounters could be taken before the court and, following a hearing, be committed to the Girls Industrial School at Delaware. The males who dallied with such girls were never singled out for comparable treatment. In the community value system, males might tempt young women at will; the young women were wholly responsible for saying No.

According to an old army song, it is "whisky, whisky, whisky, that makes you feel so frisky in the quartermaster store." Certainly not only much of the friskiness that disrupted the Athens calm but much of the violence, too, stemmed from an excess of drinking. Athens saloons provided both the stimulus and the locus of much violence. Frank Mann's "Whiskey Den" was one center. Two rural fellows who left Mann's well tanked up got into a shooting affray. On another occasion, an out-of-control patron came at Mann with a corkscrew, stabbing him near the eye. Again Mann's "refined resort," adjacent to the public school yard on West State, was the rallying point for a group that disrupted a celebratory function at Atheneum Hall at the schoolhouse.

Prostitution, too, surfaced. Periodically, the *Messenger* made passing references to the "femmes du pave," the "demi-monde," the "soiled doves," "frail companions," and the like. The town may not have discussed the issue publicly, but it knew it had prostitutes and where they were likely to be found. Whereas larger cities conducted campaigns, some organized by women, to suppress prostitution, Athens town fathers tended to look the other way unless the behavior of a prostitute or her customer caused a public commotion. In January 1873 several "femmes du pave" were haled into court for keeping a house of ill-repute. The women discreetly waived examination. No secrets were disclosed; their male patrons were secure from exposure. When an establishment became a community embarrassment, the general pattern was to fine the woman $50, grant her twenty-four hours to raise the funds, and hope against hope that she would skip town. Other times, the court made it explicit that the "frail" could choose either to do time in the local jail or to leave Athens and never return. When two of the "demi-monde" who had been run out of town rashly returned to Athens well boozed up, they were promptly taken into custody, tried, and sentenced to thirty days on bread and water by way of doing penance.

While the women were most often the ones arrested, male patrons, at least part of the time, were also charged. Louis Grones and Eli Foster, for example, paid five dollars and court costs for their adventures. James Roby, for keeping a place of prostitution, was fined fifty dollars and costs and given thirty days in jail to think about it, the same penalty imposed on several of the madams, for example, Lucy Hines and Ida Wood. When a traveling salesman complained to the police that he had been rolled by a prostitute, the court added to his distress by fining him for consorting with a prostitute. Even with periodic crackdowns on prostitution, the impression remains that the town fathers preferred to tolerate the "social evil" rather than to risk the unknown problems that might follow public disclosure of their clientele. One householder in 1870, naively or otherwise, reported to the federal census takers that two members of his household, one of whom was his daughter, were employed as prostitutes. The 1900 census lists five women as prostitutes.

When wooing got out of hand and the young unmarried woman became pregnant, the man who wooed and ran could find himself confronting a charge of forcible rape or bastardy. In some instances, at least, the accused gained his freedom by marrying the young woman at the jail. What the hapless mother-to-be thought of this solution to her plight is not recorded.

From time to time the village calm was interrupted by an egregious homicide. One such case involved a hitherto well-respected Athens business woman, who having delivered her own out-of-wedlock child, killed it, then hid the body in the chimney of her apartment. While the *Messenger* devoted a half page to relating the grisly details, the grand jury apparently concluded that if the woman had sinned, she had also been sinned against, and it declined to indict her. Shortly, the *Messenger* reported that she had removed to New York to resume her career there.

The appearance of criminal activity was sometimes deceiving, even with capital crimes. The community, and even grand juries, seemed quick enough to accuse, to attribute lethal intent when such was not supported by a thoughtful evaluation of evidence. Thus, in early December 1880 Frank Tolliver was charged with the first degree murder of Patrick Carr of Carbondale. Before Tolliver could be taken into custody, he fled. The offense was sufficiently heinous that Sheriff Tim Warden, enlisting the aid of a village marshal from Zaleski, went after his man. Warden tracked the fugitive to a remote cabin in the hills of eastern Kentucky, apprehended him, then walked his prisoner at night some sixteen miles in below-zero temperature to the nearest rail station and returned him to Athens. When Tolliver came to trial the following June, the jury acquitted him. A juror subsequently reported that had Tolliver been charged with the lesser offense of manslaughter, the jury might well have convicted him.

The crime of the era, combining sex and race and lynching, was the Christopher Davis case. A mulatto, Davis, a neighborhood farm hand, attacked Lucinda Luckey, a widow, in her home near Albany. After sexually assaulting the woman and striking her with an axe, he left her for dead. Although sustaining a fractured skull, Luckey revived, made her way to a neighbor's and named her assailant. Local citizens took Davis into custody. Although Sheriff Tim Warden took the precaution of jailing the accused in Chillicothe to forestall a possible lynching, Davis was ultimately returned to Athens. And on November 21, 1881, a mob, by ruse, gained entrance to the sheriff's home, overpowered the sheriff, broke the jail lock with a sledge hammer, then took the prisoner to the South Bridge, fastened a nine-foot rope about his neck, and tossed him over the side. For years thereafter, according to local lore, the rope adorned the office of Dr. Lash, who had acted as coroner.

Subsequently, a meeting of Albany ladies met to review the case. While they "deplore[d] a resort to mob violence," they concluded that Davis had "met a just and timely fate." Those who participated in the lynching, the first in Athens, were not punished. The ladies concluded by urging the Ohio General Assembly to make rape a capital offense. Local tradition holds that the leaders of the lynching party were prominent members of the Albany community, several of whom were relatives of Lucinda Luckey. It also seems that the lynching traumatized the black communities of both Albany and Athens. Although the populations of blacks in both communities, according to census figures, peaked in 1890, thereafter blacks drifted away.

A glance at the annual reports of the Athens Mayor's Court and the indictments of the Court of Common Pleas helps put the "crime scene" in Athens in perspective. The Mayor's Court for the year 1873–74, for example, reported twenty-four cases for the year of which three-fourths were for disorderly conduct, documenting the hijinks that annoyed the respectable. The lists of indictments of the Athens County Court of Common Pleas ran the gamut of felony offenses. In June 1880, for example, the grand jury handed up thirteen indictments. Of the ten named offenses, three were crimes against people: shooting with intent to kill, assault with intent to wound, and assault and battery. Four offenses entailed burglary or larceny. Another entailed defacing property. The remaining two cases arose out of carrying concealed weapons and arson. Analogous indictments would come forth four times a year. On this basis, then, the entire county might experience, on average, one felony against people but certainly less than two and between one and two crimes against property each month. Life and property were generally safe in Athens.

THE SOCIAL ORDER in Athens village matured in the last three decades of the nineteenth century. The rugged individualism, necessary in the earlier years, became dysfunctional with the concentration of people even in a village of two or three thousand souls. What emerged was a sense of community responsibility. Thus, the care of the mentally ill and of dependent children became a societal responsibility. At long last the State of Ohio assumed financial responsibility for Ohio University, while the university itself became more academic, more secular, and took the first tentative steps to serve a social need by training public school teachers. As the physical environment of the community continued to change, a community concern for conservation and public health began to take shape. At another level, individuals increasingly turned from self and family to organized clubs in the pursuit of social life. The village churches increased in their diversity, yet they, too, became involved in the social problems of the village. The Athens black community—in many ways a community within a community—struggled to define its place. Finally, the village had to deal with those individuals who could not, or did not, observe the conventions and norms of the community. Overall, as the village grew, it became less an aggregation of individuals sharing a common space and more an interdependent community.

"THE SPLENDID LITTLE WAR"

In April 1898, when Congress began voting on a resolution that a state of war existed between Spain and the United States, Athenians were not caught by surprise. The *Messenger* and the *Journal* had reported the developments in Cuba and the Philippines as well as in Hawaii. The *Messenger* had noted the efforts of Americans living in Hawaii to replace the government of Queen Liliuokalani with a republic of their own and their effort to secure annexation of the islands by the United States. In doing so, the *Messenger* enunciated an expansionist dogma that it would apply to Cuba and the Philippines.

The unfolding Cuban question had provoked occasional asides in 1896 as Cubans began an ongoing insurrection against their Spanish overlords. These reports acquired a more personal tone in 1897 when the *Messenger* carried a series of accounts by banker D. H. Moore, who, having visited Havana, wrote of what he saw and felt and shared the view that he did not believe that, if free, the Cubans could govern themselves.

By the end of 1897, the international caldron was close to the boiling point. Another proposal to annex the Hawaiian Republic was before the United States Senate. Enthusiastically expansionist, the *Messenger*, now edited by Fred Bush, urged annexation. On the other hand, Bush thought the time was not yet "ripe" to recognize the Cubans as belligerents. When ten weeks later the USS *Maine* blew up in Havana harbor, the *Athens Journal*'s first reaction was that the Spanish, irked at what they regarded as the unwarranted interference of the United States in Cuban affairs, had blown up the ship. Then within a week the *Journal* carried the de Lome letter in which the Spanish minister to the United States characterized President McKinley as "weak and catering to the rabble," altogether "a low politician." As a Democratic paper which might be expected to be anti-imperialist, the *Journal*, nonetheless, regarded McKinley as slow to respond to the Spanish. Athenians were told that a declaration of war could be forthcoming within a week—that is, by the end of February. When a declaration of war was not as immediately forthcoming as the *Journal* thought appropriate, *Journal* editor Curtis V. Harris sarcastically inquired: "Will the Administration ever wake up to the fact that a war exists in Cuba?"

On April 7 Athenians learned the United States had given Spain forty-eight hours to yield Cuba or face war with the United States. War came on April 21. So far as Athens was concerned, the war focused on Company B, 17th Regiment, Ohio National Guard (ONG).

Recruited after the sinking of the Maine, Company B was far from combat ready. It had three officers—Captain Frank S. Lowry, 1st Lieutenant Albert O. Sloane, and 2d Lieutenant Herbert W. Brook—and seventy-six enlisted men. In the enthusiasm of the moment, great things could occur in short order. On Tuesday, April 26, Co. B., indeed the whole 17th regiment, proceeded to camp. Departure time for Co. B was 12:25 P.M. An impromptu parade was arranged. Bunting and flags were retrieved from storage as was an old brass cannon. Three companies of men—Company L (Middleport), Company K (Hebron), and Company A (New Lexington)—arrived in Athens in the morning. Company B assembled at its Congress Street armory. The cannon "belched forth in deafening tones." The parade formed up to the accompaniment of "clanging bells and the blowing of whistles." A mounted escort of townsmen, headed by D. H. Moore, took the lead. Then, in order, the West End drum corps (a black group), members of the Columbus Golden GAR Post, the mayor, village council and other municipal dignitaries, the Athens Coronet Band, and, of course, the departing volunteers. Members of the Athens fire department, Ohio University students, and ordinary citizens also fell in line. Hastily prepared banners proclaimed "Remember the Maine" and "To Hell with Spain." The parade paused briefly at the courthouse where J. P. Wood presented Co. B with a silk flag. In a brief, but fulsome, patriotic address Wood, with good grace, alluded to April 1861, then concluded: "Boys, we bid you God speed, but we know what war means." At least 3,000 persons, the whole village, the *Journal* thought, joined in the line of march to the depot.

The recruits of Company B shortly found themselves in Chillicothe and three days later at Camp Bushnell, Columbus. "Tired, footsore, weary, and hungry," they passed through rituals that veterans of all wars can identify with, the physical examinations and the settling into army routines. What the men remembered, though, were the incongruities. At Chillicothe several "boys" of Company B succeeded in capturing a hare. They took the hare with them to Columbus where, to their chagrin, the hare was stolen and, so they speculated, was converted into somebody else's soup or served up as "hare on toast." On arriving in Columbus, Private Hollett achieved hero status as he saved a woman from injury by a runaway horse. These diversions aside, the boys were in the army. On their first Friday evening in the service, they made straw ticks for their own use.

For Athens there were two wars. The first war was the "splendid little war" of the history books—Dewey's victory at Manila Bay on May 1, Commodore Schley's destruction of Admiral Cervera's fleet at Santiago Bay in early July, the exploits of Theodore Roosevelt's Rough Riders at San Juan Hill, and General Miles's occupation of Puerto Rico. The other war—Company B's war—was from start to finish a war with the elements and with boredom. This other war was "seen" by most Athenians through the reports of Corporal Howard L. Charter, a steady, articulate non-commissioned officer of Company B. As a corporal, Charter reflected life among the enlisted men, the people who fight wars.

As Corporal Charter put it, the boys were "anxious to see something more exciting than camp life and are afraid they will never see a [Spanish] 'Don' except an embalmed one in a dime museum." As raw recruits, they had months of conditioning and training ahead of them before it would be safe to risk them or others by sending them into combat.

At Camp Bushnell, there was a degree of disorder, even chaos. Writing on May 10, Charter hailed "this perfect May day." It was as welcome "as an oasis in the Sahara." The two days preceding had been miserable. It would have been hard to find two other such days in a thousand years, Charter wrote. Rain had come down in a steady patter; wind blew cold from the north; the camp's streets were muddy, like Athens County roads in January. Water flooded the tents to a depth of as much as six inches. But Company B was equal to the occasion; outfitted in rubber boots, they kept dry. Charter assured hometown folks that "the general panacea—whiskey and quinine—put all in condition to brook another flood." As was to be expected, the stay at Camp Bushnell was an interlude and indeed the 17th Regiment, ONG, was transformed into the 7th Regiment, Ohio Volunteer Infantry, then transferred into the federal service as of May 13th. Shortly thereafter, it was sent to Ft. Alger, Falls Church, Virginia, on the outskirts of Washington, D. C.

When Company B arrived, Camp Alger, a hundred-acre facility, was "not the most inviting place in the world." In the course of the next two weeks, this "barren tract of land" was transformed into "a city of white tents," the streets "neat and clean." The military also took care to provide for a sanitary water supply and safe disposal of waste, a far cry from the Civil War camps. It was here that Company B secured its uniforms and shoes. It was mid-July before the Springfield rifles arrived. The knowing among the men recognized these as older model rifles, "inferior in workmanship and design." But thus far nobody was sick.

Remembering Civil War days, Athenians promptly organized an active Soldiers' Aid Society. One activity involved furnishing troops passing through Athens with breakfast, dinner, or supper as appropriate. This could be a major undertaking as when the thousand men of the 2d New York Volunteers were fed a lunch of sandwiches and lemonade and provided with cigars and tobacco. The 159th Indiana Volunteers got a variation—sandwiches, onions, hard boiled eggs, and coffee. Fortunately, most of the groups passing through numbered no more than a half-dozen to two dozen men. These beneficiaries warmly acknowledged the thoughtfulness of the Athenians.

In June the military ordered the 7th Regiment to recruit enough additional men to reach full strength—106 men and officers to the company. On his return to Athens, it took Captain Pratt only a matter of minutes to enlist all the men needed to fill Company B. In mid-July Corporal John Gist of Company B arrived to recruit 150 men for the hospital corps, and in the one day allotted for recruiting in Athens, he signed up 46 men. Enthusiasm for the war remained high.

As might be expected, July 4th called for a major outpouring of patriotic sentiment in Athens. A newly organized fraternal order, the Red Men, organized the day-long celebration, featuring a series of bicycle races—the half mile, mile, and five-mile. In the evening, a fireworks display was mounted from North Hill.

Two weeks later, when news of Commodore Schley's victory at Santiago Bay reached town, a spontaneous celebration took place. Bells rang. Quickly residents hung out the flags and draped the bunting. After supper the band began playing patriotic music on "the Court House Square." Shortly, several thousand people gathered, then drifted to the more spacious area around the Civil War monument on the College Green. A second band, the colored band, followed. In an impromptu speech, General Grosvenor characterized the American victories as almost "like a work of fiction," with so much destruction of the Spanish forces, so little damage to the American. Grosvenor then went on, foreshadowing the division in American society that would follow the war. He had "no faith in a Cuban Republic." The Cuban insurgents, he thought, were incapable of governing themselves, and when a government was created, it should be one "of the United States, by the United States, for the United States." His speech was followed by fireworks.

War or not, life went on on the home front. Athens High School graduated seven young ladies and seven young men. Beginning to appreciate the value of a high school diploma, fellows were completing high school in the same proportions as their sisters. The university commencement continued to be a major occasion for the community as well as for the graduates, extending over five days. Commencement week over, weekly band concerts attracted crowds to "Court House Square." Dr. William Hoover, the Ohio University mathematician, made his yearly pilgrimage to teach at Lake Chautauqua. Euchre and whist parties enlivened summer evenings. The WCTU continued its monthly meetings, although most other organizations took traditional summer breaks.

Life at Camp Alger settled into a routine. Company B was at full strength as were all twelve companies of the 7th Regiment. Supper might consist of roast beef, potatoes, beans, coffee, and bread, plain but adequate for a vigorous out-of-doors life. Camp routine was periodically interrupted by a "training" exercise—to wit, a ten-mile march to the Potomac River and a chance to bathe or swim. This refreshing respite from close order drill was negated by a forced march on the return to camp. One member of the company, Porter, suffered a slight attack of measles. But unlike the "boys" in the Civil War regiments, no one, as yet, had contracted dysentery, intermittent fever, or the like. There was ample time for pranks as when a practical jokester placed a live eel in the bed of the sleeping Earl "Pat" Gabriel. The eyewitnesses reported that when Gabriel became conscious of the eel, he departed through the "upper story" of his tent, grasped his bayonet and hurled it at the offensive eel which escaped death by seeking refuge in the nearest tree.

Far more significantly, correspondent Charter observed that relative to other units at Camp Alger, the 7th Ohio was regarded as poorly equipped and was likely to be sent back to Columbus. Training exercises nonetheless continued. There are no reports of time spent on a rifle range. Rather, the long, hot afternoons were devoted to skirmish drills. Members of one company in each regiment were deployed in the underbrush to play "the wiley Spaniards," while the other companies formed a skirmish line to go in search. Each man was armed with five blank cartridges to acquaint him with some of the sounds and smells of combat. Such activities made for "an unusually dull week."

Rumors bedeviled the men. Writing July 18, Corporal Charter thought it "practically settled" that the 7th Regiment, under the immediate command of General Butler and overall command of General Brooke, would be sent to Puerto Rico. Whether he had come to discount his earlier report that the regiment would return to Columbus or whether he and the men so wanted to see combat that they believed what they wanted to hear is unknown. Authority for Charter's report was the Washington newspapers. The men of the 7th, he claimed, were delighted. In fact, the next day General Miles sailed for Puerto Rico with two brigades, but without the 7th Regiment. By the end of July, the hopes of going to Puerto Rico had evaporated, and stories of any impending moves were regarded as "mere space fillers."

Boredom and home sickness increased geometrically. Complaints began to appear that some of the men had misbehaved when on pass in the District of Columbia. They were especially troublesome following pay day. To pass time, the boys learned new skills or practiced old ones. Jesse Blakely repaired shoes; Alonzo Barnes barbered; a number of men passed time as tailors. A few, however, acquired reputations as "reachers," which is to say they reached—stole—blackberries, enabling the rank and file to partake of berry cobbler every evening.

By the end of July the character of the war was changing. First, there was a well-founded story that the Spanish government through M. Gambon, the French ambassador in Washington, was suing for peace. Second, General Miles had landed on Puerto Rico's south coast in the vicinity of Ponce. The fighting in the Caribbean was about over. If the 7th Ohio was to leave the United States for the Caribbean, it would be for occupation duty, not combat. Third, there were disturbing rumors that yellow fever had broken out among troops at McHenry, Mississippi. Within a month, the press reported that American troops occupying Santiago were coming down with yellow fever, a "most unfortunate" circumstance that boded ill for the future. Fourth, although Admiral Dewey had destroyed the Spanish fleet, he was in no position to occupy the city of Manila until troops arrived from the United States. Indeed, Philippine independence fighters under Emilio Aguinaldo had the Spanish surrounded in the old walled city of Manila. By the time General Merritt appeared with his advance forces, the American and the Filipino leadership were thoroughly distrustful of one another. The Americans were no more prepared to turn the Philippines over to Emilio Aguinaldo than General Grosvenor was to recommend that Cuban insurrectionists assume control in Cuba. The war with Spain might be at an end, but the United States had moved into a political and military quagmire in the Philippines that would go on and on. Meantime, the men of "the gallant Seventh Ohio" were "whiling away weary, hot days amid beautiful pine groves."

As diplomats negotiated the Spanish capitulation, Company B moved to another site some three miles away. In the short run, this was a decided improvement. Each company had its own street, the camp was less crowded; two good water wells were close at hand; sanitary facilities were new. But the satisfaction quickly disappeared. "Inactive" and "dormant" were the words Corporal Charter employed to describe Company B. By mid-August, the "boys wanted to go home." Only two members of Company B were eager to enlist in the regular army. The men were "heartily disgusted with the manner of soldiering" they were called upon to perform. Seven of their number were in hospital with fever, one with rheumatism. Before August was over, the enlisted men had drafted a petition saying they wanted to go home, a petition the officers quickly repudiated. Corporal Charter, however, bluntly explained that as the officers were "drawing larger salaries than ever before, and possibly ever will, in civil life," their desire to remain in the service was self-serving. He protested when the officers termed their men "cowards." By the end of August, the new site was "this dreary and desolate spot."

For "the boys" of Company B, the end of the war came quickly. On Thursday, the 22d of September, they were sent back to Camp Bushnell, Columbus, Ohio. The following Tuesday morning they were released from service. They arrived in Athens before the band and cavalry escort reached the depot, although a crowd of citizens was waiting. At the top of Union Street hill, the band and cavalry met them and escorted them to the Courthouse, where the Reverend Mr. William Powell greeted them. The Soldiers' Aid Society hosted them to "a sumptuous dinner" at the Armory. There were more speeches. Captain Lowry replied on behalf of the men. The speeches over, the men went home. If no one achieved fame in battle, neither had anyone in Company B lost his life either in combat or from sickness. In the judgment of the *Athens Journal*, Company B had done all it had been asked to do.

If the experiences of Company B represented the war to most of Athens service men, there were others who had decidedly different experiences, although not as systematically chronicled in the local press. In August Athenians read of the exploits of James Holland, an ex-miner from Buchtel who had enlisted in the navy. Early in the war Holland had been a member of a detail that had been sent shoreward to cut the Cienfeugos cable, a marine cable that linked Cuba to Spain. A highly hazardous venture, Holland escaped with a slight wound to the neck from a Spanish bullet and a four-inch section of the cable which he had cut. It is also the case that Dr. Dudley Welch served in a field hospital at Santiago for several months before being posted to the Philippines. So, too, the *Journal* reported that three Athens County men—John Rivers, King Simmes, and Albert Lake—all of the regular army, had fallen at Santiago.

Within a month, a reaction to the war had set in. Members of the president's party had begun to question its wisdom. Joseph Foraker had concluded that the war was unnecessary; it was "the work of yellow journals and demagogues, and self-seeking politicians." Secretary of State Sherman added that the Cubans could have bought their independence. Closer to home, Charles Grosvenor, often the spokesman for the McKinley administration, was quoted from a letter he had written April 23d, that the president had been hustled into the war, that diplomacy could have settled the whole matter. However much it had been a "splendid little war," the Spanish-American War had great consequences. It left the United States a small empire, extending from Puerto Rico in the Caribbean to Guam and to the Philippines in the western Pacific. What Athenians did not know as the century ended was that their days as an innocent village were numbered.

10

The Emerging City: 1900–1920

THE PERIOD 1900–1920 marked years of unprecedented growth. The village of 3,066 inhabitants in 1900 counted 6,418 two decades later, becoming a full-fledged city along the way. The entire period was dominated by Progressivism, a movement that placed great confidence in the capacity of ordinary people to share in governing themselves, that sought to democratize the political process, and that believed government could and should adopt a wide spectrum of programs for the general welfare.

In 1910 Athens reported a population of 5,463, which under Ohio statutes qualified it to be governed as a city. The magic day for the change was January 1, 1912. Paradoxically, for a community long given to municipal celebrations—the arrival of the first canal boat, the dedication of the Masonic Hall, the laying of the cornerstone for the Athens Lunatic Asylum—there was no hoopla. One factor may be that the community had known for months that the switch was impending; by January 1912, this was no longer news. Second, the incumbent village mayor, Charles H. Slaughter, had been reelected so there was no traumatic change in personnel. Third, there was little visible change in the structure of government, while the problems of the community remained unchanged.

The mayor's position was enhanced by the promotion of Athens to city status. Executive power was lodged in the mayor and his appointees—the service director and the safety director. The mayor would no longer be compensated by fees but instead received a salary set by council; in this case $1,200 a year, not a munificent sum but for the time a salary one could live on. The other elected officials—the city solicitor, the auditor, and treasurer—were part-time positions. For supervising the city's electric and water plants, the service director received $600 a year. The safety director, with the fire and police departments to oversee, received $240 a year. Councilmen received $2 per session, with a maximum pay of $48 per year. This was a no-frills government that tested the altruism of all who held a city office. Nor did city status enhance the capacity of municipal authorities to address the city's problems.

THE PROGRESSIVE MILIEU

Public Input

Athenians quickly embraced Progressivism. Over the years, a mix of private citizens and ad hoc civic groups formulated a series of agendas for the city administration. One of the earliest groups was the Village Improvement Society, an organization of village matrons. The concern of the mass meeting of May 1903 was the cleanliness of village streets, sidewalks, and other public places. The society's street committee monitored the streets and notified the town fathers of problems as they arose; it asked for an anti-spitting ordinance, and took steps to provide trash receptacles for the streets. Next, the Society urged a program of beautification by private landowners—attention to lawns and flowers, the preservation of shade trees, and the cutting of weeds on vacant property. The committee also urged that street debris be swept up at the end of each day, thus making for pleasant evening walks.

In spring 1904 Madelyn Schaeffler outlined in the *Messenger* a broad program akin to the City Beautiful Movement then fashionable in the East. With a little effort, she argued, Athens could become the model village of Ohio. Implicit was a sense of pride in the village and belief that its flaws were cosmetic, not intrinsic. For the most part, the needed improvements were ones that individuals could and should take care of. Schaeffler urged a program of painting unsightly barns and outbuildings, of cultivating grape vines, rambler roses, and ivy to cover the otherwise unsightly areas. Sidewalks were to be straightened and laid at uniform height; she would ban posters and signs on utility poles, trees, and fences; Court Street would be cleared of its metal awnings; brick incinerators should be constructed in backyards to burn refuse. She concurred with the Village Improvement Society that the deck of South Bridge (a covered bridge) should be kept clean. Schaeffler, it is clear, would rely on private initiative to effect this cleanup.

In 1905 and again in 1907 "A Citizen" writing to the *Messenger* sought to provide a sense of direction. Praising the amenities Athens already offered, "A Citizen" went on to argue that the village needed a *system* for cleaning its streets and a fire department that had a fully-equipped truck and a trained fire brigade "always in readiness to respond." At this point, "A Citizen" looked to the village government to solve the problems.

The Athens County Taxpayers Association, H. D. Henry, president, was preoccupied with the "economical expenditure of public funds" and a "proper reduction in the rate of taxation." This came as the village government found itself incurring additional operating costs—a team and driver for the fire department, installing a public restroom at the courthouse, a street sweeper, and a storm sewer for East State Street. Subsequently, the Taxpayers Association published an analysis of the village's finances that gave the citizenry a clear picture of the village's tax base, its bonded indebtedness, and its operating costs. Concern was expressed that so much of the village's funds—60 percent—went to salaries and fees. While the Association observed that some officials were overpaid, others underpaid, no final judgments were forthcoming.

From 1915 to 1917 Athens club women, organized as the Civic Federation, acted as a pressure group. Alarmed at the number of unsupervised youth on the streets in the evening hours, they insisted on enforcement of the curfew ordinance and proposed that the whistle at the brick plant sound the curfew.

Ultimately, in April 1916, the town's business and professional community organized a Chamber of Commerce. A major part of its energy was directed at drafting an agenda for community development. Initially, the agenda entailed bringing the interurban to Court Street, creating a city hospital, building a cold storage facility to serve the area fruit industry, employing a county agent to serve area farmers, and surveying the county's natural resources.

The Chamber of Commerce was energetic. It pressured the city fathers to erect new street signs, urged a strengthening of the city police force, and promoted a city-owned site for the burning of garbage. At other times the Chamber facilitated a discussion of the merits of the commission-manager form of city government, a reform Dayton, Ohio, had adopted to handle the crisis it encountered following the disastrous 1913 flood. It is abundantly clear that once organized the Chamber of Commerce and the Athens City Council worked closely, the Chamber formulating city policy, the council enacting the requisite legislation.

Woman Suffrage

As of 1900 Athens women had acquired considerable political experience in the temperance crusade and in public school affairs. Progressivism pushed them into the mainstream of local politics. They participated actively in the campaign to secure woman suffrage and otherwise expand women's rights.

The enthusiasm that had led to the election of Mary Means and Ella Osborne to the Athens School Board in 1895 remained undiminished in the new century. Meeting in the Union Street home of Mrs. C. A. Snow in March 1901, the Athens Woman Suffrage Association elected its officers for the year and nominated Esther (Mrs. James B.) Fulton and Emma (Mrs. James) Palmer to run for school board. Two months later they listened to Dr. Maud Park Wood, then on a national tour in support of woman suffrage, and gained 120 members for the local association. Woman suffrage was a national issue, and Athens women played a role alongside women from thousands of other villages and cities. Anna (Mrs. Sam) Hobson, wife of a local banker, was chosen treasurer of the Ohio Woman Suffrage Association. Athens regularly sent delegates to the successive state suffrage conventions and from time to time hosted distinguished state and national suffrage speakers, including Laura Clay, the granddaughter of Henry Clay, Kate Gordon of Louisiana, Mrs. Percy V. Pennypacker, national president of the General Federation of Women's Clubs, and Harriet Taylor Upton, president of the Ohio Woman Suffrage Association.

If the pro-woman suffragists were active, so, too, were the antis. The *Messenger* reported the bitter debate at the State Constitutional Convention in 1912. Prominent Columbus club women insisted that "women can and do exercise their full share of influence and responsibility for the public welfare without the ballot." And as of February 1912 the antis represented the majority view in the state on woman suffrage. Within Athens city the antis were a silent majority.

Local suffragists organized debates, lectures, and forums at home to reach out beyond the already convinced. This effort was important, for the state constitutional convention had voted 76–34 in favor of a statewide referendum on woman suffrage. Candus (Mrs. Clement L.) Martzolff, herself a popular Athens Sunday school leader, first reviewed the case for woman suffrage with local suffragists. A self-possessed woman capable of sarcasm and wit, she went on a county-wide tour, packing the Public Square in Nelsonville and reporting respectful audiences at Hollister and Glouster. A pillar of the Methodist Church, she spoke before one of the men's Sunday school classes. A public debate in Athens, moderated by editor Fred Bush, drew five hundred Athenians to the county courthouse.

The vote on woman suffrage in 1912 was but one item on a broad spectrum of amendments to the Ohio Constitution. While most of the proposed amendments passed, statewide woman suffrage went down to decisive defeat. In the city of Athens, woman suffrage also lost—by a margin of 171 votes. Ironically, the rural areas of the county tended to support votes for women.

Undaunted, Athens suffragists continued their fight. Persisting, the women planned a suffrage proposal for the Ohio ballot in November 1914. And again throughout the year, debates and lectures were scheduled in Athens. In a debate before a full Ewing Auditorium, Dean Irma Voigt opposed the suffrage, arguing that as a majority of women opposed the suffrage, it ought not be forced on them. Further, alluding to the radical suffragists led by Alice Paul, she thought the suffragettes were "a menace to society." Suffragism she equated with socialism and anarchy.

Later in the summer Professor H. W. Elson joined in the attack. Woman suffrage was not needed; there were already sufficient voters. He thought rivalry between the sexes was undesirable and that attainment of the suffrage would cost women the respect of men. Candus Martzolff took Elson head on, insisting that the suffrage was a moral right, involving the idea of freedom and justice. To exclude a class of people (women) from the suffrage undercut the basic premise of the United States government that it derives its just powers from the consent of the governed. When a massive suffrage parade was scheduled at Columbus, Athens representatives carried a petition bearing 1,045 names. While the suffrage proposal lost decisively statewide, this time Athens County gave the measure a majority of 275 votes in a total of 7,865. Nonetheless, Athenians remained decidedly more supportive of prohibition than of woman suffrage.

The suffrage crusade continued. Necessarily, much of the action was elsewhere. At most, Athens women could lend their support to a cause that did not yet enjoy majority support either in Ohio or the nation. There was evidence that President Wilson was becoming more receptive, but at a glacial pace. In October 1915, while he stated that as a private citizen he would vote for woman suffrage in the New Jersey election, he declined to make it a national issue. In September 1916, with a presidential election in the offing, Wilson spoke to the national convention of the National American Woman Suffrage Association (NAWSA), the first president to do so. By this date, the Democrats had endorsed woman suffrage in principle, but chose to leave the issue to the separate states. In contrast, Charles Evans Hughes, Wilson's 1916 rival, expressly endorsed the Anthony Amendment, which would give women the vote nationwide.

As 1917 began, Ohio's governor, Democrat James Cox, endorsed presidential suffrage for Ohio women. A bill to authorize presidential suffrage in Ohio was cosponsored by M. P. Totman, representative from Athens. This was scarcely a half loaf, for presidential suffrage let women vote for president of the United States while barring them from voting for members of Congress, the state governor, or members of the state legislature. Nor would it let them vote on prohibition. As in 1914, the suffrage amendment lost heavily statewide. Within Athens County, presidential suffrage for women enjoyed a plurality of 223. But clearly Athens city had a climate far more friendly toward public roles for women than the state of Ohio as a whole. The minutes of the Pallas Club document that their members kept their fingers on the pulse of community affairs and were active in promoting all manner of civic projects.

In 1917 the tide of public opinion began to run in favor of national woman suffrage, and in January 1918 President Wilson publicly endorsed the Anthony Amendment. While the House of Representatives promptly adopted the amendment, not until June 1919 did the Senate give the amendment its blessing. Within two weeks the Ohio legislature ratified the Anthony Amendment. In August 1920 the Anthony Amendment received the requisite ratification, so that in November 1920, women were free to vote for the full slate of candidates, state and national.

THE BUSINESS OF GOVERNMENT

While progressivism emphasized promoting the public interest, a glance at the realities of Athens politics discloses a high level of very personal politics. In particular, the mayor's position gave him unusual discretion in his role as a justice of the peace, and at times the conduct of the mayor's office suggested a government of men rather than of law.

In 1906 and early 1907 the system seemed out of kilter. There were too many instances of rowdiness, drunkenness, gambling, prostitution, and juvenile delinquency. When one eleven-year-old schoolboy shook down a classmate for a dime on his way to school and then shoplifted on his way home, he was taken into custody and, although no charges were ever filed, held behind bars for a day or two "to teach him a lesson." A few days later Marshal Peter Finsterwald narrowly escaped being stabbed as he attempted to take two toughs into custody by way of ending a barroom brawl. One of the toughs had bet $50 that he could lick any man in Athens. A week later rowdies disrupted a performance of *Way Down East* at the Opera House. Early in March Athens police broke up a "gambling joint" above Fulton's grocery on Court Street. Before the month was over Kenneth Gillett, a seventh grader, slid his feet under the desk of the youngster sitting in front of him. When the youngster told him to stop, Gillett stabbed the boy in the back with a pen knife, inflicting a painful injury.

In 1906, on taking office, Mayor Gilbert Day insisted on law and order. This meant a vigorous enforcement of the closing laws for saloons—10 P.M. on weekdays and all day on the Sabbath. He not only insisted on halting gambling and prostitution but threatened to prosecute owners of property on which prostitution occurred. Mayor Day also began to enforce ordinances banning concealed weapons. All too often, men came to town, drank, then fired off their revolvers on their way home. When George W. Schawl, of Luhrig, came before the mayor for the "promiscuous shooting" of his revolver, the mayor fined him $18.90 (something like two weeks' wages) and ordered him jailed for five days.

The village also had a problem with dogs running loose. Confronted with an area-wide rabies problem, the mayor ordered the police to summarily shoot unleashed dogs, and within short order Marshal Finsterwald dispatched seventeen animals. The rabies threat was serious. A four-year-old Athens boy had been bitten in the face by a stray, and within a month six other Athenians who had also been bitten had to go to the Pasteur Institute in Ann Arbor for treatment.

The paradox of this law-and-order administration was that in June 1907 the no-nonsense mayor was sued for divorce, charged with having spent his time in gambling, drinking, riotous living, and debauchery and with maintaining lewd and lascivious women. Notwithstanding the allegations, villagers supported his tightship operation of the village government, re-electing him to office handily in November 1907.

In November 1909 Charles H. Slaughter was elected mayor. The first two years of his mayoralty passed quietly enough. As mayor, he practiced "live and let live." In fall 1913 Oliver Rowland, an attorney, bested Slaughter in a hotly contested election. Rowland had barely assumed office in 1914, when he had his predecessor arrested on a charge of stealing three slot machines that had been stored in the city jail. Just before vacating his office, Slaughter had taken the machines home. Mayor Rowland also relieved police chief Mills for malfeasance in office and for knowingly permitting the operation of houses of prostitution and the sale of intoxicating beverages.

City affairs remained in a state of chaos as Rowland failed, on technical grounds, to sustain his charges against either Slaughter or Mills. He then took another tack, charging Slaughter with embezzlement, to wit, with pocketing fines he had collected. In May 1914 a grand jury returned twenty-one charges against him.

Slaughter appears, at least in part, to have been a negligent record keeper, failing to distinguish among fines that were suspended, fines partially paid and partially worked off, fines collected in full, and those still unpaid. Public office demanded more expertise and attention to detail than Slaughter appreciated. A jury found Slaughter guilty of embezzling $200. Despite an appeal, he was ultimately sent to prison. Governor Frank Willis, however, had the last word, and in April 1915, he granted Slaughter a full pardon. In June, the ex-mayor and Council settled on a restitution payment of $422.50. Chief Mills resigned his post. Athens city government had got off to an inauspicious start.

The Legislative Agenda

While the mayor presided over council, the latter had the responsibility for making policy. Even more than in the 1890s, council had to set the terms by which the community would enjoy such amenities as electric power, fuel gas, telephone service, public water and sewerage service, paved streets and sidewalks. It would also have to take responsibility for the availability or absence of alcoholic beverages and formulate measures with respect to public health. As it proceeded to make policy, council was caught between the unwritten principle "Thou ought not tax" and the progressive article of faith that "urban governments" in particular, because they were close to the people, "could and should be activist." Government was inherently good. The *Messenger* noted in January 1903 that "progressive" villagers grumbled that past councilmen had not done anything. The villagers thought the town fathers should exercise "a sort of municipal paternalism over every inhabitant." Voters wanted an instant response by council to "every mudhole, every missing brick, and every clogged gutter." Editor Bush observed that to realize the municipal improvements villagers sought, there would have to be an increase in the tax base.

Municipal Socialism

A paradox of Athens political history was that a community that was rock-ribbed Republican flirted with and, for a time, embraced municipal socialism in the form of a publicly owned electric plant. The franchise of the privately owned Athens Gas and Electric Company expired in October 1902, and the company indicated that it would not renew its contract under any conditions. The village, at this point, was desirous of incandescent home lighting as well as arc lighting for streets, necessitating a larger electric plant. At the moment, the village stood at the upper limit of its bonded indebtedness, making it difficult to finance an electric power plant. A public debate later in the month revealed the town leadership was divided on the merits of public and private ownership.

After the Athens Artificial Ice and Electric Company made a bid to manage a municipally owned electric plant, the village council agreed to its proposal, whereupon Fred Bush of the *Messenger* launched a massive assault on the idea of municipal ownership. The village differed; a referendum in April 1903 revealed that voters favored a municipally owned electric plant by a margin of better than three to one. The proposal required a $15,000 bond issue, a $1,000 bond to be retired each year. A second referendum in July ran ten to one in favor of municipal ownership.

By mid-March 1904 the new system was in operation. On the streets the old arc lights were replaced, new incandescent lights added. Furthermore, there were orders for well over 700 commercial lights. O. B. Sloane, a retired businessman, was named manager of the plant.

As the village-owned electric plant came on line, unanticipated problems and costs emerged. The demand for additional street lights increased the village's electric bill. Initially, the municipal plant generated electric power only for nighttime use, the generator being deemed too large to operate profitably for the limited demand for daytime power. Accordingly, the village bought a smaller generator for daytime use. Next, the devastating 1907 flood knocked out the generator, leaving the village without electric power for days until the generator could be dried out and the transformers repaired. Dependent upon electric pumps, the village water system was also rendered inoperative. By December 1907 it was apparent that the flood had damaged the power plant's boilers. When the replacement boilers were lost in transit, Athens was compelled to discontinue street lighting in order to make its limited electric supply available to its commercial customers and to operate the pumps for the town's water standpipe.

As the technology of electric power generation, transmission, and use evolved, the economy of a small power plant began to be questioned. The future of the city's plant was put in doubt by an announcement in June 1911 that an English firm expected to erect the world's largest electric generating plant at Beaumont. This central generating plant would serve area coal mines, brick and tile plants, a possible electric interurban transit system, and the area's towns and villages. A series of proposals followed in the course of the next several years before any concrete steps were taken. For a time, the Athens City Council resisted the proposals, the more so as the influential Commercial Club seemed satisfied with the municipal plant. Indeed, it termed the municipal plant an "important function of city government."

When the Ohio Electric Company finally broke ground in 1914 for an 8,000-kilowatt electric plant at Floodwood, Athens again faced building a new electric plant at an estimated $45,000 and a new water plant at $65,000. In these circumstances, the attractions of municipal socialism began to pall. Ohio Electric offered to sell electric power to the city and let the latter distribute it to customers; otherwise Ohio Electric would both generate and distribute power itself.

By midsummer, the business community recognized the economic advantages of a large, centralized power plant—lower rates for commercial users and for street lights and an adequate source of power for industrial use both for the present and foreseeable future. The city could also reap additional savings by switching from steam power at the water plant to electric pumps. The community concurred. In a referendum in July 1914 townsmen rejected continued municipal ownership by an overwhelming 418 to 14. Feeling vindicated at last, editor Bush characterized the city's electric plant as "a white elephant." Athens seemed to be at the dawn of "a new era," with an adequate electric supply that in turn would assure adequate water and the feasibility of an electric interurban system. In September the city council granted the Floodwood plant a twenty-five-year franchise for electric power and a ten-year contract to serve the city water system. At last, all-night street lighting seemed financially feasible to council. In an expansive mood, council agreed to install new, decorative lights on Court Street with the possibility that the merchants might pick up the costs of underground wiring, thereby freeing Court Street of its mishmash of poles and wires.

As electric power from the Floodwood plant came on line, the *Messenger's* editorial writer looked back, equating municipally generated power with frequent power outages that had forced temporary reversions to candles, oil lamps, and gaslight. Indeed, many buildings in the first decade and a half of the new century were equipped for both gaslight and electric service. As it began operations, the power company removed its poles from Court Street and otherwise rebuilt the city's electric distribution system. Private operation, however, was not problem-free. In February 1918, a breakdown at Floodwood deprived the entire Athens community of electric power—no lights, no water, no interurban service. Toward the end of the year, Mayor E. C. Woodworth complained bitterly to the firm that its electric service had been "a little less than abominable." The town had put up with inconvenience for a year and a half. The power company excused its interruptions as the concomitants of upgrading the system.

A Modern Water System

Municipal socialism also extended to the operation of the community's water system, which was at least as problem-ridden as its electric plant. The problems were multifaceted and on-going.

Given the doubling of the town's population between 1900 and 1920, the town had to expand its water supply accordingly, a major task. The older wells along the Hocking repeatedly failed to function properly. Other wells required cleaning. Compressors and pumps failed. Repeatedly, the town had to develop new wells. Three wells opened in February 1902 increased water supply by 750,000 gallons per day. As the system made its first report in fall 1902, income appeared to exceed expense, offsetting an earlier charge by the *Messenger* that it had cost the city several thousand dollars "to buy influence, pay rake offs, and remove obstructions." Although editor Bush had offered to name names when appropriate, such a time never came.

Certainly Athenians were prodigal in their use of water. The 2,000 customers of 1903 drew water at the rate of 250 gallons per person per day, and this in an age when the weekly Saturday-night bath was still the norm. The problem was twofold: users were not diligent in turning off the taps and water was used liberally to water lawns and settle the dust on the town's dirt streets. In cold weather residents let the taps run continuously to keep the pipes from freezing. Nor was there any inducement to conserve water, for the billing was at a flat rate. This prodigal use of water had dire consequences—it ran down the town's water reservoir, strained the wells, and overtaxed the pumping station.

Periodic floods wreaked havoc, too. The 1907 flood damaged the town reservoir badly, causing it to leak water. In 1913 a shift in the channel of the Hocking and the destruction of the Herrold dam adversely affected the well field. At the same time, several private wells used by Stedman's packing plant and the ice plant failed, and these firms—with large demands for water—shifted to city water. A hydraulic elevator in the First National Bank was especially wasteful.

By fall 1913 the city had a water crisis it could not dodge. The State Board of Health ordered the city to abandon four of its wells that were too close to private homes. This order came at a time when the city was often short of water and the pumping station had been deemed outmoded for a decade. The Commercial Club rallied, discussed the matter, and reached consensus: the city needed a new well field and pumping plant; patching-up was rejected. Within days, city council voted to drill five new wells, secure a new pump capable of handling two million gallons of water a day, and make other changes. While council concluded that the only way to curb prodigal use of water was to install meters and bill customers for use, it could not bring itself to act decisively in this matter. On occasion, the drain on the city's water was so great the schools were shut down for lack of water. At other times the city reservoir ran dry. The city did, however, inaugurate a vigorous policy of collecting delinquent bills after a state auditor identified 380 delinquent accounts.

In 1915 council voted to take a second, more expensive step in providing the city with an adequate, dependable water supply. This entailed constructing a 2,750,000-gallon reservoir on North Hill to maintain pressure to homes on the many hillsides and hilltops. The cost: $64,000. By 1920 the city had a reasonable, dependable public water system. The unresolved problem was wasteful use of water facilitated by the flat-rate pricing system.

Gas

As of 1900, the Athens gas supply came from outside the village. As gas wells did not regenerate, the sources of gas were ever changing. Council had the task of negotiating with suppliers.

In 1910 the city council intervened to contract with a new supplier of natural gas—the Marietta and Hocking Valley Oil and Gas Company, the contract to run for ten years. Before the year was out, the firm was taken over by Athens Heating, Lighting and Power Company. Capitalized at $25,000, the new firm was franchised to operate within Athens to compete with Ohio Fuel Gas Company, which was both a supplier and a distributor of gas, the new firm undercutting Ohio Fuel by five cents per thousand cubic feet. At this point there were two gas companies operating within the community.

Beyond 1910 the city encountered increasingly serious difficulties with its gas suppliers. Some Ohio gas fields that had been adequate a decade earlier were now depleted; furthermore, to protect its own residents, the State of West Virginia sought to restrict the "export" of scarce natural gas to Ohio. Cost of gas production and transmission had risen markedly, but to Athenians, it seemed more than likely that the gas suppliers were exploiting the situation by threatening local communities with the loss of gas supply unless they agreed to substantial price increases.

In September 1919 Athens Mayor Erwin C. Woodworth called a conference of Hocking Valley and Southeast Ohio mayors, city solicitors, and community delegates to discuss ways and means of preventing Ohio Fuel Gas Company and the

South Court and Union streets, c. 1900. The corner embarrassed Athenians. *(Courtesy of the* Athens Messenger.*)*

North Court Street as seen from Washington Street, c. 1910. *(Courtesy of The Dairy Barn, and Archives and Special Collections, Ohio University Libraries.)*

Berry Hotel, c. 1915. The hotel of choice, famed for its cuisine and service. *(Courtesy of Margene Bush.)*

Charles Cornwell, a member of the Cornwell dynasty of jewelers, oldest Athens business operated by a single family. *(Courtesy of the Cornwell family.)*

The Union, a price-conscious store, Campbell Building, West State and Court Street, 1912. A number of area mining companies had offices upstairs. *(Reprinted from* The Arena, *1912.)*

David Zenner, founder of the Zenner dynasty, came to Athens 1853, retired 1875, died in 1891. (*Reprinted from* The Athens Home Coming.)

The D. Zenner Co. Building, built 1872. Henry Zenner remodeled the store in the new century, installing modern display windows and recessed entrances. (*Reprinted from* The Centennial Atlas of Athens County Ohio, *1905.*)

Cline's Drug Store, c. 1905. Famed for his ice cream, Cline began its manufacture, creating a market for high quality milk. (*Courtesy of ACHS&M.*)

Interior of the Bank of Athens, c. 1910. William B. Golden is left front. *(Courtesy of ACHS&M.)*

John Brown, founder of the Bank of Athens and conductor on the Underground Railroad. *(Reprinted from the History of the Hocking Valley, Ohio, 1883.)*

James D. Brown, president of the Bank of Athens from 1875 to 1934. *(Reprinted from The Athens Home Coming.)*

Athens National Bank, 1905. Athens' first skyscraper, the structure had Athens' first elevator. After Athens National and First National merged, this building became the home of the Security Bank. *(Reprinted from The Centennial Atlas of Athens County Ohio, 1905.)*

Interior of the First National Bank, c. 1905. *(Reprinted from* The Centennial Atlas of Athens County Ohio, *1905.)*

First National Bank, Court and Washington. Successor to the Bank of Ohio, First National operated in this building from 1863 to 1921. *(Courtesy of James Anastas.)*

Erecting poles for electric arc lights, Court and Washington streets, 1889. A gas light, about to be replaced, is on the corner by the bank. *(Courtesy of the* Athens Messenger.*)*

T. A. Beaton & Co., a livery stable on Court Street at Rose Avenue, c. 1875. *(Reprinted from* Atlas of Athens County, Ohio, *1895.)*

Charles Secoy's blacksmith shop, c. 1905, Carpenter and Court streets. *(Courtesy of The Dairy Barn, and Archives and Special Collections, Ohio University Libraries.)*

Central Delivery Service, 1909. *(Courtesy of James Anastas.)*

South Court Street, c. 1910. Horse and buggy are supreme. By 1920 the auto and truck are dominant. *(Courtesy of the* Athens Messenger.*)*

John Perkins, merchant and druggist, son of Dr. Eliphaz Perkins. *(Reprinted from* The Athens Home Coming.*)*

John Ballard, merchant, promoter of the Marietta and Cincinnati Railroad, and bank president. His dry goods business was largely destroyed in the 1877 Court Street fire. *(Reprinted from* The Athens Home Coming.*)*

John Perkins home and drug store. Built 1828, the structure was purchased by J. Halliday Cline in 1903 and incorporated into the Cline Building of 1903 with a new facade and a third story. It was destroyed by fire in 1912. *(Reprinted from* Atlas of Athens County, Ohio, *1895.)*

Wilson H. McKee Drug Store, North Court Street, 1900. McKee manufactured his own herbal medicines along with patent medicines. *(Courtesy of The Dairy Barn, and Archives and Special Collections, Ohio University Libraries.)*

The Masonic Hall. The preeminent building on South Court when it was dedicated in 1878. It was part of the building boom generated by the construction of the Athens Lunatic Asylum. *(Reprinted from* The Centennial Atlas of Athens County Ohio, *1905.)*

The Athens County courthouse, built 1880. This is the third courthouse on this site. *(Courtesy of Margene Bush.)*

Theodore Roosevelt campaigns from the courthouse, May 19, 1912. Few women are in attendance. *(Courtesy of Margene Bush.)*

Major Samuel M. Johnson, foreground, leads a World War I parade up Court Street, summer 1917. Johnson achieved distinction as commander of a Negro unit in France. *(Courtesy of James Anastas.)*

Bernhard Fauser's butcher shop, North Court Street, offered "Home Cured Meats," 1905. *(Courtesy of the Athens Messenger.)*

The W. H. Potter Building, c. 1905. A grocer, Potter built this building in 1875. *(Reprinted from* The Centennial Atlas of Athens County Ohio, *1905.)*

The Warren House, 1872, the hotel of choice of the late 19th century. Later called the Athens Hotel. *(Reprinted from* Athens County Illustrated, *1897.)*

Athens Fire Department, c. 1915. During the day, the horses were rented out to work on the streets. A motorized fire truck replaced the horses in 1918. (*Courtesy of James Anastas.*)

The Lawrence Building, 1909, located on the sites of Perkins's Corner and Ballard's Corner. At the same time C. S. Newsome built his undertaking parlor next door. (*Courtesy of the* Athens Messenger.)

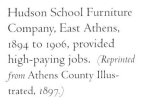

Hudson School Furniture Company, East Athens, 1894 to 1906, provided high-paying jobs. (*Reprinted from* Athens County Illustrated, *1897.*)

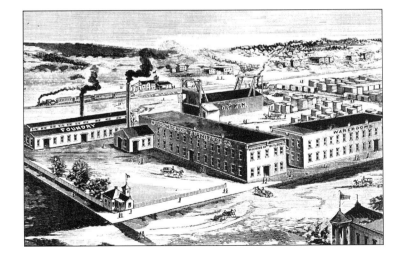

Women bookbinders at McBee Bindery, 1907. Charles McBee is in right foreground. *(Courtesy of The Dairy Barn, and Archives and Special Collections, Ohio University Libraries.)*

Men at McBee's Smith Street Machine Shop, 1907. McBee was the town's largest industrial employer by 1920. *(Courtesy of The Dairy Barn, and Archives and Special Collections, Ohio University Libraries.)*

North Hill shale quarry. Source of shale and clay for Athens Brick Company. *(Courtesy of Mary Diles and Archives and Special Collections, Ohio University Libraries.)*

Kilns of Athens Brick Company along present-day Stimson Avenue. In 1917, the market for paving brick was undercut by asphalt and concrete. Unable to operate during the war, the firm closed down. *(Courtesy of the Athens Messenger.)*

The Stedman Packing Plant, West State and Shafer streets, offered a major market for area livestock. *(Courtesy of James Anastas.)*

Circus parade, Court Street, 1915. For a century the circus attracted large crowds. *(Courtesy of James Anastas.)*

Alpha Delta Pi coeds celebrate May Day, 1914. *(Courtesy of the Athens Messenger.)*

The city recreation field, 1916, later rechristened Putnam Field. Recreation programs were supported to keep youth off the streets when school was not in session. *(Courtesy of the* Athens Messenger.)

The city beach, the Hocking River at the foot of Court Street, 1901. Supported by public and private funds, the beach was a first venture into a community recreation program. *(Courtesy of ACHS&M.)*

Boating on the Hocking River, near the State Hospital grounds, 1910. The dam at the East Mill maintained a pool that permitted boating. *(Courtesy of Margene Bush.)*

18th Regimental Band, Decoration Day, 1879. The GAR organized appropriate memorial ceremonies for the Civil War dead. *(Courtesy of the* Athens Messenger.*)*

.B. LAURIE
EORGE McG
EWIS CARPENTER
ACOB HERDER
EORGE DAVIS
HARLES PILCHER

10 GUS
11 BOB
12 WAL
13 BIL
14 SAM
15 ED
16 ED

Athens Ladies Band, 1915. During World War I, the band often accompanied draftees to the railroad station. *(Courtesy of the* Athens Messenger.*)*

Athens High School Orchestra, 1917. High school increasingly became a social center for middle-class youth. *(Reprinted from* The Arena, *1917.)*

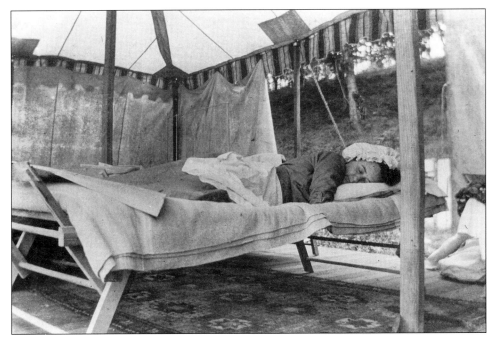

Camping along the Hocking, 1912. *(Courtesy of The Dairy Barn, and Archives and Special Collections, Ohio University Libraries.)*

The O'Bleness Bicycle Club ready for an outing. *(Courtesy of The Dairy Barn, and Archives and Special Collections, Ohio University Libraries.)*

Logan Natural Gas Company from raising gas rates above thirty-five cents per thousand cubic feet. Woodworth's solution was to lobby the Public Utility Commission of Ohio (PUCO) for assistance and to secure a thirty-five-cent rate ceiling by statute. When a spokesman for the Ohio Manufacturers Association averred that Ohio's natural gas supply was not exhausted, a West Virginia supplier refuted him and pointed out that while West Virginia's supply had declined by half, demand had increased. Henceforth, cheap natural gas would have to be augmented with expensive manufactured gas.

A game of "hard ball" ensued. Logan Natural Gas Company notified the Athens community that it could no longer supply Athens with natural gas. Its Athens subsidiary that distributed gas locally then petitioned the PUCO for permission to discontinue service. Mayor Woodworth thought: "Now is as good a time as any to determine whether or not the public shall be at the mercy of any corporation." While the natural gas producers and suppliers had a vested interest in raising rates to maximize their profits, they had a formidable ally in the "law" of supply and demand. Athens came to terms; gas rates went up.

Telephone Service

Athens did much experimenting on its way to securing a modern telephone service. As the new century began, the village had two competitive phone systems, the locally owned Athens Home Telephone Company and Central Union Telephone Company, a Bell affiliate. Clarence L. Jones was president of the Home Telephone Company. In 1909 the firm installed a common-battery switchboard, ending the use of the hand-crank to gain the attention of the switchboard operator. The firm also installed underground cables on Court Street, eliminating a network of overhead wires and a forest of poles. Finally, it purchased a building on Court Street to house its offices and switchboard.

The other company, Central Union, also shifted from the hand-crank mode of operation to a common-battery switchboard. For the business community, in particular, the existence of competing phone companies meant that to accommodate their customers, they had to subscribe to both phone services, doubling their costs, and to endure the confusion of two different phone numbers. At this level competition was not cost-effective for merchants and was awkward for others.

Increasingly, the telephone became an integral part of the middle-class home as well as of the business community. As more and more private homes installed phones, the phone companies published monthly addenda to their directories in the *Messenger*. In the interest of efficiency, Central Union requested its patrons to give the operator the phone number of the party they sought rather than the party's name. Another indication of change was implicit in the effort of the phone companies to promote an upstairs extension at fifty cents a month. In the competition between the firms, Home Telephone seems to have had the edge. Central Union, in fact, leased underground cable space in Home Telephone's conduits.

World War I brought an end to the competition. With workers and resources in short supply, the Wilson Administration initiated a broad program of rationalizing business practices in the interest of efficiency. Ironically, the rationalization of telephone service materialized only after the armistice. For Athens, the government takeover took effect December 1, 1918. Federal management of the nation's phone services was short lived, but it left a permanent impact. Central Union chose to exit Athens, and in early May 1919 the Home Telephone Company took over the Central Union operation. Athens ended the decade with a single phone company, and in this case, the home-owned enterprise was triumphant.

The Traction Line

High on the wish-list of the Athens business community was an interurban transportation service, referred to at the time as a traction line, that would reach out from Court Street to the mining camps and towns of Sugar Creek, Sunday Creek, and Monday Creek. Those living away from the village could use the inexpensive service to reach town and its stores and shops. Realizing these aspirations took time and patience; hopes were raised only to be dashed. Building such a line proved difficult and time consuming. The village council got a workout.

In 1902, 1905, and 1909, promoters came forth with proposals to build a traction line, generally to connect Nelsonville and Athens with a spur reaching up Sunday Creek to Glouster. In each case the story was similar. Local citizens were to provide the capital with which to build the line; the promoters, who were without funds of their own and without experience in operating a transit system, counted on taking whatever profits there were. The fact is that Athenians distrusted out-of-town promoters. In the summer of 1910 a separate Hocking–Sunday Creek Traction Line based in Nelsonville was proposed. The line would ultimately run from Nelsonville to Athens, a forty-five-minute trip, while one branch line would run from Chauncey to Glouster and a second branch would ascend Sugar Creek Valley. As plans matured, the company decided on an electric-powered line, using waste coal of various mines along the right-of-way to fuel its power plant.

By fall 1911 Athenians, led by C. L. Poston and the Rardin Brothers, oversubscribed the $50,000 needed to link up with the Nelsonville firm's line at Chauncey. This firm would operate the Athens end of the system. The Athenians involved included the town's major business interests: C. L. Poston, the coal baron; W. N. Alderman, Athens Brick Company; J. D. Brown, Bank of Athens; Henry Zenner, department store mogul and financial angel of McBee; F. S. Roach, the Hardwood Finish Company; L. G. Worstell, attorney of Grosvenor, Jones & Worstell; and D. H. Moore, First National Bank.

Building the line took far more time and funds than initially projected. The line coming from Nelsonville was complete to Chauncey. At that point, the estimated cost to complete the last six miles into Athens was $38,000 a mile, whereupon an English firm offered to invest $100,000, if Athenians would invest another $25,000. With thousands of dollars already committed on which there could be no financial return until the line entered Athens, Athenians raised the additional sum and construction resumed. At last at 6 A.M. on Sunday, May 13, 1915, the first traction car arrived in Athens. The terminus, though, was the corner of Second and Central. A jitney bus service transported passengers to and from the courthouse. This jitney service proved a makeshift, at best. Although a local group organized by the Chamber of Commerce talked of completing the line from Central Avenue to Court Street, the extension never materialized.

Streets and Sewers

Decisions regarding the operation of the community's waterworks and the franchising of its public utilities were dramatic, but the unrelenting day-to-day business of council concerned its streets and sewers.

The rapidly growing community always required new streets, sidewalks, and sewers. The initiative lay with the private developers who platted their diverse subdivisions, laying out the streets to suit themselves. Council's role was a reactive one—receiving petitions to pave the streets and walks, and to build the sewers. There was no mechanism for drafting an overall, coordinated plan.

In the absence of a city engineer, council had to busy itself with the details of planning as well as with contracting for construction. An inflexible bidding system precluded cost savings that might otherwise have been possible. For example, surplus dirt generated by lowering the grade on East State Street might have been used as fill on a contemporaneous project on Morris Avenue, but, alas, the projects had been sold to different contractors. The one contractor had the expense of getting rid of surplus dirt; the other had the expense of buying fill. All too often, council's planning did not start soon enough in the year to permit completion before cold weather imposed extra costs. The community's service director, who held a part-time position, was in no position to solve these problems.

Funding of streets, walks, and sewers became a far greater problem than hitherto. The old poll-tax that required male citizens to either work two days a year on the roads or else pay $3.00 was inadequate. Few citizens possessed the skills to grade streets, to lay brick, or to install sewer pipe; the $3.00 alternative generated too little to hire out the work. Nor did the system suit the urban wage-worker who lost a day's pay for every day of missed work. In practice, many men "forgot" the required work. Fred Bush estimated that fewer than fifty percent of those liable for service performed the service. Nor did the town's businessmen want the law enforced with respect to themselves, arguing that because they paid for sweeping Court Street, to collect the poll tax from them was unfair. When James McCormick, Athens Street Commissioner in 1907, served notice on some two hundred men who had failed to report for road service, the mayor refused to enforce the order, whereupon McCormick resigned.

For the most part the out-of-pocket costs of new street and sewer construction was covered by assessing the costs to the owners of adjacent property and hiring a contractor to do the work. The problems were concentrated on the maintenance of the streets and sewers, where the poll-tax labor was both unqualified and undependable. There seemed to be no solution until the state legislature authorized municipal governments to levy a tax in support of street and highway maintenance.

At times council had an activist role in the management of streets. When development pushed eastward along Stimson and Morris, the council had to negotiate a right-of-way across the property of the Athens Brick Company and to relocate the Free Methodist Church in order to link the two streets. In 1910, to create a gentler grade, the city repositioned West Union Street, trading a portion of the original street for land owned by the Rardin brothers. On the east side, because of the ad hoc procedures in platting subdivisions, the city had to intervene to straighten the north end of Watt Street and to acquire property so that at its south end Watt could reach Morris Avenue. In 1911, the town fathers once more grappled with the remnants of the old railroad cut both to the west and east of the Old Cemetery.

Successive ordinances for new streets reflect the specific parts of the community that were experiencing growth. In 1906, for example, lower Morris Avenue was being paved as far east as May Avenue; in 1909, Central Avenue and Second were being paved as were Sunnyside Drive and East Mill Street. In 1913, South Shannon was opened from Morris to State Street, linking side streets that previously had dead-ended. In July 1918, Marietta, North Shannon, North May, and Arden Place were opened.

The increased size of the community and the proliferation of the automobile brought about two minor questions that council could not evade. At the beginning of the century, the Post Office Department inaugurated house-to-house delivery of the mail, but insisted that as a condition of service houses be numbered and streets named and signed. During the latter part of the nineteenth century, in the absence of street signs, Court Street had also been referred to as Main Street. In 1901 there was a short-lived effort to officially designate it as Main Street. Council split, and it remained Court Street. At the same time, council hit on a scheme for numbering houses, one number per twenty-five feet of frontage. Years passed before the streets were uniformly signed.

Parking was a continuing problem. In 1900 the concern was to provide adequate parking for horse-drawn wagons so that Court Street would remain passable. East Union Street was thought to afford the needed space. As late as 1912, council was occupied with finding hitching posts for farmers' teams. The arrival of the auto-mobile compounded the problem. Noisy motors and horns spooked horses, caus-ing serious accidents. One solution was an ordinance requiring autos to stop on the approach of a team and thus yield the right-of-way, a solution resisted by auto operators. By 1915, as the automobile replaced the horse-drawn vehicle, the com-plaint was again directed at long-term parkers on Court Street. After a year and a half of deliberation, council decided to limit parking to thirty minutes for auto and team alike.

A more general concern was the safety of pedestrians, and the village council limited autos to a speed not much above a brisk walk. As early as 1917, council warned motorists on East State Street of a school crossing. Speed limits were periodically raised, but complaints continued that West Union and East State were "speedways." Editor Bush was only one of many motorists fined for racing with another vehicle on East State. Ultimately, the state legislature intervened to set uniform speed limits: 15 miles per hour for business districts, 20 mph in residen-tial areas, and 30 mph outside cities. Restrictive village and city ordinances were nullified.

Seen through the mists of nostalgia, small towns of the past were picturesque, quaint, idyllic. Yet, repeated testimonies over the years aver Athens streets were dirty. In early October 1903, the *Messenger* commented that the streets were as dirty as ever. Editor Bush lectured the village fathers: It was up to council "to get out with pick, shovel and horse cart." At best there were periodic cleanups, but no long-term improvement. In fall 1905, the *Messenger* renewed its complaint. The village had "as filthy, dirty streets as can be found in any paved town in Ohio." For its part, council had a complaint: many merchants swept out their stores, dumping the refuse in the gutters, although to do so was illegal. The streets were "the dumping ground for everything from home and store . . . that won't burn." When Council served notices on a select few to clean up their properties, Bush accused the council of bluffing. To 1920, the city fathers continued to embrace the notion that each property owner was responsible for the disposal of his own trash.

Merchants were especially irked by the dusty streets, dust that settled on merchandise and damaged it. The problem was aggravated by the merchants themselves, because in good weather they customarily displayed merchandise on the walks in front of their stores. To minimize their difficulty, they banded together to hire a private contractor to sprinkle the streets and asked the village for free water. Some complained that too much water was poured on the streets.

Athens began the 1900s with an ad hoc sewer system. There was no master plan; no sewage treatment. No one was in charge. The result was unsatisfactory, even wasteful. The *Messenger* suggested the village needed a full-time service director in charge. It also advocated a sewage treatment plant, featuring a series of filtration beds such as Gallipolis used.

The council was under continuous pressure to construct new sewer lines. As with streets and sidewalks, the city borrowed the construction funds, then recovered the money by assessing the costs to the adjacent property owners. When the city could not respond quickly enough, impatient residents of Grosvenor and Townsend streets bought sewer pipe on the condition that village crews would install it.

A major part of council's problem was anticipating future needs. The original ten-inch sewer on Mill Street did not allow leeway to accommodate future growth on the east side of town, a problem further aggravated by its use as a combination sanitary and storm sewer. Then, when the village undertook to build separate storm sewers, some property owners questioned whether the assessment against their property was proportionate to the benefit they might derive from it. In the end, the common pleas court settled the matter, holding that "a public" need rather than an "individual need" sufficed to legitimize the assessment of property owners for such projects, although the assessments must be proportionate to the benefits. To 1920, Athens had no overall plan for sewer expansion or for sewage treatment.

THE PUBLIC SERVICE COMMUNITY

Council's legislative agenda was ordinarily preoccupied with the prosaic, but the progressive mood of society led it to undertake a variety of new services. Some items were not especially exciting: a municipal trash and garbage disposal service or a fire department with a cadre of full-time persons. But beyond these items was the creation of a public restroom, the fashioning of a public health program, and the establishment of public recreation facilities. These were novel programs for the time, and their proponents believed that in each case there was a need that was best met by government action. In responding council expanded the sphere of local government, creating a public service community.

Trash and Garbage Disposal

Garbage and rubbish removal posed an ongoing debate over policy. There were two problems—garbage and trash removal from private homes and stores and the cleaning of streets. These were not problems council was eager to address. Throughout the nineteenth century, responsibility for disposing of ashes, trash, and garbage had rested with each householder. Council did arrange for a public dump on lower Mill Street. This did not satisfy, and in 1907, a committee of leading businessmen —Henry Zenner, J. D. Brown, and H. D. Henry—appeared before council to argue the case for regular municipal trash collection. Simultaneously, the ladies of the town, especially those of the Pallas Club, circulated petitions and sent delegations to call on council. Council resisted. In 1917 the city fathers relented to the degree that they offered to haul the trash of the poor, but pleaded municipal poverty in declining to undertake regularly scheduled, city-wide rubbish-removal service. To 1920 the city fathers continued to embrace the notion that each property owner was responsible for the disposal of his own trash.

Fire Protection

The ways of providing fire protection for the community changed moderately. Beginning in 1901, alarms to summon the volunteers were sounded by a bell at the Village Hall, having hitherto relied on the Presbyterian church bell. The volunteers were paid $1.50 per fire. Often as not, the department had to finance its equipment, relying on private subscriptions and a Christmas Ball to raise funds.

Fire protection was inadequate. In one uptown fire, it took ten to fifteen minutes for the department to respond; only four firemen showed, and when they turned on the hose, it burst. Most of the volunteers had resigned because council insisted that the firemen were liable for the poll tax. So far as the fire hose was concerned, the department lacked a proper place to dry and store it. The *Messenger* lost little time in demanding that the town fathers provide a hose tower and new hose. "Delays," it cautioned, "are exceedingly dangerous." When council took no action, editor Bush urged council to issue bonds, if need be, to buy a thousand feet of hose and to secure a facility for properly caring for it. Pleading poverty, the council declined to act; a private subscription raised the money. Shamed, council belatedly secured the requisite funds by a property levy and reimbursed those who had bought the hose.

Following its inspection of the department, a committee of the Ohio Insurance League made several recommendations to upgrade the fire department. The village should: 1) build a fire house with a hose tower and employ a man to care for the equipment; 2) furnish the department the necessary paraphernalia; 3) place all equipment under the direction of the chief; and 4) acquire a modern hook and ladder truck.

When Athens became a city in 1912, council did provide for two full-time firemen, one of them doubling as janitor for the City Building, the other assigned to street sweeping. The chief and the other volunteers were paid on a fee basis. Even so, despite the proddings of the Insurance League, the fire department continued to be under-funded, under-equipped, and under-staffed. When the department acquired two horses, "Dick" and "Frank," at a cost of $450, the animals were ordinarily rented out for street work. This meant, of course, that the horses were not immediately available during the day in the event of a fire. A year later, the department acquired a "deluge" nozzle, a device that could throw a two-inch stream of water two hundred feet vertically. Indeed, the department gave a public demonstration, shooting a stream of water over the cupola of the courthouse. Finally, in fall 1919, the department got its first motorized fire truck. Although the truck had a much faster response time than the horse-drawn rig, on its first real trial, a fire at a West Union Street hot-dog stand, the fire was out by the time the new fire truck arrived.

Public Health

By 1900 typhoid, scarlet fever, and diphtheria, which had ravaged the village off and on during the nineteenth century, seemed in check. Even so, the old scourges had not been eradicated and periodically typhoid claimed the life of a citizen. So too, diphtheria and scarlet fever recurred, with ten cases in 1904. In 1906, when diphtheria and scarlet fever raged in epidemic proportions in a forty-mile radius of Athens, the village experienced twenty-six cases of diphtheria but no deaths from either ailment.

Smallpox was another matter. Although vaccination had long been available, many adults failed to have their children or themselves vaccinated, and periodically smallpox struck, triggering panic. However, the disease was more common among those out in the county than among residents of the village. When a case did show, local authorities were generally quick to quarantine the afflicted. In 1903 four children in the Baker family came down, threatening a more general outbreak. The village promptly erected a "pest house" on West State Street in which to isolate the victims and quarantined seven homes. The Board of Health, whose rules had the force of a municipal ordinance, ordered that every villager who lacked a scar from an earlier vaccination must either submit to vaccination or be quarantined. Village doctors then went door-to-door. Two of the fifteen Athenians who contracted the disease died.

Tuberculosis was the leading killer, accounting for one death in every six in 1900. Worse yet, there seemed to be no effective way to combat the ailment. In 1912 Athens County reported the largest number of TB deaths of any county in the state of comparable size, 104 deaths.

Although no one made a point of it, the fact is that infancy remained inherently risky. In 1906 fully one death in seven in the village was of a child under one year of age. Despite the risks of childhood, no one between the ages of two and twenty had died that year. This was unusual, but the mortality rate for youngsters between five and fifteen was ordinarily negligible.

Modern medical education, medicine founded on scientific investigation, was still in its early stages, dating essentially from the beginning of the Johns Hopkins Medical School in 1893. Few doctors practicing in Athens or elsewhere during the first decade or so of the twentieth century had been trained in the new methods. Most Athenians continued to rely on old familiar home-made remedies. Such medications were supplemented by a plethora of patent remedies: Lydia Pinkham's Vegetable Compound, Fletcher's Castoria, Peruna, and E. S. Grove's Laxative

Bromo Quinine Tablets. Wilson H. McKee, an Athens druggist not to be left out of this profitable business, made and marketed his own McKee's Little Liver Pills. Medicine in 1900 was still at the survival-of-the-fittest level.

As Athens had no hospital or infirmary for its residents, the ill were treated at home. In cases of accidents, two or three local doctors might perform surgery. Thus, when George Carney broke a leg at the shale bank north of Court Street, he was taken home by carriage and there Doctors Merwin and White reduced the fracture. When there was time, the patient might be taken to Columbus, riding on a cot set up in the baggage car of a Hocking Valley train. As likely as not, the patient's doctor accompanied him or her to Columbus and performed the operation there. Thus, Mrs. Albert Swett had her appendectomy at St. Anthony's Hospital, Columbus.

The State Board of Health took note of the pollution of the Hocking as part of an inspection of the Athens State Hospital. The Athens swimming hole was also just downstream from the outlet of the hospital's sewer line. The pollution was aggravated during periods of low water in summer and by the East Mill Street dam, which impeded the flow of the river. Fred Bush suggested that the state legislature buy the dam, already damaged by a winter ice-floe, and remove it, a proposal officially advanced several months later by the village council. The legislature did not act. The problem became less serious when the 1907 flood further damaged the dam, allowing the river to run more freely.

In 1906 the village Board of Health directed a number of citizens—some of them leading citizens—to take responsibility for the stagnant water behind their homes, notably the swamp that lay below and to the east of the homes along College Street and University Terrace. The water was "a nuisance and a menace." Stable owners were enjoined to conform to public health standards and property owners adjacent to a sanitary sewer were directed to hook up to the sewer. A year later, the village health officer began a campaign for public garbage disposal. By 1910 the concern focused on public drinking cups; schools were urged to replace the shared cup with sanitary drinking fountains. In time, paper cups and tumblers replaced glassware in many soda fountains, a measure far less onerous to proprietors than complying with the regulations that required glassware to be rinsed in steam or boiling water for three to five minutes. Other regulations were directed at dairymen to assure the cleanliness of milk containers. The ubiquitous fly was targeted, an annoyance of which Maria Foster Brown took notice in the 1830s and '40s and of which Charles Jennings complained annually during his tenure at the *Messenger*. The "Kill the Fly" campaign of the *Messenger* in 1912 offered $25 to the elementary school children who brought in the most flies; they came in by the gills and pints. The flies were held to be a special danger to the health of babies.

Tuberculosis became a subject of special concern. In 1908 the American Red Cross introduced its Christmas seals to raise money for a crusade against TB, the white plague. Athens joined with a will. By September 1912 it had a local chapter that worked along with the chief businessmen's organization, the Commercial Club. The citizenry took the campaign to heart, buying some 50,000 TB stamps at Christmastime 1911. By 1916 local churches and clubs joined in disseminating information about TB and its prevention.

The effort to contain TB led to the securing of a public health nurse. Ohio's Society for the Prevention of TB sent Nurse Kammerer to Athens for one month in the fall of 1912 to work with known patients and to get a feel for what might be done. Nurse Kammerer swept with a new broom. She upbraided county officials. The County Building generally, she declared, was filthy; the law library, suffocating in dust-covered books; the men's lavatory smelled; the courthouse steps were covered with tobacco juice. Before the month was out, the building had been scrubbed down. Next, Nurse Kammerer turned her attention to public school children, noting the incidence of unhealthy adenoids and tonsils and eyes requiring corrective glasses. She also identified the presence of children living in poverty, citing one family living in an old box car, the whole family sharing a single bed. She noted other children whose diet was limited to bread and potatoes. A few children, she averred, had to go out and beg for food. Others lived in dark, damp, moldy rooms, conditions in which good health was unlikely.

Nurse Kammerer made an impression. While some Athenians might have been annoyed at the public disclosure of these conditions, this was the Progressive Era, a time when the citizenry generally regarded proposals for reform not as a rebuke but as positive measures to create a better community. In November 1914 the Civic Federation launched a subscription campaign to fund a public health nurse. By this time the Athens City School Board had employed a dentist to check children's teeth and to notify parents of needed dental work. The fund-raising campaign proceeded smoothly as the community's social and literary clubs took a hand. Local Elks subscribed fifty dollars a year and organized a charity ball. Early in December 1914 the community employed Laura V. Fisher as its first regular public health nurse with an office in the City Building. Within the first month, she had visited 116 homes, dealing with illnesses, accidents, and obstetrical cases. In 1918 a campaign was undertaken to check every child in the city under age six, street by street. A clinic was set up in the City Building.

Talk of a hospital for Athens recurred often but was less easily achieved. In spring 1906 Dr. A. B. Allen, who operated a private hospital in Glouster, spoke of founding a hospital in Athens. Discussion centered on the use of the Lawrence-Merwin house, the double house that wraps around the corner of Mill and College Street. It could provide separate wards for men and women and space for an emergency ward as well. Nothing happened. Early in 1907 it seemed possible that area miners might establish a hospital in Athens to receive accident cases. Nothing happened. In August 1909, the village seemed "practically assured" of a local hospital. An anonymous businessman was reported to have offered $12,000 to cover first-year costs. Nothing happened. Finally, in October 1916, the Civic Federation succeeded in fitting up an emergency hospital room in the City Building. It had to be a bare-bones operation. Funding relied on voluntary contributions. A benefit movie at the Majestic Theater raised seventy-five dollars for equipment. The C. L. Martzolff Sunday School Class presented twenty-four pairs of pillow cases. And so it went. Another step forward came in January 1919 when Dr. T. A. Copeland, an eye, ear, nose, and throat specialist, leased the second floor of the Athens National Bank Building for a nine-bed "hospital." He outfitted an operating room and employed a full-time nurse. Dr. Copeland made his operating room available to other town doctors for emergency surgery.

Just as the war in Europe ended, Athens experienced the "Spanish floo" epidemic. The first indications were reports of influenza spreading through New England and in various military and naval installations. Within a month Athens County was afflicted. Especially hard hit were the mining camps at Luhrig, Sugar Creek, and Canaanville, places with high concentrations of people and no doctor on site. On October 22, 1918, the State Public Health Department dispatched two physicians to Athens County. As the flu hit Athens city, university students were advised on preventive measures. On October 7 all places of public gathering—churches, movies, theaters, dance halls, and the city schools—were closed; the next day the University closed for two weeks. The Student Army Training Corps fellows alone were kept in town. Then, the university's shutdown was extended for a third week. The town was still under a ban on public meetings when the Armistice occurred. Not until mid-November were restrictions lifted. Thereafter, the homes of persons with the flu were quarantined. Christmas 1918 was to be "kissless" and "a stay-at-home day." Nor was the flu epidemic over. The flu reappeared spasmodically during 1919.

Generally, Athens City had made considerable progress in promoting public health by 1920. The death rate for the city in 1921 stood at 11.4 deaths per thousand population, comparable to the rate for the state as a whole. Even so, a disproportionate number of deaths, almost one-third, occurred among children under five years of age. Despite the evidence of the benefit the community had gained from the public health nurse, the county's doctors were unanimous in their opposition to the creation of a tax-funded county health officer. The cost for salary, laboratories, and staff could run, they estimated, $15,000 a year, a sum too high for taxpayers. The doctors thought it more prudent for the community to await better times. The community would have to continue to ponder whether to fashion a public health service to which every resident had access or else leave to the doctors the burden of providing medical care to those unable to pay.

PUBLIC RECREATION

The proper bounds of municipal involvement in public well-being was tested in the case of a municipal swimming area and a public playground. In 1914 the city fathers were persuaded that a supervised swimming area was in order. A beach was established just upstream from the South Bridge. A bath house, swings, and a raft were provided, and a supervisor engaged. Volunteers prepared the beach and stored the equipment over the winter. Private funds also paid for the equipment, the council believing that the purchase of equipment was an improper use of public funds.

The initial reaction of council was to schedule swimming for girls and boys on alternate days. They did so without reckoning with the mothers of the girls, who promptly let council understand that coed swimming was to be the policy. Such a policy, the mothers insisted, was far more likely to limit the teasing girls might otherwise be exposed to. With reservations, council accepted the mothers' advice. As the beach opened for the first time, the beach director put the fear of god into the fellows, lest any of them think of harassing a girl. Coed swimming worked fine.

A second crisis erupted in 1914 over the propriety of swimming on the Sabbath. Frank Cross, a local craftsman, rose to the occasion in a letter to the *Messenger*, pointing out that on Sundays numerous adults buzzed about the city in their autos making "smoke and dust," and that, given the six-day work week, Sunday was the only day many people had to swim. The town authorities agreed, opened the beach on Sundays, and completed a three-level diving tower. In 1919 a new beach was set up in the vicinity of White's Mill, where the water was far cleaner.

The city also tackled the problem of providing a public recreation area for youth. Land was secured in the approximate area of what was later Putnam Field. Henry Zenner took the lead in organizing an Athens Playground Association.

Through the summer of 1915, Ethel (Mrs. Thomas) Hoover and Vera (Mrs. C. L.) Jones canvassed the city for contributions for an equipment fund. Some $1,050 was collected, and as the money came in, a shelter house with dressing rooms was constructed, the land graded, and two tennis courts and two basketball courts were laid out as well as two baseball fields and two football fields. Though not completely finished by the end of the summer, the playground was put in use.

The debate over the propriety of expending public funds on a playground continued into 1916. The Presbyterians, Methodists, and Disciples joined forces to hold a community meeting at which the city school superintendent, Geoffrey Morgan, laid out the case for a public playground. Four hundred dollars was raised on the spot. The next evening, city council agreed to pay $240 for the rental of the land, while the city school board advanced $300 to hire a playground supervisor. The playground committee was to raise $1,200 in private funds for equipment. Ultimately James D. Brown offered to equip the playground at his own expense. Over the next several years, private funds were raised, usually by a Tag Day on Court Street, to raise additional funds for repairs and to augment the equipment. During this same time, council established a picnic park on North Hill, now Highland Park.

NEW SCHOOLS FOR OLD

Among Athens public institutions, the public schools were second in importance only to the town government. As Athens entered the twentieth century, elementary education was widely accepted, but as late as 1900 the high school enrolled but 67 youngsters, mostly girls. Nonetheless, secondary education was coming into its own. The school facilities, one building for grades 1 through 12, and built in the mid-1850s, were no longer adequate.

The village needed both a new high school and, given the spread of the population eastward and throughout the West End, two elementary schools. The existing school, "Old Brick," was physically sturdy, but it had, the *Messenger* declared, no more amenities than "a pig pen." Its system of heating was "almost criminal;" proper ventilation was "an impossibility," and it was overcrowded. In the *Messenger's* judgment, it was best to tear down Old Brick and build anew. The editorial writer thought that although a new school would cost $30,000 to $40,000, the community could build a new structure without increasing taxes.

What to build? Where to build? How much could the community afford?

Neither the voters nor the board of education could decide. But the *Messenger's* cost estimate was far too low. The board proposed an $80,000 bond issue which lost 2 ½ to 1. Resubmitted to the voters a month later but no longer tied to a dollar amount, the bond issue passed 2 to 1. On the strength of this, the board proceeded to issue bonds. Clinton Poston took $49,000; the Athens National Bank, the remaining $11,000.

First priority was given to erecting a high school building. Constructed by George Fenzel, the new high school building had two stories and a basement with facilities for both home economics and manual training. It was ready for fall 1907, at which time high school enrollment hit 184—a three-fold increase in seven years. Completion of the new school only served to make high school attendance more attractive. Of major importance, in spring 1909 the North Central Association of Colleges and High Schools accredited Athens High. College-bound youngsters no longer had to attend the University's academy; they could now safely attend Athens High School. By 1916 Athens High was no longer primarily a girls' school as it had been before 1900.

The high school became the center of the social life of the town's youths. The school boasted, in 1907, its first orchestra, directed at times by a student. Other students participated in interscholastic debate competition. In 1912 the first edition of the *Arena*, the yearbook, appeared. School spirit dictated that the seniors place their class flag atop the nearby standpipe. In June 1912 the Senior Play first made its appearance. The Junior Prom was already a feature. The football team and its seven-game schedule drew more attention from townspeople than from students. Baseball and basketball attracted even less attention; the basketball team of 1911, playing a three-game schedule, lost all three games. One other innovation of note was a limited senior trip to New York City. Beginning in 1915, Superintendent Geoffrey Morgan escorted a number of the boys to New York City during Christmas break. The week-long 1918 trip included a visit with New York City's Mayor Hyland and dinner with James E. West, head of the Boy Scouts of America, in addition to conventional sightseeing.

By 1920, the school had a 45-piece band, both boys' and girls' glee clubs, a small orchestra, and a jazz band. It had presented an operetta, a school-wide revue, and a senior play. Although the flu epidemic had played havoc with its football schedule, the school had organized a girls' basketball team.

Once the high school was adequately housed, the board turned its attention to the elementary schools. The board decided on two schools. For the east side, they bought the Cable property on what is now Wallace Drive; a two-story building was constructed with eight classrooms, each to accommodate forty pupils. The other children attended Central School (Old Brick) which served 350 youngsters. After 1915 those children living close to the University campus attended the university's training school, in effect giving the city a third elementary school.

Schools were more than brick and mortar. The chief concerns were the teachers' training and their salaries. Intertwined was the effort of the state to set standards. As of 1906 the state set the minimum millage for the support of schools at 6 mills and established $40 per month for eight months as a minimum salary for teachers. Teachers could not live on such wages, the *Messenger* observed. In 1910 the *Messenger* reported women elementary teachers in the village averaged $44.23 a month, high school teachers $68.00 a month. Such low wages meant high turnover in staff and a preponderance of inexperienced teachers in the classroom. The school term was 36 weeks, 180 days.

Educational quality prompted much debate. The presence of the University's Normal School, its faculty, and the Training School provided the village with a nucleus of persons professionally aware of good educational practice. One concern focused on incorporating the kindergarten into the Athens school system. The lead was taken by the Child Conservation League and the Parent-Teachers Organization. Personnel in the Normal School shared the interest and arranged for an open meeting to let one of their faculty who had experience with a kindergarten share his insights with the community.

There were occasional evidences of the quality of the Athens schools. The art program won first place with its exhibit at the 1914 Ohio State Fair. There was also the career of Ella Osborne, a first-grade teacher who had amassed forty years' experience as a teacher and was principal of East Elementary when she died in January 1916. Twenty years earlier she had been one of the first two women elected to public office in Athens. An ardent feminist, Osborne was remembered for her "gentle, kindly deeds."

In 1919 the city schools assessed their standing. The report focused on shortcomings, on an agenda for the future. Central School, in particular, had a preponderance of inexperienced teachers. Classes were too large, one first-year teacher handling forty-four pupils. The schools lacked a program to educate those we term the learning or physically challenged. The high school library lacked books of poetry, history, biography, and science. Chemistry needed to be added to the curriculum. There was no gymnasium. If anything, the problems were less severe than those many other Ohio communities faced. But working within guidelines set by the State of Ohio, the district was limited financially in its capacity to respond. A plea that would be reiterated *ad nauseam* was: "The State of Ohio must devise an adequate financial system which will enable us to build new buildings, pay increased salaries, and put schools on a sound and efficient basis."

TEMPERANCE

Just as saloons and immoderate drinking created problems for the Athens police and courts, the production, sale, and consumption of alcoholic beverages created a major political issue that absorbed time and energy for the better part of two decades. Agitation to prohibit the sale of liquor in the village was unremitting. As the Aiken Law became effective in 1906, five local saloons closed. Determined to close all the saloons, pro-temperance men organized the Anti-Saloon League, circulated a petition for a local option referendum and secured the signatures of over one-half of those who had voted in the previous election. The Rev. Mr. W. M. Boden, minister at First Christian, was the president of the local Anti-Saloon League. Aiming at a county-wide constituency, the League in fall 1907 held a meeting with delegates from eleven townships. In a special election in fall 1908 the county voted itself dry, the drys carrying every township. For the village of Athens, this meant every saloon had to close within thirty days.

The problem Athens faced thereafter was that while drys formed a majority sufficient to close the town saloons, a minority of the townsmen were determined to drink and there were businessmen willing to oblige them. The drys countered by employing private agents to locate the illegal dispensers of liquor. These agents were often aggressive to the point of entrapping their quarry, engendering much antagonism, the more so when an agent such as Orvell Hewitt was in turn charged with bootlegging. Representatives of the Anti-Saloon League who came to Athens from other communities were especially despised as busybodies.

Women opposed to the use of alcohol continued to work through the WCTU —the Woman's Christian Temperance Union. The broad-ranging reform program instituted by Frances Willard continued after her death. The gathering of the WCTU in March 1911 focused on "purity." The ladies wanted to exclude "pernicious books" from libraries; advocated a program of sex hygiene for the home, school, and Sunday school; condemned indecent billboards; took offense at a recent motion picture show with "improper features." They cited the danger of persons infected with venereal disease, hinting they should be quarantined. A year later the WCTU moved to enforce the observance of the Sabbath. Specifically, they would ban hunting, fishing, and shooting on Sunday and would prohibit manual labor and business transactions on the Sabbath. The latter prohibition was aimed especially at drugstores, news, cigar, and fruit stands, and at ice cream sales. For the WCTU, temperance was part of an overall program of social and moral reform that pre-dated progressivism.

To saloonkeepers convicted of illegally "keeping a place," the drys seemed indecently vindictive when county officials sought to collect retroactively the liquor tax otherwise applicable to saloons in jurisdictions where the sale of alcohol was legal.

In an effort to lend authority to the temperance cause, the *Messenger* printed lists of businessmen in Athens, Albany, and Amesville who opposed saloons. The fact is the community was divided and views were ever-changing. In 1909 in a county-wide referendum drys polled just shy of 57 percent of the votes cast; in 1911 they polled less than 48 percent. Athens city voted itself dry in this latter election by a margin of 87 votes in a total of nearly 1,500. Charges of a fraudulent vote count resulted in a second referendum, the city voting itself dry by a margin of 237. By early 1914 many of the other villages in the county joined Athens city in the dry camp.

From 1914 to 1918 the temperance issue was raised repeatedly and the stakes made ever higher as prohibition advocates sought first to secure statewide prohibition, then nationwide prohibition. But each such referendum placed local option at risk, forcing each local jurisdiction to campaign actively. In 1914 Athenians paraded: university students, public school children, and Sunday school members marched, "thousands," said the *Messenger*. The wets ran advertisements warning that a dry vote would threaten Athens fruit growers' market for apples for cider and other fruit for brandy. The wets won statewide, but Athens County remained dry by a margin of 3–2.

In November 1915 the wets made the issue one of individual liberty and of the integrity of home rule. For their part, Athens drys imported William Jennings Bryan. Billed as "the world's greatest orator," Bryan spoke to a crowd of 4,000 to 5,000 persons gathered at the northwest corner of the College Green. Again Athens voted dry, although the state vote was wet.

America's entry into World War I changed the parameters of the contest. The army declined to permit the sale of liquor to troops in camp, and it directed saloonkeepers not to serve soldiers in uniform when out of camp. With grain in short supply, the federal government sought to curb the production of beer. The showdown came in 1918 in the vote on the Eighteenth Amendment. In the middle of the propaganda campaign, agents of the state liquor commission staged a series of raids in Athens. When the dust settled, it was apparent that the Benevolent and Protective Order of Elks had a well-stocked cellar from which five hundred bottles of beer were confiscated; Isaac Slaughter was arrested for "keeping a place" and pleaded guilty on condition that his customers not be charged; Herb Hunley, a barber, was arraigned for ordering liquor by phone for thirsty locals from a supplier in Nelsonville, the liquor to be shipped to Athens by traction car. It was also apparent that Athens city officials had been aware for a year or so of the availability of beer at the Elks' lodge but had done nothing to enforce the law.

The Eighteenth Amendment secured the necessary ratifications. With the subsequent enactment of the Volstead Act, the lawful sale of alcoholic beverages ceased nationwide in May 1919. Agitation over prohibition, however, did not cease; bootleggers and moonshiners became major problems.

11

Toward an Urban Economy: 1900–1920

BOOMING AND EXPANSIVE were the terms for Athens economy between 1900 and 1920. The population grew as much in those two decades as it had in all the years between the arrival of the intrepid settlers of 1797 and 1900. The labor force increased proportionately, so that it numbered 2,224 in 1920. It is, however, far easier to be precise about the increase in population or in the number of workers than to assess the degree of growth attributable to each of the several elements at work.

AGRICULTURE

As a market town served by both north-south and east-west railroads, Athens continued to benefit as a processing and shipping point for the products of area farms. By 1900 area agriculture no longer had the capacity to drive the town economy; it still had an importance that spurred townspeople to make it as profitable as possible. One approach was the organization of yearly Farmers' Institutes. The *Messenger,* which had a substantial out-of-town circulation, summarized the proceedings for subscribers who had not attended. Held at the county courthouse, the sessions combined entertainment with nitty-gritty presentations on such subjects as the use of cowpeas and clover for building soil fertility and the varieties of potatoes likely to yield well in Athens County soils. At times the institutes took stands on political issues, expressing support of Theodore Roosevelt's proposals regarding railroad regulation and endorsing the "good road movement." Beginning in 1910, the institute scheduled a separate session for farm women, focusing on topics as diverse as ways of making the farm home attractive, the need for a sanitary water supply and plumbing, and the teaching of domestic science in rural schools.

A second approach was the organization of the Athens County Poultry Association in 1907. Athens merchants like C. W. Roach, who also bred chickens, participated. The thrust was that by reliance on selective breeding, the quality and value of local chicken flocks could be significantly improved. As the Poultry Association served some of the same people drawn to the Farmers' Institute, the two groups at times held joint meetings, often accompanied by exhibitions of birds, with prizes awarded for best of class.

The two decades between 1900 and 1920 marked an era in which the federal and state governments along with state colleges of agriculture and private organizations promoted a variety of specific measures to improve farm productivity. These groups recognized that the county fair had lost its edge as a means of improving farm practices. Now, the attention of the farm community was directed to the efforts of the Ohio Agricultural Experiment Station at Wooster to perfect and test new crops and farm methods. To the newly created post of county extension agent fell the responsibility for transmitting to area farmers the know-how developed at Wooster and the agricultural experiment stations in other states.

At this point, the Athens Chamber of Commerce took the initiative in bringing area farmers together to promote the recruiting of an agricultural extension agent for Athens County. For this effort to succeed, at least 270 farmers in the county had to form an organization, the Farm Bureau, and petition for a county agent. The Chamber offered to coordinate and facilitate the effort. Once organized, the Farm Bureau took charge of the project, and in June 1917 Athens secured its first county agent, Floyd DeLashnutt. When the local seed corn crop failed that year, DeLashnutt demonstrated his usefulness by testing seed corn samples for local farmers, tests individual farmers could not perform at home.

Local agriculture continued to change. Area orchards took a hit, first the peach orchards at the start of the century, then, in 1919, apple "scab." Wool producers in Canaan Township took the initiative in discussing ways of upgrading their breeding stock and in creating a mechanism for marketing their wool collectively. Area farmers expanded their dairying operations. E. C. Angell introduced the first mechanized milking device in 1913. Here, too, the state extended its activity in an effort to assure the health of the cattle and the cleanliness of the milk supply. The initial survey by the state inspectors disclosed "a considerable amount of carelessness in their [the dairymans'] operation." The inspectors directed their efforts at correcting faulty practices rather than penalizing the wayward.

Overall, Athens agriculturists consolidated small farm units into larger, more productive units. Nonetheless, agriculture in the county had peaked by 1900. Between 1900 and 1920, the number of Athens County farms declined by one-sixth and the acreage by one-seventh. With the average improved acreage per farm at seventy-five acres in 1920, few Athens County farmers could maintain a lifestyle comparable to that of farmers of the grain belt of the midwest or command sufficient purchasing power to be prosperous customers of Athens merchants. Production of corn far outdistanced wheat by a margin of three to one. The hilly land still supported herds of cattle, sheep, swine, and flocks of chickens. Of these, the cattle were easily the most valuable asset—$871,000—worth far more than the sheep, swine, and chickens combined.

ATHENS STATE HOSPITAL

The Athens State Hospital remained the major institution, private or public, in the Athens area. With 800-plus patients in 1900, it was a major economic force. The largest single employer, it bought many of its supplies locally. In 1920 the hospital reported 1,310 patients and a staff of 167, thus fueling the expansion of the local economy. As the patient load was not subject to downturns, it was a depression-proof enterprise that lent stability to the Athens economy.

The glow that the hospital had generated in its early years had dimmed somewhat. The positions of superintendent and other senior staff had become political plums, subject to swings in political affairs in Columbus. There were periodic hints that patient-care sometimes suffered, as did the efficiency of hospital administration. Troubles surrounded the administration of several superintendents. In 1907, the *Messenger* speculated whether Superintendent J. T. Hanson was incompetent or a victim of an intra-party struggle over political patronage. In 1907, the death of a patient resulted in charges of "negligence and cruelty" on the part of the hospital staff. The governor called for an investigation. In the wake of other charges of favoritism in the purchase of groceries and charges that attendants had impregnated two patients, Hanson resigned his post. To straighten matters out, Dr. E. H. Rorick, who had established his competence as a hospital administrator in earlier years, was called back to head the hospital. Within a few months Governor Harmon allegedly forced Rorick out in favor of his own candidate. Charges of patient abuse resurfaced. In one of the more sensational murder trials in Athens, several hospital staff were convicted of the beating death of a patient. Again in 1913, when County Prosecutor Woolley insisted on investigating charges of patient abuse, state authorities sought to block the investigation. Woolley stood his ground and sent the case to the grand jury. At issue was the question of permitting patients to testify before a grand jury in cases in which hospital staff members were accused of mistreating patients. Woolley prevailed.

Between 1900 and 1920, the facility changed somewhat. A cottage system was adopted, allowing for decentralized patient care; patients with tuberculosis were segregated. An auditorium, or amusement hall, was added in 1900. Gradually, the institution acquired additional land and ventured into farming and dairying operations. In 1912 it built the fine dairy barn now housing the Southeastern Ohio Cultural Arts Center. It also began to develop a championship herd of Holstein cows. The object was partly to provide work therapy for patients and partly to reduce the operating costs of the institution. Over time the hospital developed a poultry plant, piggery, orchard, and truck farm in addition to its dairy. In becoming self-sufficient in food, the hospital provided less business for Athens wholesale grocers. But as the patient population climbed, it generated increased employment opportunities for area residents, some of whom lived in the city of Athens, but many of whom lived on the hospital grounds or south of the Hocking River.

BANKING AND COMMERCE

The Athens banking structure underwent major changes between 1900 and 1920. In 1900 there were two institutions, both locally owned. The First National Bank, the older institution, had resources on the order of $600,000. Holding a federal charter, it represented the old guard, three-fourths of the stock being held by David H. Moore and Henry O'Bleness; Clinton L. Poston and Judge J. Perry Wood had served on its board of trustees. The other institution, the Bank of Athens, was still a merchant bank, the private property of James D. Brown, and not required to disclose its resources.

The first change was the organization in 1905 of a third bank, the Security Bank, with an initial capital of $25,000. Unlike the First National Bank and the Bank of Athens, which accepted checking accounts, the Security Bank limited itself to savings accounts. From the first, there was a community of interest between the Security Bank and the First National, for D. H. Moore and Henry O'Bleness, the two major stockholders of the First National, owned an important stake in the Security Bank. The ties were strengthened by the fact that the Security Bank began operations in rooms at the rear of the First National. The Security Bank prospered. By 1915, it was introducing a Christmas Savings Thrift Club. At the end of World War I, its resources stood at $434,719.

In 1905, a group of younger men—L. G. Worstell, W. N. Alderman, H. D. Henry, Fred L. Alderman, W. R. Phillips, Henry Zenner, and John E. Jones— incorporated the Athens National Bank and built the five-story structure at 8 North Court on the site of the old Market House. Fred Alderman, the cashier, set the policies that guided the bank during its formative years.

The Federal Reserve Act in 1914 changed the ground rules for banking in the United States, giving a decided advantage to banks operating under a federal charter. Accordingly the Bank of Athens abandoned its status as a merchant bank and secured a federal charter while retaining its old name. James D. Brown continued as its president. Conservative in his thinking, Brown nonetheless made innovations, introducing the first bookkeeping machine used by Athens banks in 1916. At the start of 1917, the bank reported net resources of just over a million dollars and was the largest bank in the city.

In May 1917, to become competitive with the Bank of Athens, First National and Athens National merged, with combined assets of $1,276,000. D. H. Moore and Henry O'Bleness became trustees of the new bank, which adopted the name of the younger institution: Athens National. L. G. Worstell became its president. At this point, the Security Bank moved into the former quarters of the First National Bank.

To accommodate Athenians who were building houses, either for themselves or as rental properties, the Citizens Building and Loan Society organized late in 1909. Led by F. P. McVay, it had a capital of $100,000. Behind the scenes as a trustee was J. C. Campbell. It promised depositors four percent on their deposits, double the rate of the Security Bank. As a building and loan, it dealt in first mortgages, entering business at a time Athens was completing its most expansive decade.

THE PROFESSIONAL COMMUNITY

The Athens professional community enjoyed an unprecedented growth in the first two decades of the new century. The number of dentists, physicians, and university faculty more than doubled. Only the legal profession did not increase proportionately.

Of the attorneys active between 1900 and 1920, a third to a half achieved a degree of distinction. At the top was the venerable Charles H. Grosvenor, whose Congressional service brought him national attention as a platform speaker. He was largely responsible for securing the classic post office building on West Union Street. Beyond 1907, when he left Congress and returned to live out his life in

Athens, he basked in his accumulated glory. His death in 1917 was marked by a community-wide funeral that merited the closing of the public schools, the University, and local businesses.

If Grosvenor stood first among the attorneys, others moved into the limelight. Israel (Izzy) Foster, a three-term county prosecutor and a power in the Republican party at the state level, was elected to Congress in fall 1918, the first of three terms. Joseph M. Wood and Oliver Rowland both served as county judges, while Rowland was also a mayor of Athens. Wood's brother, James Perry Wood, spent ten years in Washington as president of the Spanish-American War Claims Commission.

The dentists were never as numerous as the medical doctors or attorneys. Clarence L. Jones stands out, not because of his dental expertise, but because his fascination with the telephone drew him into the management of the Athens Home Telephone Company. Also of note is Edna Thompson, the first woman to practice dentistry in Athens, who shared an office with her brother.

Some of the far more numerous members of the medical fraternity were also torn between following their profession and pursuing outside interests. Doctors William N. Alderman and Thomas R. Biddle succumbed to the lure of business. A son-in-law of the aging Clinton L. Poston, Biddle joined the latter in the active operation of Poston's coal properties, especially the Sunday Creek Coal Company, which had large holdings in the Hocking Valley, eastern Ohio, and West Virginia. Biddle's brother, David H., came to Athens to take over T. R.'s medical practice. Alderman built the office complex across from the City Building, then went on to become an organizer and head of the Athens Brick Company as well as of the Athens National Bank. His name also crops up as an investor, trustee, or officer in a variety of other Athens enterprises. Other doctors stayed the course. John R. Sprague, whose family supplied the city and county with numerous doctors, was on the scene before World War I. As noted earlier, T. A. Copeland made his mark by establishing a private hospital for treating his patients.

MERCHANTS

Athens in 1900 was far more a mercantile community than an industrial one. Yet the character of the mercantile community changed markedly in some ways, while continuing along time-honored paths in others. Most of the businesses operated as individually-owned or family-owned enterprises or as partnerships. Few merchants, Zenner and Preston excepted, had more than three or four clerks. The small scale of operation facilitated ease of entry and ease of exit, and the individually-owned firms and partnerships were often short-lived; such firms had to reorganize each time a partner withdrew, a new partner was added, or one of the partners died.

When possible, merchants sought to free themselves of the impersonal operation of market forces. To increase their market share, merchants increasingly turned to advertising campaigns or marketing gimmicks; a few broadened their market by setting up branch outlets in other villages of the Hocking Valley. They formed trade associations to promote village growth, hoping thereby to increase their customer base or to protect themselves from risks.

Throughout the period the merchants sought ways to limit competition from businesses outside Athens. In 1902 merchants persuaded the Village Council to require licenses for sales representatives of out-of-town firms. Accordingly, one John Payne, salesman for a Parkersburg dry-goods firm, was arrested for selling goods in Athens without a license. Convicted in mayor's court, he and his employer appealed, and the court of common pleas ruled the ordinance an unconstitutional restraint of trade. Another concern was the mail-order house. While farm organizations hailed firms like Sears Roebuck and Montgomery Ward for giving isolated farmers access to as broad a range of goods as were available to big city dwellers, small town merchants with limited merchandise viewed the mail-order houses as a potent threat. They warned the community against buying goods which they could not examine in person, of trading with men they did not know. During World War I, their arguments made it a patriotic duty to support the home-town merchant; thinly veiled appeals to religion invoked the Golden Rule in support of buying at home.

At the beginning of the century village merchants organized a Board of Trade. In a wave of enthusiasm 150 persons joined within a few days. The board, however, was short-lived. For a decade and a half, 1906–20, the promotion of business interests lay with the Commercial Club. Open to all citizens, it was to promote the welfare of the community and to secure, if possible, new manufacturing enterprises. Harry G. Stalder, Henry Zenner, and H. D. Henry were among the leaders. To assist it, the group "hired" W. B. Lawrence, an active businessman, as its ten-dollar-a-month secretary. Its meetings provided a venue for discussing public policy and formulating a consensus within the business community. That Athens needed industry was an article of faith. It discussed the pros and cons of annexing the Richland Avenue district, a move that would instantly inflate the community's population, but would also entail major new costs for schools, water, and sewerage.

In 1912 the focus was on "boosting" the hometown. By way of promoting the community, the Commercial Club opposed indiscriminate posting of signs and sought clean streets. The organization did not restrict itself to talk. Believing that if a "labor train" to Luhrig were operated miners could live in town and commute daily to their work, the Club raised $3,000 as a guarantee to the railroad should the service fail to pay for itself. The club facilitated the construction of the National Guard Armory at the north end of Court Street. In 1914, with over two hundred members committed to paying dues for three years, the Club lobbied for the creation of a new, union rail depot. This was a difficult matter, for it meant abandoning the terminal at Cemetery [Shafer] and Dean [Washington] avenues, a move West End businessmen opposed as hurtful to their interests.

Retail merchants organized their own Retail Merchants' Association, primarily as a means to limit credit abuse by exchanging data on customers whose bills were delinquent. This incidentally underscores that, despite earlier efforts, a cash-and-carry policy had not been universally adopted. Merchants made common cause at other levels. A year after the Zenner company introduced its own delivery service in 1905, featuring "a handsome closed delivery wagon," merchants established a central delivery service. As the telephone came into general use, housewives phoned orders to grocers, expecting almost immediate delivery of one or two items needed for the next meal. The central delivery service proved to be an on-again, off-again operation. A new beginning was scheduled for June 1908—five deliveries a day, beginning at 7:45 A.M. Customers were warned to allow a one-hour lead time for their orders. In 1910 merchants, grocers, and butchers shifted from contracting for the delivery service to one they owned outright. During the price-crunch of World War I, merchants offering delivery service instituted a modest charge. As inflation began to push prices upward, Athens merchants employed the wartime mystique to secure the community's acceptance of a cash-only policy, to become effective August 1, 1918. They justified their case by arguing that as their suppliers had already initiated such a policy, they had to follow suit.

Food and Drug Merchants

By 1900 Athenians had lost their ability to produce their own food. Few residents had room for a cow or pig, a small flock of chickens, or a large kitchen garden. Bread-making increasingly became a lost art as did the production of home-made salves, ointments, and teas with which to treat ailing family members. As home production waned, the business community expanded, becoming increasingly specialized.

As food was a universal necessity, the number of grocers was large. For a decade, 1904–17, Eldridge-Higgins, a Columbus firm, operated a wholesale grocery operation. F. C. Stedman, however, stood out as the wholesale grocer who supplied not only Athens city retail grocers but those in the county and contiguous counties. The retail grocery trade was divided among ten merchants on or adjacent to Court Street and four others located in West End. The stores were still small, and most goods were on shelves not accessible to the shopper, although some bulk goods might be out in the open. Processed foods slowly made their appearance, and a few national producers such as Kellogg, Mazola, and Fels Naptha advertised. But national brands were uncommon. Arthur Falloon, located near Court and State, opened "a modern grocery," his claim referring to his possession of a refrigerator, enabling him to sell creamery butter, cheese, lard, and milk. Without exception, the grocery stores were Athens-owned. There were no chain stores.

With fourteen enterprises competing for the trade of a community of about three thousand persons at the beginning of the century, profits must have been slight for many, which may explain the ephemeral character of a number of these shops.

Baked goods, sweets, and meat were sold by separate firms. Two bakers and one confectioner met the community's needs for bread, pastries, and sweets at the beginning of the century. In 1914 the William S. Foutch Bakery, located in the Phoenix Building, began operations with six bakers. With a capacity of seven thousand loaves a day, Foutch supplied bread to a regional market. Meat was supplied by three Court Street area proprietors and one in the West End. Unlike in the 1870s, these were full-time butcher shops, and the animals were slaughtered off-site. The meat was custom-cut by the butcher.

Three druggists—J. Halliday Cline, Eli R. Lash, and Wilson H. McKee—were all of more than ordinary standing among their fellow businessmen. Cline had taken over the John Perkins residence-store in 1893, then remodeled it, incorporating the old Perkins building within the new structure but adding a new pressed-brick front, a modern entrance, and a third story. In February 1912 the building burned; only the four exterior walls were left intact. Cline promptly cleared the site, then rebuilt. His elegant soda fountain became a fashionable meeting place in the summer. When the Athens National Bank building was completed, the new drug firm of C. B. Henderson and Floyd Crider occupied the north room. At the end of World War I, the premises were occupied by Wilson McKee. Eli R. Lash remained in place on South Court Street. While handling a large volume of patent medicines, the druggists continued to compound some medicines on their own.

Clothing and Dry Goods

The clothing needs of women were served by a variety of specialized firms. Dressmakers continued to produce one-of-a-kind creations for milady. While millinery could be purchased at the department stores, several women operated their own millinery shops. Indeed, dressmaking and millinery, drawing on women's traditional skills, were the principal enterprises in which women were proprietors. Lizzie Hibbard and Emma Boelzner, two of the milliner-proprietors, went off to Cleveland or Cincinnati periodically to renew their stock. The essence of their enterprises consisted of individualizing the hats for their customers. Lizzie V. Cook at 35 North Court, however, was deemed the dean of the milliners when she retired in 1913, having followed that pursuit some twenty years. At the end of the second decade, the Finsterwald sisters were the leading Court Street milliners.

Dry goods and ready-made clothing were available from several stores. D. Zenner & Co., the oldest of the three department stores in town, operated the top-of-the-line store. In 1902 Zenner's establishment boasted eleven women and seven male employees. In 1905 Zenner claimed thirty regular employees. Henry Zenner, who assumed ownership of the firm in 1901, regularly shopped in New York for goods, leaving his wife in charge of the store. As a merchant, Zenner was decidedly fashion conscious, scheduling formal openings for seasonal goods; his wife oversaw the opening of the fall millinery season, an opening characterized by special evening hours, usually with music. Zenner also employed special sales gimmicks, bargains available for limited time periods.

Having started in the Potter Building at the southwest corner of Court and State, Olivian B. Sloane, in the course of nearly two decades, had expanded southward to the alley next the Warren House and remodeled the several structures to provide a more uniform facade. In 1900 he occupied thirteen rooms and had the largest floor space of the town's three department stores. When Sloane retired in 1903, his store as such ended. His successor, J. D. Raw, continued only the dry-goods business, but in 1906, a fire devastated much of the building. Rather than start over, Raw left town, and Sloane, who still owned the building, rebuilt the structure, creating a third floor by splitting the high-ceilinged second floor .

The Hickle-Kessinger store, occupying the first floor of the Masonic Hall, was purchased in 1910 by the Prestons of Nelsonville. The Prestons remodeled the building, installing a new front featuring show windows and recessed entrances. Prestons quickly became a major merchandiser.

A number of smaller stores, emphasizing low price rather than fashion, served

Athens. Most notable was Sam Sommer who continued the business started by the Seligs. As a practicing Jew, he did not open his store on Saturday until sundown, the end of the Jewish Sabbath. On the other hand, Sommer had no qualms about merchandising Christmas and Easter goods. He made a point that his special purchases enabled him to offer bargain prices.

Over the years, other dry-goods and clothing stores appeared, usually with indifferent success. Rothman's Economy Store opened in March 1906 in the new, roomy Campbell Building at Court and West State. Greenfields, which succeeded Rothmans, offended the sensibilities of the Retail Merchant Association by offering trading stamps as a come-on. Greenfield, who had come to Athens from Murray City, ended in bankruptcy. The Union took over the space vacated by Greenfield. Advertising itself as "Athens Underselling Store," it featured ready-to-wear and a money-back guarantee. Within a short time of its opening, it expanded its space; in mid-1913 it cited "the general backward business conditions throughout the country" as a reason for an unprecedented sale. At the start of 1918 The Union closed, selling off both merchandise and fixtures.

Men's clothing could be secured from department stores such as Hickle-Kessinger and D. Zenner. But Henry Nelson and I. Rosenthal operated general clothing stores, while F. S. Grones ran an up-scale men's furnishings store. Two merchant tailors, Baker and Groff and Link and Grones, sold made-to-measure suits. In 1903 Athens got a second upscale men's store when S. K. Thompson and W. K. Scott located in the Worstell Building.

By 1900 most Athenians wore ready-made shoes and had a choice of five dealers, several of whom had started as shoemakers. Two shoemakers still held on, J. B. Dalton on Court Street and William Chambers off-Court. The preeminent shoe merchant was Peter Kern, who had come to Athens in 1856 as a shoemaker, gradually added a stock of ready-made shoes, and in 1884 built the store now occupied by Mountain Leather. J. B. Selby, a long-time manufacturer of shoes, likewise joined the ranks of shoe merchants.

Household Furnishings

Athenians furnished their homes with goods manufactured elsewhere rather than with furniture fabricated by local craftsmen. Furniture could be had from Charles S. Newsom, who doubled as one of the town undertakers, or from Ellis and Hibbard. As Newsom increasingly favored his undertaking business, he sold his furniture business to R. C. M. Hastings and built the structure at 42 South Court for his undertaking parlor. When the Ellis and Hibbard firm dissolved, M. T. Ellis continued in the furniture business, while William A. Hibbard turned to selling records and phonographs. For a time J. C. Campbell sold furniture, but his interests increasingly turned to real estate promotion and development. Two new firms appeared, The Home Furniture Company and the Swanson Company, firms that along with Ellis continued into the 1920s.

Hardware

Three or four hardware merchants were generally available. Such stores sold general hardware, some furniture, and household supplies. With the development of gaslight, gas heating, a water and sewer system, and electric lighting, hardware stores expanded their merchandise to include plumbing and electrical supplies. Of the three merchants of 1898, only Frank E. Goldsberry in the Moore-Russell Building was still in business in 1913. In 1915 Goldsberry sold his business to Merill Kerr. With relatively little change in its physical layout, as the Kerr-Hunter Hardware, the store continued to 1978. Several others also took up the business. The Carpenter Hardware, originally in Nelsonville and Glouster, opened a store in Athens in 1904 (30 North Court), the Athens store engaging in both wholesale and retail sale of general hardware. So, too, H. L. Wheaton established himself at 32 South Court. When Wheaton retired in 1918, he passed the firm to his son and Merle Crooks, the latter specializing in the general hardware business, young Wheaton, in the plumbing and electrical supplies lines.

While the town plumbers provided on-site repairs to homeowners and renters, they were also merchants. In 1903, for example, Charles Demolet sold garden hose and canvas window awnings along with bathroom fixtures. In time Demolet teamed up with Charles Cornwell to provide plumbing and electrical service. By 1913, Lorin C. Nye and C. V. Strawn had entered the field. Located at 72 North Court, Strawn Plumbing would remain there until the mid-1990s, although ownership had passed into other hands.

Miscellaneous Retailers

A miscellany of individuals catered to residents' other needs. A number of barbers, eight in 1898 and fifteen in 1920, served the male community. Some barbers were black men, others white. Athens barbers organized a union, #478 Journeymen Barbers of America, in August 1905, which set standard hours, 7 A.M. to 7 P.M. weekdays and Saturdays to 11:30 P.M.—no Sunday work. They undoubtedly set standard fees as well. And they insisted that all who practiced the craft be dues-paying members of the union. Having run into customer objections to the 7 P.M. closing, they relented and agreed to remain open to 8 P.M., a thirteen-hour workday. Perhaps the most elegant of the establishments was the City Hall Barbershop of Bennett and Miller, a three-chair shop.

Four merchants featured jewelry. The D. C. Cornwell firm, the oldest, was firmly ensconced at 10 South Court. George I. Putnam, George R. Walker, and the venerable Cinny McLean offered competition, although McLean was especially known for watch repairs. As mass-produced clocks and watches were already the norm, jewelers became repairmen and salesmen rather than watchmakers. Some jewelers doubled as opticians.

As the community grew, new kinds of specialized enterprises surfaced. The need for a likeness was supplied by a series of photographers. Albert Wood operated a billiard parlor in the late 1890s, and the activity was sufficiently popular that there were four parlors in 1913. Cigars were available at several shops. Fruit stores appeared by 1913, most notably that of E. T. Abdella at Court and State. A spate of candy stores also appeared. The candy and fruit stores were also likely to offer ice cream, there being six sellers in 1913 aside from J. H. Cline. As Edison's motion picture equipment evolved, the town came to have several venues, The Opera House, the Columbia on North Court, and the Grand on West Washington. In time there was the Majestic on South Court. The Columbia and Majestic survived into the mid-twenties.

BED, BOARD, AND BUILDINGS

For travelers in 1900, Athens offered a variety of hotels. The most venerable was the Palmer House at Congress and Washington. Often remodeled, it was still in business in 1920. The Colonade, on North Court, had disappeared by 1913. The hotel of distinction was the Berry, which by 1915 had expanded to forty-four rooms and had earned a reputation for its service. The Athens Hotel, originally the Warren House, was large, but during a time when office space was in short supply, the owners stopped serving transients and instead catered to long-term roomers and rented out office space and sample rooms. By 1913 it had reverted to hotel status.

Across the alley, in the southernmost portion of the block that O. B. Sloane had put together, was the Ohio Hotel. On West Union there was for a time the Elk; farther down West Union was the Walker Hotel. Nearby Depot Street featured the Park, while in West End J. P. Thompson ran an establishment. Of the various hotels in 1912, the Berry was the town's largest. The Athens claimed thirty rooms, the Palmer twenty-eight. None of the others had as many as twenty.

Restaurants came and went. The seven eating places of 1898, mostly on Court Street, had become a baker's dozen by 1913, and the number would continued to increase. Those eateries in the West End might expect to serve railroad crews and the increasing number of miners who lived nearby. The Court Street restaurateurs had a captive trade of countrymen who came to town to trade or to conduct legal business and of the traveling salesmen and townspeople who chose to dine out. B. B. Johnson's Dining Hall in the Worstell Building was among the foremost of these. The finest cuisine, however, was to be found at Berry's Hotel.

A factor in the economy of 1900 was the village's ten saloons, essential to the well-being of the drinking men, an abomination to the town's drys, and a problem to public officials. Of the saloonkeepers, W. H. Farrell, on West Union Street, was especially important for his role as an agent for the distillers and brewers. Farrell also doubled as a restaurateur. As businessmen, the saloonkeepers were unique in that they were locked in a contest over their right to engage in business, a struggle they ultimately lost.

As in earlier years, an uncertain number of Athenian householders provided room and board to the public. The 1898 City Directory lists four boardinghouses, three of them on Dean Street and the fourth on High. Given their location, they quite likely accommodated railroad workers. A far larger, invisible economy was managed by townswomen who provided room and board to Ohio University students for part of the year. In 1900 the Ladies' Dormitory, East, and West housed but a small fraction of the student population. As student enrollments passed 1,000, even allowing for the young women housed by the university, there was a heavy demand for rooms in private homes. By 1920, when upwards of 2,000 students were in residence during the summer term, the demand for rooms pressed the upward limit of space Athenians could spare.

An even larger part of the invisible economy was the home-rental business. Athens had 1,808 households in 1920, of which 819, 45 percent, were occupied by renters. The *Messenger* gives a glimpse of the situation, reporting from time to time that a particular townsman is building one or more houses for the purpose of rental. Some of these rentals were built in the newest, most fashionable areas of the community, Sunnyside and North Hill. How widespread the ownership of these rental units was cannot be determined, but given the number of units, this business represented major amounts of investment capital.

A fundamental sector of the town's economy was the building industry. In 1800 Silas Bingham with one or two assistants might build a log house from scratch— that is, cut the necessary trees, hand saw them into the needed lengths, square them, notch the ends, and then lift them into place. House building in 1900 required a variety of specialists. E. H. Moore provided local contractors with sand and gravel for the cement work, the footers. Athens Lumber Company made or marketed cement blocks, framing materials, lath, and shingles. Its planing mill and wood shop fabricated the doors, windows, and their frames. J. C. Hewett's and J. H. Boden's Parquetry Flooring Company manufactured flooring. The Athens Brick Company produced pressed brick. Two roofers, F. P. White and B. F. Witman, competed for the roofing trade. Charles Demolet specialized in installing the fittings for gaslight, gas water heaters, and gas furnaces. Within a decade, the electrician would appear as houses began to get electric lights and, by 1915, the first electric appliances. The role of decorator appeared along with paper hangers.

At the top of the heap, as it were, were three contractors: Henry O'Bleness, who had undertaken great enterprises in the late 1870s, '80s and '90s—often out of town; Charles P. Kircher, who supervised the University's building programs— Ellis Hall, Boyd, the Carnegie Library, the gym, and Lindley; and George L. Fenzel, who gained recognition in the period after 1910. After Fenzel died, still a young man, his widow, Maud, took over and became a contractor in her own right.

Given that the number of houses in Athens doubled between 1900 and 1920 and that Ohio University more than doubled its buildings, the Athens building industry prospered.

Farm-Oriented Enterprises

Although the agricultural sector of Athens County's economy was shrinking, there were still 2,503 farms in 1900, most of whose operators depended on Athens village for logistical support.

In 1900 the village still had three blacksmiths who fabricated or repaired farm implements and shoed horses. The two harness makers and three horseshoers would hold on, even though the automobile was making its appearance. In 1913 there were a half dozen blacksmith shops. Those of Carl E. Norris and

C. W. Lawrence also dealt in buggies, carriages, and wagons. H. M. Cotton operated a feed stable. There were three harness shops, two liveries and two veterinary surgeons.

The mode of marketing agricultural products changed. In rural Athens County the general stores still traded farm produce for store goods, and the merchant had to find a market for the produce he took in trade. In the village the role of the produce merchant emerged. In 1900 C. H. Peters' produce house off West Union purchased area farm products for resale outside the county. In 1903 he closed his firm and left Athens. Subsequently, Thomas H. Craig undertook this business. At the end of World War I the Athens Poultry and Produce Company marketed area chickens. J. H. Cline and the Hocking Valley Creamery provided a steady market for milk; F. C. Stedman, a market for beef cattle and hogs. Except as these firms either solicited farm produce, cream, or livestock from outside the county or generated markets for such goods beyond the bounds of the county, they had limited prospect of growth.

Horses and Autos

Most Athenians provided their own means of getting where they needed to go, but there were times when some form of public transportation was in order. For moving packages in and out of town a variety of express services were available, of which Adams Express, the most important, had a resident agent. By 1917 Wells Fargo also provided express service to the community.

Athens Bus Line provided service principally between the depot and the town's various hotels. When, in 1915, a traction line materialized, the horse-drawn bus attempted service from Central Avenue to Court Street. Maintaining a bus schedule proved difficult since incoming trains and traction cars as often as not were late. Theodore Dean was the last driver. Forty years before, at fourteen, he had carried the mail by horseback for ten dollars a month; he graduated to driving a stage drawn by a two-horse team, then moved up to a four-horse rig. In mid-January 1919 he made his last run with a horse-drawn omnibus. His horse-drawn bus was replaced by an eight-passenger motor bus.

For the general public, especially those who came to town by buggy or wagon, a parking lot was needed to provide care for the horse or horses. Two firms specialized in storing private buggies and carriages. The community's livery stables, by contrast, rented teams, buggies, and wagons, the prototypes of Hertz and Avis. By

1913 two firms concerned with buggies, carriages and wagons, a feed stable, and five livery stables served Athens. But the auto was making inroads.

The first autos to arrive in Athens were curiosities. They had to be brought in from Columbus or Cleveland, and simply delivering them to Athens was a major undertaking. Their owners became instant celebrities, and their travels were conscientiously reported by the *Messenger*. In fact, several owners entrusted the driving and maintenance to a chauffeur. Repair garages preceded the organization of auto dealerships. As of 1913 the town boasted three garages—City Auto on East Carpenter, J. R. Lostro on West Union, and J. S. McCarter on East State. A portent of future events was the notice that Graves and Williams auto repair shop had taken over the building previously housing Charles Secoy's livery stable. C. R. White, who specialized in tin work and furnaces, by 1920 also repaired auto radiators.

In December 1913 a new auto taxi service offered Athenians "heated, warm, and comfortable" vehicles. Rides anywhere inside the town limits on paved streets cost twenty-five cents; to the top of North Hill or to the Children's Home, fifty cents. In 1914 in an effort to be up-to-date, C. S. Newsom, the undertaker, introduced a "motor hearse" that doubled as an ambulance and even transported patients to Columbus hospitals. Other undertakers followed suit.

In 1909 Robert C. Fulton, the pioneer auto dealer in the city, organized the Athens Buick Company, financed by local and outside capital. Running a close second was George W. Hopkins with a Ford agency. In these early years dealers frequently switched from one company to another. In 1916, local auto dealers staged the first auto show in town, a four-day affair at the new Armory. Fred Beasley, still in Amesville, let Athenians know that he operated a Ford agency. The Ford was already far and away the most numerous vehicle registered in the county. For the residents of the rural areas that Beasley's dealership served, the Ford was practical and affordable.

Most of the car dealers located at the north end of Court Street or adjacent parts of Carpenter, an area that had just been opened to development. John R. Lostro was the exception in locating at Court and Union. A mine manager, he had been persuaded to manage a West Union Street garage. At the time the southwest corner of Court and Union was occupied by a number of nondescript buildings. As Lostro took over the garage, he also contracted to sell the Overland, did remarkably well, and dreamed dreams. He organized a corporation, and, in 1915, constructed the brick, three-story structure that most Athenians associate with Logan's and Follett's. As designed, the structure faced West Union. The building drew attention from the start, for in digging the foundation, an older structure immediately to the south on Court Street collapsed into the excavation. When completed, the first floor was given over to displaying new cars; the second floor, to a garage, an elevator moving the vehicles between floors. Several offices were also located on the second floor overlooking Court Street.

Lostro set the pace for the rest of the decade. In 1916 he inaugurated the used-car business and eventually took space on North Court to market used vehicles. As taking delivery of new cars continued to be a major difficulty, given the absence of good roads, he tried an experiment and sent twenty-one young women to Toledo to pick up new Overlands and drive them back to Athens in a convoy. At the end of World War I, Lostro reorganized his operation, using the basement of his building for wholesaling auto parts area wide. Indeed, he hired salesmen to canvass the garages springing up in the area's hamlets and crossroads. The age of the auto had arrived.

INDUSTRIAL ENTERPRISE

Athens entered the new century firmly believing that to grow, it required new industry. Industry would provide wage jobs that would attract new residents who in turn would generate a demand for new homes, for the goods of local merchants, and for the services of local professionals. The promoters still emphasized the advantages Athens offered as a rail junction of east-west and north-south railroads, and the availability of bituminous coal, clay, shale, and timber. In addition it had the produce of the land, both agricultural and timber, to process and market.

Millers and Packers

Milling continued at both the East Mill and Herrold Mill sites, both powered by the Hocking River. In July 1901 Otto Barth of Coolville bought the East Mill, announcing his intention to erect an elevator. Barth's operation was ill-fated, for both his mill and dam were badly damaged in the 1907 flood, which also cost him his life. The new owner, Charles F. Theiss, also experienced disaster. Theiss made a number of improvements in the mill and began processing grain imported by train. But in March 1909 the mill was consumed by flames, the Athens fire department forced to watch helplessly from the opposite side of the river, which was again in flood. In 1912 there was talk of rebuilding both the "old brick mill," the one Roach had constructed, and to rebuild the dam. In fact, the Athens side of the dam was soon dynamited as a means of limiting erosion of the river's bank. The East Mill was history.

The Herrold Mill had its problems, too. In 1911 Henry Herrold sold the family mill to Edward S. White and John P. Davis. At the time of sale the mill had been idle for several years. The new owners completely overhauled it, installing modern equipment. Further, they announced that they would buy local grain. Within two months, the mill burned. White, however, in 1916, moved a mill from Meigs County to the site. The dam and forebay being in good repair, the mill was water-powered. White produced both flour and animal feed. The river-powered mills had to face a new competitor. In 1901 J. C. Campbell, a Court Street merchant with some milling experience, constructed a steam-powered mill on upper Court Street, a mill that could operate whether the river was high, low, or frozen. While Campbell owned the mill, E. D. and Herbert A. Junod operated the mill and the adjacent feed store. Competition among the millers increased still more when, in June 1917, Frank J. Beasley and Son, Amesville millers, purchased the Eldridge-Higgins wholesale grocery building on West Union and established a modern flour and feed mill capable of an output of 150 barrels a day.

A second industry with roots in area agriculture was meat packing. Local butchers had continued to buy local cattle, hogs, and poultry and to slaughter for their retail customers. F. C. Stedman, "a genial, whole soul gentleman," took meat packing to another level by operating a stockyard and slaughterhouse. In 1907 his operation, described as small-scale, had eleven cold storage rooms; his smoking room could process 45,000 pounds of meat at a time. His business was closely tied to the mining community, as he marketed much of his product in the company stores of the Sunday Creek Coal Company. Although retaining the Stedman name, the firm passed into the ownership of G. E. Tetrick. Its scale of operation, while small compared to packing houses such as Swift and Armour, provided a market for some 600 hogs and 100 cattle per week and employed 60 persons by 1918. Stedman was one of Athens' major employers.

Creameries

Several enterprises processed milk from local dairy herds. Area farmers were capable of producing more fluid milk than could be consumed locally. Given the

341

distance from the metropolitan markets, milk could be converted into either but-ter or ice cream. In 1910, the *Messenger* announced the creation of a new Athens creamery, capitalized at $10,000. Relocating from Guysville, the plant occupied a site on North Congress. Production, which had been at the level of 2,000 pounds of butter per week, was slated to increase four- to five-fold. In 1912 the firm was sold to John Carpenter and Ed Banks and operated as the Carpenter Ice Cream and Dairy.

Production of ice cream provided a second market for area cream. While most Athenians thought of Cline's as a drugstore with an elegant ice cream parlor, J. H. Cline was an aggressive, imaginative businessman. Realizing that his profits could be enhanced by making his own ice cream, he also perceived that he might whole-sale ice cream to other retailers. Since the market for ice cream was seasonal, he also produced and marketed butter. He first produced ice cream in the basement of his store, but in 1910 he built a new plant behind Preston's Department Store. His original production of 250 to 400 gallons of ice cream a day increased to 1,000. The move was fortuitous, for while his Court Street drugstore burned in 1912, the creamery, now in its own building, was unaffected. The business grew, and in 1916 the plant was expanded. Ice cream production was increased by another 300 gallons a day, butter production to 10,000 pounds a week. In 1917 the West Virginia market beckoned, and Cline undertook an even larger ice cream operation in Charleston.

Other Farm-Oriented Industries

Dependent on the rural character of the hinterland, two enterprises manufactured products for area farmers. Although wagon manufacture had long occupied a number of Athens County craftsmen, the age of the locally made wagon was end-ing. C. W. Lawrence, who had operated a wagon factory on West Union, sold out in 1904 to Eldridge-Higgins of Columbus, which remodelled the building for use as a wholesale grocery. C. S. Newsom designed an incubator for chickens in 1898 and began manufacturing it on a small scale. In 1907 Newsom took over a former livery stable to expand his production facilities. It seems doubtful that his firm took off, for Newsom remained preoccupied with his undertaking business.

Lumber Milling

Several Athenian businessmen tapped the area's timber as a basis for a manufacturing business. The timber-cutting in the county was left to local woodlot owners. As the *Messenger* noted in 1906, the forests had been "ruthlessly pillaged." A
century before some timber was cut and floated down the Ohio to find a market
and a lesser amount was processed into building materials for local use, but the
lumber business of the early decades of the twentieth century produced a variety
of wood products.

The pattern had been set in part by the Hudson Brothers School Furniture
Company, which had begun operations in Athens in 1894. It was one of the larger
employers in the village and doing well. In April 1906 the brothers' plant in Logan,
West Virginia, burned. Initially the prospect seemed to be that the firm would
salvage what equipment it could and move it to Athens. This was not to be. Their
West Virginia associates rallied to their aid, and instead the brothers abandoned
their operation in Athens and relocated in West Virginia.

The mainstay of the timber-processing enterprises were the locally owned and
operated lumber companies. The foremost was Rardin Brothers, initially located
in West End and much involved in promoting the development of the Central
Avenue area. Started about 1900, the Rardin business operated a planing mill on
Central Avenue and a builders' supply, coal, and burial vault works on Smith
Street. In 1910 the brothers bought the abandoned Hudson School Furniture
property. Daniel A. Rardin rebuilt the facility for the purpose of manufacturing
caskets, a wholly new business. There were no competitors in the region, and the
demand was steady. The firm would not only manufacture caskets but also handle
burial suits and robes as well as a complete line of funeral directors' and em-
balmers' supplies. The necessary specialists were imported; the main labor force
was recruited locally. In 1914 the Rardins relocated their business from West End.
When this move was completed, they were operating a planing mill, a general
builders' supply, and custom mill-work business on the old Hudson property.
Their land in West End was platted for sale as home sites. The firm expected to
employ between 60 and 100 persons.

Two other general lumber businesses also operated during part of this time: the
Athens Lumber Company on West Union and Sunnyside Lumber Company on
Hocking Street. The Athens Lumber Company, incorporated in 1890, utilized the
one-time facilities of the Athens Gas and Electric Co. The firm had its own drying kiln. The planing mill operated on a scale that allowed the firm to supply

the interior woodwork for buildings in Indiana, Michigan, Kentucky, and West Virginia. The firm also operated a large mill at Glouster. Management averred that its scale of operation was limited by scarcity of skilled labor. Owned at the start of the century by H. D. Henry, in 1904 the firm passed from Henry to George H. Junod and L. W. Roberts. Junod ultimately withdrew from the business, and the firm continued under the Roberts family. Sunnyside Lumber Company, founded in 1904, operated to the end of 1914. In that year, recognizing that the Athens market could not support three lumber firms, it sold out to the Rardin firm.

At least three firms specialized in the manufacture of wood products. As home buyers increasingly demanded a degree of style in their homes, windows, doors, and trim began to be manufactured off-site. The earliest specialized firm was the Veneered Door and Finish Company. A small firm founded about 1906 and capitalized at $10,000, it exported most of its product to eastern cities. In 1909 it was bought out by the Hardwood Finish Company, a firm owned by a combination of Athens investors and two outsiders, one of whom, H. H. Mechlin, the president, had large lumber interests elsewhere in Ohio and Kentucky. Daniel W. Peoples, former president of the Veneered Door Company, was employed as manager. Capitalized at $50,000, the new firm expected to employ 50 to 60 men. The firm also added to its original facility by putting up a new plant, gaining 8,000 square feet of space. The third firm was J. C. Hewitt's and J. H. Boden's Parquetry Flooring Company. Located next to the brick plant, it operated its own dry kiln and a woodworking building. Beginning operations in 1911, it employed perhaps fifteen men.

Clay Products

Although Athens village never developed a working coal mine, it had clay and shale, the basis for a substantial commercial brick industry. Well established by 1900, the Athens Brick Company secured its raw materials from the south end of North Hill, and by 1920 it had cut the hill back nearly 100 yards, opening up for development the northernmost block of Court Street as well as the lower end of Carpenter Street.

The production of brick required strong backs and unskilled laborers. And while the brick company was not the only enterprise in the village with union laborers, because of its size, it initiated Athens in the problems of labor and management. July 1904 found the plant on strike over a union shop. Management claimed it did not object to hiring union labor, but it refused to make union membership a condition of continuing employment. After other union workers in Athens declined to support the striking brick workers, the strike collapsed. Periodically other strikes occurred. That of 1906 focused on establishing a nine-hour day, while that of 1914 made pay the issue. In none of the strikes did the workers win. After breaking the 1906 job action, management upped wages by one cent an hour—a sixty-cents-per-week increase. After the 1914 strike ended, management ordered a steam shovel, thus lessening its dependence on manual labor.

The brick company faced serious competition for labor. As they could, the unskilled workers drifted off to the mines or railroads, and at times brick production was limited by a dearth of laborers. To explore a possible solution, the owners built eight four-room homes on Stimson Avenue on its own land. These were to be rented inexpensively to employees to reduce employee attrition.

As the firm introduced the community to union-management problems, it also illustrated the vulnerability of relatively unskilled wage-laborers. In February 1904 a serious fire closed operations for weeks, leaving the majority of the men without income until production could resume. Again in December 1908 an engine broke down, throwing 130 men out of work for ten weeks. In another December, a jinx month for the firm, a flywheel ran wild, breaking in pieces, and employees lost five to six weeks' work and income.

Athens Brick Company depended not on a local market but on a market reaching beyond Ohio. For a time the city of Columbus was a major customer, but bricks went to other cities as well, including Chicago. Local lore has insisted that the Indianapolis Speedway was paved with Athens-made bricks, and although the Speedway management disclaims a record of such purchases, Athens residents have averred seeing such bricks at the Speedway in the past.

The breadth of its market, however, put the Brick Company in competition with brick plants elsewhere. In 1906 Hocking Valley Coal and Iron built a brick plant at Doanville; capitalized at $1 million, it was represented as the biggest in the world. Both Glouster and Trimble developed large brick works, taken over in 1913 by a Dayton firm. As a low-priority enterprise during World War I, the Athens firm could not retain its employees nor could cities undertake new street construction under wartime regulations. Furthermore, alternative road-building materials—concrete and black top—appeared on the market. With its equipment standing idle and the future demand for brick paving blocks uncertain, the owners closed the plant and sold off the equipment.

Metals Industries

Visions of becoming a new Pittsburgh or Birmingham never materialized. Athens, in fact, had little natural advantage in industries working with metal as it lacked the requisite kind of ore and coking coal required by modern technology. Yet some older metalworking enterprises continued. The Athens Foundry and Machine Company continued its "yo-yo" experience. It was down at the start of the century. An infusion of new capital by W. N. Alderman, Fred Stalder, and Henry O'Bleness breathed new life into it for a time under the direction of E. S. Jennings. When the market for turbines dried up, the firm turned to the manufacture of mine cars and their wheels. Even so, by 1912 the scale of operation was down to no more than a dozen employees. In that year W. H. Hyde of Marietta bought out the firm. It was still operating at the end of the decade.

As modes of heating private homes changed, new devices were invented. There seemed to be a broad market for space heaters to be used in homes originally heated by open fireplaces. Lorin C. Nye invented one such stove, advertised as strong, durable, and ending the threat of carbon monoxide poisoning. These sold for as little as $3.75 or as much as $5.75. Nye's market seems to have been local only.

Still another enterprise was the Athens Stove Company, capitalized at $25,000, and organized to manufacture a "fireless stove" invented by Guy H. Hewitt, a local inventor. The firm was sufficiently successful that in spring 1915, eighteen months after its organization, it raised another $10,000 in capital to expand production, to advertise its product, and to hire traveling sales representatives. In 1916, reporting itself pleased with its progress, its output was four stoves a day. The firm seems not to have survived the war.

McBee Binder Company

If Athens was not to become the stove capital of the world, Charles F. McBee had an idea for a device that would bring order to the filing and binding of freight bills. A one-time agent of the Baltimore and Ohio Southwestern Railroad, he knew firsthand the problems of coping with the massive volume of freight bills that station agents had to handle and store. His binder was relatively simple and efficient. With financial aid from Henry Zenner, McBee and Zenner organized the McBee Binder Company. The firm began with a modest capital of $10,000, was housed in a rented building on West Union Street, and had a sales office in St.

Louis. Growth was slow but steady. From its original 3,600 square feet, by 1912 it had nearly four times that space and was adding more.

By 1916, the firm, clearly on its way up, was constructing a 40,000-square-foot structure at West Union and Smith Street. McBee provided the hands-on management of the plant; Zenner, appreciating the firm's potential, shifted his energies from his Court Street department store to the business affairs of the Binder Company, which by 1920 had become one of the major employers of the city, hiring women as well as men for factory jobs.

Other Small Industries

In the effort to diversify its economy and promote community growth, the village tried for a shirt factory. G. A. Welty, a Zanesville shirt manufacturer, expressed interest in setting up a plant in Athens on the condition that Athenians would raise the needed capital. The shirt company projected turning out two hundred dozen shirts a day, the production workers being women. The Athens investors—H. D. Henry, O. A. Sloane, and Harry G. Stalder—secured a property at 74 East State street and constructed a suitable building, now The Peddler and Packer. As production began in mid-May of 1906, talk was of 100 employees. The business took a different direction in 1907 after Welty sold his interests to Herchey-Rice, a Columbus, Ohio, firm that made overalls and work shirts. The new company proposed to shift all its shirt-making to Athens and was still thinking in terms of a production force of 75 to 100 women. The *Messenger* exulted over the prospects. In 1909 the bubble burst. The new owners secured a considerably cheaper labor force in Columbus, inmates of a Catholic home for incorrigible girls. Shortly after, the shirt factory closed down, and forty or so Athens women lost their jobs with no alternative employment available. Once more Athens investors found out-of-town "partners" to be a fickle lot. The local investors had been as little in control of their destiny as had their hourly employees.

Not every enterprise aspired to employ 100 workers, nor was the stability of a firm proportionate to its size. And Athens always had a host of small enterprises. In 1903 Athens Artificial Ice Company began operations, freeing Athens from dependency on ice harvested from nearby lakes and ponds or imported from northern communities. Financed by outside capital, the firm had its own water wells and electric and steam plants. Initially capable of producing twenty-five tons of ice a day, the firm marketed two-thirds of its product outside the community. Another industry produced soft drinks. Beginning as a partnership, the Star Mineral Water Works was incorporated in 1907. This soft-drink business took a different turn in 1917 when James Josten and others secured a license to manufacture Coca-Cola for sale in Southeast Ohio and adjacent West Virginia. A relatively exotic enterprise, the Luster Fought Company, manufactured and wholesaled flavoring extracts and family (patent) medicines. Burned out of its quarters in Albany, the firm relocated to Athens in 1911 to take advantage of Athens transportation facilities. Yet another small enterprise serving a strictly local market was J. E. Cross's Athens Dye Works.

Laundry service had traditionally been a cottage enterprise in which widows, deserted wives, and poor women washed other people's laundry either in their own home or at the home of their employer. In the late 1890s steam laundries emerged. The Athens Steam Laundry, W. S. Southerton owner-manager, came to public attention in 1919 in connection with a strike. Southerton's "laundry girls," complaining that in view of wartime and postwar inflation they could not live on $1.00 a day, asked for a hefty fifty percent pay raise. Southerton refused to budge, firing the striking women and recruiting a new labor force. This did not wholly end his problems, for a week or so later, he found himself in court pleading guilty to employing two under-age girls. The court imposed a "stiff" fine for his violation of child-labor laws.

One last enterprise was the Athens *Messenger*. As the lineal descendant of the *Mirror and Literary Gazette*, the *Messenger* was the oldest business enterprise in the area. While engaged in the business of gathering and disseminating the news, a service business, it necessarily operated a printing plant. Through the editorship of Charles Jennings, the paper had been printed on a hand-powered press, the last "power-source" being George Mathews, "a powerful Mulatto." The papers had been folded by hand. When Fred Bush took over the management in June 1896, the paper was located on the second floor of the old city-owned Market House. In 1905 the paper moved to the Law Building on West Washington. The building was expanded to house the printing plant, while the editorial and business offices crowded into the second floor. Later that year the paper added a weekly "Magazine Section" with many illustrations and a variety of feature stories: "Search for the North Pole," "The Sun's Corona," "Farm Notes," and "The Beef Trust."

Technology exerted a major impact on the paper. Introduction of a Simplex typesetting machine marked a big leap forward over dependence on compositors who set type by hand, a letter at a time. In 1905 the *Messenger* installed its first Mergenthaler linotype, making it feasible to produce a daily paper and thereby cover the news in greater detail; it also made possible a greatly increased volume of advertising by local merchants.

From the start, the publishing of the paper had been supplemented by a custom job-printing operation. In 1911 the *Messenger* split off its job-printing business, incorporating it as the Athens Printery Company. A. T. Lawhead and Edward Cooley held half the stock, with Lawhead in charge of the operation. The newspaper, for its part, introduced new, high-speed presses, and the first comic strips began to appear: first "Regular Fellows" and then "Jiggs," later renamed "Bringing up Father." No less important, at the start of 1914 the *Messenger* subscribed to the United Press Service, giving it access to the same news material from out-of-town and overseas sources that the largest papers enjoyed. Within the area the *Messenger* operated news bureaus at Nelsonville, Glouster, and Pomeroy.

By 1920 the *Messenger* was a mid-size business with some forty employees. Its linotype operators and press operators were skilled workers. At $25 to $35 a week, they were among the elite of the Athens labor force. Circulation stood at 9,400 papers daily.

Athens had had other papers—The *Athens County Gazette*, a Republican paper established in Glouster that moved to Athens in 1895, and the *Athens Journal*, a Democratic weekly. Founded as a Republican paper about 1870 by General T. F. Wildes, the *Journal* changed hands several times. In 1873 Robert W. Jones purchased it and converted it to a Democratic paper. For two decades Jones and Jennings of the *Messenger* traded insults in the manner of personal journalism of the post-war era. When Jones died, his daughter Jennie, later Mrs. A. J. Frame, continued the paper. In 1887 Thomas H. Craig acquired the *Journal* and still later, in 1899, Curtis V. Harris acquired an interest. As the *Messenger* became a daily, the *Journal* was less and less competitive. Bankrupt, the *Journal* suspended publication in 1912.

The fragile industrial base supporting Athens in 1900 had broadened markedly by 1920, although along the way there had of course been losses. Of the old businesses, the East Mill and the Athens Gas and Electric company did not survive. The School Furniture Company, which had seemed so promising in 1900, had moved out of town. So, too, had the Welty/Herchey-Rice shirt factory. The Athens Brick Company, after more than two decades, went out of business. Yet, in 1920 the Herrold Mill, rebuilt, was operating as White's Mill. F. C. Stedman's meat-packing operation was profitable; the Carpenter ice cream and dairy and the J. H. Cline ice cream and butter factory gave area farmers a ready market for their milk while creating year-round employment in the community. The Rardins had established a stable lumber and planing mill operation alongside their burial vault business. So, too, the Roberts family's Athens Lumber Company did a mill-work business. The Athens *Messenger* had expanded from a weekly to a daily while spinning off its job-printing business. Above all, there was the McBee Bindery, a firm solidly established by 1920.

KING COAL AND THE RAILROADS

King Cole of song was a merry old soul; King Coal of Athens County was a troubled soul. For Athens County, coal was the major product. Viewed from a distance, coal production soared—2,594,000 tons in 1900; 5,943,000 tons in 1910; and 6,872,000 in 1920. The reality was that output generally was in flux. In the early part of the century Athens County led the state in coal production, and through World War I coal remained a major export. On the other hand, the relationship between coal and Athens village was often tangential, anomalous.

In 1901 the *Messenger* outlined the coal industry in great detail—mine by mine. The coal market for the mines for which Nelsonville was the transportation hub was Toledo and the Great Lakes. The area was capable of exporting 750 cars daily, averaging 35 tons each. There was an equally active market in the buying and selling of coal lands. In the post–Civil War era, the mines had been small and the owners relatively numerous; at the turn of the century the mines were large and the ownership concentrated in a few hands. Thus, Thomas and Edward Johnson of Columbus sold 4,500 acres of coal land, including eight mines and four company stores, to the Pittsburg Coal Company. Clinton L. Poston, transplanted from Nelsonville to Athens, was busy buying coal lands. He was especially active in developing the coal lands in Sugar Creek.

But the times were out of joint. This was an era of robber barons, of trusts and monopolies and cartels, an era in which private ownership did not mean a competitive economy. The Hocking Valley Railroad, the Kanawha and Michigan, and the Ohio Central, the three north-south railroads serving the coal area, had common corporate owners. There were suggestions, eventually documented, that either the rail firms or their corporate owners owned coal properties as well and thus were free to manipulate coal output to maximize profits in the interest of the railroads.

In February 1902 the *Messenger* noted that area coal was not moving to market. There were 1,300 loaded cars standing idle on sidetracks. The rail firms averred they lacked the engines to move the coal to market. This situation was repeated time after time. In January 1903 the railroads blamed a national coal shortage on a lack of production. Editor Bush dissented. He charged that mine owners and coal dealers deliberately restricted production to force coal prices upward. There was solid evidence that the railroads on occasion refused rail service to mine owners who were not members of the cartel.

The manipulations of the railroads and mine owners had an adverse impact on the miners. In 1903 Continental Coal Company, owner of fourteen area mines, closed its mines, idling 2,100 miners. With the mines closed much of the summer of 1903, the workers soon exhausted their financial reserves. By fall they had at best "a hand-to-mouth existence." According to the *Messenger*, Continental could mine coal in its West Virginia properties less expensively than in Ohio. Hence, it had closed down its Hocking Valley and Sunday Creek mines. From a national economic viewpoint, this was a rational decision; to the Hocking Valley it brought extreme economic distress. To mitigate the distress, area miners proposed to share work in those mines still open with laid-off workers. The "facts" presented in the *Messenger* had to be weighed carefully by the public, for the *Messenger* also reported that West Virginia mines were closed and that owners were preparing to open new mines in the Hocking Valley. The leadership of the Ohio Mine Workers Association in Columbus claimed that there were too many mines in Ohio, too many miners.

In the midst of this turmoil and confusion, the first mines were opened in the Canaanville area. With mines at Canaanville to the east, Continental Coal to the north of the village, the Johnson mines on the far side of the Hocking, and the Luhrig mines west of town, the future of Athens as a coal center seemed made. Fred Bush predicted this would have "a telling effect on the business of the town."

It did, but not the impact Bush envisioned. By this time most of the coal mines were absentee owned. The profits flowed to Columbus or Pittsburgh or New York, to stockholders wherever they lived. The notable exception was C. L. Poston, who had relocated in Athens. At the start of the century Poston sold his mining properties to the J. P. Morgan syndicate, but he always retained his rights to the coal per se. As the Morgan group came under the assault of the anti-trust laws, Poston quietly acquired more and more coal lands, especially along Sugar Creek, while also serving as a director of the Sunday Creek Coal Company, one of the largest coal-mining firms in the nation. In 1905 Sunday Creek Coal Company established its general offices in the Campbell Building, consolidating its office personnel previously located at Glouster, Corning, and Nelsonville. Two of its mining engineers also moved their offices to Athens as did the payroll office. In 1911 Poston organized the Poston Consolidated Coal Company, a considerably smaller enterprise than his Sugar Creek or Sunday Creek enterprises. To protect himself, Poston had coal interests elsewhere as well. Sunday Creek Coal had major holdings in West Virginia, while Poston joined Calvary Morris, son of the one-time Congressman, in a major coal operation in Jefferson County, Ohio.

As the Canaanville Coal Company began operation, it too established its general offices in Athens. Indeed, by 1913, seven coal firms maintained offices in Athens. To this extent, Athens secured "a piece of the action." And the "piece" grew as new mines opened close to the community and miners made their homes in West End, accounting for roughly one-third of Athens population growth between 1900 and 1920. Recognizing the possibilities, D. A. Rardin and Dr. William Alderman publicized the need for fifty or more new rental houses suited to miners and their families.

Yet this was only one side of the story. In a fundamental sense the Athens community was usually on the periphery of the coal business without the power to direct the course of its development. This was especially evident in three crucial areas—the nature of the coal business, labor relations, and the relationships among the mine owners, the railroads, and the government.

Coal mining was initially labor intensive, and it seldom assured workers economic security. The per capita income of Ohio miners in 1905 was $268 a year, far less than a living wage. Miners worked an average of only two days a week. Given the harsh economic circumstances of the miners and given that many of them belonged to a union, the wonder is that strikes were not more frequent or more violent.

In 1906 the miners did strike. Machine-mining, which was replacing hand-pick mining, required a wide range of specialists who were not automatically interchangeable. Where a union could maintain a common front, it could stand up to the owners, if the latter did not have alternative non-union properties from which they might secure coal to fill contracts. In any event, the proliferation of work specialties made the negotiation of wage scales an enormously difficult task. Differences in the thickness of the coal seams affected the cost of production, and the varying qualities of the coal affected the selling price, further complicating wage negotiations. The strike of 1906 lasted some twelve weeks. In this case Sunday Creek Coal carried its striking workers on credit all but the last two weeks of the strike.

In November 1907 the miners at Luhrig struck. Circumstances had changed; the nation was in the midst of a business panic, and owners, short of cash, offered to pay workers in script issued by the Cincinnati clearing house. Allegedly the script was secured by $1.20 in securities for every dollar in script; but skeptical miners refused it; indeed, the script was not legal tender, and there was no legal obligation for either miners or businessmen to accept it, although at least two dozen Athens firms accepted it in payment for goods and services.

Mining in the Hocking Valley—including Sugar Creek, Sunday Creek, and Monday Creek—continued to be marked by repeated work stoppages. In some cases the miners struck; other times owners locked the workers out. At times mines were set afire. Again the strikes caused great hardships. The *Messenger* reported that "grim death stalks the district." The area gained notoriety.

In the conflict between miners and mine owners over wages, there was a factor the miners refused to confront. The Ohio miners had long argued they should be paid for all the coal they dug out; in fact, they were paid for the coal after it was screened—for the coal that had wide market acceptability. The remainder—pea and nut coal—was left to the owners to market for whatever they could get. From the owners' point of view, Ohio miners were prone to produce dirty coal; too much of the coal loaded and sent to the surface was unsalable and made Hocking Valley coal less desirable than West Virginia coal. Indeed, the 1914 strike was over this issue, and the owners agreed to pay for coal on a "mine-run" basis but at rates somewhat lower than they would have paid for screened coal. The miners had one point in their favor. Machine-mining produced far more fine coal—pea and nut grades—than did the hand-pick method. Yet the miners were expected to take a cut in wage because of this.

By 1915 the cumulative labor troubles, the closing of mines, and the apparent loss of market share prompted an exodus of miners from the Hocking Valley. The *Messenger* reported miners departing for West Virginia and Kentucky. Hocking Valley coal was on the ropes. Sunday Creek Coal Company was closing its company stores, confessing it could not compete with West Virginia coal. The Pere Marquette Railroad, a long-time purchaser of Hocking Valley coal, was switching to West Virginia coal, claiming a saving of 35 cents a ton; The Big Four Railroad was switching to Eastern Kentucky coal. With the future of Hocking Valley coal interests turning dark, Continental Coal elected voluntary receivership. Nicholas Monsarrat, Jr., one of the best coal engineers in Ohio, stepped in as its manager. Meanwhile, when the spring of 1916 revived the demand for coal nationwide, it seemed likely that West Virginia coal would again seek the East Coast market, leaving the Great Lakes market to be served once more by Hocking Valley coal. Before spring 1916 was out, miners and operators came to terms on wage rates that seemed likely to permit profitable operation of Hocking Valley mines. Mines began to re-open. By October the railroads were complaining that speculators were holding loaded cars on sidings, hoping thereby to profit from rapidly escalating coal prices.

As the United States entered World War I, the nation's economy was stretched as never before and neither the federal government nor the private owners of the coal-mining or the railroad industries were equipped to meet the crisis. In August 1917 President Wilson began setting the price of coal state-by-state. Other products, too, became subject to price controls. By early fall 1917 there were acute shortages of coal. Athens Brick Company partially closed down when its coal order was shipped to Bucyrus, Ohio. Once more, Hocking Valley mines closed because they could not secure shipping, while the railroads hauled West Virginia coal through the valley en route to Great Lakes ports. At the same time the Hocking Valley Railroad had loaded cars standing on every available siding. To supply Athens City with coal, the traction company, which had several cars of its own, hauled coal into Central Avenue. In January 1918 a severe cold wave further impeded the movement of coal while greatly increasing the demand for home use. Governor Cox's efforts to get coal moving were rebuffed by federal officials as unwarranted interference. Cox's analysis—that the coal shortage was owing chiefly to mismanagement by railroad officials—was on target. Notwithstanding the difficulties in moving coal, Athens County did produce coal. For 1917 Athens County, with a production of 6.3 million tons, stood second in the state. For July 1918–June 1919, it again turned out 6 million tons, finishing third in the state.

The war over, labor troubles resumed. In 1919, the United Mine Workers mounted a nationwide coal strike, idling 8,000 miners in Athens County alone. Athens city's place was ambiguous. By 1920 at least eight coal operators maintained offices in Athens; management decisions were made elsewhere. The livelihoods of some 350 persons living in the city were directly connected to mining. Yet the city escaped the violence and distress that out-of-town mining communities experienced. The mines were the sites of the violence, and the 350 mine-related workers formed a small fraction of the city's work force.

Railroads and Anti-trust

The interest of the railroads in coal was two-fold. First, approximately 24 percent of the nation's coal output was consumed by the steam railroads, which had to have a stable supply of coal. Second, nearly the whole of the Hocking Valley Railroad's business consisted of the transportation of coal. For their own protection, the railroads were driven to control the supplies of coal.

The ties between the railroads and the mine owners gave Athenians a front row seat in observing the operation of anti-trust law. Two levels of law operated, state and federal. Ohio corporation law expressly forbade railroads either to own or operate mines, although a mining company might operate a railroad, if it chose. Federal law was expressed in the Interstate Commerce Act of 1887 and the Sherman Anti-trust Act of 1890, which prohibited monopoly and business practices in restraint of trade. In 1900 the federal courts were still defining the Sherman Act. That N. D. Monsarrat, Jr., was manager of the Sunday Creek Coal Company while his father was president of the Hocking Valley Railroad suggested a cozy community of interest between the two firms, yet the situation did not violate the Sherman Act itself. The nature of permissible conduct under federal law was clarified by the Hepburn Act of 1906, which made it illegal for a railroad to own coal properties.

Tracing the enforcement of state and federal anti-trust laws against the railroads operating in the Hocking Valley is often confusing. The laws asked the railroads to put at risk their access to the fuel they required to operate their trains, and, in the case of the coal railroads, like the Hocking Valley, put at risk their access to their principal cargo—coal. Similarly, the laws left the coal mining firms in the lurch. They no longer had assurance that a railroad would haul their coal to market. This was no mere theoretical possibility. In 1912 the independent coal operators, miners, and business interests of the Hocking Valley area alleged that railroads charged lower rates for Kentucky and West Virginia coal than for Hocking Valley coal, depriving the latter of markets they had once enjoyed. Still more to the point, the refusal of the Hocking Valley Railroad to serve New York Coal's mines prompted the latter to bring suit in federal court, asking $250,000 in damages. The coal company alleged that the Hocking Valley and the Toledo and Ohio Central declined to serve any but the mines of Continental Coal Co. About the same time, the Norfolk and Western and the Chesapeake and Ohio railroads issued orders prohibiting the delivery of West Virginia coal to Toledo or other Great Lakes ports, an order illustrating the power of a railroad to unilaterally affect the coal market. These latter orders, of course, operated greatly to the advantage of Ohio coal producers.

In view of the economic imperatives the railroads dodged full-faith compliance with the anti-trust laws as long as they could. And they were attacked over and over again in both Ohio and federal courts. Official investigations were launched and dragged on. A 1914 decision of an Ohio court gave the Lake Shore, the Hocking Valley, and the Chesapeake and Ohio sixty days in which to divest themselves of shares in Sunday Creek Coal. To retain a degree of control, they sought to sell the shares to a syndicate of mine operators led by J. S. Jones of Newark, Ohio, and Chicago, Illinois. After the deal fell through, Jones acquired Sunday Creek for himself, closed all but a half dozen of the mines, then re-outfitted ten of the most productive, better preparing them to compete profitably.

The gambit didn't work, for when the railroads finally cut Sunday Creek Coal loose, they did so in ways that saddled it with $6,000,000 in mortgage bonds, a debt it could not liquidate. Within a month Sunday Creek Coal's creditors were in court seeking its liquidation. Nearly two years later the U.S. circuit court took jurisdiction away from state courts and bankruptcy courts and gave a New York firm the first claim against the coal company's assets. In July 1918 Sunday Creek Coal was auctioned off. The firm that was auctioned off was, in law, the Sunday Creek Coal Co. of New Jersey. It was bought by the newly organized Sunday Creek Coal Company (Ohio) which also acquired the assets of the Buckeye Coal and Railway Company and the Ohio Land and Railway Company. The new firm possessed several hundred houses, a large store, two mines, a hospital and theater at San Toy—a property considered the most valuable mine property in Ohio. The reincarnated Sunday Creek Coal Company seemed to have a promising future under its owner, Clinton L. Poston. For the moment the railroads had lost their ability to control Hocking Valley Coal production.

Oil and Gas

The possibility of quick fortunes from exploiting area gas and oil often beckoned to local interests but as often betrayed them. As the *Messenger* phrased it, the village experienced a spell of "oil excitement" in 1909 as local, Columbus, and Parkersburg interests took leases on land east, north, and west of Athens. A hastily organized Athens Oil and Gas Exchange did "a lively business" in leases and stocks in oil and gas properties. Falling in line, the *Messenger* began printing a column of oil stock prices in April 1909. There was sufficient promise of a profitable oil field in Bremen, well to the north of Athens. A second field in nearby Waterloo township drew attention of the Ohio Oil Company as well as a variety of New Marshfield investors and E. C. Logan of Athens. Interest in Strouds Run, where some marginal wells had been developed at the end of the 1890s, revived. Extensive leasing occurred with the expectation of drilling to follow. The whole episode can be summarized in two words: expectations unfulfilled.

Much the same can be said of the flurry of interest in gas wells. Gas there was. The problem was that the supply did not prove dependable. In 1905, for example, in Glouster the pressure in the wells declined; one well played out completely and the community was forced to convert back to coal for fuel. In Marshfield and Albany there were substantial gas strikes. In 1911 Athens became drawn in as Sunnyside Gas Company—owned by a combination of Marietta, Glouster, and Athens men—brought gas into the city along East State Street, took over the holdings of the Athens Heat, Light and Power Company, and supplied the Hardwood Finish Company and the Athens Brick Company with gas. Early in 1912 the firm was bought out by Marietta and Hocking Valley Gas and Oil. In August 1912 the Athens Gas and Oil Co. reported "a strong gasser"—a two-million-cubic-feet-a-day well at Factory. For a brief time gas was found in commercially profitable quantitites, but the output was not sustained, and Athens businessmen did not make a killing.

THE LABOR FORCE IN 1920

A review of the Athens labor force in 1920 puts the city's economy in perspective. In quantitative terms Athens labor force in 1920 numbered 2,224, roughly 75 percent were white and male; 20 percent were white females; not quite five percent were blacks.

Changes in the character of the labor force after 1900 were uneven. Because of the changes in the categories used by the census and the appearance of new kinds of employment, comparisons are not precise. Even so, several generalizations are possible.

First, by 1920 Athens had become modestly involved in the coal industry. Whereas only four persons were expressly identified with the industry in 1900, the 1920 census identifies at least 306 miners, a substantial addition to the labor force. While the coal literally and figuratively fueled other industries, the coal left the Athens area, and, except as it generated income for the railroads that hauled it away, it had not, as had once been predicted so confidently, turned Athens into another Birmingham.

Second, white-collar occupations such as the professions, managers and proprietors, and clerical and salespersons increased handsomely. Increasingly, enterprises owned by one person or group of persons were managed by others, resulting in a substantial proliferation of managers, overseers, and superintendents. Athens now had a few firms that required foremen to supervise their labor forces. In the management of business, owners increasingly employed male specialists—bookkeepers, accountants, and cashiers—to monitor and record the financial transactions. Males were not employed, however, as secretaries, typists, stenographers, or receptionists. Although still primarily individually owned or partnerships, retail businesses had expanded to the point that numbers of salespersons were required; 81 males claimed that job description, and another 42 were "clerks." Grocery stores and the department stores, in particular, sought such help.

The 1920 Census distinguished a category of employment termed public services—officialdom. There had always been public officials, many of whom lived in Athens, the seat for the village, the township, and county. They were more numerous in 1920 than earlier for many posts that had been part-time and reimbursed by fee-for-service had become full-time and salaried. So, too, the number of persons directly responsible for safeguarding the peace increased. Athens City now had four policemen—two for daytime, two for nighttime. But Athens was also home to township marshals, the sheriff, and a number of private watchmen.

Paradoxically, between 1900 and 1920 the number of common laborers declined while the number of operatives increased. The most probable explanation is that as jobs became specialized, workers acquired a degree of expertise on the job and thus passed from the category of common laborer to one or another of the categories of semi-skilled operatives. As Athens became a city, it was not overwhelmed by an industrial proletariat. Employment patterns reflect an economy that was more commercial than industrial. Even so, it was an economy in which coal mining, the McBee Bindery, and the University had been the major elements in stimulating growth.

The occupational distribution of black males in 1920 suggests why the black community was shrinking. More than a half century after emancipation, seventy percent were employed either in service work or as operatives. Their Baptist pastor, Charles Hart, was the only professional man in the black community. Four men claimed proprietorships and three held white-collar employment. But far more worked as bellboy, janitor, porter, shoeshiner, and waiter. All too few had found a niche in Athens.

Their wives and daughters fared no better. One black woman managed a hotel; another taught school. Most of the other black women earned a living in a personal-service occupation washing or cleaning up or otherwise seeking to make somebody else comfortable.

The 463 white females in the labor force represented a doubling of the number of women in the Athens labor market in two decades. But this is misleading in part, for in 1900 the female labor force included a substantial number of girls; in 1920 girls under sixteen were no longer present. While the numbers of women engaged in professional occupations increased enormously, women were still excluded from the professions of doctor, lawyer, clergyman. The overwhelming majority of professional women were teachers, some of them at Ohio University. In the business world, women were gaining a degree of independence in that they worked away from home under the direction of non-family members. As salespersons, they interacted with the general public. Some women still relied on the traditional female skills to secure employment as dressmakers, seamstresses, and milliners, but McBee Bindery offered factory employment to women and several women held positions of forelady.

A measure of how far women had come is seen in the role of domestic servant. In 1870 domestics lived in their employer's home, and many were girls under age eighteen. Aside from teaching, domestic service had been almost the only employment available. In 1920 only one-fifth of the working women were in domestic and personal service. Most of those who were in domestic service lived at home, going out during the day to their jobs and returning home at night. Such work had become specialized: the women were employed as waitresses, cooks, dishwashers, laundresses. There were, in fact, approximately equal numbers of women teachers and personal service workers.

Athenians may still have thought that woman's place was in the home, but in 1920 close to one-third of the women ages twenty to twenty-four were employed. For single women the rate was close to 50 percent. And the labor force rate remained on the order of 20 percent for women age twenty-five to forty. Probably half of the children born in Athens in the 1920s had mothers who had at one time worked in the labor force.

OHIO UNIVERSITY: THE ELLIS YEARS

When the new century began, Ohio University occupied the enlarged College Green and was housed in five structures—The College Edifice, East, West, the Chapel, and Ewing. Although, the university's enrollment in fall term 1900 was on the order of 400, fewer than 100 students were in the four-year degree program. There were 20 full-time faculty. Twenty years later all was changed. College buildings stood on the far side of the streets bounding the College Green. Fall-term enrollments had pushed above 1,000; summer term enrolled over 2,000. The full-time faculty numbered 74. If not entirely the result of the leadership of President Alston Ellis, this growth had been guided by him.

The growth of Ohio University had two components. The transcendent feature was the university's maturing as an educational institution—the initiation of new academic programs and the professionalization of its faculty which accompanied the growth in student enrollments. The other component was the changed role of the university as a force in the Athens economy. In this respect the expansion of the university's academic programs, especially the founding of the State Normal School, the regularization of adequate state subsidies for operating expenses, and the beginnings of a dormitory system had a critical impact on the university's place in the city's economy.

Alston Ellis

Alston Ellis succeeded the retiring president Charles W. Super in July 1901 and would serve nearly twenty years. Long years of experience in Ohio public education as principal, superintendent, and a member of the Ohio Board of School Examiners, along with five years as president of the Colorado College of Agriculture equipped Ellis to deal with problems of curriculum, buildings, and securing recognition for the university. Once on the job, he revealed himself to be a bit of a martinet, a man quite capable of standing at a window in the College Edifice, watch in hand, to make certain that faculty arrived at their offices by 8:00 A.M. and did not depart before 4:00 P.M. Furthermore, he proved inordinately vain, a man who wore "more medals than a stallion at a county fair." Courting flattery, he was heard to say: "I'll take my taffy now and less epitaffy after I'm gone." A spin-off of Ellis's predilection for display was the introduction of caps and gowns and academic processions at graduation. For himself, Ellis chose a gown of green and white. If Ellis exhibited a goodly measure of human foibles, they were just that—foibles. He proved to be an able administrator, a builder.

The Normal School

Given his long ties to public education, Ellis perceived the need to expand the number of trained teachers available to Ohio schools and to upgrade teacher training. This was a big order. The university had offered teacher training since 1886.

But what had been a step forward in the mid-1880s was no longer adequate in 1901. Within weeks of assuming the presidency, Ellis had the trustees pledged to the creation of a fully-equipped and qualified normal school supported by a state tax levy. The Seese Bill, sponsored by representative Charles F. Seese of Summit County and Aaron Price of Athens, provided for founding normal schools at Miami and Ohio University. Senator David H. Moore pushed the bill through the Ohio Senate, and in March 1902 the bill became law. The act assured Ohio University an additional $35,000 a year in income and the prospect of additional enrollments. For his part, Ellis spent much time in Columbus lobbying for the measure. Jubilant townsmen, students, and faculty met him at the train on his return from Columbus. A mass meeting honored him with band music, the singing of university songs, and speeches by local luminaries. The ecstatic Judge J. Perry Wood declared this new state subsidy worth more than a million-dollar endowment. He predicted enrollments would double in two years. Fred Bush editorially made the point that the whole community stood to gain because the new normal school students would spend thousands of dollars in the city.

To flesh out the Normal School, a variety of additions to the curriculum were introduced: programs of teacher-training for the elementary and secondary grades as well as training for school administrators. These programs had to be structured to serve students who entered the school with no more than a common school education as well as those who were high school graduates. In practice, the normal school students took many courses in common with the four-year college students, yet administratively there were two roughly parallel institutions, the Normal School directed initially by Dean Henry G. Williams and the Liberal Arts College directed by Edwin Watts Chubb. In 1911 the Normal School curriculum was further expanded by departments in agriculture and domestic science, programs designed to train teachers who could help youth in rural schools make the most of their rural environment.

The attention lavished on the Normal School stimulated the college itself to grow and expand its offerings. By 1912 courses in stenography, typewriting, and accounting were pulled together and a certificate was granted for completion of a two-year commercial course. The baccalaureate programs were realigned. The Ph.B., Bachelor of Philosophy, degree was dropped; the Liberal Arts College, henceforth, awarded only the A.B. and B.S. degrees. The baccalaureate degree provided for an academic major requiring twenty semester hours in one subject and a total of 120 hours for graduation. Here were the essential elements of the twentieth-century academic program.

The university also initiated a music school that maintained public visibility through its performances. In 1906, led by James P. McVay and featuring a chorus of seventy-five, the school presented Balfe's *The Bohemian Girl*. Three years later, 1909, the major offering was *Il Trovatore*, the first effort to produce grand opera on campus. When the college presented Mendelssohn's "Elijah" oratorio at the Methodist Church, the *Messenger* hailed it as the greatest musical event in the history of the college.

A unique aspect of the university's work was its extension program. The program had begun well before Ellis came to Athens. Individual faculty, having established that there was a clientele, went to outlying communities weekly to give instruction. Ellis's view of the program was ambivalent. At first he embraced it. Clement Martzolff, who had roots in the area and a facility for reaching local people, had charge. Among other places, the program reached Logan, Nelsonville, and Pomeroy. In 1914 there were requests for forty-four courses. When officials at other colleges questioned the academic integrity of such off-campus instruction, Ellis reconsidered, and the program was discontinued. But here was the forerunner of the Ohio University off-campus instructional program.

Closely tied to the Normal School was the Summer School. Summer term had been instituted in 1892 as a private venture by professors Eli Dunkle and David J. Evans. By the time Ellis came on the scene, the program was well established. Summer 1901 enrolled 102 students; by 1920, there were 2,163. A program begun to supplement faculty incomes and utilize university facilities an additional six weeks ended by drawing more students than any other program, albeit for only six weeks. It provided a real service in upgrading the educational preparation of those actively engaged in public school classrooms.

Inauguration of the Model School enabled normal school students to gain hands-on classroom experience, practice-teaching. Initially located in the basement of Ewing Hall, the school was moved to Ellis Hall. In an arrangement with the Athens School Board, the Model School was assigned an area of the village from which it enrolled students, in effect giving the community a third elementary school, cost free. The university's Model School enrolled roughly 320 students.

Bricks and Mortar

The existing buildings of 1900 could not accommodate all the new programs nor the additional students. In 1902, even before the state legislature had appropriated the money, Frank L. Packard, a Columbus architect, drew plans for a normal school building. Built in three sections, the main unit facing University Terrace was completed in 1904, the north wing in 1907 and the south wing a year later. Taking credit for the new building, Ellis persuaded the trustees to give it his name. A tradition was born—to name new buildings for men still alive and in office. The long-dead Manasseh Cutler had to continue marking time until 1914 before his contributions would be recognized. Rufus Putnam waited even longer.

Next came a separate library building. The existing 16,000-volume collection had been squeezed into a third-floor room of the College Edifice. Through the personal efforts of General Grosvenor, Andrew Carnegie contributed $30,000 for the yellow-brick building facing Park Place, dedicated in 1905. Carnegie stipulated that free use of the library be assured "to all Athens' citizens, school teachers, and school children." In 1913 Carnegie advanced additional funds to expand the already overcrowded building.

Bigger enrollments required new dormitories. The mores of the day required a protective, home-like environment for women students. Accordingly, in 1906 the Margaret Boyd dormitory was constructed at the southeast corner of the College Green, housing 88 women. In 1908 the University purchased the Ladies' Hall, remodeled and expanded it to house 100 women. In 1916 the building was named Solomon Howard Hall. Finally, the university undertook to build the central section of Jacob Lindley Hall. Opened in 1917, it housed 120 women. The wings had to wait until after World War I.

East and West, built in the 1830s to house students, came in for extensive repairs and remodeling, but only after the trustees were dissuaded from tearing down East to make room for the Carnegie Library. By August 1907 the two historic structures were being remodeled. Internal partitions were replaced or moved and verandahs, three decks high, were built across the front of each, "an ornament" said to add to their usefulness. When the remodeling was completed, East was occupied by the new Department of Civil Engineering, while West offered practice rooms for the School of Music. Both buildings continued to house some male students.

With an eye to the future, the trustees began buying property in the vicinity of the College Green. Thus, it acquired the Putnam property on President Street. It was especially interested in acquiring properties on East Union, South Court, Park Place, and University Terrace. Of special importance for future expansion, property on South College adjacent to Howard Hall and the Johnson Welch property on University Terrace were acquired. Subsequently, the Welch house was moved back from the street, clearing the land adjacent to the street for the Agricultural and Domestic Science Building. For a time, the Welch house was used by students ill with contagious diseases.

In 1912 the trustees began the structure now called Gordy Hall to house the Model Training School. Sensing the importance of the sciences, President Ellis called for a Science Hall to be located on President Street and to house courses in chemistry and physics. The building was dedicated in 1911. Not the least of the University's additions was the purchase of Ellis's home at 23 South Congress Street to be the presidential home, henceforth provided free of charge.

The expansion of the physical facilities posed another problem. The College Edifice, East, and West had been heated room by room with fireplaces, a method no longer efficient or economical. At this point, 1906, a central heating plant for the university was built. Subsequently, the University began the first of its heating tunnels. By 1911 the University not only heated all its buildings from the central plant but was preparing to produce its own electric power in 1913. Such progress was not without its critics. The heating plant belched smoke "drenching nearby residents with flakes of soot." Growth of the university's physical plant necessitated a staff to operate it. To run the heating plant required three stationary engineers; to care for the buildings, six janitors, three carpenters and painters; and, reflecting a gentler, more innocent age, a single night watchman.

Funding, Status, Reputation

Repeatedly, Ellis had to deal with the questions of Ohio University's role as a state institution. The view that Ohio could afford but one comprehensive state university persisted. Before President Ellis could persuade the legislature to furnish an adequate level of operating support, he had to confront the hostility of the Ohio State University. In 1906, the legislature considered the Lybarger Bill, which would have limited Ohio University and Miami University to teacher education. Up in arms in opposition to the Lybarger Bill, 150 Athenians gathered at the courthouse to protest. On hearing that the bill had been defeated, the village had "a grand jollification," parade, and bonfire.

The Eagleson Act (1906), however, which limited Ohio and Miami to normal school programs, the liberal arts, and the master's degree, passed. The Ohio State University would be the comprehensive university for the state. Ohio and Miami would be funded at the rate of .015 mill for normal school education and .025 mill for liberal arts education. The Sleeper and Seese Acts were repealed; given the value of the property on the state's tax duplicate, Ohio University could now anticipate a certain annual income of nearly $86,000, a grand leap forward.

This was not the end of the issue. Ohio State renewed the contest in 1914 as it sought to become the University of Ohio. In this effort it had the support of Henry S. Pritchett of the Carnegie Foundation for the Advancement of Teaching. In Pritchett's judgment Ohio University and Miami University were not "real universities." Ohio was a mixture of college, normal school, and academy. Miami was deemed "a fairly good college" with the same mixture of normal school and academy. Ohio bristled, pointing out that it had come legitimately by its name a half century before the Columbus institution was founded. This issue withered away in the course of World War I.

The University got unwelcome publicity from other sources. First, there was concrete evidence that neither Augustus J. Frame, the university treasurer, nor Leonidas M. Jewett, the university auditor, had performed their duties in a systematic, competent manner. When Frame, "one of the best known and most highly respected men in Athens County" died early in 1906, his accounts were short by over $7,000. Worse, Frame had kept his personal funds and those of the university in the same cash drawer. In the investigation that followed, it also became clear that auditor Jewett had "made no pretense towards keeping any books and he has no check whatever upon the Treasurer." Indeed, the business affairs of the university had been conducted in a most haphazard manner. Debts had been incurred without regard to the funds currently or soon to be available with which to pay expenses. Funds had been expended without reference to the purpose for which they had been appropriated.

Nor did the university's trustees help the school's image. The *Messenger* reported a hue and cry regarding "graft and conflicts of interest" among the trustees. The objection was to trustees who were also on the university's payroll as employees. Trustees who lived in Athens had long engendered suspicion that they ran the university to benefit themselves and their friends. They compounded the university's difficulties in 1906 when they failed to open bids of several contractors in a public meeting, preferring instead to announce only the winning bid. Nor did President Ellis enhance his stature when, after a four-week tour of eastern universities to study their practices, he returned to Athens and appointed a committee to gather squirrels with which to populate the College Green in imitation of Harvard Yard.

Overall, Ellis was on the right track. He instituted sound business practices. One innovation was the appointment of a purchasing agent, a move that gave the university a firmer grip on its expenditures and curbed the freedom of department chairs to initiate purchases on their own. The Summer School was taken over by the university, while the university abandoned the operation of its own bookstore.

The office of Alumni Secretary was created, an office that would gradually generate modest financial support for the institution. In 1913 Ellis created the office of dean of women to deal with the housing, personal, and social problems of the women students. The office went to Irma Voigt, who would fill it until 1949.

The Ellis era ended without warning. During the war years, Ellis had hinted at retiring but had been persuaded by the trustees to remain at the helm. Then, on Sunday evening, November 14, 1920, having gone to church as usual, he returned home and suffered a fatal heart attack. To the trustees, Ellis had been a superb achiever. He had been "at his best when presenting a case before the legislature." He was "logical and forceful." According to historian Hoover, he was "at his worst when dealing with his faculty." Thirty years later, the memory of Ellis still stirred controversy in faculty circles.

By 1920 Ohio University played a significant role in the Athens economy. The university's subsidy from the state grew from $55,232 in 1901 to $170,919 in 1910 and $186,000 for 1919–20. The faculty constituted an important segment of the community's professional class. The thousand-plus students the school drew to Athens in 1920 stimulated sales for local merchants, generated incomes for local landladies and eateries, and created employment for those who staffed the dormitories and dining halls and maintained the buildings and grounds. The students also provided a secondary labor force for the town, performing many of the townspeople's odd jobs. At last the University was beginning to fill the vision of Manasseh Cutler and Rufus Putnam. Students, faculty, and staff constituted one-sixth of the Athens population in 1920. The University had become a major economic force within the city. Ohio University and Athens owed much to Ellis.

In MOVING TOWARD an urban economy, Athens city had fortuitously developed a diversified economic base. In processing the timber, milk, beef, pork, poultry, and grain of area farmers, it provided the rural areas with a steady, accessible market for their goods, while creating a base for several village firms. The State Hospital, continuing to grow, also brought stability to the Athens-area economy since its patient load and its staff remained independent of fluctuations in the nation's business cycle. Ohio University had been an especially dynamic factor in the community's growth, as the state assumed a more realistic position in funding the operating expenses of the school, and because, in championing teacher education, it created a new, rapidly growing student clientele. The development of mining in Athens Township also spurred the city's growth, first through the number of workers employed in mine-related jobs, and secondly, through the additional persons employed in Athens who produced goods and services for the area's mining communities. The town's experience with industry had been mixed, but in McBee Bindery it had a locally owned and managed industry with a potential for growth. The community took satisfaction that it had caught up with Nelsonville in population.

Above all, the enhanced population and the level of affluence sustained by the diverse economy and the growing university had operated to fashion an urbane society.

12

An Urbane Society: 1900–1920

As ATHENS MOVED into the twentieth century, it developed a degree of urbanity. To be sure, the community was segmented. The black community continued to shrink, while the university student community exploded in numbers. The city's own youth developed, for the first time, a sub-culture centered about the high school. As in earlier generations, the church was a vital organization in the lives of many members of the community, but there was also evidence that some members of the community could not, did not practice the values endorsed by the community's mainstream, producing a wayward community. The increasingly secular character of society was apparent in the stresses that often shattered interpersonal relationships.

THE BLACK COMMUNITY

Ironically, as Athens progressed from village to city, adding substantially to its population, its black population declined. The "colored" population, to use the phrase of the day, had, in fact, peaked at 317 in 1890, dropped to 279 in 1900, and stood at 220 in 1920. This is not a subject the white community took note of. The community's blacks, for the most part, were of the underclass, and except when blacks got in trouble with the law, they remained largely invisible.

In 1920 the black community showed signs of stress. There were 57 children under 15 years of age and 24 elders 60 years and over. These dependent classes relied for their support on 43 males in the prime of life—ages 25 to 50. In addition, the black community included 15 youths age 15 to 24 who were breaking into the labor force and 7 men in their fifties who were winding down, persons who could look after themselves. Those males in the prime of life had a considerable burden, made heavier by their inability to secure professional, mercantile, or managerial employment.

On the other hand, black males found the marriage market was favorable: there was a considerable excess of females in the age range 15 to 24. This may reflect the migration of young men to other communities in search of work; it may also reflect the dislocations produced by World War I. Among the males 25 through 66, there was also an excess of women. The excess of adult males resulted in a rise in female-headed households, from 27 percent in 1900 to 33 percent in 1920. Furthermore, the number of black householders whose wives had entered the labor market had also increased: 1 in 1900, 6 in 1920. Adult black women often had to support themselves and their children as best they could.

At a time that Jim Crow laws elsewhere discriminated against blacks in access to public transportation and public accommodations, there is no evidence of an overt campaign in Athens to discourage or harass the blacks. But nothing in the combination of forces that sparked the growth of the Athens community as a whole offered the blacks an inducement to remain in Athens, much less to urge other blacks to come live in Athens. The blacks responded by migrating away from Athens.

THE TEEN COMMUNITY

If adults had problems, so did teens. Beyond 1900, the transition from child to adult became more complex, although not necessarily more protracted in duration. An eighth-grade education generally sufficed for a youngster entering the adult world in 1870; not so in 1900. A fellow might secure employment in 1900 on the strength of having eight years of schooling, but such an education would not support continuing upward mobility in later years, and even in 1900 the professional, business, and managerial world favored youth who worked easily with words and numbers, who had a familiarity with the basic sciences. Employment, though, was deferred to the late teens. Programs were needed, then, to bridge the gap.

One expression of the teen culture was the Boy Scout movement. In a carefully orchestrated move, the *Messenger*, in July 1915, endorsed the scout movement editorially as an outlet for the energies of exuberant boys and a deterrent of delinquency. With Europe at war, it seemed important to disavow any connection between the scouts and the military. The next day the paper announced that at a meeting at the Commercial Club, five patrols had been organized. In the course of the next two years, the movement took hold. By September 1917, Athens had its third scout troop. The interlocking ties of Athens institutions is further illustrated in the sponsorship of the troops—one by the Presbyterians, one by the Methodists. That the movement was maturing became apparent with the awarding of the Eagle rank to Floyd Brown in February 1919. By the year's end, Gordon Bush, Robert Jones, and William Moler had also attained the Eagle rank.

The rise of a teen culture is particularly evident in the appearance of the first substantial generation of middle-class youth who attended high school, who spent most of their waking hours away from home but in the company of other youths in a school environment. It is during these years that the term "adolescent" came into use, and "adolescence" became a recognized phase in the transition from childhood to adulthood. In these circumstances, the high school became the organizer and focal point of the social and cultural life of Athens young people: the athletic contests, the school plays, the musicals, the informal games, and the infatuations, crushes, and romances. It should be kept in mind that this teen culture was still a class phenomenon, for only a minority of the youth completed high school.

THE UNIVERSITY STUDENT COMMUNITY

Student life at Ohio University took a distinct turn after 1900. The decades-old literary societies, the Athenian and the Philomathean, continued their annual competitions. Partisan members attended and whooped it up, so that Ewing Auditorium was "comfortably filled." Nonetheless, student interest drifted elsewhere. The "Joe College" spirit prevailed in all-night clashes between freshmen and sophomores. In 1907, for example, the class flag was hoisted atop Ewing; a hapless freshman was tied up and painted a cardinal red. Juniors, entering the fray, mediated by painting some sophomores white.

The focus of college social life shifted to the fraternities and sororities. At the turn of the century, there were three venerable fraternities—Beta Theta Pi, Delta Tau Delta, and Phi Delta Theta—and one sorority, Pi Beta Phi. Other Greek societies emerged as the student population grew—Chi Omega, Alpha Gamma Delta, and Alpha Xi Delta. Fraternities began to acquire their own houses, beginning with Beta Theta Pi, who first rented a house on South Court, then in 1912 bought a thirteen-room home of their own; three years later Phi Delta Theta began construction of a fraternity house on West Mulberry. The proliferation of sororities brought uniform rules for rushing. The sororities bound town and gown together to a degree as townswomen, acting as patrons of the sororities, entertained the young women in their homes.

Women students pursued a social-cultural life of their own aside from sororities. In 1913 they organized a women's league. The power among the women's organizations was the YWCA, committed "to promote growth in Christian character and service" among the coeds. The young women also organized their own annual skit-shows to raise money for women's scholarships.

Housing women students remained a particular concern. Despite the acquisition of Howard Hall and the building of Boyd and Lindley, many women lived in private residences. In 1914 President Ellis took note that Athens landladies often regarded their coed tenants as troublesome. The young women bothered landladies with minor problems, failed to take care of their rooms, and were not "seasonable" in the hours they kept. All too often the landladies were annoyed with the young men who hung around of an evening. To deal with problems related to women's housing, the university created the position of dean of women in 1913. Dean Irma Voigt saw two dimensions to resolving the problem: first, the need of an "accredited" list of rooming accommodations suitable for coeds, and second, a set of rules of conduct for the young women. As early as 1910 a faculty committee met with women students, urging them to be more discreet when in the company of fellows. On learning of this, the fellows reacted angrily, painting a variety of slogans on the walls of Boyd Hall: "Hands Off," "Touch Me Not," and "Back, Base Man." Ultimately, women students were subjected to regulations that set curfews that kept them off the streets at night. Nor could they entertain young men in their rooms or go motoring with young men.

As one group of students felt the need for institutionalizing the spirit of brotherhood and sisterhood, another group, espousing the ideal of independence and referring to themselves as "barbarians," organized the Ohio Union. They proposed to have a reading room. Otherwise, a campus YMCA served male students and the college community generally. Early on, the young Thomas Hoover headed a student employment office, matching students who wanted part-time work with townspeople seeking students to care for their lawns, gardens, furnaces, and horses. In fall 1913 the YMCA took over the employment office and maintained a list of available student housing.

Allied to the YMCA and the YWCA was the Student Volunteer Movement (SVM). Organized in fall 1911, the Ohio chapter encouraged and supported students desiring to become foreign missionaries. In 1913 the *Messenger* reported that a number of Ohio University students were headed for work in foreign missions.

Although many students identified with the YMCA, the YWCA, or the SVM, the mood of the campus was increasingly secular. Students did not rush to attend daily chapel. In fact, chapel attendance was no longer required; perhaps one-sixth to one-quarter of the students attended. With student enrollments approaching the seating capacity of Ewing Auditorium, President Ellis abandoned daily chapel altogether.

Student life found other forms of expression besides the literary societies, fraternities and sororities, and sports. While townspeople enjoyed their dances on Court Street, students focused on the annual Junior Prom. Indeed, they thought the new gym was just the place for the dance of the year; the trustees demurred, and the dance was held at the smaller club rooms of the Athenian Club. With sixty couples or so attending, the students were adequately provided for. As with some of the town dances, nothing would do for the 1910 Prom but an out-of-town ensemble from Columbus. For their part, seniors experiencing the first pangs of nostalgia as they prepared to depart their alma mater, were solicited to support a memorial to their class. Hence, students contributed to a campus gate at the foot of College Street (1912), a clock for the Cutler Hall cupola (1914), and a contribution toward the Cutler Hall chimes (1917).

Despite the entrance of John Newton Templeton and Edward Roye to the university in the early nineteenth century, Ohio University had few black students in attendance thereafter, and it was 1912 before Martha Jane Hunley enrolled, becoming the first black woman student. Although she claimed Wilmington, Ohio, as her hometown, in fact, her father was an Athens barber. Barred from college dormitories, Hunley lived in a private home on South High Street. She majored in English and literature and minored in home economics, graduating summa cum laude in 1916. Subsequently she married Charles Blackburn, son of John R. Blackburn, Ohio University's first black trustee, 1884–1891. Martha Jane Hunley-Blackburn devoted most of her working years to teaching home economics.

International Students

Although most of the student body came from Southeast Ohio, the university often had a small number of foreign students. At the beginning of the century, for example, there were the two Yoshisaka brothers from Japan, and in 1908 the college enrolled three Japanese and four Chinese students, one of whom, at least, was American-born. By 1910 the Chinese students had organized their own club associated with the Chinese Student Association of North America. The intention was to promote cultural and social contacts with American students and to promote the welfare of fellow Chinese. Summer 1912 found eight Chinese in attendance, some American-born but others from Singapore and Sumatra as well as China proper.

Although East Asians accounted for most of the foreign student population from 1900 to 1912, Leon Horsep Boghasian, an Armenian with a Tehran address, attended in 1911; in 1913 there were four Brazilians, a student from Honduras, four Chinese, a Japanese, an Armenian, and a Greek from Egypt—an even dozen.

An occasional international student was drawn into student affairs, as indicated by the participation of W. K. Limm, "a Chinese of ability," in the 1913 Literary Society oratorical competition. His plea for the recognition of the new Chinese Republic was printed in toto by the *Messenger*. The Yoshisaka brothers, on the other hand, found their peace of mind disturbed when some miscreant threw a rock through their window, hitting one of the brothers. Angry and frightened, they promptly quit the campus, although the older brother, a graduate student, returned for a second year before transferring to Purdue University. In fall 1912 a Brazilian student had the misfortune to be caught in the rivalry between incoming freshmen and the sophomores and was beaten up, his face "bruised and abraded," as the *Messenger* phrased it. Other expressions of hostility toward foreign students lay in the efforts of the Phi Delta Theta chapter to exclude "Japs" from membership in their fraternity.

THE CHURCH COMMUNITY

At the beginning of the twentieth century, five churches—First Presbyterian, First Methodist, the Disciples of Christ, Mount Zion Baptist, and St. Paul's Roman Catholic Church—provided the community's religious leadership. In the course of the next two decades, several new church bodies would appear.

Roman Catholics

The Roman Catholic community in 1900 enjoyed the newest, finest church building in town. Its position in the community was somewhat ambivalent. On one hand, its membership, strongly rooted in the Irish and German immigrants of the nineteenth century, was augmented by their American-born children. Their numbers were growing; their economic and social position had markedly improved over that of the parish founders a half century before. In June 1915 Father John Joseph Fagan, the first Athens native to become a priest, conducted his first mass at St. Paul's.

In 1904 Father J. B. Mattingly, who had guided St. Paul's as it built its new church and rectory, was transferred to Logan. He left with the parish debt-free and with the respect of the Protestant community. Of Mattingly's successors, Father James Banahan stands out for his leadership. When he was seriously injured in a 1915 auto accident, the church felt keenly the temporary loss of his services. In 1917 Father Banahan enlisted as an army chaplain, expecting to serve with the Athens men sent to Camp Sheridan, Alabama. The army being the army, Father Banahan was assigned elsewhere. His place at St. Paul's was taken by Father Elwood Berry.

Theological and liturgical differences between Catholics and Protestants led St. Paul's and the Protestant community to move along parallel tracks rather than join in cooperative ventures. One evidence of this was in the use of the revival. In November 1905, for example, the Reverend Father Richard Barrett, from Cincinnati, led a revival, a nightly event with music provided by St. Paul's choir. Some 500 persons attended the closing meeting.

While the Masons, Odd Fellows, and Elks drew members from the churched and non-churched, St. Paul's organized its own fraternal society, the Knights of Columbus. One appeal of the various lodges had been the provision of burial insurance, but another had been the religious character of its secret rituals. If Catholics had difficulties with the Protestant flavor of lodge rituals, they solved the problem by organizing their own.

For the first time overt anti-Catholicism surfaced in Athens. In spring 1909 Lewis King, a Holiness evangelist, stirred a hornet's nest in Nelsonville with his immoderate accusations. When he asserted that all Catholic women were unchaste, he was charged with slander. The night he was arrested, three Catholic women confronted him and whipped him with buggy whips. After a court appearance in Athens, a crowd exceeding 1,000 persons welcomed him back to Nelsonville. Subsequently, a Holiness crowd gathered at the courthouse in Athens to hear anti-Catholic speeches. The county prosecutor, Israel Foster, sought unsuccessfully to disperse the crowd. Father Banahan appeared, spoke, and pacified the crowd.

Anti-Catholicism did not go away. When the management of the Athens Opera House and municipal officials became aware that the Reverend Jeremiah J. Crowley, a known anti-Catholic, had been booked to lecture on a Saturday evening in September 1913 and twice the next day, the Opera House management sought to break the contract. A *Messenger* article praised the United States as a country that permitted religious choice and condemned Crowley for stirring up religious antagonism for personal profit. When Crowley appeared at the Opera House, Chief of Police Mills barred him from speaking, citing a recent incident at New Lexington that had degenerated into a near riot. Crowley's sponsor then took him to Glouster, Chauncey, and Mechanicsburg. His presentation, at the latter, the *Messenger* reported, was "coarse, vulgar, vituperative, and threatening." Undoubtedly, some Athenians shared anti-Catholic views, but the community leadership moved aggressively to bar the public denigration of the Catholic members of the community.

Presbyterians

The act of building St. Paul's proved contagious, and in early 1901 the Presbyterians plunged into raising funds for a new church edifice. Within a year they had their plans in hand, had torn down the old structure, and laid the cornerstone for the new. Dedication of the cornerstone occasioned a community celebration, with music and speeches; school dismissed for the occasion. Designed by Frank L. Packard of Columbus, the new structure featured steel-gray pressed brick with white limestone trim. The pipe organ, said to be one of the largest in southeast Ohio, cost $3,000. The church auditorium and adjacent chapel accommodated 600 persons (the church reported a membership of 144). The stained-glass windows especially pleased the congregation.

The euphoria induced by the new building ended when George Walton King, the able pastor who had seen the congregation through the construction process, resigned. Finding an acceptable successor proved difficult. Eventually the Reverend J. Marshall Thurlow was called. A current of unease continued to manifest itself. In part this may have reflected a near obsession of some members with the temperance movement and the Anti-Saloon League. Anxiety over securing a suitable parsonage was resolved by the purchase of a home on North College. The most overt source of unease was a vigorous discussion of whether to abandon the Court and Washington Street site and relocate away from the downtown noise; the church stayed on Court Street. After seven years on the job, the Reverend Mr. Thurlow resigned to be replaced by Abbott Y. Wilcox of Marietta, a man of more than ordinary talent.

The Presbyterians exhibited a number of interests; clearly the curbing of alcoholic beverages was one, and in this they worked with the Woman's Christian Temperance Union. There was much concern with the Sunday school program, which drew five-sevenths as many attendants as the main Sunday worship service and was as much for adults as for children. There was also a strong interest in missions, both domestic and foreign. The Christian Endeavor Society of the church maintained contact with a mission at Moxahala in Perry County. The congregation also developed a tie with the national church's mission in Persia, and in 1913 Caroline Holmes, on leave from the Persian mission, spoke in Athens, wearing Persian garb. Four years later, when the Christians served by the Persian mission came under assault, the Reverend Mr. Wilcox took the lead in raising funds for Armenian and Syrian Relief.

Under Pastor Wilcox the Presbyterians took a leap forward in church finance; they inaugurated the every member canvass. There had been criticism in the past that too few had shouldered the financial burden and that too little attention had been given to the support of missions. The innovation worked. The number of pledges more than doubled, and the level of giving increased by 50 percent. At another level, the Presbyterians promoted a Good Friday service, emphasizing "Seven Words from the Cross." In this the Disciples of Christ also participated. Another innovation was a father and son dinner at the church: "creamed chicken with all the fixings."

Pastor Wilcox enjoyed the support of fellow clergy to the degree that in October 1918 he was elected Moderator of the Ohio Synod, that is, to the highest office in the state organization. Not for twenty-nine years had an Athens pastor held this position.

First Methodist Church

Boasting 770 members in 1905, the Methodist congregation was the largest in the village and felt the need for a new building. The church prided itself on the fact that three of its own, David H. Moore, Charles C. McCabe, and Earl Cranston were bishops of the church. The three men had not only grown up in Athens, but Moore and Cranston had been schoolmates before the Civil War.

In presenting the proposal for a new building to their congregation, the Methodist leadership summoned their three bishops to lend a hand. They began their building-fund drive with over $21,000, mostly gifts from C. L. Poston and Eliakim H. Moore. They had also acquired the W. E. Day property that lay immediately to the south of the old church, an acquisition that enabled them to position their new structure so that it would face straight up East Washington Street. Some of the joy of anticipation was dulled by the death of their pastor, W. L. Slutz, less than a month before the final service in the old church. Slutz's son Earl, a recent graduate of Drew Seminary, was on hand and filled in until an established minister could be assigned.

With their new church building completed in 1908, the Methodists exuded vitality. They organized a men's society "to promote the spirit and practice of Christian brotherhood." To be sure, they had a Ladies' Aid Society, one of whose memorable actions banned the wearing of women's hats during the Sunday service. The special forte of the church was its Sunday school. Indeed, the latter was so spectacularly successful that it tended to overshadow the church itself.

On Rally Day 1911 the Church anticipated a Sunday school attendance of 1,000, roughly one-fifth of the community. The expectation was within reason, for it had counted 875 attendees the previous Sunday. Despite its new building, to accommodate the Sunday school, the church was forced to use at one time or another the Opera House, a nearby movie theater, the offices of the Commercial Club, and even the Mayor's office. Sunday school was not for women and children only. Males often outnumbered female Sunday-school attendees by two to one. On Mother's Day 1915 the Sunday school reported 4,178 attendees, of whom nearly 3,000 were males 16 years old and over.

Class Six, a Sunday school class headed by the charismatic Professor Charles Copeland, had a life of its own. On the Mother's Day referred to above, his class for adult men drew 2,837 attendees, 900 of whom had to stand outside the church sanctuary. The Class developed its own executive committee to coordinate the class activities. In 1916 it sponsored the week-long Chautauqua program for the community, had its own ball team, and its own choir. The substance of its Sunday morning meetings was Bible Study, yet attendance came to be an end in itself. Class Six challenged analogous mega-classes in Nelsonville, Lancaster, and Huntington, West Virginia, to see which could, over a period of months, draw the largest attendance. The *Messenger* published the score week by week, and the Class ran advertisements urging Athens men to attend Sunday school. To stimulate attendance guest speakers were invited on occasion. One July Sunday in 1916 the guest "teacher," Ohio Governor Frank B. Willis, reminded the class that Sunday school stood for "the best ideals in America: frugality, thrift, honesty, faith, optimism, and patriotism." Perhaps inevitably, the group got burned out. With Class Six attendance lagging, the *Messenger* observed: "Class Six Has Lost Her 'Pep'."

Central Avenue Methodist Church

As Athens grew, the religious scene became more diverse. Early in the new century Methodists in the West End organized a congregation of their own. It was, after all, a formidable walk from Central Avenue to College Street, decidedly unpleasant in inclement weather. In August 1903 a group of West End Methodists organized a "melon social" at the Daniel Rardin residence, a benefit anticipating the formation of a church in West End. Three years passed before the group secured recognition. Promptly the new church secured an architect and organized a building committee. The building was to be a concrete block structure, concrete block being a new building material at the time.

In guiding the building to completion Addie Rardin Haney was the moving force and the Reverend Mr. Samuel J. Bishop, the founding pastor. By the time of its dedication, October 17, 1909, the building was debt-free. Although in the shadow of the older, established First Methodist Church, the Central Avenue congregation made a respectable showing, drawing 195 persons to its Sunday school in March 1913.

Disciples of Christ

In the mainstream alongside the Presbyterians and Methodists was the Disciples of Christ, the Christian Church. Small in size, it was big in activity and enthusiasm. The congregation took special pleasure in April 1902 in the fact that it was debt-free.

As with the Methodists and Presbyterians, the Disciples of Christ Sunday school was dynamic. On Easter Sunday 1905 it reported an attendance of 286 and an enrollment of 371. Clearly its Congress Street building was too small, and that fall the congregation engaged John Rardin to raise the building by four feet in order to construct a basement with Sunday school rooms. The fact is, it had a young congregation. Its cradle roll listed 92 infants, the Sunday school, 456, the Christian Endeavor Society, essentially junior-high and high-school age youth, 164. It was also a congregation of modest means, able to pay its pastor but $1,250 a year, a condition that contributed to a frequent turnover in pastors.

In many ways, the program of the Disciples was much like those of the Presbyterians and Methodists. The Disciples employed the revival, usually in January and February. Featuring a Portsmouth minister, the 1910 revival packed the church and ran three and a half weeks. Its Higley Class, a smaller version of Class Six at First Methodist, often made front-page news. A Thursday evening meeting of the class drew seventy-five men to a debate on the retention of Bible reading in the public schools. The class, whose motto was "Better Men for Athens," held a monthly business meeting. It, too, challenged Sunday school classes in other Christian Churches to a contest over attendance. The Disciples also provided their members contact with exotic areas abroad. In June 1903, for example, they heard from Mary Kelly, who spoke on a Sunday morning of her experiences in China and of the Boxer Rebellion in particular.

Ultimately, the Disciples, having added greatly to their membership, proceeded with a new building. In 1913 they secured an option on the Josiah "Si" Allen property at Congress and West State Street. Later in the year, they hired their architect and dreamed big dreams—Sunday school rooms to accommodate 1,800 pupils! a gym! a cost of $40,000! The plan seemed daunting. Two years later they sat down again to discuss a new building; a month later they broke ground. Misfortune stalked them. Minutes before the cornerstone was to be laid, a prominent parishioner, speeding to the ceremony, was killed in a bizarre accident almost in front of the church. The ceremony was called off. Then, three months before the building was completed, their pastor left to take up YMCA work with American troops on the Mexican border. At last, when the church held its first service in the new structure, other town ministers and President Ellis participated in the service. As completed the church was said to seat 1,250 persons; its cost, $42,000. The dedication, in April 1917, passed off without incident.

Mount Zion Baptist Church

The congregation of Mount Zion Baptist Church also heard the call for a new church, an enterprise posing far more problems than the more affluent congregations faced. They had determination and Edward C. Berry. The successful hotel proprietor had the know-how and drive to carry the project to completion. Berry acquired the northeast corner of Carpenter and Congress for the new building. Ground was broken in September 1905. When the cornerstone was placed in November, the Methodist and Disciples pastors participated. It took nearly four years to complete the building, but when it was formally dedicated in September 1909, the other Protestant churches extended their Christian greetings. President Ellis spoke. The new building dedicated, the pastor, the Reverend Mr. George

Washington, resigned to go to Oberlin. In the six years he had served in Athens, the *Messenger* reported he had been "a power for good," "a public speaker of merit, a man of force and consequence."

Episcopal

As the new century began, the Episcopalians once more attempted to found a permanent congregation in Athens. In 1907 the new Episcopal bishop, Boyd Vincent, decided to test the waters of the Hocking Valley. Athens was but one of several posts served by a single missioner, the Reverend Mr. Alfred W. Buckland. Anticipating his appointment, several Athens women organized a Ladies' Guild. The organizing committee, led by Ellen (Mrs. Johnson M.) Welch, was all women. Organized Wednesday, May 8, 1907, the new congregation took the name Church of the Good Shepherd.

As a mission, the Athens group had the services of a priest every other week, using the old chapel of Ohio University for its services. Of the successive missioners who served Good Shepherd, A. J. Wilder and Willard D. Stires stand out. Capitalizing on the work of his predecessors, Wilder built churches at Logan and Nelsonville. Athens lagged, but a building site was secured at the corner of State and Carpenter. When Wilder left in 1916, the lot was paid for, and the building fund held $4,000.

In May 1917 Good Shepherd, then pastored by Willard D. Stires, was ready to build. The cornerstone was laid, but with the United States having entered the European war, the church found completing its building slow going. Indeed, when the congregation began to use the building in the fall of 1918, the interior was not yet completed. The dedication was deferred to October 1920 with Bishop Boyd Vincent officiating.

Other Church Societies

Other church groups operated around the periphery of the mainstream churches. The Salvation Army, based at Marietta, came to Athens on occasion to raise money for its programs on behalf of society's downtrodden. In 1910 the Christian Scientists leased a room in the Campbell Block where they held services Sunday mornings and Wednesday evenings; following a decade of preparation, in 1920 they incorporated with a view to becoming a permanent feature of the local scene. The Free Methodists, a holiness congregation, seldom drew the attention of the *Messenger*, but in fact it had suffcient membership to erect its own structure on Stimson Avenue, a building it occupied until long after World War II. In 1919 a Mission Church operated in quarters on West Washington Street. In March 1919 the Baptists began to organize, meeting in the University's Music Hall. The Bassett (Baptist) Church in Alexander Township was disbanding, and that congregation provided the nucleus for the Athens congregation. Reported to have about 100 members in 1919, the group looked forward to building its own church edifice in Athens. This move did not work out.

While Athenians typically expressed their religious feelings through one or another church organization, they had other outlets. The summertime camp meetings at Coolville and Lancaster continued. These drew less attention from the press than in the late nineteenth century, but they persisted. Although the campgrounds faced competition from Chautauqua, the Coolville Camp in 1905 reported the largest meeting in its history and again a very large turnout in 1912.

Revival-style religion had a strong appeal to Athenians in the years before World War I. The Fife Brothers, itinerant evangelists in the mode of Billy Sunday, came to Athens in March 1913 at the behest of the Disciples. They made a particular point of a musical ministry that utilized the Billy Sunday Song Book. From the first meeting, they mesmerized their congregations; attendance was so overwhelming that the Fife Brothers ended up turning people away. Their meeting on the 15th moved to the Methodist Church, which likewise proved too small for the 1,300 persons who appeared. On the 17th a decision was made to build a tabernacle at Court and Carpenter. Constructed in two days and capable of seating 2,000 persons, it had gas heat, electric lights, telephone service, a nursery for very young children, and a baptistry. It was filled, and "hundreds" were still turned away. The Fife Brothers were a phenomenon. They continued to hold forth nightly until April 6. As they concluded their ministry in Athens, they claimed to have registered nearly 500 converts.

At another level Athens provided a site for a major convention of the collegiate leaders of the Student Christian Movement. Delegates from thirty colleges were present. This was the time when John R. Mott was promoting "The Evangelization of the World in This Generation." There was a strong sense that this was do-able. President Ellis spoke to the group. The major speaker was the still young Sam Higginbottom, missionary to India, then making his reputation for work with lepers.

As exciting as the summer camp meetings, the Fife Brothers' revival, or the conference of the Student Christian leaders were, the day-to-day collaboration of the mainstream Protestant churches of the town was more important. The multi-denominational Sunday School Union, begun in the nineteenth century, continued. The Sunday school teachers of the member denominations met to get further training in common. More frequently, the cooperation between churches was expressed in union services that enabled the pastors of the Methodists, Presbyterians, and Disciples of Christ to take vacations while maintaining a continuity of worship services. They also held union services at Thanksgiving and Christmas. The Protestant clergy formed a county ministerial association, the first program of which examined the new American Revised Standard Bible. This recognition of mutual interest among Athens mainline Protestant churches found its counterpart at the state and national levels in the formation of the Ohio Council of Churches and the Federal Council of Churches of Christ. Reverend A. Y. Wilcox of the First Presbyterian Church had a hand in the organization of the Ohio Council.

Given the magnitude of Sunday school attendance and the number of church edifices constructed during these two decades, it would seem that more than half of the Athens population identified with one or another of the community's churches.

THE WAYWARD COMMUNITY

From time to time Athens was rocked by serious acts of violence. The most notable of these incidents were the near lynching of Richard Gardner, the shooting of Marshal Finsterwald, and, as the press termed it, the "war on the streets" of Athens.

Near Lynching

In May 1900 Athens came within an ace of experiencing its second lynching. The near-victim, Richard Gardner, a Negro, charged with the rape and murder of fifteen-year-old Ethel Long of Austin, Ross County, had been lodged in the Athens County jail for protection. Anticipating trouble, Athens Sheriff Carl Porter made careful plans. On the evening of May 30 groups of angry men congregated along West Union and the streets of the West End. A few minutes before midnight, a mob of possibly two hundred men swept up Union Street to Court Street and surrounded the jail. "Above the din of the hysterical howls of the mob" the cries could be heard, "We are going to hang the nigger!"

Judge Joseph M. Wood tried to dissuade the mob by telling them that Gardner was not in the jail. Disbelieving, the mob demanded to see for itself. The judge then allowed a committee of the mob to inspect the jail; Gardner was not in his cell. In fact, Sheriff Porter had secreted Gardner, securely manacled, with three deputies in the courthouse cupola. With the mob in confusion, he had dispatched a carriage from the alley next the jail, allowing the mob to believe that Gardner was in the carriage. Believing that Gardner had been taken off, the mob dispersed. Then at 3 A.M., when the streets were deserted, Gardner was brought down from the cupola, and Sheriff Porter and Marshal Peter Finsterwald departed with their prisoner for Trimble. After breakfasting there, they boarded the morning train for Columbus, where Gardner was placed in the Franklin County jail to await his trial in Chillicothe.

On returning from Columbus, the sheriff rounded up eight of the ring leaders of the mob, charging them "with unlawfully, maliciously and forcibly attempting to break into the county jail and with intent to kill Richard Gardner." When several leading citizens—F. C. Stedman, T. H. Craig, D. H. Moore, and J. D. Brown —posted bond for the men, prosecution was abandoned. Gardner was subsequently tried in Chillicothe, found guilty, and executed.

Finsterwald's Shoot-Out

An event Athenians long remembered occurred in Gallipolis. In late January 1902 Harvey Williams and John Lisle, employees of John Lambourne's photo gallery on West Union, planned to rob a wealthy woman who lived in Gallipolis. The nefarious duo confided their plans to a pair of acquaintances, who, rather than become accomplices, tipped off Athens Marshal Peter Finsterwald.

Finsterwald promptly recruited Athens County Sheriff Andrew Murphy, and the two took a train to Gallipolis, expecting to lie in wait for the two would-be robbers. Instead, the robbers, who had changed their plans, got to Gallipolis first, and Finsterwald and Murphy walked into a near trap. In the ensuing shoot-out Lisle shot Finsterwald in the chest just above the heart, although the marshal still managed to drill Lisle. When the gunfire ended, Finsterwald appeared to be mortally wounded. Lisle was dead, eight bullets in his body. Williams was also dead. Sheriff Murphy was uninjured.

Subsequently, Lambourne was arrested as a possible accomplice. The robbery was apparently undertaken to finance a counterfeiting operation to which Lambourne was a party. Finsterwald was brought back to Athens, presumably to die. But as tough as he was "fearless, dutiful, and big-hearted," Finsterwald recovered. Four weeks following the shooting, he was back on the streets of Athens.

War in the Streets

A "bloody encounter" between members of the Ohio National Guard and regulars of the United States Army on an August evening in 1904 resulted in one death and several wounded. The two units were encamped near Athens for summer-training exercises. Strained relations between the national guardsmen and the regulars had existed for a number of days. The turning point came on the afternoon of the day of the encounter when several guardsmen, acting as military police, arrested a disorderly member of the 27th U.S. Infantry in an Athens saloon. In resisting arrest, the soldier had emptied his pistol, and the guardsmen had "clubbed him into insensibility," then bound him hand and foot.

That evening a number of regulars made their way to town, a hundred or so assembling in the schoolyard next to High and West State streets. Forming a column six abreast, they came marching down State, turned right into Court Street, and then west on Washington. In front of the sheriff's residence, they turned on the provost guard. Almost instantly, the regulars broke ranks and began firing on the guardsmen. In a hail of one hundred or more shots, Corporal Charles Clark was killed, Sergeant William Blessing seriously wounded, and privates Ohl, Heald, and Pond injured. All were members of D Company, Fifth Regiment, ONG. Their assailants were all members of the 27th Regiment, U.S. Infantry. The firing lasted only a minute or so, but the damage had been done.

Following an intensive investigation by the Athens County coroner, five regulars were charged in the unlawful killing of Corporal Clark. Three of the accused were jailed. Only reluctantly were the other two released to the sheriff's custody. Altogether nine soldiers were indicted for the shooting. In January 1905 John L. Lott was found guilty of assault with intent to kill, for having clubbed private W. R. Ohl. Six others were sentenced to thirty days in the Columbus workhouse, fined $500 and costs. For its part, the army stonewalled the case. The killer was given a good conduct discharge; all the others, honorable discharges. No one faced a courtmartial.

SOCIAL VALUES

While Richard Gardner, Harvey Williams, John Lisle, and the 27th Division were outsiders, Athenians also resorted to violence. Failed relationships, whether between husband and wife or between lovers, produced a variety of crimes. In many cases, the public record offers only a raw statement of such an event—the body of a newborn baby found in a vault on Morris Avenue; a charge against E. A. Secoy for aborting a sixteen-year-old Athens girl; the sentencing of Dr. John W. Tippie of Trimble to a year in prison because a woman whom he aborted died from the chloroform. What the record does not reveal are the circumstances that led a woman to kill her newborn infant or to prefer an abortion to bearing a child.

Periodically, the tranquility of the community was disturbed when marital infidelity ended in a crime of passion. Thus, when Emmett Mason found his wife in bed with Frank Blackstone, he killed the latter with the weapon of convenience, a beer bottle. In another instance, John Carmichael deliberately shot John Ellis four times, twice in the heart and then, with Ellis on the ground, in the head; Ellis had allegedly broken up Carmichael's marriage. In yet another case Harvey Graham was shot dead in his own doorway by one Mort Willis. The latter averred that Graham had been overly familiar with Mrs. Willis for several years. Fed up, Mort Willis terminated their relationship.

The community recoiled in horror at homicide. But Athens still toyed with "the unwritten law" that excused a husband for killing his wife's lover. When Carmichael advanced this argument at trial, prosecutor Israel Foster instructed the jury that it was not a valid defense in law, and Carmichael was convicted and sentenced to life imprisonment. Three years later, Foster joined the trial judge, all of the trial jurors, and six hundred Athens citizens in petitioning the Ohio governor for Carmichael's release. When the governor pardoned him, the *Messenger* editorially commented on the vitality of the "unwritten law."

The "family values" of this era expected marital relations to be confined to marriage. While the community was not inclined to look for trouble, persons who engaged in extra- or premarital sex, if not discreet, could find themselves in court. On occasion, the community prosecuted persons for fornication or adultery per se. In 1909, for example, when Etta Rawson and William Matthews were convicted of adultery, both were given jail time. The arrest of Mrs. Sam Moore for adultery with Homer Hunkerford had a different outcome. Neither was a paragon of virtue. Mrs. Moore had a reputation for having lived with a number of men, and her husband, who was suing her for divorce at the time, had custody of their children. His reputation was hardly spotless; he was suspected of being a chicken thief, while she had allegedly fenced the stolen birds. Before prosecution proceeded, the lady's husband secured a divorce and the custody of the children; Hunkerford and his lady-love married in Parkersburg.

Then, as now, physical abuse was hard to prove, the more so when the victim denied he or she had been abused. The court was faced with a difficult case in 1911 when two daughters, fourteen and fifteen, charged their father with incest. Their mother, however, promptly appeared in court, an infant in her arms, to ask the court to reduce the bond for her husband and to express the belief that her husband was innocent. One of the daughters responded that the mother was aware of her husband's behavior. The Court had less difficulty dealing with Oliver Glaspy, charged with three counts of incest with his twelve-year old sister. The charge was dropped; Glaspy was already serving time in the reformatory at Mansfield.

Cases of fathers who abandoned or failed to provide for their children (including those born out of wedlock) were more common. Such offenses were routinely resolved by requiring the errant father to post bond to assure future financial support. When Harry Bennett failed to provide the promised child support, Bennett was brought back into court and was ordered to pay $4.00 a month, a token amount.

Engagements were not to be taken lightly. Among the middle classes, a male who wooed a girl, became engaged, and then backed off, could find himself in court. Lettie Coe thought it would take $10,000 to heal her broken heart when John J. Woolley, newly elected Athens prosecuting attorney, spurned her. One imagines that her attorney I. M. Foster, who had just been ousted from office by Woolley, pursued the case with uncommon vigor. In a similar breach of promise suit, Mrs. Mary Vincent estimated the damage to her heart at $15,000.

The course of true love did not invariably run smooth. In 1901 divorce actions constituted a large part of the civil suits filed during the year. Adultery by the husband was alleged twice as often as adultery by the wife. Desertion, neglect, drunkenness, and cruelty also contributed to marital breakdowns. What the record does not disclose is whether the antisocial behavior alleged in the divorce action arose from the pure cussedness of the "guilty" spouse or was the response to unstated actions of the "innocent" spouse or those of a third party. What is clear is that not all men were proper gentlemen; not all women were proper ladies. Certainly, local judges protested against the propensity of couples with marital problems "to rush into the divorce court upon the slightest provocation." Judge Joseph M. Wood, having granted fourteen divorces in fall term 1901, resolved to make divorce more difficult, chiefly by insisting on a higher level of evidence of the marriage's failure. In the year July 1902–June 1903 the court denied a divorce in one-third of the cases it heard.

As in earlier years, the community had to deal with juvenile delinquency. Those who dropped out of school were most likely to be at loose ends. Rowdiness continued to the point that town fathers, disturbed over the lack of parental guidance, periodically mandated a curfew intended to keep youngsters at home in the evening. On a more positive note, in tacit recognition that the job market no longer guaranteed a ready occupation for adolescents, the town fathers supported a public playground and organized sports. Even so, some youngsters were antisocial.

Periodically, the *Messenger* noted cryptically that a young woman, a school-age girl, who had offended community sensibilities by truancy and premarital sexual activities had been committed to the Girls' Industrial School. Being "ungovernable" by her parents was sufficient grounds for committing a wayward girl to the GIS; it was not, however, grounds for committing her wayward male companion. Even the Athens post office took a puritan stance. It protested the practice of those young women who chose to receive mail at general delivery to avoid home delivery of personal mail and disclosure of their correspondents.

But there were youth who turned to petty crime. In summer 1914 a rash of breakings and enterings ended with the arrest of Freddie Duppler, age ten, and Jamie Vernon, age thirteen. The younger boy was discharged to his mother, who relocated to another town; the older youth was committed to the Boys' Industrial School. Only days later two other juveniles were held for beating a third lad. Both assailants were drunk. The younger of the two was also sent to the Boys' Industrial School. The older boy was fined and jailed.

Most of the adult crimes Athens experienced involved misdemeanor offenses against public order and peace. Much had to do with drunkenness. In February 1901 Mayor Rose instructed village police to arrest all inebriates found on the streets on Sundays. Previously, a tipsy citizen in the company of a sober friend had been ignored. Repeatedly, over the years, the saloonkeepers declined to observe the closing laws. In November 1901 sixteen Athens liquor dispensers were arrested and convicted for Sunday sales. Sunday sales were especially repugnant to the Athens church-going respectability, and those who violated the law often faced stiff fines and sentences as harsh as twenty days in jail.

After Athens voted itself dry, some saloonkeepers became bootleggers to accommodate those with unquenchable thirsts, persisting in spite of fines. Eddie Banks, a Nelsonville saloonist, who brought liquor into Athens, had, by January 1908, been found guilty three times and fined $200 each time. A Parkersburg liquor firm advertised its wares, offering to accept mail orders and to ship liquor by express. Two unnamed Athens women provided same-day service, taking orders, going to Parkersburg by train, suitcase in hand, and returning with the goods.

Local sellers resorted to artful dodges. Jim Bobo, who ran a restaurant on Dean Avenue, was discovered to have five bottles of beer in his basement, beer his wife had procured in Parkersburg. The Bobos admitted to having the beer, but claimed it was for family use, not for sale in their restaurant which shared the same building. Disbelieving, the court fined Jim Bobo $200 and costs.

Another Dean Street tavernkeeper argued that while she had sold three drinks in a one-hour period, that such sales were too few to constitute a liquor trade. The State Supreme Court, which heard the case on appeal, held that she had, indeed, been engaged in the liquor trade and, thus, owed a tax of $985.71. In 1913, an unrepentant Jim Bobo was once more in trouble for bootlegging. "Notorious" for his activities, he was jailed, pending trial. The court drove a hard bargain, denying him custody of his son until he could give the court evidence that he was leaving Athens. As evidence, the court wanted to see a receipt for the rental of a home outside the Athens area and evidence that he had shipped his household goods. Bobo moved to Chillicothe. Judge Rowland could be flexible. Faced with two repeaters, he gave one a choice of thirty days in jail or permanent removal from Athens. The other he fined fifty dollars and sent to jail for thirty days, jail time to be worked off on the streets in leg irons.

A second category of offense against public order was prostitution and white slavery. Clearly, Athens had a demimonde element. As in earlier years, Athens judges were generally content to impose a token fine and costs on a convicted prostitute and either let the woman flee town (in which case she could be charged with contempt of court if she ever returned to Athens), or explicitly order her to leave town. Those who conducted a house of prostitution could expect a fine and court costs as much as triple the penalties imposed on "inmates." A crackdown in spring 1904 rounded up ten women—five madams, five inmates. Two of the madams were in court once more early in 1905 in the company of six other women. A raid of April 1909 netted one Ella Butts, a madam who had been arrested in the April 1904 raid. The male patrons of the 1909 raid were fined $11.25 each; Ella Butts, $25 plus costs. In 1913 Clara Reynolds, a repeater, was in court as a madam; her fine, $25 plus costs.

In 1918 a midnight raid on a house on South Lancaster Street resulted in the arrest of three women. That the house was in sight of the schoolhouse evidently was too much for the city fathers to stomach. The madam was fined $100 plus costs, but a sixty-day jail sentence was suspended on condition that she abandon the business. Two inmates of her establishment, both married women with children, were fined and ordered to keep out of Athens. A raid on the Ohio Hotel in May 1919 also raised the hackles of local authorities. The hotel had initially rented rooms to Ohio University coeds, then gradually replaced them with women of the street passing as coeds. In general, the prosecution of prostitution seems to have been episodic, and, although the "johns" were on occasion prosecuted, the police tended to regard the prostitute's conduct as more reprehensible than that of her customer. In exiling women, the courts in effect traded Athens' prostitutes for the exiles of other communities. At best, enforcement restricted the business of prostitution. It did not abolish it.

Occasional evidence of white slavery involving underage girls surfaced. In March 1909 an Athens man was charged with transporting two underage girls to a house of prostitution in Columbus; his alibi: the girls had asked him to take them to Columbus. Such cases could be more complicated, for when a fourteen-year-old girl from The Plains was found to be an inmate of a Front Street house in Columbus, she was in the company of her mother and her aunt. A year later, when sixteen-year old Laura Thomas was arrested for prostitution, she implicated Cora Hawkins, a local madam, who was planning to place Thomas in a house in Columbus. Hawkins, who already had a police record in Athens as a madam, was fined $100 and costs for contributing to the delinquency of a minor; her house was declared a public nuisance and ordered closed. Young Thomas was remanded to the Girls' Industrial School, Delaware.

Some crimes arose out of personal disputes, most of which ended in little more than shouting matches. A brouhaha in Africa Alley (now Depot Street) involved a number of black women who hurled epithets and flailed one another with broomsticks. When summoned, the police challenged the ladies to swear out warrants or to desist. They stopped fighting, ending the battle of the broomsticks.

At times there were unprovoked assaults as when W. J. Warrener, editor-publisher of the Athens *Tribune*, was assaulted on his way home late one night. Then again, there were occasional shootings with intent to kill. Ben Six was so indicted, but on trial he convinced a jury that he had shot one Pearl Smith (a male) to forestall Smith from attacking Harvey McCulley. Six was fined fifty dollars plus costs for assault and battery.

There were, of course, crimes against property. The new century began with a rash of petty break-ins at Court Street businesses, prompting editor Bush to complain that in turning the town's street lights off at midnight, the town fathers were leaving the village "to the tender mercies . . . of the criminally inclined." Reflecting the fact that Athens had not shed all of its rural roots, George Baker and William

Harden were but two of several who stole chickens. Marshal Finsterwald nabbed a traveling salesman who, in the guise of canvassing house to house, stole small items and sums of money. A break-in at the J. C. Loos jewelry store in 1914 was executed by smashing a display window and looting the display. The case had a ludicrous element to it, for the thieves left a trail of the stolen trinkets up Washington Street. When one of the thieves sought to fence part of the loot he had managed not to drop, he was turned in, then implicated his colleague. The latter confessed and led the police to the remainder of the loot.

From time to time gambling was a problem. Wheels and boards, devices used for chances of winning cigars, as well as slot machines and dice games were common. In 1911 Mayor Slaughter ordered a shutdown of all gambling within the town. As with drink and prostitution, there were persons driven to gamble and businessmen willing to oblige. Eight persons were rounded up on a Saturday evening at the Court Street residence of "Soupy" Graham. They were engaged in poker and crap shooting.

A confirmed criminal like Jay Withem was rare. From youth, Withem had a reputation of stealing anything he wanted that was not nailed down. As an adult, he was regarded as "one of the worst criminals and most daring." He had been difficult to apprehend; he had sawed his way out of the Athens County jail, and Athens police were extremely upset when, after he had been incarcerated in the state penitentiary, prison authorities had placed him in an "honor gang," from which he promptly walked away. Almost a year passed before county authorities apprehended Withem a second time and returned him to prison.

WORLD WAR I

War was in the air all through the first half of 1914. But the focal point was Mexico. Contending factions of Victoriano Huerta, Venustiano Carranza, and Pancho Villa kept the Mexican government unstable, while provoking repeated incidents along the United States–Mexican border. The assassination of Archduke Ferdinand by a Serb nationalist on June 28, 1914, at Sarajevo illustrated that Mexico was not the only troubled country. The *Messenger* explained that the assassination was attributed to a "general plot" in which there was a conflict of German influences and Slav nationalist aspirations in the Balkan provinces of the Austro-Hungarian Empire. A day later, the paper reported that Moslem Croats had descended on Mostar, Herzegovina, killed 200 Serbs, and fired the city. There the matter ostensibly rested until July 24, when the United Press at Berlin declared:

"World War Probable Over Austrian Action." The repercussions of the general war that swiftly followed increasingly shaped life in Athens. Within a week European news preempted most of the first page of the *Messenger.*

War and Rumors of War

As the war in Europe began, the Athens County fair proceeded, while the county election campaign peaked in early August. But by mid-August observant housewives were aware that meat that had sold for 13 cents a pound a week earlier, now sold for 15 cents, a 15 percent increase in one week that foreshadowed future inflation and suggested that Athens was vulnerable to the impact of events transpiring thousands of miles away and with which it had little or no connection.

For months the effect of the war on the city was sporadic, diffuse, limited. In September the state superintendent of schools directed that all Ohio school children sing the "Star Spangled Banner" at 9 A.M., September 14, the centenary of the piece. New flagpoles were provided for both Central School and East Side School. In April 1915 the war acquired a more personal character as Elsie Druggan, an American Red Cross nurse in German-occupied Belgium who hailed from Morris Avenue, began to share her experiences in the columns of the *Messenger.*

Throughout 1914 and 1915 Athens retained much of its insularity. When William Jennings Bryan resigned as secretary of state, the *Daily Messenger* solicited the views of local leaders. Mayor Oliver F. Rowland thought the resignation would show the Germans that "we mean business." Captain J. B. Allen added that Bryan had been consistent in his views and had shown "considerable fortitude" in resigning. These were views of staunch Republicans who scarcely concealed their feeling that President Wilson had been too mild in his treatment of the Germans. W. A. Carpenter, in a thoroughly political reaction, expressed the hope that Bryan's resignation would split the Democrats. The *Daily Messenger* itself lamented America's unpreparedness. By this time, Athenians were already playing "It's A Long, Long Way to Tipperary" on their phonographs along with "When You Wore A Tulip and I Wore a Big Red Rose." The war was still marginal to everyday life.

If the war in Europe remained on the horizon, the *Messenger* nonetheless kept the community apprised of developments. It was filled with reports of the repeated bombing of England by German zeppelins and the devastating impact of the *untersee* boats. The sinking of the *Lusitania* on May 7, 1915, had an added dimension for Athenians. Continuing the fur and hide business his father had begun nearly a century before, Hull Foster, Jr., lost $10,000 in furs that went down with the ship.

By August 1916, Athenians were alerted that the five-cent loaf of bread was gone for the duration; it would cost a dime.

Troubles with Mexico continued and with more immediate consequences. In April 1914 the United States ordered its fleet to blockade Mexican ports and occupy the port of Vera Cruz. Fed up with the banditry of Pancho Villa, in March 1916 the United States began preparations to invade Mexico to capture the elusive guerrilla leader. When the call-up of the Ohio National Guard units came in June 1916, the two Athens units—Company L and a Machine Gun Company— were not mobilized. Why these units and the 7th Regiment of which they were a part were not summoned, the *Messenger*, if the editor knew, never shared with the community.

The war in Europe became perceptibly closer as, in early February 1917, the United States broke diplomatic relations with Germany. By mid-March war talk seasoned with speculation began crowding all else from the front page. The Germans had resumed unrestricted submarine warfare. The Ohio National Guard was preparing. Selected guard units were mobilized by the state. Seven units of the 7th Regiment were assigned to guarding area bridges, rail terminals, and public buildings. At a mundane level, Thor Olson, the university's star wrestler, was winning some matches, losing others. Hemlines on dresses for the forthcoming season were to rise to mid-calf length, and skirts would be less full than in the past to conserve material. The need for residents to plant gardens was spelled out. And at the end of March 1917, with the prospect that a declaration of war was no more than a week or so away, Athens businessmen closed ranks, announcing their support of Woodrow Wilson.

On the eve of the declaration of war, some 10,000 people gathered in Athens for a flag-raising at the new Armory at the north end of Court Street and an accompanying parade. With Fred Bush, editor of the *Messenger*, as chair of the occasion, 3,000 persons marched, including the Athens Band, Company L, the Machine Gun Company, the GAR and Women's Relief Corps, the Spanish American Veterans. Father Banahan of St. Paul's gave the invocation—in short, an inclusive community celebration. Congress declared war on Gemany the next day.

The Home Front

Athens plunged into the preparations with enthusiasm. Immediately, the American Red Cross, which would do much that the Soldiers' Aid Societies had done in the Civil War, began organizing. Frank Roach, longtime grocer, was designated "Food

Dictator" by the county commissioners to encourage increased home food production and the conservation of existing supplies. Athenians were advised to watch their garbage cans and to prepare for future food shortages and even meatless days. Governor James Cox touted the merits of "war flour," meaning whole wheat flour.

As might be expected, the forces of patriotism were increasingly evident. When two Holiness Assembly ministers from Mechanicsburg took exception to rendering homage to the flag, one was made to salute and kiss the flag; the other was dunked several times in a watering trough for horses, then marched up and down Court Street. Likewise, a Harry Henry of Amesville, having received a draft exemption that some locals thought unwarranted, was seized on Court Street by members of Company L and doused with water. So, too, when Harley Nice expressed the uncharitable wish that an acquaintance, Ellis West, a recent draftee, might fall victim to a German bullet, a mob of forty men hunted Nice down and ducked him in a horse trough at "Flat Iron Square," that wedge of land at the intersection of State Street and Mill Street.

These explosions of intolerance reflected a degree of paranoia and fear that unassimilated enemy aliens, Austrian- and German-Americans, were of doubtful loyalty. Those at Canaanville were expressly referred to. And, indeed, in some rural areas of the county the flag was desecrated repeatedly. That the German-born and German-Americans might well organize such activities was widely accepted. The Reverend B. D. Evans of the Methodist Church lent his considerable powers of persuasion and the authority of his calling to fan hostility to the Germans. He pointed to the horrible brutality of the Germans—the rape and mutilation of civilian populations. The Kaiser he portrayed as the "anti-Christ." That Evans had visited the Western Front added to his credibility and made him a favorite speaker. Ordinarily, Athenians supported their country freely from love of country per se; wartime expressions of patriotism were increasingly made under duress to retain a personal aura of respectability.

From the beginning Athenians on the home front demonstrated their loyalty by their support of the successive War Bond Loans and War Savings Stamp Drives. All told, there were four drives, ending with the Liberty Loan Fund at war's end. Each community was assigned a quota which was then sub-allocated to specific local financial institutions. Professionally prepared copy for the local press spelled out the official reasons why unstinting support should be forthcoming. In the first bond drives, enthusiasm for the war sufficed to bring forth spontaneous purchases.

Typically, the first day or so of a drive started splendidly, after which the drives seemed to stall and consternation set in; with the community's self-respect on the line, a final surge of enthusiasm brought forth the lingering funds and, its goal well exceeded, Athens would be at peace with itself. In the third bond drive, the village surpassed its quota by $70,200. By October 1918 with ready savings already transferred to war bonds in the earlier drives, the sell was harder. Names of subscribers were published. The Daughters of the American Revolution and the newly organized Boy Scouts were recruited to go door-to-door to solicit. Firms like McBee developed a payroll deduction program for the purchase of bonds. The venerable banker James D. Brown used his skills to "sell" the drive, and Fred Bush lent the drive the authority of the *Messenger*. At times the War Bond Committee pled, cajoled, even harassed reluctant subscribers. This included publishing the names of men of property who, in the opinion of the committee, had not subscribed their fair share.

While the War Bond Drive asked much of citizens, the funds were, after all, loans to the government and at worst inconvenienced the lenders by temporarily reducing their liquid assets. In contrast, the War Chest Drives and analogous fund raisers required gifts in support of the diverse programs of the American Red Cross (ARC), the Young Men's Christian Association, and the Knights of Columbus. Initially these organizations conducted independent drives, but by early 1918, some coordination was necessary to eliminate repetitious appeals. The campaign of February 1918 aimed at raising $100,000 within the county, a large sum even by post–World War II standards. To spur contributions, a full-page ad reminded donors that these sums were needed to support those directly engaged in combat with the Germans, people who had "nailed a babe to a barn door." "Athens," the ad went on, was "no place for a piker patriot." When the goal was not immediately met, the fund committee reviewed the contributor list to see if the pledges were appropriate, and, if not, solicitors were sent back to encourage such donors to raise their pledge. Athenians were expected to give, cheerfully if possible, but nonetheless to give.

To support its nationwide activities, the American Red Cross, in mid-June 1917, began a $100,000,000 War Relief Fund—$1.00 per person for the country. Athens city easily met its goal. In less than a month, the city had some $15,000 in pledges, close to $3.00 per capita.

Giving was in terms of time as well as of funds. With a plethora of social and cultural organizations, Athenians had a variety of mechanisms through which to express themselves. The chief was the American Red Cross. A local chapter was organized and in operation within days of the start of the war. Although women played a major leadership role, the Red Cross was coed. On April 18, 1917, it announced a desire for 1,000 members for the county, and the energetic Dean Irma

Voigt took responsibility for getting the local group officially chartered. In another week the ARC was organizing squads to sew bandages, make surgical dressings, knit sweaters. Sewers were sought for a half-day-a-week, the work to be done in such public spaces as church basements. All 600 women students currently attending Ohio University enrolled in ARC-designed classes, getting instruction in first aid, home nursing, and dietetics.

At year's end, the ARC had a suite of five rooms in the Athens National Bank Building—two rooms fitted up for 157 women volunteers. Their products included pajamas and bed sheets for hospital patients as well as napkins, wash. cloths, sweaters, socks, and the ubiquitous surgical dressings. "Out-of-town" women accounted for a "big part" in the production of sweaters and socks for the servicemen.

The YMCA as well as the ARC had access to servicemen at home and abroad, though the YMCA operated on a far smaller scale. As college resumed in fall 1917, OU students undertook to raise $4,000 among themselves as part of the national YMCA fund drive. And it was in connection with this fund drive that the Reverend B. D. Evans did some of his speaking on his return from a one-month tour of the war zone in France. His Sunday night program on the "YMCA Story in France" was followed the next two days by a door-to-door solicitation of the city.

Nothing made the home front so aware of the war as did creeping inflation. British and French demands for foodstuffs pushed prices upward from the first weeks of the war in Europe. When America entered, prices escalated ever faster, 3 percent in the month following the declaration of war. The country was told to "further cut down food," of the need to further share its food with the Allies. A spate of regulations sought to assure that available supplies were stretched out. To get white flour, one had to buy specific quantities of flour substitutes—corn meal, hominy, rice, and oatmeal. Recipes for white bread substitutes were distributed. There were annoying shortages of sugar. To limit speculation the futures market in coffee was suspended.

As prices rose, tempers flared. The shortages that annoyed the many, a few regarded as opportunities to make large profits. A landowner might ask an inflated rent for the use of otherwise unused land. Farmers were suspected of withholding their 1917 wheat crop from market to get higher prices. Store owners here and there overcharged. Eventually, in mid-1918, food prices were fixed, both wholesale and retail, and rationing of sugar began. Beef might be served in public places only at the noon meal and no more than four days a week. Housewives were restricted to $1\frac{1}{4}$ pounds of beef per family member, per week. Thus, the government intruded in the basic economic equation set by the forces of supply and demand.

Access to coal was as troublesome as the food supply. For Athens this was a double problem: access to coal itself as well as the impact on the area job-market. One dimension of the problem was seen in September 1917 when President Wilson set coal prices at a level lower than the cost of production. Many Ohio producers claimed to hold contracts for delivery of coal at profitable pre-war prices, and they insisted on honoring those contracts. As public institutions, forbidden to offer more than the official price, were threatened with an inability to buy coal, state officials speculated publicly about the need of the State of Ohio to buy coal lands and produce its own coal supplies.

Another dimension to the problem was the railroads. Ohio coal dealers and manufacturers were unnecessarily dilatory in emptying coal hoppers, creating a minor shortage of cars. Far more serious to the Athens area, railroads found it more profitable to haul West Virginia coal to Toledo for the lake trade than Hocking Valley coal. As a result, hundreds of cars, fully loaded with coal, sat on sidetracks, and mines in Athens and Meigs counties, despite unprecedented demands for coal, closed down, leaving miners without an income. To the reader of the *Messenger*, it was also apparent that the Wilson Administration suffered divided counsel, seriously limiting its ability to get coal moving. Athenians experienced the paradox of living in a major coal-producing region, yet facing a shortage of coal for home use.

The Military at Home

The principal aspect of the war was preparation of army and navy forces with which to engage the Central Powers. Before the war ended, some 1,700 Athens County lads would be drawn in along with the county's first women soldiers and sailors. Despite the earlier concern for the nation's preparedness, or lack thereof, the county's experience with the military was largely pragmatic.

As the nation entered the war in April 1917, there were wildly optimistic guesses as to the length of time before local soldiers would engage the enemy face-to-face. In fact, in Washington officials were seriously divided regarding the merits of National Guard units, volunteers, and draftees. Certainly, few Americans fully appreciated all that had to be done before American forces could engage an enemy located in Europe.

A draft bill, calling for the registration of males between twenty-one and thirty years of age, was before Congress within a week of the adoption of the war resolution, but not until June 5 did men register for the draft, 439 men in the City of Athens. The draft itself occurred in July, with Gomer Lewis of Athens being the first on the list. The first contingent of draftees, then referred to as "selects," was summoned to report to Chillicothe on September 5, nearly five months after the declaration of war.

In the interval Athenians focused on their two national guard companies. Here, too, developments occurred in slow motion. More than three months passed before Company L and the Machine Gun Company were mobilized for federal service. For soldiers and civilians alike, the mobilization was a gala occasion. The community hosted an "old fashioned" picnic at the fairgrounds on July 24. A half-dozen brass bands were promised; Nelsonville and Glouster entertained the crowd with a ball game. Ten thousand came to picnic and watch the two military companies drill. As a token of its goodwill, the community presented Major Samuel M. Johnson with a fine bay cavalry horse and equipment, an old Civil War tradition. On August 1 the two guard companies were sworn into the federal service.

The fact is that weeks and months of behind-the-scenes planning was required before the federal government could begin to train either the draftees or the guardsmen. Aside from preparing training camps, cadres of officers had to be trained, and two successive groups of officer-volunteers, chiefly men in their thirties, were recruited and converted into ninety-day wonders. The Athenian officer candidates went to Ft. Benjamin Harrison, Indiana. The first of these men received their commissions in early August. Included were Ohio University students, most of the 1916 college football team, men obviously below the age preference.

For its part, Congress had to decide whether to rely chiefly on volunteers as it had in the Civil War and Spanish-American conflict or to rely on the draft to produce the requisite number of troops. The refining of criteria for military service continued to the end of the war. In late August 1917 the Congress finally defeated a measure that would restrict overseas service to volunteers. Further, the military had to decide how to use the national guard units. Army leaders in Washington provoked considerable dismay when they decided that both guard officers and the rank and file might be reassigned to other units. Unlike in the Civil War and Spanish-American War, local units were not sacrosanct organizations that would go off to war together and come home together at war's end. In September 1917 the War Department replaced the divisional staff officers of the Ohio National Guard units, and many company-grade officers were supplanted by officers trained at Plattsburgh (New York), actions that Ohio National Guard authorities in Columbus viewed as an outrage. To get a single, reasonably trained division abroad by year's end, a handful of men were drawn from guard units across the nation. Accordingly, thirty men were transferred from the two Athens guard units to the 4th Regiment, 42d Division, the Rainbow Division. The transfer was unannounced in advance, and the departure of these men occurred before many townsmen were aware of it. By November the 42d Division, now with twenty men from Athens County, had arrived in France. These men would see much action before they returned home.

Through September 1917 Company L and the Machine Gun Company continued to occupy the armory. Close order drill and company parades alternated with other army routines. The 7th Regiment Band came from Zanesville to give impromptu concerts at the courthouse incidental to playing for company drills, and, on occasion, they offered formal concerts at Ewing Hall. The thirty-piece band charged a thirty-five-cent admission fee, offering the audience a potpourri including the "William Tell Overture" and Bandmaster Henry F. Stenim singing "If You Ever Get Lonely." At this level, the war was a social occasion for Athenians. To keep troops busy, ball games also provided entertainment for townsmen. But above all, there was interminable waiting for orders.

Early in October 1917, both Company L and the Machine Gun Company were directed to recruit to full strength. Company L was to have 150 men, the Machine Gun Company, 170. This meant further delays while the new enlistees were integrated with the old. The upside was that in mid-October the units departed for Camp Sheridan, Montgomery, Alabama. Some 7,000 persons, more than the total village population, showed up to see the troops depart. Zenner's Department store mounted a huge flag on its facade, while other merchants displayed bunting along Court Street. Loring G. Connett, a local florist and graduate of Athens High School and Ohio University, was in command of Company L. Within a month, Company L's personnel were reassigned, scattered among one or another of three batteries of the 136th Field Artillery, and Captain Connett was made adjutant of the First Battalion. The men faced an additional sixteen weeks of training before being ready to go over seas.

The first "selects" were ordered to report to Chillicothe on September 5. The draft presented an anomaly: in the midst of all the hoopla, the effusive patriotism, and the calls for self-sacrifice, enormous numbers, over 50 percent, of the draft registrants claimed family dependency exemptions, and the *Messenger* printed their names and reasons. (For the nation the proportion ran as high as 80 percent.) From this point on, draftees were called to service. The first quota was 120, the second group, 48.

Initially, draft regulations scooped up the unemployed and those without dependents, then to complete quotas, those "easily spared," a not very objectively defined group. Businessmen, the third category, were allowed time to wind up their affairs. Married men, the fourth category, were deferred until all of the preceding classes had been called to service. Shortly, these criteria were refined and amended.

The revised regulations, more realistic and pragmatic, allowed local boards to assess the degree of hardship the draft would impose on the select's family and on the economy.

In March 1918 a second draft was conducted of men ages 18 through 45 who had not been subject to the initial registration. At the same time, the spotlight of publicity was focused on those in the initial draft who did not report. Again, where patriotism did not flow freely, public pressure forced compliance. The numbers departing Athens began to surge—125 in early May 1918, 144 toward the end of the month, 143 in late June, 217 in July. Civil War and Spanish-American war veterans and Boy Scouts escorted the men to the station.

Until July 1918 all the selects had been white. Blacks were first called in mid-July 1918. Religious services were held at Mount Zion Baptist Church to honor the men; Mayor Rowland spoke as did the Reverend C. T. Isom, their minister turned chaplain. En route to the station, The Plains Band led a Court Street parade. Members of the Knights of Pythias provided an escort and the departees were "warmly applauded" along Court Street. A week later the balance of the colored "selects" was sent off, some 29 men in all.

The recruiting of women was in abeyance until 1918. In September the government indicated a need for trained nurses for army service. Two women, Grace Riley and Annabelle Seiple, were already in training; Athens County's quota called for 22 more. Another 40 women volunteered for service in the United States Navy. Within a few hours Kathryn Cuckler, Dicie Cuckler, Katharine Dias, and Ruth Souder passed the navy physical and were sworn in, in Parkersburg. Not to be outdone, Nona Casley, Catherine Dice (Beckler), Nellie Brooks (Griswald), and Dorothy Putnam went to Parkersburg to enlist. To Dicie Cuckler went the distinction of being the first to be ordered to duty. Twenty-two years old and an OU graduate, she was assigned clerical duties at Norfolk, Virginia, as were most of the women.

From the beginning of the war President Ellis had wanted Ohio University to offer students some form of military training. By November 1917 some 200 students were receiving close-order drill. Efforts to have an officer assigned to campus were unavailing. Not until fall 1918 did the War Department have a program in place for college students: The Student Army Training Corps (SATC) and the Student Naval Training Corps (SNTC). The university enthusiastically embraced these programs. Students who enlisted received $30.00 a month plus tuition, laboratory expenses, and board and room. They were also furnished uniforms, guns, and health care and would live under military discipline. Howard Hall was used as the dining hall for the volunteers, and local businessmen put up the funds for a barracks built on campus along Union Street. The structure, to house 250 soldiers, was ready for occupancy by October 10. The men were sworn in October 2. These plans, of course, presumed that the war would go on well into 1919 and perhaps longer. In fact, members of the SATC received their uniforms in time to wear them publicly the day after the war ended; they were all discharged and at home by the end of 1918.

The Military Abroad

The overseas experiences of the Yanks from Athens varied enormously. For the few, service was largely an individual affair. Israel Putnam, the fifth—a direct, lineal descendant of "Old Put"— joined the U.S. Marine Corps and was thus deprived of the companionship of other Athens lads while in the service. So, too, many of those who enlisted as officers or who went through officer candidate schools—men like Prof. Clinton MacKinnon, Prof. D. L. Jefferson, Byron Wolfe, Jr., and J. H. Comstalk—were assigned to units whose ranks contained fellow Athenians only by chance. The city also lost one of its dentists, Dr. J. T. Merwin, who entered the Army Medical Reserve Corps. R. Phillip Rose, an industrial chemist and son of Mrs. E. T. Rose, was appointed captain in the Sanitary Corps. A small number of Athenians with an interest in aviation served in Italy. Leo Pierce of the Athens post office became an aviator. Charles D. Barnhill, another aviator, was based at Foggia, Italy.

Parents, wives, brothers and sisters, girlfriends, and neighbors might be especially concerned with the fate of particular soldiers, but the community as such retained a special interest in the units to which members of Company L and the Machine Gun Company of the old 7th Regiment, ONG, were assigned.

Much attention focused on the Rainbow Division. In January 1918 Arthur Evans confided to his parents: "By Jacks! I've paddled around in the mud and slop until I've begun to grow webbed feet." But all was not mud. He soon reported eight to ten inches of snow on the ground. The Frenchman he thought "a very congenial kind-hearted person," but the French were "about 100 years behind" the Americans.

The 42d Division was at the front by February 22, 1918, and in early March it went into combat. The *Messenger* reported they had "walloped" the Germans. The 166th Regiment took its first casualty, a Chillicothe fellow, in mid-March, and before March was out, the division had been gassed, although reportedly no one had been hurt. As late as June 1918 Wilbur Reeves, of Carpenter, with fifteen lads from the Machine Gun Unit, reported that while his unit had been gassed, there were no casualties; later he became one. The boys, he said, played ball near the artillery while the latter were firing.

In July 1918 the Germans launched a major drive on Paris. Americans on the front between the Aisne and Marne rivers, the 42d Division among them, were in the line of attack. Fighting alongside the French, American troops straightened out the line from Soissons to Chateau Thierry and then pushed across the Marne. By month's end the Germans were represented as having their backs to the wall. The struggle was one of mutual annihilation. When Athens received news that the French had taken Soissons, an impromptu celebration followed. As church bells pealed, the streets filled up within minutes. Boy Scouts, with two flags and a drum, began marching through the streets and three to four hundred people fell in line behind them, the impromptu parade ending in front of the courthouse. Clement Martzolff and the Reverend B. D. Evans spoke. Superintendent Geoffrey Morgan led the singing of "America." After the singing of the "Star Spangled Banner," the elated groups adjourned.

To August 1918, the Americans were brigaded with French units. Then in August, with seven American divisions in France, General Pershing fashioned an independent field command on the Marne front. Thereafter, many but not all Americans fought under American direction. During summer 1918, American troops poured into France by the tens of thousands. In September one and a half million Americans were reported to be in France; a month later, 1,840,000. As American participation escalated, so did the tempo of combat, but hometown folk often learned of the participation of specific units only after the war had ended.

The 42d Division remained in the center of combat through the bloodiest of campaigns from September to November. The Company L lads in the 166th Regiment took casualties: Lawrence Conrath of Richland Avenue, enlisted at 16, was dead at 17.

Interest also centered on the 37th Division, in which those Athenians who had been shipped to Ft. Sheridan, Alabama, were assigned. It arrived in France in June 1918. The 136th Field Artillery, with its contingent of old Company L men, was at Camp Upton, New York, in mid-June, still awaiting shipping orders. The 83d Division, containing selectees from the May 1918 draft, by the end of July was reported to be in Italy.

Even in the midst of war, Athenians, some of whom had perhaps not yet experienced combat, were also struck by the differences in their new environment. Every French home was of stone. "The funniest thing is that the houses and barns are all together." The people were friendly, and there were "some good-looking girls." Perhaps the oddest things they encountered were the wooden shoes.

Until late August 1918 the 37th Division, containing some 300 Athens Countians, remained behind the lines, adjusting to the sights, sounds, and smells of a battle area. Their first real taste of war was an air attack on July 25. The 37th Division found itself on the western end of the allied front, and in the last weeks of war it was in the midst of the campaign to drive the Germans from Flanders and to force the evacuation of Ghent. The 37th Division and the 135th Machine Gun Batallion had first entered the trenches at Baccarat, then moved into the Argonne Forest, where they made an advance of 15 kilometers, held St. Mihiel for a week, and finally engaged in the big push in Flanders. Captain Rafael Johnson's company, the 135th Machine Gun Battalion, was one of four American units chosen to escort King Albert of the Belgians and his Queen to reoccupy their throne in Brussels.

To the end of the war, hometown folks heard little of the activities of the 136th Field Artillery, for once overseas, it had been brigaded with a British unit. It had ended in the thick of combat in Belgium, being in continuous action from October 21 to November 11. The unit experienced few casualties.

The German resistance collapsed with unanticipated suddenness. At the end of September, the *Messenger* reported the Americans had penetrated the Hindenberg Line northwest of Verdun. Bulgaria and Austria already had "peace feelers" out. On September 29 Bulgaria surrendered; on October 3 the Ottoman Government reportedly quit. On October 7, the Kaiser was said to be asking President Wilson to arrange an armistice, and a discussion of peace terms began both in Washington and among the Allies. By November 1 a people's government took over in Vienna.

The Armistice

Shortly before noon on November 7, Athens church bells and factory whistles began to blow, signaling the end of the war in Europe. When it hit the streets, the *Messenger* confirmed that the Allies and Germany had signed an armistice at 11 A.M. The news was no surprise. For a week the paper had been filled with reports on the negotiations. The news was greeted with "wild joy." The student soldiers and sailors spontaneously paraded. As townsmen gathered at the courthouse, parents of the "boys over there" were overcome. "Tears mingled with smiles." In the evening "a monster open-air celebration" was held under the auspices of the Chamber of Commerce—a parade and a program in front of the Masonic Hall on Union

Street with Judge Sayre, Superintendent Morgan, and President Ellis. The latter expressed his regret that the Germans had not been "beaten to their knees and completely humiliated in the dust." The celebration, the *Messenger* declared, had been "the greatest day of all days in the history of Athens." Late that evening, the United Press repudiated its report of the armistice. The war was still on.

On the 11th, President Wilson confirmed the end of the war. Athens felt a sense of relief, but the community was emotionally drained. Youngsters made noise; autoists tore up and down the streets, but the oldsters stayed home. On the 14th, a sense of jubilation surged on the report that the "Rainbow Boys (the 42d Division) May Be Home By Christmas." This was pie-in-the-sky speculation, but it underscored that the Athens lads abroad would be returning. A community celebration of the war's end scheduled for November 15 was put off until Thanksgiving because of the "floo"—Spanish influenza. And it would be put off again and again.

The war was a stage on which some Athenians performed remarkable feats. Among the first was Kossuth T. Crossen of Albany and Carbondale. A medical doctor, Crossen chose to serve in the infantry, going to France as a First Lieutenant, 102d Infantry. Serving alongside French troops in a raid, he was first cited March 12, 1918, "for admirable courage and energy" and awarded the Croix de Guerre. Writing home a short time later, he declared: "The only good Hun is a dead one." Promoted to Captain, Crossen was mortally wounded in July, becoming the first officer from Athens County to die in France.

In May 1918 Athenians learned that Wallis Stewart, Guysville, a member of the 166th Regiment, 42 Division, had also been honored with the Croix de Guerre. No details were given. Just before the end of the war the *Messenger* reported that Samuel M. Johnson, Athens attorney and erstwhile officer of Company L, had been cited for leading his men on the field of battle. Detached from the 7th Regiment, Johnson had the relatively unique experience of leading a Negro unit in combat. In the Champagne, he and his men captured a German trench, 100 prisoners, an arms dump, 30 machine guns, and 2 howitzers. Now a Major of the 372d Infantry, Johnson also received the United States Distinguished Service Cross for his "extraordinary heroism" as well as the Croix de Guerre with palm and the Legion of Honor from the French Government.

The community took pride, too, in the recognition accorded Captain Rafael Johnson, the younger brother of Sam Johnson, and two of his enlisted men, Carl Lovett and Norman Ervin, both of Nelsonville, who received decorations at the hands of the Belgian Government. The 135th Machine Gun Battalion, of which they were members, had performed extraordinarily well. And then there was Sergeant C. J. Hayden, 339th Infantry Regiment, on whom the British Government bestowed the Distinguished Conduct Medal for his "great initiative, coolness, devotion and courage" while serving with British forces in Russia.

By World War I Louis Rodolph de Steiguer was a remote figure to all but the oldest Athenians. The *Messenger* had closely followed his career in the navy from the time he departed Athens for the U. S. Naval Academy in the mid-1880s. As a career officer he had pioneered in the field of naval gunnery fire control. During World War I, de Steiguer, a Captain, commanded the U.S.S. *Arkansas* and was one of the senior American naval officers who accepted the surrender of the German fleet at Scapa Flow. For his wartime services he received the Distinguished Service Medal. He went on in the 1920s to command the Atlantic fleet, the navy's senior command at sea, and retired in 1933.

While the war brought fame to some, it brought injury and death to others. The deaths of Lawrence Conrath and K. T. Crossen have been noted. When news of the demise of Floyd Bolin, the first Athenian to be killed in combat, was received, the Athens community shared his mother's grief with a community memorial service. Israel M. Foster spoke for the military groups, L. G. Worstell for the American Red Cross. The *Messenger* provided an extended account of the service.

By the day of the armistice the Athens community had been shielded from the full impact of the war. At war's end, 12,000 deaths had been reported for the entire nation, and only five were of men from Athens County. But this figure was deceiving, for there had been almost continuous, intense combat from late September to November 11, and the War Department lagged seriously in identifying casualties by name. It was spring 1919 before the last families received the notices of the death of kin. While the "Sammies" largely escaped the dysentery, typhoid, and malaria that had claimed so many lives in the Civil War, the death of Fred Jordan at Camp Custer (Michigan) of the "floo" foreshadowed a devastating epidemic that would afflict military and civilian populations alike. When the final military casualty figures were all in, the *Messenger* reported that a total of 61 men from the county had died while in the service. It estimated another 110 had been wounded. The casualties sustained in World War I were a small fraction of those experienced in the War between the States. Few men had been in combat more than a few months. Medical care was better. But as in the earlier war, more men died from disease than on the battlefield.

After the War

The Armistice left a modest agenda of unfinished business. One item was the disposition of the $111,978.43 held by the Athens County War Relief Association. The leadership earmarked $50,000 for relief in 1919, leaving nearly $62,000, which it suggested could be used to build an "Athens County Memorial Hospital" in honor of the Athens men who had served in the war. The hospital would be open to all residents of the county. The *Messenger* enthusiastically supported the proposal. Opening the Copeland Hospital made the proposal moot. In the early 1920s the funds were divided among the veterans' organizations.

The Athens chapter of the American Red Cross took on one final task, treating those returning veterans whose trains halted briefly in Athens for fuel and water. The railroad provided train schedules and the number of troops on board. The treats included bread and jelly, apples and oranges, and popcorn. In February some 8,400 service men were served; in March, 12,800; in April, 19,656. By May, most of the "boys" were back. On a Friday early in August 1919 the Red Cross wound up its war work, relinquishing its space at the Athens National Bank Building and selling its sewing machines. Its final report stated that the canteen at the depot had served 106,590 soldiers.

Another item of unfinished business was the final Victory Loan drive. The national goal was $4.5 billion and was advertised to care for the soldier boys abroad, to bring the boys home, to pay war insurance claims, to rehabilitate the wounded, to sustain the veterans hospitals, and to pay war debts. With the country in the midst of converting to a peacetime economy and an unusually high proportion of men unemployed, reaching the goal proved "a difficult task." But in the end, Athens again met its quota.

The highest priority deservedly went to welcoming the troops home. This proved a protracted exercise, for the troops dribbled back home, usually company by company, and at times units or parts of units arrived unexpectedly, sometimes in the middle of the night. And while the welcoming committee might have its agenda for a proper welcome, soldiers anxious to embrace wives, girlfriends, and mothers had their own priorities. The model was that designed for the return of the Athens contingent of the 135th Field Artillery, scheduled to arrive on April 9, 1919. The welcoming committee planned to meet the train and have the fellows form ranks and parade to the courthouse, led by parents and the Athens High School Band. The fellows would be treated to a dinner at the Chamber of Commerce Rooms followed by a dance at the Armory. While all town girls might attend, the only males at the dance would be the members of the 135th. In fact, on detraining, the boys rushed to their girlfriends, wives, and mothers, and the band marched back to Court Street by itself.

When Company L, 136th Field Artillery returned a few days later, a similar format was adopted. But all went awry. With but three-hours notice, only twenty-five of the fellows arrived at midnight in a drenching spring rain. The town bells sounded to summon the citizens, while latter-day Paul Reveres drove through the streets to give the cry "The boys are coming home at midnight." Efforts to notify the citizenry by telephone resulted chiefly in the collapse of the entire phone system. Despite the rain, the band fell out as did hundreds of citizens and parents. The "old royal spirit" prevailed. Over the next several days other members of Company L trickled back to town. The banquet and dance had to be rescheduled. Still much attached to their one-time commander, the men asked Major Sam M. Johnson to be the principal speaker when their banquet finally came off. Johnson spoke bluntly, reminding them they "could not live forever on this hero stuff." He urged them to go back to their old jobs or to school as soon as possible.

Not only were the returnees welcomed unit by unit as they arrived, but various community organizations also staged their own welcome homes. The Knights of Columbus threw a banquet for their membership at the Masonic Hall. Sisters of veterans of the 37th Division entertained their brothers. The Elks and the Knights of Pythias likewise treated their returning lodge members. The Methodists hosted all the returning veterans in town, except those of Company L and the Machine Gun Battalion whom they had already treated. With 150 veterans attending, this was reputedly the largest homecoming reception. This was the reception that welcomed the "selectees" who had been far more dispersed in their military service than the members of the city's two National Guard units. By mid-1919 Athenians were free to look to the future.

A MORE URBANE ATHENS

Athens moved perceptibly toward a more secular, more worldly society between 1900 and 1920. One of the side effects of the Spanish-American War had been to focus attention on such exotic places as Cuba, Puerto Rico, Hawaii, and the Philippines. The focus was sustained as Charles Grosvenor joined William Howard Taft in an official mission to the Philippines, and Grosvenor subsequently shared his views in the *Messenger* and in person. Local attorney J. Perry Wood was appointed to the Spanish War Claims Commission, and he recruited several Athenians to work for the Commission. Frank Lowry, Albert Graf, and Dr. Dudley Welch, among some 40 other Athenians, were scattered from Manila to Mindanao as part of the United States Army during the Philippine Insurrection, while Professor E. E. Baker spent several years in the Philippines helping to set up a public school system for the islands. And all of these people shared their insights with fellow townsmen via the *Messenger*.

China and Japan also drew attention. C. D. McGrath wrote home of his experiences as a businessman in Yokohama. David H. Moore, having been elected a bishop of the Methodist Church, was posted to China and Korea. Several Athens women, including Eva May Raw and Mary Kelly, went to China as missionaries. Mary Kelly and Flo Hedges related their eyewitness reactions to the Boxer Rebellion. Raw shared her on-the-scene views of the 1911 revolution from Nanking.

As in earlier years, a handful of the Athens affluent vacationed abroad. Lena Slatterly and daughter May took three months to tour England, Holland, Germany, Switzerland, and Italy. Traveling within the United States, visiting the successive national expositions at New Orleans and St. Louis, summering at resorts and spas, and wintering in Florida or California gave dozens of Athenians direct experience of other communities.

World War I, of course, uprooted hundreds of Athenians. Soldiers went off to camps across the country, and of these, roughly half also went to France for at least a few months, observing, if not always understanding, the cultures of others. In addition, numbers of civilians went off to other communities to work for a time. By the end of the war, Athenians were far more cosmopolitan than ever before.

The rise of competitive football and baseball did much to make Athenians develop a sense of community consciousness. The university and Athens High School organized football teams that allowed a handful of young men the exhilaration of competitive sports and provided entertainment for large numbers of fans, students, and townspeople. President Ellis attended pep rallies and on one occasion blasted the faculty as "tightwads" because so few joined in the mass-migration to Oxford for the Miami game. Both university and high school games merited front-page stories. When the *Messenger* could say of a game that [Roger] "Jones booting and good work . . . tell the story," it not only reported the game, but it identified with the team and the star of the day. The community's self-respect was on the line. The town shared in the suffering and mourning when high schooler John Porter died following a freak accident in a game with Nelsonville. The event revived memories of nearly two decades before of another football accident that had claimed the life of Ralph O'Bleness.

Baseball, even more than football, focused attention and loyalties away from self and family to a wider social group. The playing season was longer and teams had a broader community base. In 1902 Athens had a good team, the "Ebonies," "colored boys" who could draw 300 persons to their games. Inter-city rivalries were played up. The games were events. The Athens-Jackson contest at Jackson merited telephonic bulletins inning-by-inning, posted at Cline's Drug Store. Athens won and on returning home, the team was met at the station by a band and escorted about the village in an impromptu parade. Baseball was ubiquitous; kids played in vacant lots and in the streets; the north and south ends of College Street and the intersection of Court and Park Place were favorites. The young women organized teams, too, competing with out-of-town teams.

Baseball was not just a fun game; organized competition required funding for equipment, uniforms, and travel. Not uncommonly, the pitcher and catcher received a modest stipend even when everyone else played for free. The village took vicarious satisfaction in the careers of several young men who played professional ball for teams at Paris, Kentucky, and Chillicothe and Columbus, Ohio. "Crum" Kahler and Josh Devore, who made it to the big leagues, became local heroes. Kahler had a sore arm and Devore, at 5' 6", was pushing his luck in National League competition. But at key moments, the scrappy Devore drove in runs or made brilliant catches, had a talent for drawing a base on balls, and was a terror when on base, on one occasion stealing four bases in a single inning.

By 1911 Athens youngsters were playing ball not only in the streets and on the high school and university teams, but on teams representing Sunday school classes, labor unions, the brick plant, and post-office clerks as well. A proposal came forward to lay out a proper diamond on Mill Street beyond the railroad tracks. At this point the town chose sides. Mill Street residents feared a ballfield would attract a "disorderly crowd" and bring their neighborhood into disrepute. Town churches opposed the prospect of Sunday baseball and thought of it as contrary to "the culture and moral tone" of the city. Council divided 3–3 on an ordinance prohibiting Sunday baseball. One adamant but anonymous opponent of baseball mailed a letter to council threatening to burn the grandstand and fence should they be built. The threat was passed on to the United States Postal Inspector. Months later city council moved to ban Sunday baseball for pay.

Other entertainment came to the city. The minstrel show was passé, but the circus still made its rounds. Robinson's was greeted in 1901 as "ever popular, ever welcome." But over the next two decades, it lost its aura. The performances became jaded and the show was compromised by the drifters and con artists who seemed inseparable from it. By 1918, the *Messenger* thought of Robinson's as having always had an unsavory reputation. When Pawnee Bill's Wild West Show played Athens in 1907, the *Messenger*, rather than bubbling over in anticipation, recalled that on his previous visit, in the course of demonstrating his legendary marksmanship, Pawnee Bill had shot the fingers off his wife's hand. Buffalo Bill Cody appeared twice, but on his last visit, the aging Cody rode in a coach.

Although old ways were still good ways, they were passing. New ways were appearing. At the popular level, the local YMCA leadership condemned the "mushing," the "hugging and kissing habit," of young men and women at parties. It was bad, "this dark and dangerous 'mush party.'" Nor was Cardinal Farley pleased with the new dance, the tango. Other examples of the new were experienced as curiosities. The first aircraft that passed over at night was a dim outline of "a long cigar-shaped shadow high in the sky." Charles Nye's wireless outfit on South High was accepted matter-of-factly.

Athens drew a variety of speakers; they ranged from Albert Bushnell Hart, distinguished Harvard historian, speaking on the Balkans to John Spargo lecturing on socialism, and Maud Ballington Booth, leader of the American branch of the Salvation Army, and hailed as the "ablest woman orator in America." But there were other celebrities to be seen and heard: Theodore Roosevelt on a campaign trip speaking from the courthouse steps in 1912; John Mitchell, the United Mine Workers' president; and "Uncle" Joe Cannon, the autocratic speaker of the United States House of Representatives.

Musical tastes expanded. While the century was still young, John Philip Sousa, "the one real and only," gave a Saturday matinee performance. The Mendelssohn Quartet returned. A high point, however, was the appearance of Ernestine Schumann-Heink. "Elegantly gowned," she was an "engaging and gracious personality" as well as a great singer. Eight hundred Athenians attended her concert at Ewing Auditorium. Only half that number came out to hear the Pittsburgh Festival orchestra present Smetana's "Moldau" along with the "Quartet from *Rigoletto*." At a more popular level, Victor Herbert's *The Red Mill* appeared at the Opera House in 1911 and his *Princess Pat* in January 1918.

A wide variety of theater also played Athens. Shakespeare was offered—*The Taming of the Shrew*, *The Tempest*, and *Hamlet*. But Athenians were now open to other fare, too. As large theater chains arose, a succession of national touring companies were abroad, some of which played the Opera House. In October 1909 the Sam and Lee Shubert organization sent *The Road to Yesterday*, which charged from twenty-five cents to a dollar and a half for admission. Other plays included *Buster Brown* (1911), Ed McWilliams and Frank Crumet in *The Three Collegians* (1913), plugged as a ragtime act, *Peg o' My Heart*, which played in Christmas season 1913, George Bernard Shaw's *The Chocolate Soldier*, and *Daddy Long Legs* with a New York cast. The

Opera House was not Broadway, but Athenians had intermittent access to a sampling of contemporary theater.

Unquestionably, the movies made a big impact; during much of the second decade, there were three theaters operating, each exhibiting three different feature pictures a week. The motion picture provided the day-to-day fare of the Opera House, yielding place as needed for live theater and concerts. To house the new Majestic Theater, precursor of the Athena, the Bethel grocery store was evicted. In 1919 it was enlarged to seat 600 patrons. This generation of Athenians saw the movie evolve. As late as 1914, "Etta of the Footlights" was a special feature, a four-reeler for five cents. The movies became longer; repertoire groups gave way to stars, of whom Mary Pickford was one of the first. And she appeared repeatedly—"A Good Little Devil," "Lena and the Geese," and other forgettable shows. On opening, the Grand promised first-run movies for five cents—three-reelers—featuring the likes of Charlie Chaplin, Fatty Arbuckle, Mabel Normand, and W. C. Fields. Within a week of its opening, the Grand offered Chaplin in *The Tramp*. Not to be outdone, the Columbia offered six reels of Chaplin's work, a retrospective. And at the end of the Great War, Athenians were treated to a pioneer cowboy epic: Zane Grey's *Riders of the Purple Sage*. Indeed, during the decade 1911–1920, Athenians were treated to Dorothy and Lillian Gish, Geraldine Farrar, Douglas Fairbanks, and Ethel Barrymore. Initially D. W. Griffith's *Birth of a Nation* seemed too strong fare for Ohioans, and even after two years, when the Ohio Board of Censors finally allowed the movie to be shown, Athenians for some months had to go either to Cincinnati or Columbus to view it. When finally exhibited in Athens in December 1917, lower floor seats at the Opera House went at $1.00 and $1.50 each.

Not all movie fare was elevating. Theda Bara's *Sin* was billed as "a startlingly realistic screen drama." Much theater fare focused on girls who fell from grace, the producers hoping to get past the movie censors either on the premise that the movie illustrated that the wages of sin were death or as a sociological study of human behavior. In a few cases, a women-only screening of a controversial movie was offered. While most adults were abstractly aware of the demimonde, the movie made it visual and thrust it before the citizenry, advertising it in the *Messenger* as well as on the streets in the center of town. The movies flaunted the risqué at a level Athens had never before experienced and illustrated publicly behavior that previously Athenians had been compelled to seek out surreptitiously. Although theater managers elsewhere operated on Sunday until the Ohio Supreme Court declared Sunday movies to be illegal, no movies profaned the sabbath in Athens.

Another medium shaping and broadening popular culture was the phonograph.

The curiosity of the late 1890s became a commonplace of the middle-class parlor by 1914. A Columbia highboy was available for $75.00, only $2.50 per week; a table-top model was available for $25.00. From the start Victor and Columbia records offered twenty or so new releases once or twice a month. If the sound was not high fidelity, it had improved enormously from that produced by Edison's first machines. As even the cheapest machines were beyond the means of wage workers, the music that was issued was intended to appeal to the middle class. Columbia's "China Town, My China Town" was a stiff 65 cents—half a day's wage. By 1917 Hawaiian music was the rage; "Aloha Oe" and "My Honolulu Hula Girl" were available. For children, Thornton Burgess narrated his own "Bed Time Stories," or one could choose "Peter Rabbit." At the other end of the spectrum, one could secure recordings of the "Sextet from *Lucia*" or Ignace Paderewski's performance of "Minuet in G." The phonograph, like the motion picture, transcended regions. Mass produced and distributed, a Paderewski recording, like an Ethel Barrymore film performance, was within the range of dozens of Athenians who never could have gone to Columbus or Cincinnati to experience such stars in person. Athenians participated in the mainstream of American culture.

POSTSCRIPT

Had Rufus Putnam been able to visit Athens in 1920, the terrain would have been strange. The primeval forests, through which Putnam had made his way to Athens, had been cleared, replaced by cultivated fields. Natural vegetation had given way to cultivated crops, although paradoxically the major crop was corn, an Indian staple. Deer, bear, panthers, wolves, and turkeys had been displaced by cattle, swine, sheep, and poultry. As bad as Athenians thought the rural roads were, the road from Athens to Amesville and on to Marietta was wide enough to accommodate a wagon. By railroad Athenians could travel between Athens and Marietta in three hours or so; at an earlier time it had been an overnight venture. Within the village, the plat of the old town might seem familiar enough to Putnam, although it had been altered. Streets that Putnam had laid out on a plat map were now bricked and flanked by sidewalks. The trees that lined the streets or that stood in yards would have been chosen and planted to suit the residents' convenience.

The lifestyle of Putnam's generation was shaped, often limited, by the natural environment, but Athenians of 1920 were, by comparison, the masters of the environment. Putnam's generation had relied on wood for fuel; Athenians now heated homes with coal or gas. The homemade candle had been displaced by the electric light, although some older homes may have still used gaslight. Electricity permitted a level of light at night unimagined by Putnam and extended the workday when needed. When used in the telegraph and telephone, electricity opened Athens to instant communication with the rest of the world. Steam engines, barely known to Putnam, had become practical, useful machines freeing man from dependence on animal, wind, and water power. Wind power and water power had functioned as much at nature's dictate as at man's. Steam worked when and where man directed it. The steam engine permitted sustained travel at speeds faster than any man or animal could attain and generated power beyond anything man or animal could muster. The price was a transformed eco-system.

If most Americans had lived in a rural milieu in the nineteenth century, in the twentieth, the majority lived in an urban community. With 6,400 residents in 1920 Athens stayed in the mainstream. During the previous century, it had shared the rural and small village experience of the majority of Americans. Henceforth, it would share the urban experience of the new majority, its political energies focused on designing and managing an infrastructure suited to its needs as a small city. The concentration of people within the corporate limits alone made it increasingly imperative for the municipal government to assume responsibilities that individuals could no longer handle. Athens did not have all the answers; no community did. Finding the bounds, for example, between areas of health care to be left to the individual and the areas in which public authorities should intervene for the common good—the slaughtering of meat, sanitary standards in restaurants and soda fountains, and the role of the public health nurse—engaged much attention. Civic interests won out over the individual.

From the first day of settlement the men of the community, all whites, had been citizens. While at the time no one seems to have thought about it, women had limited contractual or political rights. And most American blacks were slaves. The Civil War had ended on terms that made the blacks free and granted them the rights of citizens and the right to vote. Women, as they engaged in out-of-home activities, had an increasing impact on public affairs in the village, and well before the nineteenth amendment was adopted, Athens women played an active role in civic affairs. By the end of 1920 women, too, possessed the right to vote and hold public office.

Initially the local economy was marked by production for home use and otherwise shaped by the ability of local merchants to market farm surpluses while supplying staples of food, clothing, and household goods that could not be produced locally. By 1920, Athens was fully engaged in a nationwide market economy. The city's economy was diversified, the State Hospital, the University, the mines, and the railroads, and McBee Bindery being the major employers.

For all its economic progress, the community faced a major paradox. In the beginning each family, of necessity, had been self-reliant, largely limited to the goods and services it could produce for its own use, but otherwise self-directed, self-employed. By 1920 factory production had replaced home production, and while the level of living was infinitely higher, the greater portion of the population was dependent on an employer, often an outsider, for income. The newer way of life often placed the needs of society in conflict with the interests of the individual.

The community of 1800 had been isolated. By 1920 the community was surprisingly cosmopolitan. Significant numbers of citizens were well-traveled, some by virtue of their affluence, others courtesy of the armed forces. The university faculty added to the variety of well-educated citizens. The movie and phonograph—alongside the stream of visiting speakers, musicians, and theater companies—enabled Athenians to share a common culture with the rest of American society. The automobile, still at the threshold of its utility, promised a degree of mobility that would extend the area within which citizens might operate, further expanding their social and cultural horizons.

At long last the college, the *raison d'être* of the Athens settlement, had come into its own. It had shaken free of domination by the Presbyterians and Methodists. It had freed itself of the role of landlord to Athens village and to Athens and Alexander townships, a tie that had kept the university strapped for cash either for capital or operating funds for successive generations. Charles Super had succeeded in getting regular annual appropriations from the Ohio legislature; Alston Ellis, in embracing teacher education, had attracted a volume of students to Athens that made the university an economic force that had contributed to pushing the community from the status of a village to that of a city.

In 1920 the village years were behind Athens; for the future Athens would explore an urban experience.

Bibliographical Essay

In uncovering the record of Athens' past, the issues of the successive Athens newspapers have provided the foundation. They begin in April 1825 with the *Athens Mirror and Literary Register* (1825–30), followed by the *Western Spectator and Athenian Chronicle* (1830–37), the *Hocking Valley Gazette and Athens Journal* (1837–44), the *Athens Messenger and Hocking Valley Gazette* (1844–61), and the *Athens Messenger* or some variant thereof from 1861 to the present. The *Athens Journal* (1875–1909) provided a dissenting view from the dominant Republican tone of the *Athens Messenger*. The newspapers, on microfilm, are found in the Microforms Division, Alden Library, Ohio University, Athens, Ohio.

As a corrective to writing a history as seen through the eyes of successive newspaper editors, I've relied on the United States Manuscript Census. The data included varies from decade to decade, but I transcribed the census of 1820 to 1920 inclusive, excepting the 1890 census, which was long since destroyed, and the 1910 census, which is all but untranscribable. The census beginning in 1850 lists each individual by name and provides a wealth of personal data. I have been able to work with printouts that present the data in alphabetical sequence, that list individuals by race, sex, and *age*, and that list individuals by race, sex, and *occupation*. The cross-tabulations that result have permitted me to make informed generalizations about sub-elements of the Athens community and to calculate school attendance rates, labor force participation rates, the occupational distribution of the labor force, and the character of the black community. The census materials are from the National Archives, Microcopy, Microforms Division, Alden Library, Ohio University.

At critical points, I verified spellings of names, family relationships, and dates of birth and death from the indexes to burials at Athens' three cemeteries: West State Street Cemetery (1993), Mt. Calvary Cemetery (1994), and West Union Street Cemetery (1995). These are accessible either at the Athens County Historical Society and Museum (ACHS&M) or at Alden Library's Special Collections and University Archives. By printing the data for West State Street Cemetery (the town's oldest cemetery) in order of death dates, I was able to calculate ages at death and make informed judgments about the mortality of infants, children, and adult women and men for various time periods in the nineteenth century.

The manuscript collections of Ohio University offer insights into the activities of specific groups. The records of the Athenian Literary Society (1818 to 1920) and the Philomathean Literary Society (1822 to 1920) give insight into the topics of interest to Ohio University undergraduates in the pre-intercollegiate athletic era. The records of the Athens Reading Club (1871–1920), the Tuesday Club (1902–1920), and the Pallas Club (1895–1920) tell much about the intellectual interests of the community's movers and shakers. The records of the Woman's Music Club of Athens, Ohio (1914–1920) spells out the musical interests of women vocalists, pianists, and instrumentalists who met regularly to perform for one another and once a year gave a public recital. All of these materials are to be found in Alden Library's Special Collections and University Archives.

Necessarily in a work covering a broad spectrum of topics, this study has depended on the research of others. I propose here to direct the reader to those materials of greatest utility.

Indians. Martha Potter-Otto's *Ohio's Prehistoric Peoples* (Columbus: Ohio Historical Society, 1968) is general, not technical. James L. Murphy's *An Archeological History of the Hocking Valley* (Ohio University Press, 1975; Revised ed., 1989) is by the archaeologist who dug some of the mounds in the Athens area. It is comprehensive.

Founding of Athens. A first-hand account of the founding of Athens can be found in *The Life, Journals, and Correspondence of Rev. Manasseh Cutler, LL.D.*, edited by William Parker Cutler and Julia Perkins Cutler, 2 vols. (Athens: Ohio University Press, 1987). Useful sources for the early history of Ohio include Ray Allen Billington's *Westward Expansion: A History of the American Frontier* (the second edition is cited here; New York: Macmillan, 1960), Allan W. Eckert, *The Frontiersmen* (New York: Bantam Books, 1970), and Theodore Pease, "The Ordinance of 1787," *Mississippi Valley Historical Review* 25 (1938). Among nineteenth-century accounts, two books by Samuel P. Hildreth are of interest: *Pioneer History: Being an Account of the First Examinations of the Ohio Valley, and the Early Settlement of the Northwest Territory* (Cincinnati: H.W. Derby and Co., 1848), and *Biographical and Historical Memoirs of the Early Pioneer Settlers of Ohio* (Cincinnati: H. W. Derby and Co., 1852).

Athens Village. For the earliest settlers, Charles M. Walker's *History of Athens County, Ohio* (Cincinnati: Robert Clarke & Co., 1869) is by the son of Dr. Ezra Walker, an Athens County pioneer. The first general history of the village, it concentrates on the founding generation and provides biographical sketches. Walker's *History* also contains several brief but rewarding first-hand accounts that are easily overlooked. These include: "Reminiscences furnished by Chauncey F. Perkins" who came to Athens in 1801 at age nineteen and relates his impressions of Athens to 1814, pp. 576–92; Julia Perkins Pratt's "Journal" of the Eliphaz Perkins family migration June 1799–December 1799, pp. 154–57; and "The Autobiography of Thomas Ewing," which tells of his first years in Athens County, beginning May 1798, pp. 395–403.

History of the Hocking Valley, Ohio (Chicago: Inter-State Publishing Co., 1883) regurgitates some of the Walker *History* and updates Walker's account. It has a narrative of the historical development. William E. Peters's *Athens County, Ohio* ([Athens]: n.p., 1947) is by a civil engineeer, lawyer, and history buff; Peters spent thirty years or so studying, collecting, and writing about Athens County. His *Athens County* needs to be consulted but with discretion. His works, at times, are idiosyncratic. Charles H. Harris, *The Harris History: A Collection of Tales of Long Ago of Southeastern Ohio* (Athens: The Athens Messenger, 1957) offers a collection of feature stories on Athens families and pictures of their homes. Harris was a *Messenger* reporter.

Elizabeth Grover Beatty's and Marjorie S. Stone's *Getting to Know Athens County* (Athens: The Stone House, 1984) approaches the county's development in topical fashion, drawing in part on Beatty's first-hand knowledge of the community and in part on Stone's skill as a researcher. It contains a detailed bibliography and stands out as carefully researched and critically written.

Periodically Athenians were moved to present a "snapshot" of the community. While these are uneven in quality, each has some utility. The *Atlas of Athens County, Ohio*, edited by D. J. Lake (Philadelphia: Titus, Simmons & Titus, 1875; reprint, ACHS&M, 1992) has plat maps for each township, maps of each hamlet, and idealized illustrations of homes and portraits of a few of the elite of the third quarter of the nineteenth century. J. C. Tipton's *Athens County, Picturesque, Industrial, Commercial, 1797–1897* (Athens: Messenger & Herald, 1897) is in the same tradition but contains far more illustrations and biographical sketches. *The Centennial Atlas of Athens County, Ohio* (Athens: The Centennial Atlas Association, 1905; reprinted, Ohio University Press, 1975, 1996) offers a potpourri of sketches of local businesses, Athens families, and historical sketches. They are of uneven quality but represent what Athenians knew of one another at the turn of the century.

The Athens Home Coming Reunion, June 14 and June 15, 1904 was a souvenir of the Ohio University Centennial homecoming. Compiled by Captain A. H. Mattox, it is full of laudatory sketchs of "Men of Athens," but is useful for the photographs of these community leaders.

A. B. Walker's "Reminiscences," (Athens, Ohio: October 1876; reprinted by ACHS&M, 1990) is by a son of Dr. Ezra Walker. His account is especially useful with respect to the salt business.

Fred H. Sands has two papers on banking in Athens: "The History of Banking in Athens County," 15 pp., and "An Athens Institution: The Bank of Athens, 1857–1963," 9 pp., (1963). Both are found at Alden Library Archives and ACHS&M. A banker by profession, Sands was a latter-day associate of James D. Brown, founder of the Bank of Athens.

Susan L. Mitchell, *The Hewitts of Athens County, Ohio* (Westland, Mich., 1989) is a well-researched study of the Hewitt family with special emphasis on Moses Hewitt, of whom the author is a descendant.

The most useful work on everyday life in early Athens is Harriet Connor Brown's *Grandmother Brown's Hundred Years 1827–1927* (Boston: Little, Brown & Co., 1929). This well-thought-out biography of Maria Foster Brown by her daughter-in-law gives much of the flavor of life in Athens in the 1830s and 1840s.

Buckeye Rovers in the Gold Rush: An Edition of Two Diaries, Revised and Enlarged Edition, edited by H. Lee Scamehorn, Edwin P. Banks and Jamie Lytle-Webb (Athens: Ohio University Press, 1989), contains the parallel accounts of Elza Armstrong and John Banks during their participation in the California gold rush.

It Happened in Athens County (in the early 1900s), compiled by Mildred Bleigh (Athens, Ohio: Mildred Allen Bleigh, Fall 1987) is a 293-page compendium of clippings from the Athens *Messenger* organized topically. It is fine for the casual reader and often serves as a quick index to the *Messenger.*

Athenians at War. There are official rosters for soldiers in the American Revolution who lived in Ohio, Ohio Soldiers in the War of 1812, and Soldiers of the State of Ohio in the War with Mexico. Patricia Fife Medert's *Raw Recruits and Bullish Prisoners: Ohio's Capital in the War of 1812* ([Chillicothe]: Ross County Historical Society Publication, 1992) is a good narrative account of Ohio's role in the war. It provides the context within which the Athens militia companies of the Gregory Brothers served. Whitelaw Reid's *Ohio in the War, 1861–65* (n.p., Moore Wilstach & Baldwin, 1868) in volume 2 gives a listing, regiment by regiment, of the officers along with a brief regimental history. "To Leonard from Fanny To Fanny from Leonard. A Collection of Letters exchanged by Leonard Jewitt and his wife Fanny Elliott Cooley While He Served in the War Between the States," compiled by Grace Jeffers Greiner (n.p., n.d.), reveals much about the problems of women on the home front and the experiences of buck privates engaged in resisting the bushwhackers of western Virginia and in the Shenandoah campaigns. This is at the ACHS&M. Thomas F. Wildes, *Record of the One Hundred and Sixteenth, Ohio Infantry Volunteers in the War of the Rebellion* (Sandusky, Ohio: I. F. Mack & Bros., 1884), is by the unit's long-time commanding officer. Wildes and Leonard Cooley were in the same unit. "Diary for the Year 1862, Duncan A. Huling, 18th Regiment Ohio Volunteer Infantry," transcribed by Philippa B. Benson; Introduction by Robert L. Daniel [ACHS&M, 1993], treats the reactions of one private to events in Kentucky, Tennessee, and Alabama, including the battle of Stone's River.

Coal. The place of coal in Athens history rests on several accounts. Douglas Crowell's *History of the Coal Mining Industry in Ohio,* Bulletin 72, Department of Natural Resources (Columbus: Department of Natural Resources, 1995) provides an overview as seen by a state agency and has the most authoritative list of coal production figures. Eugene H. Palka, *Artifacts of the Coal Age: Athens County Region* (Thesis, Ohio University, March 1986; ACHS&M, 1988) focuses on the structures that have survived the coal mining era. Most useful are Ivan M. Tribe's works: *Little Cities of Black Diamonds: Urban Development in the Hocking Coal Region, 1870–1900* (Athens: Athens Ancestree, 1986; ACHS&M, 1989) and *Sprinkled with Coal Dust: Life and Work in the Hocking Coal Region, 1870–1900* (Athens, ACHS&M, 1989). This is a social and cultural study of the coal areas adjacent to and north of Athens. There is no study based on company records.

Canals and Railroads. Harry N. Scheiber, *Ohio Canal Era: A Case Study of Government and the Economy, 1820–1861* (Athens: Ohio University Press, 1969) is a model of its genre. It provides the statewide context for the building of the Hocking Canal. David H. Mould's

Canals and Railroads in the Hocking Valley Region of Ohio, 1825–1875 (Dissertation, Ohio University, August, 1989) provides a focused look at the Hocking Valley Canal. John E. Pixton, *The Marietta and Cincinnati Railroad, 1845–1883: A Case Study in American Railroad Economics* (University Park: The Pennsylvania University Studies, No. 17, 1966) is clear, concise, and informative. It is complemented by John R. Grabb's *The Marietta and Cincinnati Railroad and Its Successor—the Baltimore and Ohio. A Case Study of This Once Great Route Across Ohio, 1851–1988* (Chillicothe: John R. Grabb, 1989). Less analytical than Pixton, Grabb captures the impact of the railroad on people and communities and provides photographs. An indispensable source on the Belpre and Marietta and the Marietta and Cincinnati railroad is Robin Lacy of Athens.

Education. The fullest account of education in Athens is to be found in the successive Athens newspapers; otherwise Thomas N. Hoover's *The History of Ohio University* (Athens: Ohio University Press, 1954) is an excellent work based on a careful reading of the university's records. Two chapters relating to student life at the university were omitted from Hoover's book but exist in typescript form at the Ohio University Archives, Alden Library. William E. Peters, *Legal History of the Ohio University* (Cincinnati: The Western Methodist Book Concern, 1910) reprints assorted documents relating to the chartering of the University and the protracted legal actions involving the leaseholds and conflicts over ownership of the Commons.

The Catalog of Ohio University (Athens, Ohio: 1804–1970) provides specific details as to faculty, students, and graduates year by year. *The Athena* (1905–1920), the student yearbook, records the development of student clubs, fraternal societies, and athletics. *The Athena* has some contemporaneous pictures of the campus. *The Arena* (1912–1920), the yearbook of Athens High School, similarly reveals the development of the high school as the center of adolescent society.

Religion. The histories of Athens churches are uneven in quality. The records of the Presbyterians are fullest. The "Session and Trustee Records" (1818–1920) are accessible in the Ohio University Archives, Alden Library. John Spaulding, *From Plow to Pulpit* (New York: R. Carter & Brothers, 1874) has a chapter in which Spaulding highlights his five-year pastorate in Athens in the 1830s. Mary Connett, *History of the First Presbyterian Church of Athens* (Athens: First Presbyterian Church, [1959]) is brief but based on church records.

The records of the First Methodist Church were destroyed in the mid-1950s fire. Clark E. Williams, "Early History of the First Methodist Church, Athens, Ohio" (Typescript, Athens, Ohio: February 1966), 81 pp., is by a member of the congregation and one-time archivist of Ohio University who made use of the church records prior to the fire.

Robert L. Daniel and Harry H. Peckham, *The Good Shepherd of Athens 1907–1987* (Athens: Church of the Good Shepherd, 1987) is in two parts. Peckham wrote Part I, "The Mission Years, 1907–1957" and relies in part on his participation in the church. Daniel's account, Part II, "The Parish Years, 1958–1987," relies on church records as well as on personal familiarity with the parish.

Catherine McQuaid Steiner and Bruce E. Steiner's *Faith and Family: Saint Paul's Catholic*

Church, Athens, Ohio: The Nineteenth Century (Athens: ACHS&M, 1995) is a meticulously re-searched, superbly written account of the parish, its priests, and parishioners, a model for other churches to emulate.

There are brief histories of two other congregations: Blanche Walden Deweese, "A Brief History of the First Christian Church of Athens, Ohio" (Typescript, 1965–67) at the ACHS&M and Waid C. Radford, *A Methodist History, Celebrating Thirty Years of Methodism in Central Avenue Church* (Athens: Athens Printing Company, 1936).

Reference Materials. A plethora of assorted reference materials can be found at the Athens County Historical Society and Museum and the Archives and Manuscript Collections of Alden Library, Ohio University. These include birth records, marriage records, death records, and obituaries from Athens newspapers.

Feb. 28, 1997

Index